To Every
Nation under
Heaven

THE NEW TESTAMENT IN CONTEXT

Friendship and Finances in Philippi
THE LETTER OF PAUL TO THE PHILIPPIANS
Ben Witherington III

Walking in the Truth: Perseverers and Deserters
THE FIRST, SECOND, AND THIRD LETTERS OF JOHN
Gerard S. Sloyan

Church and Community in Crisis
THE GOSPEL ACCORDING TO MATTHEW
J. Andrew Overman

Letters to Paul's Delegates
1 TIMOTHY, 2 TIMOTHY, TITUS
Luke Timothy Johnson

Embassy of Onesimus
THE LETTER OF PAUL TO PHILEMON
Allen Dwight Callahan

Community of the Wise
THE LETTER OF JAMES
Robert W. Wall

To Every Nation under Heaven

THE ACTS OF THE APOSTLES

Howard Clark Kee

THE NEW TESTAMENT IN CONTEXT
Howard Clark Kee and J. Andrew Overman, editors

TRINITY PRESS INTERNATIONAL
Harrisburg, Pennsylvania

Trinity Press International, P.O. Box 1321, Harrisburg, PA 17105
Trinity Press International is a division of the Morehouse Group

Library of Congress Cataloging-in-Publication Data

Kee, Howard Clark.
    To every nation under Heaven : the Acts of the Apostles / Howard Clark Kee.
        p.   cm. – (The New Testament in context)
    Includes bibliographical references (p.   ) and index.
    ISBN 1-56338-221-0 (alk. paper)
        1. Bible. N.T. Acts – Commentaries.   I. Title.   II. Series.
    BS2625.3.K44   1997
    226.6′077 – dc21   97-41513
                                                                            CIP

Printed in the United States of America

97 98 99 00 01 02   10 9 8 7 6 5 4 3 2 1

Contents

Introduction

Acts is unique among the New Testament writings in at least four obvious ways: (1) It is the only narrative account appended to a canonical gospel. (2) It is the only surviving, widely accepted report concerning the activities of the followers of Jesus who are designated apostles. (3) It includes the only details we have about Paul's life and thought apart from what can be inferred from his surviving letters. (4) It is a unique source for reports of what other apostolic leaders did, most notably Peter and James. In addition to these unique features, Acts is distinctive within the New Testament in the extent to which it employs the literary modes and methods of communication that dominated the Greco-Roman world, as well as in the degree to which it reports the involvement of the early Christians with the first-century Jewish and Roman authorities. The thoughtful reader of Acts must ask why and how an early Christian author chose the literary, conceptual, and sociocultural strategies reflected in this book to convey his message to his readers, and what the author's broader and deeper aims, which clearly went beyond simply passing on information about the origins of Christianity, were. By attention to these details and dimensions of Acts, one can discern the distinctive objectives and method of communication of the writer of Luke-Acts and thereby perceive how the community here addressed is being called to understand the message and the strategies by which it can reach out effectively "to every nation under heaven" (2:5).

Traditional Theories about the Origins of Acts

The attribution of the Gospel of Luke and the Book of Acts to Luke the physician, an associate and companion of Paul

1

mentioned three times in the New Testament letters (Col. 4:14; Philemon 24; 2 Tim. 4:11), is affirmed in later second-century sources, such as the fragmentary Latin Canon of Muratori,[1] the writings of Irenaeus, bishop of Lyons, and Clement of Alexandria. The Muratorian Canon asserts that Luke wrote "the third book of the gospel" while he was accompanying Paul, and that he had not seen Jesus "in the flesh." It also reports that he wrote the "Acts of all the apostles," including what he had directly observed, but omitted later events, such as the death of Peter and Paul's journey to Spain, plans for which are announced by Paul in Rom. 15:24, 28. In Irenaeus's *Against All Heresies* (3.1-4) he notes the shift from third person to first-person-plural narrative style — "we" — in certain sections of Acts,[2] and interprets this as showing that a companion of Paul wrote this document, combining his own personal observations with reports passed on to him by others. Irenaeus assumes that, just as Luke provides important supplemental information about John the Baptist and Jesus in his gospel, so in Acts Paul's companion has passed on important traditions, now available only through this source. Clement of Alexandria likewise affirms the Lukan authorship and historical reliability of the Gospel of Luke and Acts.

Origen, the remarkable late second/early third-century scholar from Alexandria, assumed the Lukan authorship of the third gospel as well as Luke's direct association with Paul, as reflected in Acts, which he understood to have been written by Luke as well.[3] In the fourth century, Eusebius likewise affirmed that, although Luke wrote his gospel on the basis of the testimony of others, his source for Acts was "information with his own eyes, no longer by hearsay."[4] Jerome (late fourth/early fifth century) described Luke as "the most learned in the Greek language among all the evangelists, since he was a doctor and wrote his gospel among the Greeks," and as the one who "composed the Acts [activities] of the Apostles as he had seen them."[5] These basic beliefs about the origins of Acts have survived down to the present day, in spite of challenges to their credibility from critical scholarship over the past two centuries. This study of Acts, however, will focus primarily on the special aims, concepts, and strategy of its author, rather than on his identity. Possible clues to the author and the sociocultural context in which he wrote are offered throughout, however.

History of the Interpretation of Acts

Rather than offering a compendium of modern scholarly interpretations of Acts,[6] the aim here is to highlight certain distinctive features of the history of the interpretation of this unique early Christian writing over the past two centuries.

Johann Salomo Semler, in his later eighteenth-century study of the origins of the Christian canon of scripture, advanced the hypothesis that there were two wings of the early church: the Petrine group of "Palestinian-based Jewish Christians," and the Pauline group, which was oriented toward outreach to Gentiles.[7] Encouraged by Hegel's philosophical notion that truth evolved through dynamic tension between a thesis and its antithesis, Ferdinand Christian Baur (1792–1860) produced a series of essays in which he described the radical bifurcation of Christianity from the outset into Petrine (Jewish-oriented) and Pauline (Gentile-inclusive) wings. Assuming the existence of this structure, Baur proposed that the Acts of the Apostles "is the apologetic attempt of a Paulinist to facilitate and bring about the *rapprochement* and union of the two opposing parties by representing Paul as Petrine as possible" and thus to "throw a reconciling veil" over the differences between the two groups.[8] This bifocal structuring of Christian origins became known as the Tübingen School, which had radical adherents. It also elicited from others sharp criticism for what were perceived to be unhistorical assumptions, and for its inability to recognize the basic presuppositions on which it operated and which were perceived to predetermine the results.

Bruno Bauer dismissed as unhistorical all the gospels, Acts, and the so-called letters of Paul. The aim of Acts, as he perceived it, was to show how Christianity shifted from its ethnic origins as a Jewish sect to become a universal religion, still building on the Old Testament tradition, but open to participation by Gentiles.[9] Franz Overbeck, in his thorough reworking of W. M. L. de Wette's commentary on Acts, described Acts as an attempt to universalize Christianity after Pauline Christianity had faded and Jewish Christianity was gone.[10] He theorized that a major aim of Acts was to gain favor with the Roman authorities, and to draw attention to Paul's status as a citizen, which was honored by Roman officials. The apologetic nature of the writing along political and cultural lines, together with what Overbeck saw as its nonfactual content, led him to assign Acts a mid-second-century date, by which time this legendary portrait of Paul was drawn in a style that served as a model for the second-century apologetic Christian literature. Many of those who did not subscribe to Bauer's or Overbeck's theories about Acts concluded that Acts was written to show how a movement that began within Judaism preserved features of that tradition even when it became a predominantly gentile enterprise.

A very different mood and strategy were dominant in British scholarship of the nineteenth century. James Smith's popular writing, *The Voyage and Shipwreck of St. Paul*, published in 1848, set the pattern for treating Acts as a reliable historical account.[11] Henry Alford's commentary on Acts attributed the work to Luke, the companion of Paul, and assigned it the date of 63 C.E., based on the reference in Acts 28:30 to "two years" stay in Rome.[12] The huge, popular *Life and Epistles of Paul* by W. J. Conybeare and J. S. Howson (published initially in 1852 and reprinted as recently as 1959) adduced literary and archaeological evidence from the eastern Roman Empire to provide the context for the events depicted in the letters of Paul and in Acts.[13] J. B. Lightfoot sought to discredit the theories of the Tübingen School about the ideological factors that shaped Acts, and to show how classical-historical and archaeological evidence confirm the accuracy of the Book of Acts. He concluded that Acts was free of geographical, historical, or cultural error.[14]

In volume 1 of *Hastings' Dictionary of the Bible*, A. C. Headlam summarized the dominant British views of Acts at the end of the nineteenth century:

1. Luke and Acts were by the same author, a companion of Paul, and were written to describe accurately the life and message of Jesus and the spread of the church.

2. This objective influenced the materials the author chose to include.

3. His artistic aim is clear, but does not undercut his historical accuracy.

4. In Acts 1–11 he was dependent on eyewitnesses; his sources from Acts 12 to 19 are excellent; and from Acts 20 to 28 he was an eyewitness, as evident by his use of "we" in the narrative.[15]

This basic point of view was affirmed in 1915 by W. M. Ramsay:

> The more I have studied the narrative of Acts, and the more
> I have learned year after year about Graeco-Roman soci-
> ety and thoughts and fashions, and organizations in those
> provinces, the more I admire and the better I understand.
> I set out to look for truth on the borderland where Greece
> and Asia meet, and found it here. You may press the words
> of Luke in a degree beyond any other historian's, and they
> stand the keenest scrutiny and the hardest treatment, pro-
> vided that the critic knows the subject and does not go
> beyond the limits of science and justice.[16]

In general terms, a similar position was adopted by the eminent
German historian of early Christianity Adolf von Harnack, who
asserted that Acts is a genuinely historical work in more than
just its major features; it is "trustworthy also in the majority
of details it contains. From almost every possible angle of historical criticism it is a solid, respectable, and in many cases, an
extraordinary work."[17]

Probably the most enduringly significant critical study of Acts
has been the multiauthored volumes produced by F. J. Foakes-
Jackson, Kirsopp Lake, and H. J. Cadbury. These five volumes
were published under the title *The Beginnings of Christianity,
Part 1: The Acts of the Apostles.*[18] Volume 1, however, with its descriptions of "the Jewish, Gentile and Christian backgrounds,"
is wholly outdated by more recent textual and archaeological
discoveries. But volume 2, on the literary and linguistic background of Acts, is still of considerable value, as is volume 3
with its analysis of the Greek text of Acts. Extremely useful
are the contributions of Henry J. Cadbury: the commentary on
Acts, volume 4, and the notes supplementing the commentary
in volume 5, although many of the latter need revision in light
of more recent finds. Still valuable are Cadbury's own studies,
where he sought to demonstrate that both the Gospel of Luke
and the Acts of the Apostles were conceived from the outset as
part of the larger work, and that the methods of the author's
contemporary Roman historians are employed by him.[19]

Martin Dibelius engaged in an extended series of analyses of
Acts, including possible use of sources and the literary style of
the book, especially of the speeches it contains.[20] He classified
the narratives in Acts on the basis of his form-critical categories

(legend, tale, anecdote), but refused to offer any judgment as to their historicity. The single historical feature that he identified was an itinerary of Paul's travels which the author utilized in Acts 13–21, but like other ancient historians, he is understood to have reported events in terms of what they signified to him and his prospective readers rather than what actually occurred (124). The "we" passages in Acts share the basic style of the rest of the book and are not first-hand reports (136). The speeches serve the purpose of the historian rather than recounting what was actually said (147). Jacques Dupont adopted a similar position in his analysis of Acts, which led him to conclude that it is impossible to define the sources used by the author, since the author has put "the imprint of his vocabulary and style everywhere."[21]

In the essay "On the 'Paulinism' of Acts," first published in 1950, Philipp Vielhauer asserted that the theological perspective of Acts differs significantly from that of Paul, in that Acts affirms the natural knowledge of God, it promotes conformity to Jewish ritual requirements (such as circumcision) and participation in Jewish festivals, and its christology is pre-Pauline.[22] The unity of the church, with its inclusion of Jews and Gentiles, is based on "the given unity of the human race,"[23] rather than on Paul's concept of the body of Christ. Acts does not offer primary historical evidence about earliest Christianity, but rather is a depiction of the author's subsequent perspective on the nascent early catholic church.

Other approaches to Acts include studies in which, like Vielhauer's, Luke-Acts was treated as primarily a theological construct. For example, considerable attention has been given in recent decades to Hans Conzelmann, whose book titled *Die Mitte der Zeit* ("The Mid-Point of Time") was assigned in its English translation the prosaic name *The Theology of St. Luke*.[24] His thesis was that the author of Luke-Acts replaced the earliest Christian expectation of an imminent end of the age[25] by depicting three epochs of history: (1) the period of the law and the prophets; (2) the time of salvation: the earthly career of Jesus, which is the "mid-point of time"; and (3) the present age, which will extend for an indefinite period until the parousia. A more radical approach to Acts was offered by Ernst Haenchen, who asserted that the main subject of Acts is the word of God and its growth, as it is proclaimed by humans and authenticated by God through signs and miracles.[26] He considered Luke to be inferior to Paul as a theologian, and a proponent of early catholicism, with a tendency toward requiring conformity to legal and ritual observances.[27] He thought that the author of Luke-Acts was not a historian of early Christianity in the modern sense; indeed, modern concepts of history were nonexistent then. Haenchen's outline of Acts is (1) the coming of the Spirit and the preparation for worldwide mission (1:1–8:3); (2) launching of the gentile mission (8:4–15:35); (3) the Pauline mission to the Gentiles (15:36–21:6);[28] (4) defense of Christianity and the arrival of the gospel in Rome (21:27–28:31). Haenchen viewed Acts as one significant facet of the diverse subsequent development of early Christianity, and it is to be regarded as of historical value only in the limited sense that it documents one aspect of that diversity within ancient Christianity.

A useful collection of essays that represents some of the various approaches to the understanding of Acts in the middle of the present century is that prepared by L. E. Keck and J. L. Martyn in *Studies in Luke-Acts*, written by an international group of scholars representing a spectrum of points of view, including contributions by Vielhauer, Conzelmann, and Haenchen from Germany, C. F. D. Moule from England, and H. J. Cadbury from the United States.[29] Meanwhile, defenses of the traditional view of Acts as the product of Paul's companion, Luke, have continued to appear, especially in the British world, such as W. L. Knox, *St. Paul and the Church of Jerusalem* and *The Acts of the Apostles*, and one commentary by F. F. Bruce.[30] Bruce seeks to show that not only are Acts and the Pauline letters compatible, but that the latter are illuminated by the Acts account.

Analyses of the literary model(s) used by the author of Acts have been stimulated by the continuing work of Charles Talbert, whose study *Literary Patterns, Theological Themes, and the Genre of Luke-Acts* focused primarily on the Greco-Roman literary models that served the author of Luke-Acts. Talbert proposed that the closest analogy to Acts was that of the popular lives of philosophers: "Luke-Acts belongs to that type of ancient biography in which the life of a philosophical founder is followed by a list or narrative of his successors and selected other disciples."[31] The members of the Society of Biblical Literature Luke-Acts Group continued and refined this mode of literary analysis and comparison, which has been traced and appraised in essays edited by Mikeal C. Parsons and J. B. Tyson.[32]

The emphasis on biography as the model for Acts has been challenged by David Aune, who insists that Luke and Acts embody a history of the origins and initial development of Christianity.[33]

Gerd Lüdemann has offered a brief survey of the historical value of Acts and a partial commentary divided into sections, tracing the literary and conceptual development of the tradition embodied in it and setting out the historical results of his analysis. He undertakes to discern the "historical value of the traditions in Acts," rather than the historical value of the book of Acts as a whole. To achieve this goal, he separates Lukan redaction from the tradition on which it builds, and seeks to determine the historical value of the latter. The chronological framework has to be constructed on the basis of the letters of Paul, and alone can serve as "an indispensable presupposition for ordering and evaluation of the traditions of Acts." For historical evaluation of those parts of Acts which have no counterpart in the Pauline letters, one can be guided only by analogy from Luke's use of tradition in his gospel and from those parts of Acts which converge on the letters of Paul.[34]

The scholarly ambiance for the study of Acts has been significantly altered in the past fifty years by the work of Roman historians, who have drawn on literary, inscriptional, and archaeological evidence, as well as social-scientific methods, to sketch in fresh ways the context of the early empire in which Christianity arose. Among these undertakings are the two monumental volumes by David Magie in which he details the ethnic, social, cultural, and administrative features of Roman rule in the regions where much of Paul's missionary activity was carried out. Important social histories include *The Roman Empire: Economy, Society, and Culture*, by Peter Garnsey and Richard Saller, and *The Social History of Rome* by Geza Alföldy.[35] An effort by an ancient historian to increase understanding of Roman jurisprudence and administration in New Testament times is that of A. N. Sherwin-Wright in his *Roman Society and Roman Law in the New Testament*. The conclusion drawn from his assessment of Acts within the context of Roman law and society is that "the confirmation of [its] historicity is overwhelming," that although it is as much a "propaganda narrative" as the gospels and as liable to "similar distortion," "any attempt to reject its basic historicity even in matters of detail must now appear absurd."

He further affirms that "Roman historians have long taken it for granted."[36] The same conviction about the historical credibility of Acts is evident in the recent study by the British classicist Stephen Mitchell, whose sketch of Christian origins in Asia Minor builds on an integration of evidence from the Acts of the Apostles and letters of Paul, which he contrasts with "a needless accretion of doubt" on the part of New Testament scholars.[37]

A series of insightful essays by Jacob Jervell addresses the issue of community definition in Luke-Acts along sociological lines.[38] Halvor Moxnes likewise undertook to provide perspective on Luke (with implications for Acts) along socioeconomic lines.[39] In contrast to these responsible analyses, some of the efforts to employ insights from the social sciences in the understanding of Acts have been hampered by the tendency to coerce the evidence by framing it within certain abstract categories offered by the social scientists, such as "honor and shame," or "patron and client," and by offering sweeping generalizations about "Mediterranean culture."[40] A more fruitful approach seems to be careful analysis of the diverse communities that served as sociocultural contexts for the early Christian writings, including the one in which Luke-Acts was produced. This is accomplished most fruitfully by using insights from the social sciences to heighten awareness of implicit and explicit factors, rather than by imposing abstract categories on the documents. An important work in this mode is by Philip F. Esler, *Community and Gospel in Luke-Acts: The Social and Political Motivations of Lucan Theology.*[41] My own study of the range of community models in Judaism and early Christianity, *Who Are the People of God?* seeks to show — among other models — the distinctive aims and structure of the community in which and for whom Luke-Acts was produced, with its intent to establish and foster an ethnically and culturally inclusive community.[42] Insightful analysis of Acts in terms of the social and political conflicts in which the apostles became engaged in these narratives is offered by R. J. Cassidy. He shows the continuity between the social and economic challenges of Jesus as depicted in the Gospel of Luke and those involving Paul throughout the narrative of Acts, not only in Palestine, but also in the cities of Asia Minor and Greece, and ultimately in Rome.[43]

Important thematic studies of Acts include David Tiede's treatise in which he shows how pervasive in these books is the theme that what has happened to and through Jesus is in fulfillment of God's redemptive plan as set forth in the scriptures. Insightful examination of the content and purpose of the speeches in Acts against the background of Roman literature and rhetoric is offered by Marion L. Soards in *The Speeches in Acts: Their Content, Context, and Concerns.*[44] The use of scripture in Luke-Acts is analyzed illuminatingly in a recent work by Craig Evans and James A. Sanders, and in a superb, more specialized study by Gert J. Steyn.[45] Steyn's analytical approach involved discussion of the biblical text base employed by the author, which he takes to have been very close to the text of the Septuagint as reconstructed by modern scholarship. He shows that a major aim of the author was to prove that Jesus was the fulfillment of the Messiah expected by Jews as evident in their scriptures, and that the mission to the wider gentile world is likewise justified on the basis of the scriptures. He points out that the most explicit appeals to scripture are in Luke's special material, in both the Gospel and in Acts, and especially in the speeches in Acts, the primary purpose of which is to use rhetorically the historical and prophetic information drawn from scripture in order to persuade the hearers/readers to change their minds and acknowledge Jesus as God's Messiah.[46] An analogy has been pointed out by Thomas Romer and Jean-Daniel Macchi between the strategy of the author of Acts and that of the Deuteronomist in the Jewish scriptures, whose aim has been seen as setting the divine promise of the land and the covenant over against the perpetual disobedience of the people, who are constantly being warned by the prophets and servants of Yahweh. These challenges, claims, and insights are seen as being expressed by the author of Acts primarily in the programmatic speeches he presents.[47]

Perceptive studies of the historical method employed by the author of Luke-Acts are those of Colin J. Hemer and Gregory E. Sterling.[48] Hemer deals with broader interpretive questions about the relationship of Acts to other New Testament sources, while Sterling's work includes a perceptive analytical survey of a wide range of historical writings from the Greco-Roman period, as noted below in our discussion of Acts as history.

A group of essays edited by Earl Richard deals with general introductory questions, as well as with methodological, exegetical, theological, and thematic matters. Another useful collection of essays on Luke-Acts has been edited by C. H. Talbert under the title, *Luke-Acts: New Perspectives.* Substantive essays on Luke-Acts appeared in David Aune's *The New Testament in its Literary Environment,* especially "Luke-Acts and Ancient Historiography" and "The Generic Features of Luke-Acts."[49] The most comprehensive series of studies of Acts to be produced since the Foakes-Jackson, Lake, and Cadbury series, *The Beginnings of Christianity,* Part 1, more than half a century ago, is appearing currently under the title *The Book of Acts in Its First-Century Setting* in a projected six volumes, the series editor for which is Bruce W. Winter. The subtitles of the three volumes that have been published are vol. 1, *Ancient Literary Setting;* vol. 2, *Graeco-Roman Setting;* and vol. 3, *Paul in Roman Custody.*[50] The potential impact on Acts studies from this extensive and substantive series is very great, and specific insights have been drawn upon in details of this commentary.

Acts as History

What is history? As one looks back over the centuries to the Greco-Roman period when Acts was written, it is clear that there is no single, simple, timeless answer to that question.

In the Greco-Roman period, there was no normative model for writing history, but certain recurrent features can be traced in its historiographical antecedents and subsequent development. As Gregory Sterling has pointed out, the earlier Greek historians were primarily ethnographers, seeking to describe the land, history, and customs of other people who came under Greek scrutiny or control, with special attention to marvelous or exotic features of these peoples' traditions. A major interest of these historians was to demonstrate the superiority of the culture they were depicting.[51] In the third century B.C.E., Berossus wrote his history of Babylonia to show the superiority of its culture, as Manetho had done earlier for Egypt. The features of these indigenous cultures are depicted in terms of the dominant contours and terminology of Hellenism. Jewish historians, such as Eupolemos (295–143 B.C.E.?) and Artapanos (ca. 250 B.C.E.), adapted this method in their effort to show that the insights and values of Greek culture derived from or were inferior imitations of the Jewish heritage. What emerged from this process of depicting and assessing the past was what Sterling has called "apologetic historiography," of which Josephus's works are prime examples in their effort to picture the Jewish traditions in a positive way that is compatible with Roman culture.[52] There is no effort on the part of these apologetic historians to achieve objectivity in reporting events and utterances. Instead, the writer has a clear set of objectives in mind, and the material is shaped to serve those goals.

In the second-century C.E. treatise by Lucian of Samosata on *How to Write History*, he appeals to Thucydides from the fifth century B.C.E. for the principle that history must convey to the reader what is true and useful, to enable people in the future to learn from the past. The facts are to be displayed and allowed to speak for themselves. The material should be arranged so that the events reported are illuminated as vividly as possible. The preface will indicate the features that will engage and instruct the readers. The speeches are to be written to suit the person and his subjects as fittingly as possible, although the historian may at the same time serve the role of author and demonstrate his own eloquence.[53] It is these kinds of procedures by historians which seem to have provided the model for the historical effort undertaken by the author of Acts.

A major heritage of the Enlightenment, on the other hand, was the devotion to objectivity which scholars were called to achieve. Historians were to present *facts!* As it really happened ("wie es eigentlich geschehen ist")! Historians were supposed to free themselves from prejudices as they adduced with complete objectivity the evidence for their historical reconstructions. While this principle is still widely uttered, it has come to be recognized as an unrealistic goal. Instead, there is an increasing recognition of the formative influence of the assumptions operative in the mind of the historian and of the community for whom the evidence is organized and presented. This kind of insight has been formulated and clarified by discussions over the past three decades in the field of sociology of knowledge.[54] Accordingly, what is essential in analysis of historical evidence, as well as in any historian's reconstruction of the historical situation, is careful attention not only to what is overtly stated but also to the underlying assumptions implicit in the material under examination. The latter are the basic convictions held by the historical writer and assumed to be shared by the reader of the document. The models of reality, human and divine, which are taken for granted by the historian, profoundly influence and indeed shape the way in which the historian offers the evidence and in terms of which meaning is assigned to the historical reconstruction.

Of course the modern historian is interested in the question of probability that reported events actually occurred or that statements have been attributed faithfully—or at least credibly—to the person being quoted. The aim in historical inquiry is seen to be not objective evidence in some absolute sense, however, but sensitive perception of the claims that the historian is seeking to convey to the reader. Questions of certainty of occurrence or accuracy of quotations are secondary to questions of intended meaning. The primary issue in analysis of a historical report is not, Is that the way it actually happened? but, What meaning is the report seeking to convey? A corollary of the latter question is, What are the assumptions about reality shared by the author and his initial intended readers?

•

As a consequence of that theory of historiography, which this commentary shares, the focus is on meaning in the historical context rather than on the modern quest for what is perceived to be objective historical factuality. This commentary aims to consider the various facets of the context in which the writer and his initial readers lived and thought: the religious assumptions, the political framework and structures of power, and above all the sociocultural features of the author and the initially intended readers. What we see in Luke-Acts is a prime example of what has been referred to as "apologetic historiography." The author of Acts is seeking to show how the claims concerning God, Jesus, and the divine purpose for God's new people have been disclosed and how their effective power has been operative in the careers and message of Jesus and the apostles, particularly Paul. Accordingly, there is seen to be an intended balance between information and propaganda.

The question remains, When was this history written? There are numerous indications in the Gospel of Luke that that version of the gospel tradition took shape some time after the fall of Jerusalem and the complete Roman takeover of the city and the region. Only in Luke 21:24 does the reference to "Jerusalem trodden down by the Gentiles" appear. The familiar weeping over the city by the "daughters of Jerusalem" is likewise distinctively Lukan (23:28–31). In the hearing of Jesus before the council in Jerusalem, Luke alone among the synoptics omits reference to Jesus' coming again, and mentions only the seating of "the Son of Man...at the right hand of the Power of God" (22:69). The implication is that the coming of Christ in triumph is not expected soon, but instead there is celebration of his present enthronement in glory. This matches the primary focus in Acts on the importance of the continuing outreach of the good news into the wider Roman world and beyond. When this evidence is juxtaposed with the obvious in-depth skills of the author to employ for his objectives the modes of communication and to articulate the sociopolitical issues of the Roman world, the conclusion that the work was produced early in the second century is plausible. Within Judaism the rabbinic system was evolving at that time, drawing on the Pharisaic tradition[55] — a phenomenon reflected in Acts' representation of the sage role of Gamaliel in the *synedrion* (5:33–39)[56] as well as the report of Paul's having studied in Jerusalem under this major rabbinic teacher (22:3). While the evidence is not decisive, its cumulative impact is to point to a date for the composition of Acts in the latter part of the first century, if the author was in fact a companion of Paul, or the early second century, if the author was using but enhancing such eyewitness sources.

Acts as Literature

In addition to the influence on the author of Acts from the historical methods of the Greco-Roman period, one can discern how other important modes of literary communication have also been employed in this work. The literary elements include speeches, letters, formal decrees, and dramatic narratives; the impact of the Septuagint on the literary style of the work is evident as well. An illuminating analysis of Luke-Acts along literary lines is that of David E. Aune in his comprehensive work, *The New Testament in Its Literary Environment*. He notes that the we-passages (which are discussed below in the commentary) have their counterpart in other historical writings, where the author has personally participated in the action, or claims that he did.[57]

Speeches

In hellenistic historiography, 20-35 percent of the narrative is occupied with speeches,[58] but in Acts the proportion of the text devoted to speeches is twice that of Tacitus's *Annals*, four times that of Josephus's *Jewish Wars*, and sixteen times that of Polybius's *Histories*.[59] Clearly, the speeches in Acts are of major importance. Soards notes that, while they manifest kinship in form and rhetorical style with Greco-Roman historians, they display more direct influence from the LXX, and less influence from the hellenistic-Jewish historians.[60] In the thirty-six speeches in Acts, the recurrent themes are the following:

- Divine authority: God is at work to bring to fruition his purpose in the world.

- Jesus is the divine agent through whom that purpose will be achieved.

- The present time is critical, linked with the past but pointing to fulfillment of God's purpose in the future.

- Essential for the accomplishment of that plan is the role of the witnesses: the apostles, the Spirit, Stephen, Paul, in contrast with the false witnesses.

- The testimony of these witnesses points to the continuity with the legal traditions of Israel, as set forth in scripture, with what has happened through Jesus and the Spirit, and the future fulfillment.

Those who deliver these speeches are predominantly Peter and Paul, although others offer important presentations. Twenty of the major speeches have been classified by Gert J. Steyn, with indications of those that specifically quote from or build on the Septuagint, and those that lack appeal to scripture (see Table 1).

Clearly it is the central concerns for the faith and practice of the people of God, understood in terms of the divine redemptive purpose through Jesus Christ, which are spelled out in Acts by means of the speeches. There is no appeal to scripture in addresses to governmental officers or to those with no knowledge of Jewish scriptural tradition, such as the Areopagites in Athens. All these speeches are analyzed in detail in the commentary below.

Table 1. Major Speeches in Acts

Subject		Source
Petrine		
1:16–22	The choice of Matthias	Psalms
2:14–41	Peter at Pentecost	Prophets, Psalms
3:11–26	Peter at the Temple	Torah
4:8–12	Leaders of the Nation	—
5:29–33	*Synedrion*	—
10:34–43	Baptism of Cornelius	—
15:6–11	Apostolic council	—
Pauline		
13:16–48	In Antioch Prophets	Psalms
14:14–18	In Lystra before non-Jews	—
17:22–33	In Athens before non-Jews	—
20:18–35	In Miletus	—
22:1–21	Defense speech in Jerusalem	—
23:1–6	Defense speech to the *synedrion*	Torah
24:10–21	Defense speech before Felix	—
25:6–12	Defense speech before Festus	—
26:2–32	Defense speech before Festus and Agrippa	—
28:25–28	Defense speech to Jewish leaders in Rome	Prophets
Other speeches		
4:23–31	Prayer of the community	Psalms
7:2–53	Stephen before the *synedrion*	Torah, Prophets
15:14–21	James at the Apostolic council	Prophets

Source: Steyn, *Septuagint Quotations*, 25.

Biography

Although the Gospel of Luke is clearly a kind of biography, one might ask how appropriate it is to categorize as biography the two-volume Luke-Acts, since Acts lacks any fully developed biographical features, even of Paul. Charles Talbert has provided a useful classification mode for biographies in Greco-Roman literature, which includes a type analogous to Luke-Acts, however. His typology of biographies of philosophers and rulers is based on social function:

1. a model to be imitated;

2. a correction for a false image of a philosopher;

3. discrediting a false teacher;

4. the life of a philosopher combined with the survival of his school;

5. the hermeneutical keys to a philosopher's teaching.[61]

He notes that in some of these biographies the hero displays divine features, or is linked with a deity, and may be seen as the embodiment of the value system that has been disclosed to the community.[62] Luke-Acts fits best the fourth of these categories, with its depiction of the life of the founder and the formation of the community that promotes and in some ways embodies his teachings, although the evidence for this model is slim.

Romances and Dramatic Narrative

In the past half century a number of perceptive studies have been published by classicists and ancient historians on the ancient novel or romance, a type of literature that flourished in the early centuries of the Common Era.[63] The genre has been accurately described by Thomas Hagg as follows:

> Gods, oracles, cults of different kinds are organically integrated into the course of events in human experience. In Xenophon [in his *Ephesiaca*]...there is hardly any important stage in the action that is not accompanied by an invocation, a prayer, a sacrifice or a hint at some involvement with a god. And in Heliodorus the missionary tendency in favor of the Helios cult is unmistakable....It is also quite possible that direct allusions to mystery rituals, to be understood only by the initiated, were hidden in the texts.[64]

An effort has been made to demonstrate that the romance was the model for the author of Acts, on the assumption that romances — including Acts — were written primarily as entertainment.[65] What is far more likely, however, is that some of the romances were written as propaganda for cults. They include fascinating narrative and engaging discourse, with their powerfully erotic accounts, but their ultimate aim seems to have been to persuade and propagate the cult, not merely to entertain. Detailed features of some of the romances — such as miraculous deliverance from a dangerous sea voyage in Xenophon's *Ephesiaca* — have their counterparts in Acts, but more important is the correspondence between Acts and the romances as instruments to promulgate certain religious claims.[66]

Of major significance for the author of Acts is a common feature of historical narrative in the Greco-Roman period: dramatic episodes, often involving divine action.[67] As Aune notes, this activity takes the form of divine guidance, visions, oracles, divine intervention, and fulfillment of prophecies.[68] In the romances of this period as well as in Acts, these stories function not as amusing diversions, but to confirm and demonstrate the active presence of the divine in the lives of the devotees. Again, the basic question about these stories is not "Did they really happen?" but "What meaning does the writer intend to convey through these dramatic accounts?"

Letters

References to letters in Acts show that they served as authorization of action or clarification of issues, originating with the leaders of institutions or movements. In 9:2 and 22:5, Paul is reported as having been granted authority from the high priest to transport members of the group regarded as deviant ("the Way") to Jerusalem for trial and punishment. After his conversion, Paul and associates are given a letter from the church and its leaders in Jerusalem addressed to the Syrian churches setting out the minimum obligations for Gentiles there who have joined the community (15:23–29).[69] This decision conveyed by letter is confirmed in Acts 21:25.

An analogous decision communicated by a letter is the report of the judgment of the Roman official in Jerusalem concerning the charges brought against Paul by his Jewish opponents. Written by the chiliarch (or tribune), it is addressed to the Roman procurator (*hegemon*) in Caesarea, the official seat of Roman authority in the province. The governor confirms Paul's innocence of the charges as a violator of Roman law, or as a disturber of the peace. The implications of these letters as formal pronouncements for the legal status of Luke's Christian constituency are clear: one articulates the qualifications for participation in the new community, and the other exonerates the members from the charge of violation of Roman law.

Influence of the Septuagint on Style
and Content of Acts

The careful and thorough analysis by Gert J. Steyn of the use of the LXX in Acts leads him to conclude that this is by far the major source of Old Testament quotations in Luke-Acts, as opposed to those who have proposed that testimonies or florilegia were used by the author. He observes that all the explicit quotations in Acts are found in the speeches, which he notes are the creation of Luke.[70] As scholars have long recognized, both the style and the content of the unique Lukan stories of the preparations for the birth of Jesus, of his birth, infancy, and childhood, reflect the influence of the Septuagint. The birth of John the Baptist to an elderly couple clearly parallels the birth of Samuel, and their roles in preparing the leaders of God's people are analogous (Luke 1; 1 Samuel 8–10, 15–16). Mary's song of gratitude (1:46–55) resembles that of Hannah (1 Sam. 2:1–10), while Zechariah's prophecy about his son John (Luke 1:67-79) is a mosaic of phrases from the LXX of the psalms, prophets, and law. Details of Jesus' launching the mission to Gentiles (4:14–30) are matched by Luke with stories of Elijah and Elisha (1 Kings 17–18; 2 Kings 5). Jesus' inaugural sermon in Nazareth is prefaced — only in Luke (4:16–21) — by a direct quote from the LXX, and the claim that the prophecy is now being fulfilled. In these stories (Luke 1–4), not only the content of the LXX is reflected, but also the narrative and semantic style of the LXX translators.

In the post-resurrection appearances of Jesus in Luke, there is the claim — unique in the gospel tradition — that through Jesus are being fulfilled the promises set forth in the threefold Jewish canon of scripture: "the Law of Moses, the prophets and the psalms" (Luke 24:27, 44). Once again this seems to reflect the classified grouping of the translated Jewish scriptures in the LXX. In Acts 1:14–21, Peter's explanation of the outpouring of the Spirit consists of the extended quotation from the LXX version of Joel (2:28–32). Documentation for Jesus' resurrection (Acts 2:24) is offered by Peter from the LXX of Ps. 16:8–11. Other full quotations from the LXX occur when the new community must deal with official hostility (Acts 4:25–26; from Psalm 2), when Philip explains to the Ethiopian eunuch the death of Jesus (8:32–33; from Isaiah 53), when the inclusion of Gentiles is confirmed (15:15–18; from Jer. 12:15; Amos 9:11; Isa. 45:21), and the final statement about the official disbelief of Israel (28:26–27; from Isa. 6:9).

Summary of Literary Models in Acts

Thus the astonishing skill of the author of Luke-Acts is evident in the combination of elements from two cultural traditions which are accomplished in this work: the style and content of the Jewish biblical tradition as preserved in the LXX, and the adroit adaptation of the literary and conceptual modes of the wider Greco-Roman tradition which are utilized in the narrative and speech sections of Acts.

Acts as Theology

From the instruction to the apostles by the risen Christ (1:3) to the testimony of Paul in Rome (28:23), the message of the kingdom of God is a central feature in Acts.[71] What is involved in the "kingdom" or better "rule of God" is spelled out in detail throughout the book.

The Sovereign God

In 1:8 instruction concerning the kingdom is given by the risen Christ to the apostles, who are the nucleus of God's new people. It is God who is calling everyone to share in this new reality of God's sovereignty (2:39) and thereby adding to the number of participants (2:47). It is on them that he bestows his Spirit (11:17), summoning Gentiles as well as Jews to share in this community. The emphasis throughout Acts is on the sovereignty of God, and the multiple ways in which he works to accomplish his will. God fixes the time and season (1:7), and acts with incomparable power (2:11) to achieve his purpose in the world (2:20, 22). What takes place is the outworking of the divine plan (2:23), which has been foretold through the prophets (3:18) and is certain of fulfillment (3:21). No human or demonic force can withstand that purpose (5:38–39), since God is the ultimate active subject in human history (Acts 7), as the history of Israel shows in Stephen's sketch of the experience of God by the patriarchs and Moses. Yet God has no earthly dwelling place (13:17–41).

God's agent of renewal and fulfillment of his purpose in the world is Jesus. God raised him from the dead (2:32, 3:26, 4:10), and established him as Lord and Messiah (2:35; 3:13, 15). Jesus was Messiah because God anointed him — that is, God chose Jesus and empowered him by the Spirit to carry out the divine purpose (10:38). God has exalted him by raising him from the dead (2:32, 3:26, 4:10, 5:31), and has designated him to be the judge of the living and the dead (10:42). (Jesus' distinctive role is summarized below, under "Jesus the Messiah.")

How does God work in the world in order to achieve his purpose for his people? He is in control of times and seasons (1:7), so that the course of history is the outworking of his plan. He shapes what we would call both human and natural events in order to effect his will in human history, and especially in the life of his people, as demonstrated by dozens of miraculous events — both punitive and renewing — especially in the vivid story of the voyage, storm, wreck, and deliverance of Paul in Acts 27–28. God also works in such invisible and seemingly mechanical ways to effect his will as through casting lots (1:24–26), and in such dramatic ways as enabling his people to perform healings and other signs and wonders (4:30). The prime evidences of his sovereign work in the world, however, are visible in his having exalted Jesus by raising him from the dead and establishing him as Founder and Savior of his people (5:31), followed by the outpouring of the Holy Spirit upon them (5:32).

Jesus the Messiah

There is in Acts no reference to the virgin birth of Jesus; his mother is merely mentioned as a member of the new community in Jerusalem after his ascension (1:14). He is described as a male human (*aner*) whom God attested through the mighty works, signs, and wonders which he performed (2:22). As a consequence of his having been anointed (*echrisen*) by God with the Holy Spirit and power, "he went from place to place doing good works and healing all those who were overpowered by the devil" (10:38). He was exalted by God when he was raised from the dead (5:31) and revealed to the chosen band of his followers (10:40–41). Then God exalted him to heaven, where he may be seen by the faithful at God's right hand (7:55–56), as well as by those, like Paul, who are entering the community of faith (9:5, 10, 15, 17). As the exalted one, he offers repentance and forgiveness of sins (5:31). His entire career and redemptive role are in fulfillment of God's plan for the renewal of his people, beginning with Jesus' ministry of preaching following his baptism by John, including his healings and exorcisms, his death and resurrection, his appearances to his followers, his commandment to them to send out the good news "to the end of the earth" (Acts 1:8). All this redemptive activity culminates in his function as judge of all (10:36–42). God's demonstration of his choice of Jesus as the human agent to serve as judge of all humanity took place in the divine action when he was raised from the dead (17:31).

Peter declares that all that God is doing through Jesus has been attested through the prophets (10:43). Indeed, the role of Jesus in God's plan is repeatedly asserted to have been foreseen by certain persons in ancient Israel, as is evident from scripture. David foresaw Jesus' victory over the powers of death and his exaltation to the presence of God (2:25–36). Jesus' central role in the building of God's new people was foretold in Ps. 118:22 (4:11). According to Paul's sermon in 13:16–41, his resurrection was in fulfillment of the psalms and the prophets (Ps. 2:7, 16:10; Isa. 55:3). Even the disbelief with which some greet the message about Jesus is in accord with prophetic insight (13:41; Hab. 1:5). This process of interpreting the significance of Jesus by appeal to the Hebrew scriptures is indicated in Acts as standard procedure for Paul, as evident in his address to the Jewish meeting in Thessalonica (17:2–3).

The names, titles, or roles assigned to Jesus in Acts are in part found in other New Testament writings as well, but are in part unique. As elsewhere in the New Testament, he is known in Acts as the Lord Jesus (7:59, 9:5, 11:20, 26:28), or simply the Lord (9:29, 35) or Savior (13:23), but he is also referred to as Lord of All (10:36), and as the Holy and Righteous One (3:14, 7:52). In Peter's speeches reported in Acts 3 and 4, he names Jesus as "servant" or "child," but the term used there is *pais*, rather than *doulos*, which is Paul's designation of Jesus in the Christ hymn of Phil. 2:7.[72] The most remarkable title of Jesus in Acts is *archegos tes zoes* (3:15), "Founder [or Author] of life," implying that he is the original example or model of what God intended human life to be, as is demonstrated by God's having raised him from the dead. The good news concerning him is a call to "repentance toward God and faith in our Lord Jesus" (20:21). It has the potential to turn both Jews and Gentiles "from darkness to light and from the power of Satan to God," bestowing on them "forgiveness of sins" and "a share in those who are consecrated through faith" in Jesus (26:18).

The Holy Spirit

It is only in Luke's gospel that the Spirit of God is explicitly linked with Jesus' role as the Messiah ("anointed") who has been sent by God to call together the new community, with its members from among the poor, the captives, the blind, and the oppressed (Luke 4:16–21). And only in Acts 1:8 among all accounts of the post-resurrection appearances of Jesus is the promise of the Spirit articulated. The baptism with the Holy Spirit, as promised in the gospel tradition (Mark 1:8; Matt. 3:11; Luke 3:16), is experienced on the Day of Pentecost (Acts 1:5, 8; 2:4), as predicted by the prophet Joel (2:17–18) and fulfilled through the risen Christ (2:33). All who respond in faith to the good news will share in this experience (2:38). The Spirit works in concrete ways to meet the needs of God's people: Peter is enabled by the Spirit to offer his defense before the council (4:8), and through the Spirit the apostles can speak the word of God boldly (4:31). On the other hand, for the members of the community to practice deceit is to lie to the Holy Spirit (5:3, 9). Those who are obedient are given the Spirit (5:32, 8:15–19), which empowers the chosen messengers (6:3–5) and enables them to speak with wisdom (6:10), to see the exalted Son of Man as they confront martyrdom (7:55–56), and to be guided as they carry out their mission work (8:29, 39). Paul is filled with the Spirit at conversion (9:17), and the Spirit comes on those who heard Peter's message (10:44), including the Gentiles (10:45, 15:8). In Ephesus the Spirit enables elders to serve as overseers (*episkopoi*) in the community (20:28). Barnabas, Paul's important aide and companion, is described as a good man, full of the Spirit and of faith (11:24).

The Spirit is also seen as acting in direct ways in the lives of the apostles and the people of God. Peter is explicitly directed by the Spirit to take the gospel to the Gentiles (11:12). The church in Antioch is told by the Spirit to set aside Barnabas and Saul for the mission to the Gentiles (13:2, 4). It is the Spirit that directs Paul to go to Jerusalem for the confrontation with the religious and political officials there (20:22). It is the Spirit that instructs the apostolic council in Jerusalem not to impose laws on the gentile Christians (15:28). But the Spirit also gives warnings of the hardships and suffering God's people will experience in the course of their service for Christ. Paul is warned by the Spirit of the imprisonment and affliction that he will undergo (20:23), and the disciples in Tyre are told by the Spirit to advise him not to go to Jerusalem (21:4). The prophet Agabus foretells by the Spirit Paul's capture there and his being turned over to the gentile powers (21:11). Quoting Isa. 6:9–10, Paul tells his hearers in Rome that the disbelief of some of them is in accord with the message of the Spirit through this prophet (28:25–26). Most dramatic of all the works of the Spirit is the initial one depicted in Acts 2, when the members of the new community are enabled by the Spirit to "speak in other languages," so that listeners from ethnic groups based across the ancient world attest, "We hear them speaking in our own languages the magnificent deeds of God" (2:6, 11). The good news transcends ethnic and linguistic boundaries through the power of the Spirit, reaching out to people from "every nation under heaven" (2:5).

The New People of God

From the outset in Acts, the inclusive nature of the new people of God is affirmed. In response to the disciples' inquiry whether Jesus was about to "restore the kingdom to Israel" (1:6), he announces to them their role as witnesses, not only in Judea and Samaria, but to "the end of the earth" (1:8). The potential participation of those from every nation and tribe is foreshadowed in the Pentecost event, when the people gathered at the time of the outpouring of the Spirit have come "from every nation under heaven" (2:5). When the Spirit comes on those gathered in Jerusalem, there is an explicit appeal to the prophetic promise that it will be poured out "on *all* flesh [humanity]" (Joel 3:1–5; Acts 2:17). The Spirit is to be accessible not only to those present and their children, but also "to all that are far off" (2:39). There is a reminder of the promise to Abraham that God's covenant will include blessing for "all the families of the earth" (Gen. 12:3; Acts 3:25). God has prepared no other agent than Jesus for human salvation throughout the whole of creation "under heaven" (4:12). The vision of Peter which represents participation in God's people involves all kinds of creatures, and all are declared clean (10:10 –16). The rules for participation in the new community set aside the purity laws that separated Israel from the other peoples of the world (15:28 –29). The Acts narrative describes those sharing in the life of the new community as including Jews of both Hebrew and hellenistic background, those from Palestine and the Diaspora, Samaritans, God-fearers and gentile inquirers, an Ethiopian eunuch, a Roman military officer, a Greek jailer, a prosperous Greek businesswoman, even a few Athenian intellectuals, as well as those Jews and proselytes who had formerly been committed to strict legal piety as the chief criterion for participation in the people of God – most notably Saul/Paul, the Pharisee.

The community has only minimal rules for participation (15:20, 28 –29), some division of labor between missionary and administrative responsibilities (6:2–4), and a structure for making policy decisions (15:22–29). Although there are not detailed descriptions of the sacramental practices, there is a pervasive theme of baptism as essential for membership, and references in passing to the eucharist or breaking of bread. The latter includes mention of the apostles' having eaten and drunk with the risen Christ (10:40) and Paul's breaking bread with the community in Troas (20:11). Just before the shipwreck on Paul's journey to Rome, he is pictured as taking bread, giving thanks (*eucharistesen*), breaking it and eating (27:35), which of course recalls the eucharist. However, the sacramental modes of the community's life are for the most part simply implicit in Acts.

Paul as Portrayed in Acts

The dismissal of Acts as a historical source for knowledge of Paul nearly a half-century ago[73] has been countered in more recent years by those who have more confidence in Acts as offering reliable historical evidence.[74] More important for understanding Acts than flat judgments about its historical reliability in its portrait of Paul are those studies that examine the framework of meaning in which the author of Acts has placed his account, and how this affects his depiction of Paul. Robert L. Brawley and J. C. Lentz Jr. have shown how the apologetic aims of Luke have shaped the image of Paul and his message as they are presented in Acts. Brawley makes a case for apologetic features of

Paul as seen in Acts. He has not abandoned his mission to Jews, but the rejection he has experienced from some of them is seen as foretold in scripture (Isa. 6:9–10), and it has motivated him to turn to Gentiles as well. This dual activity is legitimated in ways that have their counterpart in hellenistic literature: divine approval, access to divine power, high motivation, benefits to others, a high level of culture, and ultimate reliance on ancient tradition. The mission to Gentiles is a divinely authorized stage beyond the mission to Jews.[75]

John Lentz proposes "that Luke portrayed Paul as a man of high social status and moral virtue" who "possesses high social credentials and personifies what would have been recognized by the first century reader/hearer of Acts as the classical cardinal virtues."[76] This is accomplished not only by direct descriptive words and phrases, but also by emphasizing Paul's high social status through the use of common rhetorical devices and through the author's literary methods in construction of the narrative. The factors that determined status in the later first century C.E. included pedigree, education, social level (slave, freed, or born free), occupation, wealth — but above all character, judged by one's possession of virtues that match those fostered in the Stoic tradition: *phronesis, sophrosyne, dikaiosyne,* and *andreia.* Paul's higher status level is confirmed implicitly in Acts by his being assigned an escort of 500 soldiers (23:23), the deference to Paul by the centurion (27:3), and the distinguished group of hearers that assembles to listen to his case (25:12, 23). The wisdom given by the Spirit is depicted as akin to the hellenistic ideal of *sophrosyne.* Paul is described in Acts as "a man of wealth, good birth and education, who was proud of his standing in the city of Tarsus, relied upon the advantages of an inherited Roman citizenship, and was a strict Pharisee." As such, he "exemplified an ideal man of status and virtue." Paul's social status and moral virtue are portrayed so as to serve as propaganda appealing to Greeks and Romans of high standing. But also of paramount importance for Luke is the divine exaltation of Jesus, as the founder and central focus of the new community.[77]

Such an approach to Acts does not dismiss its contents as unhistorical, but highlights the importance of the biographical, narrative, and literary-rhetorical style of the book, and their counterparts in the Greco-Roman culture of the time, as essential features of the aim of its author.

The Text of Acts

The ancient Greek manuscripts of Acts, in addition to a seemingly random set of textual variants, include a group that has a somewhat distinctive type of text. When it first came to scholarly notice, this different version of Acts was found in Codex Bezae (known as D), which contains the New Testament in Greek and Latin. Accordingly, scholars designated this type of Acts text as the "Western text," to differentiate it from the text found in the most highly regarded Greek manuscripts from the eastern Mediterranean world: Codex Sinaiticus (*aleph*) and Codex Vaticanus (B), as well as in some ancient Coptic versions. The designation "Western" was given because Latin was the dominant language of the western Roman Empire. An older influential analysis of the text of Acts from this perspective was that offered by J. H. Ropes in volume 3 of *The Beginnings of Christianity*.[78] The textual variants represented in the Western text were seen as intended to smooth the syntax, to replace ambiguous pronouns with specific nouns, to expand the titles of Jesus, and even to correct some factual details, as when Derbe (20:4), which is not in Macedonia, is replaced by Douberios, which is there, as well as to alter some crucial features.[79] The distinctive features of the Greek text in Codex Bezae match the details found in the Latin version, which was clearly the more important form of the text for the users of D.[80] Some textual scholars use the term "non-Western interpolations" to refer to passages not found in the Western text, but that do appear in the oldest textual witnesses, and according to this theory have therefore been added to the non-Western texts. But the majority of scholars consider these distinctive passages found in D and kindred manuscripts to be later additions. More likely is the theory that they were omitted by later copyists because they were difficult, either logically or theologically.

W. A. Strange has offered a comprehensive and perceptive survey of *The Problem of the Text of Acts*.[81] He describes three stages in the study of the text of Acts: (1) the pre-1939 period, when the Western text was seen as an interpretive modification of the original version; (2) the post-1945 period, when the details of this text were perceived as the result of efforts — probably begun in Syria — to ease and clarify the original, and to widen the distance between Judaism and Christianity;[82] (3) more

recent scholarly analysis confirms that the Western text is to be
seen as the end-product of a long process of interpretation and
modification which continued down to the third century C.E.[83]
Building on this diverse scholarly tradition, Strange offers a
plausible explanation for the origin of the Western text as found
in the Greek manuscripts, the bilingual Codex Bezae, and the ancient Coptic versions: these copies of Acts included marginal or
interlinear notes on the text, which later were incorporated by
scribes into the text itself. The Western text has the quality of
a brief commentary at many points, dealing with such narrative
features as entrances and exits, explaining motives for actions,
providing edificatory notes,[84] and emphasis on apostolic wisdom
(6:10–11). Galen, the second-century C.E. physician and scholar,
differentiated between properly written books, *syggrammata*, and
commentaries or working drafts of books, which might represent
a confused text to the reader. Later editions of works by members of a circle of followers of the original author or by friends,
pupils, patrons, or subsequent readers would likewise alter and
add to the text. Strange concludes that our access to the work of
the author of Acts in the so-called Western text "is by way of his
editors, who were also his earliest interpreters."[85]

In our analysis of Acts, we shall work from what seems to be
the oldest text, as attested especially in Vaticanus and Sinaiticus.
Significant or interesting variants from the non-Western tradition will be noted as well, however. The text for this translation
is that of the most recent Nestle-Aland edition of the Greek New
Testament.[86]

Translation Principles

This commentary is based on a translation of the Greek text
which builds on the principle of dynamic equivalence: What
is the equivalent in contemporary English of what the original
writer intended to convey to the reader in the sociocultural context in and for which this document originated? One must take
into account not only the linguistic and literary styles employed,
but also in the case of Acts the cultural influences and traditions
of the community for and to which the writer is addressing his
work. The literary conventions that are taken for granted in Acts
include not only the biblical modes of communication embod-

ied in the LXX, but also the rhetorical and literary styles that were in use in the wider context of the Greco-Roman world in the first and second centuries of the Common Era. These features are noted in the commentary but also, where possible, reflected in the translation. The distinctive terminology of the author is highlighted where appropriate, as in the term used repeatedly in Acts for the new community, "the Way."

With the aim of increasing understanding of the terminology concerning persons, places, and things that play crucial roles in the Acts narrative, at relevant points throughout the commentary there are excurses that seek to define and show the specific connotations of these terms as they appear in the text.

Prelude: Promise and Transition (1:1-26)

1:1-5: Introduction to Volume 2: Preparation for the Ascension of Jesus and the Outpouring of the Spirit

The first report I made, O Theophilus, concerning all the things which Jesus began to do and teach, until the day when, having given instructions though the Holy Spirit to the apostles whom he had chosen, he was taken up [to heaven]. To them also, after he had suffered, he presented himself alive by many convincing proofs, appearing to them over a period of forty days and saying things concerning the kingdom of God. While he was sharing lodging[1] with them, he instructed them not to depart from Jerusalem but to remember the promise of the Father "which you heard from me: that John baptized with water, but you will be baptized with the Holy Spirit after not many days."

Like the Gospel of Luke, this work is addressed to "Theophilus" (Luke 1:3), who is assigned the honorific title *kratiste*, which was used for persons of high official or social status. "Theophilus" is not otherwise known, but may have served as patron for the author of Luke-Acts. But there is also the possibility that his name, which means "friend of God," is used here as a symbol for friendly support that some of the early Christians were receiving from those in the upper social and cultural levels of Roman society. The reference to the "first report" is to the Gospel of Luke, the introduction to which corresponds significantly with this introduction to Acts, but also differs in some details:

Since many have set their hands to provide an orderly account of the events which have been fulfilled among us, just as those who from the beginning became eyewitnesses and servants of the word transmitted them to us, it seems good to me, after having investigated carefully everything from the beginning, to write for you, most excellent Theophilus, an orderly report, so that you might understand the certainty of the matters concerning which you have been instructed.

Here in the preface to the Gospel of Luke is highlighted the claim that the account of the birth and career offered in the gospel as a whole rests on evidence from those who were "from the beginning" eyewitnesses of these events. The report that constitutes that gospel goes beyond the death and resurrection of Jesus to include accounts of his subsequent appearances to his followers, recounting the activity and teaching of Jesus until the time of his ascension — an event described briefly and in somewhat different detail in Luke 24:50–51. The only features detailed there are Jesus blessing the apostles (24:20) and his parting from them as he was taken up to heaven (24:51). His activity and teaching are described as having "begun" during his earthly life, but the "instructions" which he subsequently gave to the apostles are now said to have been conveyed "through the Holy Spirit," the divine agent that will continue to foster and empower God's work in the world following Jesus' ascension. They were promised this endowment of divine strength (*endusesthe ex hypsous dunamin;* 24:49) and are now to remain in Jerusalem until this occurs. The beneficiaries of this outpouring of God's power are those selected (*exelexato*) by Jesus to fulfill this unique role.

Excursus on "Apostle"

The English term "apostle" is simply a transliteration of the Greek word *apostolos*, which means "one who is sent forth." In classical Greek it was the title for an envoy or a military commander. In the synoptic gospels it is sometimes used with reference to the core of Jesus' followers, who are twelve in number (Matt. 10:2; Luke 6:13), although the far more common term for Jesus' co-workers is "disciple" (*mathetes*). In Luke's Gospel, however, the disciples are explicitly said to have been "named apostles" (6:13).

The Markan parallel (Mark 3:14) lacks this term in what is most probably the oldest version of this gospel tradition, although the importance of the term is indicated in the fact that a number of ancient codices include at this point the phrase, "whom he named apostles." The number 12 is symbolically significant as the number of the tribes of Israel, and in the New Testament broadly this tradition of the twelve points to the new people of God, or the "new Israel," whose initial core of leaders are twelve, and who are designated "apostles." In Luke 9:1-6 the twelve are sent out to exercise authority over the demons and to cure diseases, and on their return they are designated — in Luke's account — as "the apostles." In the Q tradition, following the report of Jesus' woes against the Pharisees (Luke 11:37-48) is the promise by the Wisdom of God of the sending of prophets and apostles, or in Matt. 23:54 of the commissioning of "prophets and wise men and scribes." The latter terminology fits best Matthew's interest in portraying Jesus as the one through whom the true understanding of the law is given to the true Israel,[2] for which the leadership consists of the twelve disciples who are sent out to overcome the demons and cure diseases, and designated as apostles (Matt. 10:1-2). Similarly, in Luke 6:13, the chosen twelve are "named apostles" since, for Luke, the authoritative apostolic role is of central importance. In Luke 17:5 Jesus' core of followers are referred to simply as "the apostles," as they are when they are at table with him for the Last Supper (22:14), in contrast to their designation as "disciples" in Mark 14:17 and Matt. 26:20. In the final chapter of Luke, the women who have found the empty tomb report this to "the apostles" (Luke 24:10), while in Matthew the core of Jesus' followers after his resurrection are still referred to as "the disciples" (Matt. 28:7, 16).

For Paul, the role of "apostle" was restricted to those who had "seen the Lord," following his resurrection (1 Cor. 9:1), as he indicates in the list of apostles offered in 1 Cor. 15:5-7. His own vision of Christ was probably understood by him as an inner experience, as Gal. 1:16 indicates: "He revealed his Son *in* me."[3] The term "apostle" appears thirty times in Acts; the meaning of each of these in the varied contexts is considered in notes below.

●

The reality of Jesus' having been raised from the dead has been given multiple attestation to these chosen witnesses/agents over

an extended period: "forty days" —the same length of time that
preparations were being made for earlier events in the history
of the covenant people of God: the forty days that the flood
continued in the time of Noah (Gen. 7:4-17), that Moses was
on the mountain when God sealed the covenant, and that the
land of Canaan was spied out before the tribes of Israel entered
(Num. 14:34). His message to them concerned "the kingdom of
God," which occurs thirty-seven times in the Gospel of Luke,
and which is a central feature of the message from the beginning
(1:3, 6) to the end of Acts (28:23, 31). The bodily presence of the
risen Jesus with his followers is implicit in his "lodging," or eating (*sunalizomenos*), with them during this period, as he charged
them to remain in Jerusalem while awaiting the fulfillment of
God's promise. The appearances in Jerusalem contrast with the
disciples' "seeing" Jesus in Galilee as promised in Mark (16:7)
and the report of his commissioning them there in Matt. 28:16-
20.[4] The symbolic significance of Luke's account is clear: What
will occur through the coming of the Spirit is the reconstitution
of God's people in the city —the formal social center and structure where God has long been present among them, especially in
the temple. Participating in John's baptism in the gospel account
meant that individuals gave public testimony to the need for
purification and covenant renewal of God's people. That divine
program of renewal is about to begin a new phase with the outpouring of the Spirit. Only in Luke (3:4-6) is the quotation from
Isa. 40:3 extended to include the promise that "all humanity will
see God's salvation." This potentially universal participation is
about to be dramatically and symbolically demonstrated in the
Pentecost event (Acts 2:1-42) in fulfillment of the prophecy of
Joel, when baptism "in" or "by the Holy Spirit" is to take place,
involving "all humanity" (*epi pasan sarka*).

1:6-11: The Ascension of Jesus

When they had come together they kept asking him, "Lord, is
it at this time that you will restore the kingdom to Israel?" And
he said to them, "It is not for you to know the times or the
opportune moment which the Father set by his own authority.
But you shall receive power when the Holy Spirit has come
upon you, and you shall be witnesses of me in Jerusalem, and

in all Judea and Samaria, and to the end of the earth." After having said these things, and while they were watching, he was taken up and a cloud took him out of their vision. And as they were staring into heaven while he was going — Look! two men were standing by them in white robes, and they said, "Galilean men, why are you standing looking into heaven? This Jesus who was taken up from you into heaven will come in just the same way as you saw him go into heaven."

The apostles' question to Jesus as to whether this is the time when he will "restore the kingdom" recalls two prophetic passages where the hope of restoration is phrased (in the LXX) using forms of the term found here: *apokathistaneis*. In Ezek. 16:53–58 there is an ironic prediction of the "restoration" of the status of Samaria and Sodom, that is, as victims of divine punishment. But 16:59–63 then turns to the renewal of God's covenant, which will result in his people truly knowing the Lord and receiving forgiveness. In Mal. 4:5–6 is the promise of the return of Elijah. Only in Luke is there mention of the outreach of Elijah and Elisha to non-Israelites (4:25–27), but here the restoration is expected for "Israel" only. The outreach to be performed by the apostles is then specifically announced by Jesus: "in all Judea and Samaria, and to the end of the earth."

The ascension of Jesus into the presence of God is connected with a "cloud,"[5] which in Old Testament tradition is regularly linked with the presence of God as he reveals himself to humans, announcing and then accomplishing his purpose for his people. Jesus' present status — with God in heaven — as well as his future return in triumph are here articulated by the divine messengers as they address those who were his original followers from "Galilee," who saw his death and his risen presence in Jerusalem, and are called to begin there the outreach of the good news to the end of the earth. This will culminate in his return from *heaven* in the unspecified future.

1:12–26: The Choice of a Replacement for Judas

Then they returned to Jerusalem from the mountain which is called Olive, and is a sabbath journey away from Jerusalem. When they came into [the city] they went to the upper space

where they were staying: Peter and John and James and Andrew, Philip and Thomas, Bartholomew and Matthew, James
the son of Alphaeus, and Simon the Zealot and Judas, son of
James. These were all joined in a fully shared commitment in
the Place of Prayer, together with the women and Mary, the
mother of Jesus, and his brothers.

And in those days Peter arose in the midst of the brothers
and spoke, there being a crowd of about one hundred and
twenty in the place: "Brother men, it is necessary that the
writing be fulfilled which the Holy Spirit predicted through the
mouth of David concerning Judas, who became a guide for
those who arrested Jesus, because he was numbered among
us, and he was granted a share in this service. But this fellow
then bought a field with the payment he got for his evil act.
And after he had fallen down flat, he split open in the middle
and all his bowels spewed out. This became known to everyone who lived in Jerusalem, with the result that the field was
called in their own language 'Hakeldama,' which means 'Field
of Blood.' For it is written in the Book of Psalms, 'Let his residence become empty [Ps. 69:26], and may there be no one
in his dwelling place.'

"And, 'Let someone else take on his responsibility' [Ps.
109:8].

"So of those men who were with us during the time when
the Lord Jesus went in and out among us, beginning from the
baptism of John until the day when he was taken up from
us, one of them must become with us a witness concerning
these things." And they proposed two: Joseph, called Barsabbas (who was also called Justus), and Matthias. They prayed
and said, "You who know the hearts of everyone, show us
which one of these two you have chosen to take the place
in this service and apostleship from which Judas turned away
to go to his own place." And they cast lots for them; the lot
fell to Matthias, and he was joined with the eleven apostles.

The mountain called Olive is a high hill about a mile long, paralleling and overlooking the temple mount, from which it is
separated by the Kidron Valley. Since it is over 200 feet higher
than the temple hill, the activities in the temple courts were
plainly visible from there. From the top of its ridge one can
also see eastward down into the Wilderness of Judea and the

roads leading up from Jericho. Jesus is said to have pronounced judgment on Jerusalem from that hill (Luke 19:37–44). Ezekiel pictured the cloud of God's glory resting there as it departed from Jerusalem (Ezek. 11:22–23). The prophet Zechariah expected God to return there to reestablish his rule in Jerusalem (Zech 14:1–9). It was from a village on this hill, Bethany, that the ascension is said to have occurred (Luke 24:50).

It was only a short distance from this hill back to Jerusalem, where the apostles had been staying in the time following the crucifixion and post-resurrection appearances. Building on the rule in Num. 35:5 that the pasture lands around a city should extend for 2000 cubits (about four-fifths of a mile), this was the distance Jews were permitted to go on the sabbath. "Upper space," which is mentioned only in Acts (1:13; 9:37, 39; 20:8), refers to sizable accommodations on the higher levels of buildings which could serve multiple purposes: in this case, the needs of the new community in the various places where it took root. These accommodations provided residence for guests, such as the eleven[6] who were "staying" there. The group's being "fully devoted" to prayer (*proseuche*) is usually understood as referring simply to their praying individually and corporately, but this narrow interpretation ignores the fact that the gathering of the community in the place of prayer is seen here to have involved the devotion of the new Jerusalem community to the apostles' instruction, to the fellowship, to the share in the breaking of bread, as well as to prayer (2:42, 46; 6:4). This understanding of *proseuche* matches well its use in Judaism of this period as a designation of the place where the faithful community gathered. The group was the *synagoge;* the place where they met was the *proseuche*, the place of prayer.

Excursus on Place of Prayer

A strong case for *proseuche* as the designation by Jews of their meeting places was offered by Martin Hengel.[7] Although Hengel suggested that the former was the term used for meeting places by Jews in the Diaspora, while "synagogue" was the term employed in Palestine, the only synagogues found in the Diaspora date from the third–fourth century C.E.,[8] and the only allegedly Second Temple period synagogues found in Palestine (at Gamla, Masada, and Herodium) appear to be merely multipurpose assembly rooms that lack any distinctive features of a building used for primarily ritual purposes.[9] It is significant that Josephus and Philo use the term *proseuche* with reference to places of assembly in a broad sense. A prime example is from Josephus's *Life* (277–93), where the whole community gathers (*pantes synagontai*) in the *proseuche* to deal with legal matters and to attend to requests. In Josephus's *Contra Apionem* (210) he describes Moses as having erected prayer houses (*proseuchas*) in the various precincts of the city in Egypt. In the *Antiquities* (14.258) he reports that Julius Caesar gave permission for Jews to build *proseuchas* near the sea. Philo tells how Flaccus allowed troublemakers to place pagan images in the *proseuchai*, and gave them permission to destroy these structures (*In Flaccum* 41–48). The implication is clear that in first-century C.E. Judaism, in Palestine as well as in the Diaspora, *proseuche* was the characteristic term for Jewish gathering places, and that they were not merely houses of worship but served wider social functions for the Jewish community.[10] Similarly, in the writings of Josephus, *synagoge* is used with reference to the assembled group, rather than the structure where they gathered. Perhaps the most revealing passage in Josephus on this issue is in the *Antiquities* (19.305) where the Roman legate is reported to have written a letter of protest to the leading men of Dora who had defiled the synagogue of the Jews there by setting up in it an image of Caesar. Petronius declared that these desecrators had prevented the Jews from "being [*einai*]"[11] a synagogue (*synagoge*) by their action of transferring this religious object into the Jewish meeting; Caesar's image should be placed in its own shrine rather than in the place (*topos*) where the *synagoge* met.

It is plausible, therefore, to infer that *proseuche* in Acts carries this connotation in more of its occurrences than in 16:13, where the term is regularly and translated as "place of prayer," and unambiguously refers to the Jewish meeting place. The initial clue to the broader connotations of the term is provided in 1:14 by the convergence of three basic terms to depict the gathering of the new community: the members participated fully (*proskarterountes*) in the new commitment; they did so with unified convictions and experience (*homothumadon*); their common actions and experience took place in the *proseuche* = "the place of prayer." Throughout Acts there is a range of community-defining actions linked with prayer and the place of prayer. The shared life and thought of the community are said to be operative among them as they take part in the rites of baptism and breaking of bread, as well as in the apostles' teaching and the prayers (2:42). It is also experienced when they gather in the courtyards of the temple, although the "breaking of bread" does not take place there but in their homes (2:46). In Acts, prayer itself is not a pious exercise but an instrument for decisionmaking and action. In 1:24 the apostles join in prayer to decide who should replace Judas, just as they do in the choice of deacons (6:6). Cornelius demonstrates the appropriateness of his being welcomed into the new community because from the group gathered in his house prayers and alms ascended as a memorial to God (10:1–4). Indeed he was observing the traditional Jewish ninth hour of prayer when the vision came that his prayers and alms were acceptable before God and that he was to receive a messenger from the Lord (10:30–33). Later, it was in a trance as Peter prayed that the vision came advising him not to treat other humans as ritually unclean (11:5). Peter's escape from prison is reported to the community gathered together for prayer in the house of Mary, mother of John Mark (12:12). It is likewise when the community in Antioch is gathered for prayer and fasting that Barnabas and Saul are chosen for the wider mission to Gentiles (13:2–3) and that elders are appointed by them in the newly founded churches in Asia Minor (14:23). The nucleus of the community is represented by Paul and Silas as they pray and sing at midnight in the jail at Philippi (16:25), the result of which is an earthquake and the conversion and baptism of the jailer and his entire household (16:26–34). Paul's farewell to the Ephesian elders takes place in the context of the community gathered for prayer (20:36), as does his final meeting with the men, women, and children of the community at Tyre (21:5). The place of prayer is thus portrayed in Acts as the setting for the celebration and broad experience of the shared life of the new community.

•

An important element among those participating in this common life are "the women."[12] Jesus' "brothers," with whom Luke 8:19–21 implies that Jesus had some tension during his public ministry, are now part of the community as well. The unity of the community is epitomized in Acts by the term *homothumadon*, "with a common purpose," which appears ten times

in this book, and only once elsewhere (Rom. 15:6). It connotes single-mindedness — hence, a group gathered with one, overarching common purpose.[13]
The first statistic for the size of this community is "about one hundred and twenty," which is perhaps symbolically ten times the twelve original core of disciples. "Peter" is clearly the initial leader and spokesman for this group, as he will be on several subsequent occasions when other major issues are addressed: the interpretation of the outpouring of the Spirit (2:14–39); his declaration in the Portico of Solomon concerning the role of Jesus (3:12–26); his explanations to the Jewish leaders in Jerusalem concerning the agent by which healings were taking place (4:8–12) and the significance of the death of Jesus (5:29–33); justification for inclusion of Gentiles in the new community (10:34–43) and for not insisting on circumcision of male gentile converts (15:6–11). Thus it is Peter who articulates the principles and the scriptural basis for the inclusiveness of the new covenant people. The textual variants for the reference to the community (1:15) include not only "brothers," but also "disciples" and "apostles," but male dominance is clear in Peter's term of address: "Brothers." The term shows, however, the familial nature of the group, as opposed to a hierarchal structure or a mere agglutination of individuals.

Jesus' betrayal by Judas was no chance event, but it was "necessary" that it occur in order to bring to fulfillment God's plan[14] for the death of Jesus, and because it was foretold in scripture. The passage referred to is, of course, Ps. 41:10, which describes the infidelity of a close friend, and is alluded to in Mark 14:18 but quoted only in John 13:18. His membership among the disciples was authentic and his "share" in their work was ordained by God. Thus his betrayal of Jesus was the dastardly act of an insider. The description of his ghastly death and his burial in the field he had purchased with the blood money he received are quite different, however, from Matthew's account of Judas's suicide and burial in the field assigned for burial of the impoverished or abandoned, though both accounts refer to it as the "Field of Blood,"[15] which in Aramaic is *Akeldama*. The known presence of blood in the field rendered it impure, just as by the Law of Moses a woman had to undergo an extended period of purification following the flow of blood connected with childbirth (Leviticus 12). This made the field off limits for the law-observant. Peter describes the replacement of Judas as in accord with scripture, quoting Ps. 69:25 and 109:8.[16] The qualifications for the apostolic office are detailed: one must have been a participant in the group that followed Jesus throughout his earthly career, from baptism to ascension, and hence a witness of his resurrection. In the letters of Paul, the requirements are said to be fewer: to have seen the risen Jesus, and to have demonstrated an effective ministry of the gospel (1 Cor. 9:1). In Acts the twin roles for the leaders of the new community are service (*diakonia*) and apostleship, the second of which clearly carries authoritative implications in Acts. The divine will in this decision about replacing Judas is determined by "lot," and the role is assigned to "Matthias," who is not mentioned elsewhere in the New Testament.

Chapter One —————————————————————————

The Launching of the Inclusive Community (2:1–5:42)

2:1–13: The Outpouring of the Holy Spirit at Pentecost

And when the Day of Pentecost had fully arrived, they were all together in one place. There suddenly came out of heaven a noise like the impact of a powerful wind, and it filled the whole house where they were sitting. There appeared to them divided tongues, as though of fire, and one of them sat on each of the apostles. They were all filled with the Holy Spirit and began to speak in other languages as the Spirit gave them the ability to speak.

There were Jews residing in Jerusalem, devout men from every nation under heaven. When this sound happened, the crowd came together and was confused, because each one of them heard them speaking in his own language. They were puzzled and amazed, and said, "Aren't all of these who are speaking Galileans? Then how is it that each of us hears them in our language in which we were born? Parthians, Medes, Elamites, those who live in Mesopotamia, Judea and Cappadocia, Pontus and Asia, Phrygia and Pamphylia, Egypt and those parts of Libya which belong to Cyrene, both Jews and proselytes, Cretans and Arabs — we hear them telling in our own languages the magnificent deeds of God." They were all astounded and puzzled, and were saying to each other, "What is the point of this?" But others sneered and said, "They are loaded with new wine."

The emphatic verb *sympleroo,* "fully arrived," which is used here in connection with the Day of Pentecost, is wholly appropriate, since the calculation of that festival was somewhat complicated. The first step in the festival series was the offering of first fruits, the initial crops that were harvested toward the end of the growing season (Lev. 23:9–14). This was to take place on the day following the sabbath. Then seven weeks and one day (the sabbath) later, there was to be an offering of new grain and bread made from the first fruits in celebration of the completion of the harvest. No work was to be performed on this fiftieth day (which in Greek is *pentekoste*), but a holy convocation was to take place, with a sin offering of lambs and an elevation offering of thanks to God for the crops (Lev. 9:15–21). It was on this day that the whole community in Jerusalem was gathered in one place (*epi to auto*). The coming from heaven of a sound "like the impact of a powerful wind," which was the coming of the Holy Spirit on the faithful, involves the equivalent of a play on the Greek word *pneuma* and the Hebrew *ruach* for which "wind" is a common translation. Both words can mean "spirit" in the sense of invisible power, divine (Num. 24:2; Isa. 61:1; Luke 4:18) or demonic (Luke 6:18; Acts 5:16), however, as well as wind perceived as an invisible physical force (Gen. 8:1; Ps. 1:4). The "tongues as though of fire" recall the apocalyptic visions seen by Enoch of the dwelling place of God in the heavens, which is depicted as "surrounded by tongues of fire" and as "built of crystals" between which are "tongues of living fire," with "rivers full of living fire" encircling it (1 Enoch 14:9, 71:5-6). In the prophetic tradition, fire is the symbol of God's judgment (Amos 7:4), which is to involve the purging of God's people by "a spirit of burning" (Isa. 4:4). Clearly what the fiery tongues here depict is the divine presence that has now become accessible through the Holy Spirit.

What is explicitly involved in this account is the divine enablement of the apostles through the Spirit to begin to interpret the good news about Jesus to those of other ethnic and linguistic groups than the Jews. The potential for this worldwide outreach of the gospel is dramatically evident in the list of ethnic and geographic origins of those who are present in Jerusalem when the Spirit is poured out on the apostles. They are said to be "Jews, devout men from every nation under heaven." Their reason for being in Jerusalem was not curiosity, but piety, rev-erence, devotion (*eulabeis*). The range of their places of origin is specified. The Parthians, Medes, and Elamites were from the regions north and east of the Persian Gulf and the Tigris–Euphrates Valley (present-day Iraq, here designated as Mesopotamia), and reaching across what is now Iran, from the eastern border of Turkey to the western part of Afghanistan. Cappadocia and Pontus were in central and northern Asia Minor, the latter bordering on the Black Sea. The eastern half of the Mediterranean coast of Africa was represented by Egypt, Cyrene, and parts of Libya. Asia and Phrygia were names assigned at various times to the central section of Asia Minor, while Pamphylia was the district along the south-central coast. The designation of various people includes Romans, who were visitors or "temporary residents" in Jerusalem, and people from the Greek island of Crete[1] and from the huge Arab-speaking area east and south of the Jordan region. Those present at this extraordinary event include both "Jews and proselytes," and possibly pious inquirers, as *eulabeis* (2:5) perhaps implies. What these diverse people have in common is having witnessed that the apostles — through the Spirit that has been poured out — were enabled to overcome the linguistic differences that divided their hearers and to report in the language of each the "magnificent deeds of God." The reactions of the hearers range from astonishment and profound curiosity to scorn. Are those who speak in this way messengers of God or drunken idiots? What is God seeking to convey through them? It is in direct response to this varied assessment of what is happening that Peter addresses his opening remarks.

Excursus on "The Jews" in Acts

The term "the Jews" (*hoi ioudaioi*), which occurs more than fifty times in Acts, carries two different sets of connotation for the author. The reader must be aware of this distinction in order to sense the intent of the various texts, since they are about evenly divided between these two meaning groups. The first type of usage is the only one used in the first eight chapters, but is recurrent throughout the rest of the book. It represents "the Jews" as the community committed to the Jewish tradition, preserved in the law and the prophets, and providing the ground for the covenant relationship with God. The second type, which predominates from chapter 18 to the end of the book, depicts "the

Jews" as primarily the Jewish leadership in its efforts to exterminate the early Christian movement, to which it assigned the label "the sect of the Nazarenes" (24:5).

"The Jews" as a community are depicted in sympathetic terms by the narrator beginning with 2:5, where they are identified as "devout men from every nation under heaven," who are now "residing in Jerusalem." It is as fellow "Jews" that Peter first addresses them on the Day of Pentecost (2:14) when he presents his explanation of what occurred in the outpouring of the Holy Spirit, based on an appeal to the Jewish prophet Joel (2:16–21). Throughout Acts, various individuals who enter the narrative are identified as Jews: Timothy (16:1), Apollos (18:24), even Paul (21:33, 22:3, 26:4). Included among the "devout" now in Jerusalem are "proselytes" (2:10), just as will be the case in Jewish communities in the Diaspora (e.g., in Thessalonica; 17:4). This special ethnic-religious identity of the Jews is recognized not only by members but also by hostile individuals or crowds: the Emperor Claudius (18:2, 5) and the crowd in Ephesus (19:33–34). The distinctive identity of the Jew is established and maintained through the group's conformity to the Law of Moses, of which the most visible features are ritual and dietary restrictions, which prevent free social interchange with non-Jews (21:20–21). Recognized by nonmembers is that there are ongoing definitional debates and disputes within the community, as Paul notes in his address to King Agrippa (26:2-3). This is an essential feature of the portrayal of Jews in Acts, since the author wants to make the case that Jesus and the movement he has launched embody the true fulfillment of the prophetic hopes and promises of Israel. Paul's final statement in Acts, which is to the Jewish leadership in Rome, declares that the real cause of his imprisonment is the controversy over "the hope of Israel" — a conflict that was foreseen by the prophet Isaiah (6:9–10 = Acts 28:26–27) and that has led to the rejection of Jesus and the new definition of the covenant community, which includes participation by the Gentiles (28:28). It is this controversy over the criteria for participation in the community and the "kingdom of God" (28:30) which is at the heart of the conflict with "the Jews" in Acts.

The second type of portrayal of the Jews — the Jewish leadership in its hostility toward the Jesus movement as a threat to the integrity of the covenant people — is first evident in 9:1-

2, where Paul appears in Damascus with written authorization from the high priest to take back to Jerusalem for trial by the Jewish authorities any men or women in the Damascus synagogues who were "disciples of the Lord." The Roman-designated governors and rulers in the region are seen as seeking to ingratiate themselves with the Jewish leadership by assisting in the repression of the followers of Jesus (12:3, 24:27, 25:9). In the cities of Syria and Asia Minor the Jewish leaders mount an initiative to crush the Jesus movement that has been launched by the apostles (13:45, 50; 19:33–34), as is also the case subsequently in Macedonia and Greece (18:12, 20:3). The charge against Paul is encapsulated in 21:28, where his teaching is said to be hostile to "the [covenant] people, the law, and this place [the temple]," which he has now been accused of having "desecrated" by bringing a Gentile into the holy court accessible only to Israelites. The attempt to kill him is thwarted by the intervention of the Roman tribune (21:31), but the schemes to murder him continue throughout Acts (23:12, 20, 27; 24:18). Significantly, it is the high priest who articulates before the Roman governor the accusations of the Jews against Paul (24:5–6), in which he is later joined by the priestly leaders and the "foremost Jews," who then plot to murder Paul in ambush as he is being taken to Caesarea by the Romans (25:3). A central feature in the ironic scenario of Acts is that it was the continuing accusations against Paul by the Jewish leaders —which the Roman governor characterizes as groundless (25:18) —that created the dilemma that could only be resolved by acquiescing in Paul's request to have his case transferred to the place that he was "determined in the Spirit" that he should go (19:21).[2] The hostility motif in Acts is not toward Jews or the Jewish tradition, but toward the leadership that seeks to thwart the proclamation by the apostles that Jesus is God's agent of hope for the covenant people as set forth in the law and the prophets.[3]

2:14–36: Peter Declares That God through Jesus Is Fulfilling His Promises to David and the Prophets

Peter stood with the eleven, raised his voice, and said to them forcefully, "Fellow Jews and all who reside in Jerusalem, let this be known to you and pay attention to my words. These men are not drunk, as you assume, for it is only three hours after sunrise. But this is what was spoken through the prophet Joel:

'It will happen in the last days,' God says, 'that I will pour out my Spirit upon all humanity, and your sons and your daughters shall prophesy. Your young men shall see visions, and your old men shall dream dreams. Even on my male slaves and my female slaves, in those days I will pour out my Spirit, and they shall prophesy. And I will give wonders in the heaven above, and signs on the earth below: blood and fire and steaming smoke. The sun shall be changed into darkness, and the moon into blood, before the great and astounding Day of the Lord comes. And it shall be that everyone who calls on the name of the Lord will be saved.' [Joel 2:28]

Fellow Israelites, hear these words: Jesus the Nazarene, a man approved to you by God through the powerful and marvelous acts and signs which God performed through him in your midst, as you well know – this man who by God's predetermined will and foreknowledge was delivered up, you lifted up and nailed to a cross by the hand of those outside the law. God raised him up, having set him free from the pains of death, because it was impossible for him to be held by its power. For David says about him,

Through everything, I saw in advance the Lord always
    before my face,
For this reason my heart was glad and my tongue
    rejoiced,
So now my earthly life will be lived in hope,
because you will not forsake my soul in Hades,
nor will you give up your devoted one to see destruction.
You have revealed to me the ways of life.
You will make me full of joy with your presence.
[Ps. 16:8–11]

Fellow members, it is right for me to say to you with all boldness concerning the patriarch David that he died and was buried, and his tomb is among us to this day. Because he was a prophet, he knew that God had sworn to him by an oath that someone of his offspring would sit upon his throne. Seeing this in advance, he spoke about the resurrection of Christ:

> He was not forsaken in Hades,
> nor did his body see destruction. [Ps. 16:10]

God raised up this Jesus, of which all of us are witnesses. Having been exalted at God's right hand, and having received from the Father the promise of the Holy Spirit, he has poured out this which you now see and hear. For David did not go up to the heavens, but he says,

> The Lord said to my Lord,
> Sit at my right hand,
> until I put your enemies as a footstool under your feet.
> [Ps. 110:1]

So let the whole house of Israel know beyond a doubt that God has made him Lord and Christ, this Jesus whom you crucified."

Peter, as spokesman for the apostolic group, speaks "forcefully" to this crowd of inquirers and skeptics whose origin or whose present residence is in Jerusalem. He dismisses the proposal that the strange languages in which the apostles speak indicate that they are drunk, especially since it is only nine in the morning ("three hours after sunrise"). Instead, he claims that the prophecy of Joel has now been fulfilled (Joel 2:28–32).[4] Unlike the Hebrew text, which says that this event will happen "afterward," or the LXX, which dates it "after these things" (*meta tauta*), the quotation in Acts is modified to include the phrase "in the last days." What has happened with the outpouring of the Spirit is seen in Acts as a major event in the sequence of divine actions by which God's purpose for his people is being accomplished. The inclusive intent of this event is made explicit: men and women, young and old, slave and free, will now share in access to the message from God given through the Spirit. Moses had expressed the hope that the gift of prophecy might be available for "all God's people" and that "the LORD would put his Spirit upon them," but there is in the Old Testament no report that this occurred — only the hope that it might, as expressed by Joel. In the tradition of ancient Israel, the ability to "prophesy" does not mean primarily foretelling the future, but involves becoming the instrument of divine communication to the human race. Joel declares that this capacity will be widely available when the Spirit comes upon "all humanity." The successive phases of the outreach of the new community "to the end of the earth" (1:8) are pictured in Acts as the outworking of this prophetic promise, and are highlighted in 10:1–11:18 and 15:1–35, and explained in the speeches.[5] The mode of address from God through the Spirit is not merely verbal, but is also to include "visions" and "dreams," as well as prophetic utterances. Confirmation that these messages originate with God is to be provided in the form of celestial and terrestrial marvels, including terrifying signs of divine judgment in the heavens and on earth: blood, fire, smoke, darkness. The synoptic accounts of the crucifixion agree in reporting that events of this kind have taken place. They report darkness over the whole earth (*ge;* Luke 23:44–45; Mark 15:33; Matt. 27:45) and the divine tearing of the temple veil (Luke 23:45; Mark 15:33; Matt. 27:51a). Matthew's account adds the details of an earthquake and the saints rising from the dead at the moment of Jesus' death (Matt. 27:51–53). *Blood* is mentioned in John's account of the crucifixion (19:31–37). The passage from Joel links these factors with God's disclosure of his redemptive purpose for his people, which will be the final preparation for and culminate in "the great and astounding Day of the Lord." Central for the whole narrative of Acts are the "signs" and "wonders."[6] The consequence of these manifestations of the Spirit of God will be the opportunity for people from every ethnic and national group to share in the new era for the new people of God — in other words, to "be saved." The sole qualification for sharing in this renewal is to "call on the name of the Lord." In the explanation and the argument from scripture that follows in Peter's address it is clear that "the Lord" is Jesus. To "call on his name" means to identify with him, and to rely upon his person and power to accomplish God's cosmic purpose for the renewal of his people and of the creation. How God has been at work through Jesus to make this possible is explained in Peter's subsequent remarks.

Peter's words are addressed to "Fellow Israelites." It is clear that there is no intention to replace Israel as the people of God, but instead to redefine the basis for participation in the covenant community, which is no longer perceived as requiring conformity to the Law of Moses or traditional ethnic requirements. The "powerful and marvelous acts and signs" attributed to Jesus in the gospel tradition are the consequence of God's own action through him, as is asserted by Jesus in such passages as Luke 11:20, where he claims to perform exorcisms "by the finger of God." Here he refers to the same instrument that brought the plagues on the Egyptians prior to Israel's exodus (Exod. 8:19). God's redemptive activity through Jesus is not an impulsive or improvisatory solution for the human situation of disobedience and estrangement from God. Rather, Jesus was "delivered up" to his cruel death on the cross by the "predetermined" plan of God, which was not only foreknown but fixed by divine intention. Although his death was the consequence of his rejection by the Jewish authorities, the execution itself was "by the hands" of the Romans, who were wholly outside the law's decrees or community definition of Israel. Peter is not depicted here as offering any doctrinal interpretation of the death of Jesus, such as one finds in the gospel tradition (Mark 10:45; John 15:13) or in Paul's letters (Rom. 3:24–25). Here the emphasis is on the triumph over death achieved through Jesus, which is now available for those who recognize him as God's agent for human renewal.

God, by raising Jesus from the dead, not only "set him free from the pains of death," but also showed that death does not exercise universal power over humans to bring them to sorrow and destruction. The extended quotation from Ps. 16:8–11 is attributed to David, as are all the subsequent psalms quoted in Acts, but it is perceived as a prophecy concerning the destiny of one of his "offspring," rather than the expectation of his own personal escape from Sheol (*Hades*)[7] and the pit of destruction. Clearly Peter perceives Jesus to be the one through whom this victory has already been achieved, when "God raised" him from the dead, and thereby overcame the "power" of death.

The final verse quoted by Peter (2:28 = Ps. 16:11) goes beyond victory over death to give assurance of new insights and new experience of a life of joy in the presence of God. Resurrection is here seen as not merely a return to pre-death existence, but access to a new kind of life that includes admission into the "presence" of God. Although David is understood to have foreseen this transformation of life, Peter makes clear that he did not himself experience it. David's place in a past era is emphasized by the reference to him as "patriarch." The fact of his death and burial (1 Kings 2:10) are said to be given concrete confirmation by the existence of his tomb in Jerusalem.[8] Here also David's expectation of victory over death and the grave are aspects of his prophetic role, not what he expected to experience personally. The claim here is that David both foresaw *in advance* and consciously spoke about the resurrection of Christ. What David is seen to have looked forward to in the psalm was the enthronement of one of his descendants, since he was given this promise:

> The Lord swore to David a sure oath
> from which he will not turn back:
> One who is the fruit of your loins
> I will set on your throne. [Ps. 132:11; in LXX, 131:11]

But beyond this hope of a successor on his throne, David also is said in Psalm 110 to have learned that one who was his "lord" would be told by God to remain at God's "right hand until I put your enemies as a footstool under your feet" (Ps. 110:1). Who the "enemies" are is not specified here, but the implication is that those who collaborated to have Jesus put to death — and perhaps death itself[9] — have now been overcome through God's having raised Jesus from the dead. The apostles all shared the experience of seeing Jesus risen from the dead. They now await the defeat of the powers that oppose Jesus and God, confident that the Christ who is seated at God's "right hand" will ultimately overcome all those evil powers. There is for Peter no question that God has already established Jesus in the twin roles as "Lord and Christ": the agent of God's rule in the world, and the Messiah chosen and anointed by God to fulfill that triumphant role. The supreme irony is that this Lord and Christ, the instrument of God's sovereign rule in the whole of creation, has died by the ignominious Roman mode of execution: crucifixion.

2:37–47: The New Community Begins to Take Shape

> When they heard this, they were all cut to the heart and said to Peter and the rest of the apostles, "What shall we do, brother men?" and Peter said to them, "Change your mind! And each of you should be baptized for the forgiveness of your sins, and accept the gift of the Holy Spirit. For the promise is to you and your children, and to all who are far off, all of whom the Lord has invited."

And he bore witness by many other words, saying, "Preserve yourselves from this crooked generation." Those who accepted his message were baptized, and there were added [to the community] on that day about three thousand people. They were united in the community on the basis of the teaching of the apostles, of the fellowship, of the breaking of bread, and of the prayers.

On each one of them there came fear, because signs and wonders took place through the apostles. All who believed were together, and they had everything in common. They sold their possessions and their substance and divided up the results as anyone had need. Daily they gathered as one in the temple, and broke bread together at a home. They shared food with joy and singleness of heart, praising God and having cordial relations with all the people. Daily the Lord added to this group those who were being saved.

The people's response of sorrow and contrition to Peter's assignment to them of responsibility for participation in the death of Jesus moves them to ask of the apostles what is the proper way of dealing with their shared guilt for participation in this shameful event. These penitent inquirers' identification with the apostles is apparent in their addressing the latter as "brothers." Peter's answer involves four related factors: (1) They are to "change their minds," not merely to be sorry (repent) for their part in this tragic event of Jesus' death. (2) They are to give public evidence to their participation in the new community by accepting "baptism." (3) This change in understanding and experience of the community-defining ritual promises to put them in a new relationship with God and each other, by their experiencing the "forgiveness of sins." (4) The inward confirmation of sharing in this new people of God will be their acceptance of and manifestation of the "gift of the Holy Spirit."[10] This opportunity is open to Peter's hearers and their offspring, as well as to those who by birth, ethnic or cultural status, religious tradition, or moral condition might seem to be totally alienated from a place in the life of God's people. The one essential factor is for them to recognize that it is "the Lord our God" who is inviting them to share in the common life of the reconstituted community of faith. The alternative to this response to the good news is to go on living by the norms and values and perceptions of the majority of their contemporaries. Instead, they now have the opportunity to escape that sad destiny which awaits "this crooked generation." It is with this mournful description that the disobedient children of Israel are characterized in the Song of Moses (Deut. 32:5) and in Ps. 78:8. Paul echoes the same indictment of the faithless and the wicked in Phil. 2:15. Now they have the invitation to participate in the new life that awaits God's people, and to give public testimony to their new commitment by receiving baptism.

The astonishing results of this invitation are embodied in the "three thousand" who join the new community. Their participation is not casual or temporary. Rather, they "took a firm stand" in what they have heard from the apostles. It is given concrete public expression by their sharing in the instruction that the apostles continue to offer, in the common life of this new people of God, in the central common act, "the breaking of bread," which has implications for past, present, and future: (1) it looks back to the last meal of Jesus with the disciples; (2) it celebrates now his continuing presence with his people; and (3) it looks forward to the time when they will "eat and drink at my table in the kingdom, and sit on thrones judging the twelve tribes of Israel" (Luke 22:28). The community's common life of commitment to God and their concern for each other and for the wider world are pointed to in the final element in this description: "the prayers."

The "fear" that is said to have come on each of the members is not fright, but awe as they confront the divine mystery of what God has done and is continuing to do through Jesus and the work of the Holy Spirit in their midst. The concrete evidence of this divine activity in their midst comes through the "signs and wonders" that God continues to perform through the apostles, as happened earlier through Jesus. A dramatic example of this kind of activity is described in the opening section of the next chapter (Acts 3:1–10).[11]

What is emphasized here in the summary statement about the emergent new community is its unity in the midst of the diversity of those who have joined. They are not physically assembled in Jerusalem, but they share a range of factors: their convictions about Jesus, and what God is doing through him; their experience of renewal and of the power of the Spirit; their sense of shared destiny and mutual obligation. Concrete expression is given to this last feature in the joint actions of the members in

selling their "possessions" and pooling the compensation they
receive. And they do so in such a way as to provide as a group for
the special needs of each member. The locus of the community
is dual: They join in the worship of God in the great shrine open
in its outer Court of the Gentiles, and in the areas of the temple
reserved for the faithful of Israel, including proselytes who have
accepted circumcision and conform to the purity laws. All of this
sacred complex has as its primary focus the inner court, where
God was believed to dwell invisibly, and which was accessible
only to the high priest. But the new community joyously experiences its distinctive identity in the privacy of homes, where they
join in the eucharist. It is in this act that the sincerity of purpose and "singleness of heart" are experienced. Their common
life is filled with gratitude to God for having worked through
Jesus to call this community into being, but it is also the basis
for "cordial relations" with outsiders, who are impressed by the
inclusiveness, the generosity, the joy, and the great hope that
binds them together. The result of both the public proclamation
and the vivid image of this new community is that every day
men and women come forward to join this new people of God,
who are daily experiencing and manifesting the process of transformation and renewal of human life concentrated in the simple
phrase "being saved."[12] The agent through whom this renewal
of the community is seen as taking place is "the Lord," who is
responsible for the steady increase in membership of this new
people of God. Up to this point, the results of the emergence
of this community have a positive impact on the outsiders ("all
the people") who observe what is happening and are favorably
impressed by the unity of the group, by their continued commitment to the biblical and sacerdotal traditions of Judaism (as
is evident in their regular participation in the worship activities
of the temple), by their generosity to the poorer members of this
new movement, and by the blend of joy and total commitment
that characterizes them.

3:1-10: Peter Heals a Lame Man at the Temple Gate

> Peter and John were going into the temple at the hour of
> prayer, which was the ninth hour [after sunrise]. A certain man
> who had been lame from birth was being carried along. Those

[who brought him] would put him daily at the gate of the temple which was called Beautiful, so he could beg alms from those who were going into the temple. When he saw Peter and John about to enter the temple, he asked for alms from them. Peter, as well as John, looked at him intently and said, "Look at us." He looked hard at them, anticipating that he would receive something from them. But Peter said, "I do not have silver or gold, but what I have, I am going to give you. In the name of Jesus Christ of Nazareth, rise up and walk!" Taking hold of his right hand, he raised him up. Immediately his feet and ankles were strengthened, and leaping up, he stood and began walking. He entered with them into the temple, walking and leaping and praising God. And all the people saw him walking and praising God, and they recognized that he was the one who sat for alms at the Beautiful Gate of the temple, and they were all filled with astonishment and amazement at what had happened to him.

The apostles' continuing involvement in and disciplined commitment to the worship traditions of Israel are evident in this report of Peter and John about to enter the temple at three in the afternoon, or nine hours after sunrise. In the Law of Moses there is no schedule for daily prayers, but there are prescribed times for offering daily sacrifice: morning and evening (Exod. 29:39–40; Lev. 6:20). This is confirmed by Josephus as still the norm in the first century C.E. (*Ant.* 14.4.3). The best evidence for a set pattern of prayers comes from Daniel, who is described as praying three times a day from the windows in the upper room of his house in Babylon which face Jerusalem, even though the practice has been forbidden by royal decree (Dan. 6:10). The "hour of prayer" alluded to here implies either a formal practice or at least a well-known custom, but in either case a traditional gathering of the pious in the temple courts.

The apostles' choice for entering the vast temple complex was the Beautiful Gate. Scholars have debated which gate to the temple enclosure the author has in mind, since this designation is not found in ancient descriptions of or references to the temple. When Herod rebuilt the temple, he retained the traditional east-west orientation of the central section, with the Holy of Holies to the west, surrounded by the Court of Israel and the Court of Priests to the east. Surrounding the temple was the vast enclosure, the Court of the Gentiles, major access to which was from the south through the so-called Portico of Solomon, an enormous colonnade with a great gate, steps, and a bridge linking this part of the temple with the aristocratic section of Jerusalem to the west. The older and poorer part of the city was to the south of the temple hill. Probably it was through the grand gate opening into the Portico of Solomon that the apostles are pictured as entering, and by which the lame man was placed to collect alms.[13] Through this gate would enter not only the pious, but tourists who were drawn from all over the Roman world to see this monumental temple.

The lame man had been crippled from birth, so there was no hope of his recovery by human means. His existence was dependent on the assistance of those who carried him to the temple area, and the generosity of those who gave him money for survival. The response from Peter to his begging for "silver or gold" is a total surprise, but he is depicted here as reacting without hesitation to Peter's instructions. The instrument which effects the healing of the man is "the name of Jesus Christ of Nazareth." This title combines several elements: (1) the given name of this man, Jesus, which is a grecized version of one of the traditional leaders of God's people, Joshua, an Ephraimite (Num. 13:16; 1 Chron. 7:20-27), who led the people in battle (Exod. 17:8-13), spied out the promised land (Num. 14:6-10), and then was commissioned to allot the land among the tribes (Num. 34:16-29) and lead them in to occupy it (Deut. 31:7-8), as described in the Book of Joshua. (2) The inclusion of the designation of Jesus as the "Christ" (messiah) implies the source of his power as the anointed (in Hebrew, *meshiach*) agent of God, including the healing power that came upon him when he was anointed by "the Spirit of the Lord" (Luke 4:18-21; Isa. 61:1-2). (3) The acknowledgment of Jesus' humble origins in human terms is indicated when the little-known Galilean village of Nazareth is specified by Luke as "their [the holy family's] own home town" (Luke 2:39), even though Jesus was born in Bethlehem, the city of David, as result of the Roman decree in connection with the imperial census which required families to return to the place of their ancestral origin (Luke 2:2-3). There is a dramatic irony in the configuration of these features of Jesus' origins and the astonishing power that is manifest in the healing of the lame man through this *name* (see excursus on "the Name" in Acts, p. 63.

The instant renewal of the lame man's lower limbs evokes joy from him, serves as tangible evidence for onlookers of the divine power that has healed him, elicits astonishment from the passersby who perceive the transformation that has occurred in the condition of this familiar former cripple. An explanation of what has happened and what it signifies is essential, and is offered by Peter.

3:11–26: Peter's Speech in the Colonnade of Solomon

As he was clinging to Peter and John, the whole crowd — utterly astonished — ran together to them in the colonnade named for Solomon. When Peter saw this he responded to the people:

"Israelite men, why are you amazed at this, or why do you fix your gaze on us as though it was by our own power or piety that we made him walk? The God of Abraham, the God of Isaac, the God of Jacob, the God of our fathers [Exod. 3:6, 15] — he is the one who glorified his servant, Jesus, whom you handed over [to the Romans] and denied in the presence of Pilate, even though he had decided to let him go. You denied the holy and righteous one, and asked for a man who was a murderer to be released to you. You killed the Founder of Life, whom God raised from the dead, of which we are witnesses. And by faith in his name — his name has made strong this one whom you see and know — and the faith that is through him [Jesus] has given to him this complete health which is evident before all of you.

"And now brothers, I know that you acted in ignorance, just as your rulers did. But God, who announced beforehand through the mouth of all the prophets that the Messiah would suffer, fulfilled it in this way. So repent and turn, in order that your sins may be wiped out. In this way from the presence of the Lord there will come upon you the times of renewal, and he will send the Messiah designated in advance for you: Jesus, whom heaven must keep until the times of complete renewal which God told about through the words of his holy prophets ages ago. Moses said, 'God your Lord will raise up a prophet like me from among your brothers. You will listen to all the things that he will speak to you [Deut. 18:15–16]. And it shall be so that every individual who does not give heed to that prophet will be totally thrown out of [my] people' [Deut. 18:19; Lev. 23:29]. And all the prophets including Samuel and those after him spoke about and announced these days. You are the sons of the prophets and of the covenant which God established with our fathers, saying to Abraham, 'And in your offspring shall be blessed all the families of the earth' [Gen. 22:18, 26:4]. For God, having raised up his servant [child], sent him first to you, in order to bless you by turning each of you away from your evil deeds."

Since the Portico of Solomon in the temple gave entrance to the Court of the Gentiles, which was the only part of the temple complex where non-Israelites could go, the detail that the crowd converged there prepares the reader of Acts symbolically for the important claim that Peter is to articulate in this speech: that "all the families of the earth" are to have opportunity to share in the blessings that God will offer (4:25). Even so, the group now addressed by Peter consists of the traditional participants in God's dealings with his people: the "Israelite men." He tells them that they should not be astounded at what has happened, and they should surely not attribute to the apostles the ability to perform such a cure, as though it were a consequence of some special private powers that they possessed, or even a divine gift as a reward for their personal "piety." There is no human capacity — therapeutic or spiritual — which has enabled them to effect this cure. Rather, this event is but another manifestation of the power of the God who revealed himself to the patriarchs and the people of Israel who descended from them (Exod. 3:6). The agent through whom the healing occurred is Jesus, who came as God's "servant" or child (Isa. 52:13, 53:11), but whom God has "glorified." That glorification took place through God's having "raised [Jesus] from the dead." The apostles, through their encounter with the risen Christ, are "witnesses" of this marvelous act of God.

The death of Jesus is interpreted in Peter's sermon in terms of two pairs of dual factors. The first set defines the shared responsibility for his execution: Pilate was ready to release Jesus, but the Jewish leaders asked that he be executed and a clearly guilty man ("murderer": Judas) be released. Pilate cooperated, and Jesus was crucified by the Roman mode of execution of criminals. The second set of factors is spelled out in the rest of the speech. While the Jewish leaders are depicted as guilty for their share in the death of Jesus, what they did has had results totally unforeseen by them. These consequences include the fulfillment of the prophetic pronouncements, the coming of "times of renewal," the taking away of "sins," and the share by those from "all nations" in the life of the people of God. Neither the Jewish nor the Roman leaders were aware of the divine plan and its cosmic consequences that their humanly despicable plot to destroy Jesus would achieve.

The supreme irony of what was done with and through Jesus and its import for humanity is concisely expressed in the charge that these leaders "killed the Founder of Life." The term *archegos* can mean "prince" or "ruler," as well as "author." But the basic force of the term is "originator," or "founder," pointing to an agent who begins something new. What Jesus has launched is a whole new mode of human existence: obedience to God, conformity to his cosmic purpose, triumphant over death and the powers of evil. This is *life* as God intended it to be for humans, and it has become accessible to God's people through the death and resurrection of Jesus. It is now seen to be actual and in process of availability for rapidly increasing numbers of the faithful. The crucial requirement for participation in this new kind of life is trust in the *name* of Jesus:[14] in his historical being, in the authority God gave him, in his suffering and death, and in God's vindication of him by raising him from the dead. "Faith" is not merely "in" Jesus, but has been made possible and accessible "through him."

The prophetic foretelling of Christ's "suffering" is declared here, but it is not detailed at this point as it is in Acts 8:32–33.[15] These prophecies were fulfilled by the unwitting, hostile reaction to Jesus on the part of the religious leaders. If those who sought to destroy Jesus change their attitude toward him, their "sins" will be removed through the death of Jesus, and will no longer be a barrier or a disqualification for their entering a right relationship with God. This program of human renewal through Christ is to culminate in the future, and the coming of those "times" is to be eagerly awaited as they come from God. Then the Messiah will be sent back to the world and to those people whom God has designed to be in special relationship with him, and then will be the time of "renewal" of the whole creation, as foreseen and foretold by the prophets through the earlier ages. Meanwhile, Jesus is portrayed as in heaven with God, awaiting the new era ("times") when the creation will be totally transformed in conformity with God's will and purpose. This message of human and cosmic renewal came through the primary one who has spoken God's message to all of human-kind: Jesus, who here is identified with the "prophet" whose coming is foretold in Deut. 18:15–16. He will address the whole human race: those who heed his word will participate in the renewal; those who refuse to "give heed" to his message will be fully and permanently excluded from a share in the life of God's people (Deut. 18:19; Lev. 23:29). The first of the series of "prophets" that culminates in the coming of Jesus is here said to be "Samuel." His special place in the divine plan for his people is evident from his birth to a woman (Hannah) who had been unable to bear children, "because the Lord had closed her womb" (1 Sam. 1:6). Like Mary (Luke 1:46–55) she bursts into song when God enables her to bear a child (1 Sam. 2:1–10). Her offspring, Samuel, is the one who anointed David as king of Israel — the one through whom the true royal line was established (1 Sam. 16:1–13), and the one whose offspring the prophets declare to be the one who will rule over the renewed city of Jerusalem, the people of God, and the whole creation.[16] The promise of the covenant that will be open to "all the fami-lies of the earth" goes back to Abraham (Gen. 22:18, 26:4), but God sent Jesus and his message "first" to the people of Israel and those who have turned to the God of Israel. Representatives of them are now gathered in the courtyard of Solomon, which gives access to the presence of God which was believed to be in the most holy place in the temple. To them goes the initial appeal to share in God's blessing available for those who "turn" from their misdeeds and reliance on corrupt or misguided means for gaining access to God. Their trust must be in this "servant" whom God has "raised" from the dead.

4:1–22: Peter and John before the Council

While they were speaking to the people, the priests and the captain of the temple guards and the Sadducees came and stood by them, greatly annoyed because they were teaching the people and declaring that through Jesus was the resurrection from the dead. They laid hands on them and put them in prison until the next day, since it was already evening. Many of those who had heard their message believed, and the number of men became about five thousand.

And it happened on the next day that the leaders and the elders and the scribes were gathered in Jerusalem. Annas was the high priest, and Caiaphas and John and Alexander, as well as all who were of the high-priestly family. Making [Peter and John] stand in the middle of them, they began to interrogate them: "By what sort of power, or by what name[17] did you do this?" Then Peter was filled with the Spirit and said to them, "Rulers of the people and elders, if this day you are asking about the good deed done to this ailing man, by which he was made well, let it be known to all of you and to the whole people Israel that it is through the name of Jesus Christ the Nazarene — whom you crucified, whom God raised from the dead — it is by him that this man now stands before you healthy. It is this [Jesus] who is 'the stone which was counted as nothing by you builders, which has become the head of the corner' [Ps. 118:22]. There is no salvation in anyone else, since there is no other name under the heaven that has been given to humans by which we must be saved."

When they saw the fearlessness of Peter and John and grasped that they were uneducated and amateurs, they were amazed and recognized that they had been with Jesus. When they saw the man who had been healed standing with them, they had nothing to say in response. After having ordered them to go outside of the council, [the members] discussed among themselves, saying, "What shall we do to these men, because the miracle which took place through them has become known to all who live in Jerusalem, and we are not able to deny it. But in order that this may spread no farther, let us warn them not to speak any more to anyone in this name."

When they had called them, they instructed them not to speak or teach in the name of Jesus under any circumstances. But Peter and John replied and said to them, "Whether it is right in the sight of God to listen to you rather than to God, you decide. For we are unable to keep from talking about what we have seen and heard." After further threatening them, they let them go, since they did not find any way to punish them because of the people, since all of them glorified God for what had taken place. Indeed, the man on whom this sign of healing took place was more than forty years of age.

Excursus on "The Name" in Acts

Onoma ("name") is far more frequent in Acts than in any other book of the New Testament, and in half of its occurrences it refers to Jesus. Unlike our contemporary culture, for which a name is merely an arbitrary label, "name" in the Lukan usage connotes both identity and authority. In the tradition of ancient Israel, Yahweh, the name of God, was essential not only to differentiate the God of Israel from other gods and goddesses (Deut. 5:7), but it attested to God's supreme and eternal power, his special relationship to Israel, and his timeless control over the historical life and leadership of his people (Exod. 3:13–15). This is dramatically evident in the experience of Abraham, as depicted in Gen. 12:1–3, 15:7–15, 22:15–18, and carried with it the assurance of descendants and blessing to be extended to all the nations of the world. It is this name which was also revealed to Jacob, together with promises of possession of the land, abundance of blessings for all nations (Gen. 28:10–17), and subsequently to Moses at the burning bush (Exod. 3:1–12). In response to Moses' direct question about God's name, it was revealed to be "Yahweh" (Exod. 3:13–15). The power of Yahweh and his special relationship to his people, Israel, was celebrated in the Song of Moses (Exod. 15:1–18), and reconfirmed when Israel encountered God and received the terms of the covenant at Mount Sinai (Exod. 20:1–21) and became visible in the holy cloud there (Exod. 24:1–18). When the covenant was renewed (according to Deuteronomy 5), the name of Yahweh was again disclosed and the people were called to total obedience and exclusive devotion to him (5:22–33), although the existence of other gods was not denied (5:7). The divine name continued to be a central factor in defining the covenant community.

For the author of Acts, the name that embodies transforming power to renew God's people is, of course, the name of Jesus. This name functions in Acts in at least four different ways:

1. The name as the basis of community identity. The primary function of "the name" in Acts is the identity of the new community, which is in process of formation as a result of the

life, death, and resurrection of Jesus. It involves a radical re-
definition of participation in the covenant, as compared with
the ethnic and ritual standards in Judaism following the failure of the nationalists in the Maccabean period, and again in
70 c.e. The Jesus movement as described by James in Acts 15
builds on the Jewish biblical and historical traditions, but in a
radically different direction. The "people holy to the LORD" are
said to have been "chosen out of all the peoples on the earth
to be his people" (Deut. 14:2), implying that from among all
nations on earth, God chose Israel as his own special people.
But using some of the words from the passage in Deuteronomy,
while building on Amos 9:11-12 from the LXX, the import of
Deuteronomy is reversed: What is announced is not preferential status for an ethnically or ritually separate group as God's
people, but a new community is being called into existence, the
membership of which includes men and women from among
all the peoples on earth. This divine enterprise is described in
Acts 15:14 as God's purpose to "take from among the Gentiles
a people for his name." This understanding is confirmed by the
quotation from Amos in the LXX version which declares that the
rebuilding of the "dwelling place of David" will have as its objective "that the rest of humanity may search for the Lord, and
all the nations which invoke my name upon them" (Acts 15:16-
17; Amos 9:11-12). Those who share in the new community are
identified as those who are called by the name of Jesus (9:14).

2. The name as the instrument of healing and renewal. When
Peter is called to account for having healed the lame man at the
temple gate, the main point of his case is that it is through faith
in the name of Jesus ("the holy and righteous one," "the Founder
of Life") that he was made strong (3:14-16). The question to
Peter from the leaders of the council treats as virtual synonyms
the "power" and the "name" through which this healing took
place. Peter's response matches this: it is his claim that "through
the name of Jesus of Nazareth" the man was cured (4:7, 10).
The joint prayer of the community (4:23-30) reiterates that it is
through "the name of [God's] holy child, Jesus" that God's hand
has been extended to heal and to perform "signs and wonders."
An effort to exploit the power of the name of Jesus by "itinerant
Jewish exorcists" is reported in 19:13, but the evil spirits are not
subdued by the name on the lips of nonbelievers (19:15).

3. The name as the focus of preaching and teaching. The

council, in its opposition to the Jesus movement, forbids its leaders to continue "to speak or teach in the name of Jesus under any circumstances" (4:17–18). The apostles appeal to God for support of their inescapable responsibility to speak in that name (4:20). The council's prohibition to "speak in the name of Jesus" is reiterated, and is accompanied by a beating of the apostles (5:40–41). After Paul's conversion, he spends time in Jerusalem preaching "fearlessly in the name of the Lord" (9:28–29). Peter's sermon in the house of Cornelius concludes with the declaration that "all who trust in his name receive forgiveness of sins" (10:43).

4. Preaching the name of Jesus leads to martyrdom. Paul is called not only to carry the name of Jesus among Gentiles and their rulers, but also to "suffer for the sake of the name [of Jesus]" (9:15–16). When the Jerusalem council decides to back the gentile mission, note is taken that those who are to lead it — Barnabas and Paul — have already "risked their lives in behalf of the name of our Lord Jesus Christ" (15:25–26).

The "name of Jesus" is thus a central focus for a range of aspects of group identity, mission, and responsibility of the leaders in the new community as it is depicted in Acts.

•

The random gathering of fascinated listeners to Peter in the outer courtyard of the temple is supplemented by a group of officials and others concerned for the purity of the temple and profoundly upset by Peter's message. The latter group includes three distinct elements, each with a different concern but united in their opposition to Peter's message, which supplants the temple as the primary agency by which God calls together his people. First are the "priests," who are responsible for the sacerdotal activities in the temple, including the maintenance of ritual purity. The second participant in the coalition of opponents is an individual: the *strategos*, who may have been captain of the temple guards or, more likely, the head of the Roman forces based in the tower overlooking the temple complex, whose task was to maintain civil order in the sacred precincts. This title was originally used for the military commanders, both generals and admirals. It became equivalent to the Latin *praefectus*, the title for the chief officers responsible for maintenance of civil order.[18] The third factor among the hostile observers was the Jewish group called Sadducees, whose name may mean that they considered themselves to be the truly "righteous," which in Hebrew is *tzaddiqim*,[19] or that they claimed to be descendants of Zadok, the high priest in the time of David (1 Kings 1:26). One can infer from Josephus that this group was not a formally organized movement but was composed of members of wealthy families who were linked with the priests and who rejected what they regarded as late, strict, or otherwise unsatisfactory modification of the Jewish legal tradition, such as the Pharisees' belief in the resurrection (cf. Mark 12:18; Luke 20:27; Matt 22:23, 34) and their insistence on strict conformity to the legal requirements.[20] The Sadducees' continuing link with the priests is directly indicated in Acts 5:17. In the rabbinic sources, however, they appear as the major opposition party, initially against the Pharisees and subsequently against the rabbis, who launched the synagogue movement, first as a supplement and then as an alternative to the worship of God in the temple. But in Acts 23 they are pictured as collaborating with the chief priests and the temple authorities in their opposition to the Jesus movement.

The official — but apparently impromptu — opposition from the Jewish leadership is seen as not hindering the positive results of the apostles' testimony, so the size of the new community grows from two thousand (2:41) to "about five thousand." The accused apostles are imprisoned overnight, presumably because the legal proceedings could be conducted only in daylight.

The Jewish officials who attend the formal hearing of Peter and John represent a spectrum of roles and statuses within Judaism in the first century. The term here translated "their leaders" (*archontas*) is not a precise designation: the linking of these leaders with "scribes" and "elders" is a variant of what one finds in the synoptic tradition, including Luke, where the "chief priests, scribes and elders" are joined in opposition to Jesus.[21]

Probably here in Acts, *archontas* refers to the leading priestly figures who had control of the temple and its precincts. This inference is confirmed by the designation of those who are in charge of the hearing: "Annas the high priest," with others of "the high-priestly family." The priestly leadership was determined by the Roman governors resident in the region at any given time. For example, Annas (or Ananus, as Josephus calls him) was installed as high priest by order of the Syrian governor Quirinius in 6 C.E., and served until 15 C.E., when he was deposed. Later his five sons succeeded to the post, down almost until the time of the temple's destruction by the Romans.[22] The date of Annas's term as high priest reported by Josephus does not fit with the narrative in Acts, but there may have been confusion between him and one of his son-successors. Appointment to this central Jewish post was not primarily by succession within the family, but by decision of the Roman governor. Nothing is known for certain about the identity of those here associated with the high priest: "Caiaphas," "John," and "Alexander." Caiaphas is mentioned in John 18:13, where he is identified as Annas's son-in-law, and as "high priest in that year." "John" may be a reference to Jonathan, whose brief term as high priest was in 36–37 C.E. There is no further mention of "Alexander" in ancient Jewish or early Christian sources. The "high-priestly family" appears to have been very large, and its connections extensive, although the choice of the specific one to serve as high priest rested with the Roman authorities. The interrogation of the apostles is launched by this high-priestly group with the question as to the nature of the "power" which they exercise, and the identity of the source of this power: "by what name?" In keeping with the overall outlook of the author of Acts, it is by "the Holy Spirit" that Peter is given power and wisdom to respond to his interrogators.

The leaders are addressed by Peter as "rulers of the people and elders." The term "the people" is obviously a reference to the traditional Jewish community, although the definition of God's people and the criteria for participation therein are going to continue to be redefined radically in the events and insights reported subsequently in Acts. The elders are here seen as fulfilling their traditional roles in making community decisions and carrying out judicial decrees.[23] Peter declares that the issue involved in the adjudication as a consequence of the healing that took place is not a matter of violation of Torah or Roman law, but concerns rather a good deed, an act of kindness done to an "ailing man."[24] The explanation that Peter offers for this extraordinary event is addressed not merely to the council of elders and the priestly leaders, but also to the "whole people Israel."

The initial point that Peter makes is to designate as a "good deed" the act of healing for which he and John are being investigated. The source of power that made possible this astonishing deed is "the name of Jesus of Nazareth," as he declares not only to the authorities examining him but also "to all the people of Israel." The irony is that this man's recovery of a sound, healthy body has taken place through a tragic event: the death of the one whom the authorities "crucified." The reaction to Jesus on the part of the official leaders was to connive with the Romans to have him put to death, even though he was not literally "crucified" by them, as Peter states. God's response to this act of rejection of Jesus by the coalition of religious and imperial antagonists was to "raise him from the dead." This same power of God that raised Jesus from the dead has now been at work to make "healthy" this man whose life was for forty years hindered by his physical disability. Analogous to this unexpected renewal of the lame man is the sequence of events by which Jesus, the rejected "stone," has become the foundation ("headstone") for the new community which God is now in process of building.[25] This is the unique possibility for human renewal: there is no other authority or agent — "name" — by which one can enter into the life of this forgiven, cleansed, renewed ("saved") community of God's people. The healing of this cripple is both sign and symbol of the renewal that is possible through Jesus.

On the basis of careful scrutiny, it is apparent to the professional religious and community Jewish leaders in Jerusalem that these men, who are raising such serious and effective challenges to the more traditional perceptions of Jewish identity and the criteria for participation in the covenant community, are not trained or disciplined in some ongoing mode of Jewish religious tradition: they are "uneducated and amateurs." Compounding the leaders' difficulty in assessing the situation is the clear evidence of the effectiveness of the enterprise in which these apostles are engaged, and of the extraordinary power at work through them, as is apparent from the healings they are enabled to perform. They are at a loss to offer any cogent criticism. A consultation of the Jewish leadership is called, which is here referred to as the *synedrion*.

Excursus on the *Synedrion*

Many scholars — Jewish and Christian — have by and large simply assumed that this council is virtually identical with the Sanhedrin, whose activities and guidelines are sketched in the mishnaic tractate by that name. An effort to show this continuity is that of Hugo Mantel, in his *Studies in the History of the Sanhedrin*. His basic thesis is that the title *Nasi*, which was given to the head of the Great Sanhedrin in rabbinic Judaism, "is at least as old as the Zugat [the pairing of leading scholars, which is assumed to go back to at least 150 B.C.E.] and perhaps older." While admitting that his thesis is not supported by any text, he proposes that the title *Nasi*, which was held by the presidents of the Great Bet Din (House of Justice) in the days of the Zugat, was inherited from the previous high-priestly incumbents in that office. His conclusion on the basis of these hypotheses is that dating back to at least the Maccabean period there were two judicial institutions in Israel: the Great Court, which wielded supreme religious authority and legislated on religious issues, and is the prototype of the rabbinic Sanhedrin; and the political court of the kings and high priests (which he designates as the "small Sanhedrin"), which dealt with political issues and which came to an end with the destruction of the temple in 70 C.E.[26] This entire construct is purely theoretical, lacking any documentation earlier than the second- to sixth-century rabbinic texts, but it was created in order to lend the value of historical precedent to the developments within the rabbinic period. A similar view of the *synedrion* is found in rabbinic scholarship prior to Mantel,[27] and was adopted by Eduard Lohse in his article on the subject in the Kittel *TDNT*. He prefaced his reconstruction by an admission that the only texts to support his depiction of this institution are from the much later rabbinical material.[28]

A far more judicious analysis of the pre-rabbinic nature and function of the *synedrion* is that of Anthony J. Saldarini in his article on "Sanhedrin" in the *Anchor Bible Dictionary*.[29] He asserts that the *synedrion* was a central council in Jerusalem, the membership, structure, and powers of which are not clear in the sources, and which probably varied with the changing political circumstances. He notes, however, that the *synedrion* was a typical feature of the Greco-Roman world, and was comprised of the leading citizens of each region, based on heredity, wealth, power, and position in the community. Subject to the ultimate power of the regional governor, the *synedrion* met as a body to fulfill legislative, executive, and judicial functions in relation to the welfare and control of the populace in its section of the larger empire, and did so in terms of indigenous legal tradition. This fits the evidence from Josephus, the New Testament, and even from some of the rabbinic sources. To assume that the dominant rabbinic representation of the Sanhedrin as an assembly of scholars and learned judges, debating points of law and establishing halakhic policy for the Jewish community, existed in the hellenistic-Roman period he regards as "anachronistic." And the notion that there were two Sanhedrins —political and religious — he describes as "improbable in the extreme."

Curiously, Solomon Zeitlin began his analysis of *synedrion* by showing that the term is widely used in Greek literature for a council or assembly — at times consultative, at times decision-making.[30] That fact has been demonstrated by J. A. O. Larsen, who noted that Macedonia in 167 B.C.E. had no central government, but was divided into four republics (*merides*), each of which had its own *synedrion* as the chief organ of government. The existence of these republics is attested by coins, and an inscription from the Flavian period refers to the first and fourth *merides*, and mentions the *synedrion* of each.[31] In the Septuagint, *synedrion* is used to refer in general terms to assemblies and conclaves,[32] but in the later historical books it is the term for the royal council (2 Macc. 14:5) and is apparently synonymous with *symbolion* (4 Macc. 17:17). The counselors who are consulted are called *ton synedrion* (4 Macc. 5:1). Judith refers to the *synedrion* of Holofernes, but the council in Jerusalem is called the *gerousia* (11:9).

Josephus reports that under Queen Alexandra (78–69 B.C.E.) a body of elders (*presbyteroi*) asked her for information about her plans and tactics in light of the threat of a Roman takeover of Palestine. But it is not until the Romans took control that five regional *synedria* were established by Gabinius, the Roman *strategos* of Syria: in Jerusalem, Gadara, Amathus, Jericho, and Sepphoris.[33] Hyrcanus was reinstated as high priest, and placed in charge of the temple (*kedemonia*), but civil administration was assigned to the aristocracy (*prostatia ton ariston*). Significantly, their role is described as *epoliteuonto*. As Antipater and his son, Herod, grew in power and were assigned royal roles, the challenge to them as kings of the Jews came from those whom Josephus describes as *hoi en telei ton Ioudaion* and *hoi protoi ton Ioudaion*. It was the *synedrion* who had the right to execute violators of Jewish law. When Herod was summoned before this body, Sextus, governor of Syria, gave orders to Hyrcanus to see that the members did not condemn him.[34] Clearly, the *synedrion* was not constituted as the ultimate authority on Jewish religious matters, but was a political agency established by and subject to the regional Roman officials. This group is also referred to in the sources as *boule* (council) and *gerousia* (elders).

After the failure of the second revolt of the Jewish nationalists under Bar Kochba, with the rise to religious power on the part of the rabbis,[35] a successful effort was made not only to establish an ultimate authority on redefining Jewish identity and piety but also to give the newly established central body both credibility and prestige. A convenient and important tool in achieving these aims was the choice of a venerable and prestigious designation for this authoritative and guideline-setting body. That objective was in large measure achieved by assigning the new corporate entity the title of the old hellenistic term for a regional council, *synedrion*, but to give it greater credibility for Jews seeking to differentiate themselves from Greco-Roman society and culture by transliterating the name into semitic form: Sanhedrin.

•

The members of the *synedrion* recognize that it is through the "name" of Jesus that these simple followers of Jesus claim to have accomplished the extraordinary public event (*gnoston semeion*) that has occurred in the healing of this lame man. If the apostles are not challenged, they could continue to spread that name beyond the whole population of Jerusalem, which now knows what has taken place in the name of Jesus. What happened through the power of that name is portrayed by Acts as matters of public knowledge that cannot be denied. The only hope of the council is to prohibit the invocation of the "name" of Jesus by the apostles for achieving their purposes through preaching, teaching, or healing. Peter and John courteously but unequivocally articulate a contrast between the charge they have received from God and the orders that have been given by the council. The apostles' unambiguous claim is that God has instructed them to speak and act in the name of Jesus. The council has no authority to punish them, and the populace as a whole has reacted favorably to what has been done among them in the name of Jesus. From the council come only threats, but from the people came only praise to "God" for the amazing act of healing the "forty-year-old" man. The difference between the response of the official leadership and that of the people as a whole is here pictured as total.

4:23–37: The New Community Celebrates God's Support

After they were set free, they went to their own group and informed them of the things which the chief priests and the elders had said to them. When they heard this, united as one[36] they raised their voices to God and said, "Absolute Master, you who made heaven and the earth and the sea and everything that is in them, who said by the Holy Spirit through the mouth of your servant, David, who is our ancestor,

> " 'Why were the Gentiles so haughty,
> and why did the people conspire about such empty matters?
> The kings of the earth established themselves,
> and the rulers convened in the same place
> against the Lord and against his Anointed One.'
> [Ps. 2:1–2]

"In truth there were gathered in this city against your Holy Child Jesus, whom you anointed, Herod and Pontius Pilate, along with the Gentiles and the people of Israel, to do the things which your hand and your purpose had determined in advance would happen. And now, Lord, show your concern over their threats and give to your servants complete boldness to speak your message, while you reach out your hand to heal, and signs and wonders occur through the name of your Holy Child, Jesus."

And when they had prayed, the place in which they were gathered was shaken, and they were all filled with the Holy Spirit, and spoke the message of God with boldness. The heart and soul of the large number of those who believed were as one, and no one said that any of their belongings were their own, but that all things were shared in common. With great power the apostles conveyed their witness of the resurrection of the Lord Jesus. And grace was great upon them all. There was no one in need among them, for as many of them as

were owners of lands and houses sold them, brought the prof-
its from their sales, and laid them at the feet of the apostles. To
each was given according to individual need. Joseph, who was
called Barnabas by the disciples (which means "son of help"),
and who was a Levite, sold a field which belonged to him,
brought the money, and placed it at the feet of the apostles.

The formation of a distinctive community of those who see in
Jesus the agent of renewal of God's people is evident in this reference to those to whom Peter and James go upon release by the
religious authorities: "their own group" (*idious*).[37] The complete-
ness of this new unifying identity is indicated in greater detail
in 4:32-34 (see below). The religious officials' prohibition of the
use of the "name" of Jesus is reported by the apostles to the
gathered community, whose instant reaction conforms to that of
Peter and John: the refusal to be silent about words and actions
in this powerful name.

The mode of address to God in the community's prayer,
despotes, is infrequent in the New Testament, though the word is
used several times to refer to secular masters who own slaves.[38]
Simeon's prayer — when Jesus is brought to the temple by his
parents — called on God by this title. 2 Peter 2:1 and the parallel passage in Jude 4 warn against those impostors within the
community who deny their "only Master and Lord" (*despoten kai
kurion*). In Acts 4:24 there is affirmation of the complete sovereignty of God,[39] which is now manifest in what he has done
through Jesus and is doing for and through the apostles. Even
what appeared to be a tragedy resulting from the coalition of
authorities that sought to destroy Jesus is now to be seen as
essential to the outworking of God's plan. Evidence for this is
offered through the quotation from Ps. 2:1-2 of the conspiracy
of earthly rulers to oppose the Lord and his anointed (*christos*). The participants in this corporate hostility to God's plan
are specified: Herod (the puppet ruler put in power by the Romans),[40] Pontius Pilate (the incumbent Roman prefect in Judea),
and their two groups of collaborators, Gentile and Jewish.[41] The
target of this combined attack by the earthly powers is Jesus,
who is here identified as "the holy child" (or "servant"), which
presumably builds on the theme of the Servant of the Lord
in Second Isaiah,[42] although there is no mention at this point
of his suffering or death. There is a supreme irony here: the

scheme by these powers to terminate the impact of Jesus has resulted in the launching of his message throughout the world and the manifestation of healings and other "signs" that confirm the divine origin and purpose of the movement. All this was "determined in advance." The continuing evidence of God's initiative and support for the work of the apostles is tangible in the tremors that occur and the Spirit-provided courage with which they proclaim the message about Jesus.

Further tangible evidence of God's power and purpose at work within the new community is provided by the continuing growth of their numbers, and their pooling of material resources and sale of personal property for the sake of the welfare of all the members, regardless of economic status. The distribution of support for the needs of members was controlled by the apostles. A crisis for this combination of spiritual and tangible unity was created by the stark contrast between the generosity of Joseph and the devious, self-serving actions of Ananias and Sapphira. The blend of cultural background and influences within this new community is dramatically evident in the description of Joseph: though he has a traditional Jewish given name (Joseph) and role within ancient tradition (Levite),[43] his nickname (Barnabas) is Aramaic, and his place of origin is Cyprus, where there was a sizable Jewish population in the second century B.C.E., as is indicated by 1 Macc. 15:23. Here he is an exemplar of fidelity to the principles that bound in unity the new community.

5:1–11: Ananias and Sapphira Die for Their Deceit

A man by the name of Ananias, with his wife Sapphira, sold a property, and with full knowledge of his wife, he kept some of the sale price for themselves, and so took only a part of it and put it at the feet of the apostles. Peter said, "Ananias, why did Satan fill your heart so that you deceived the Holy Spirit and kept part of the money from the sale of that piece of land? When it belonged to you, the value continued to be yours, and even when it was sold, it was under your control. Why did you let such a deed enter your heart? You did not lie to humans, but to God."

When Ananias heard these words, he fell down and breathed his last. Great fear came on all who heard this.

The young men got up, wrapped up his body, took it out and buried it.

It happened after an interval of about three hours that his wife came in, not knowing what had taken place. Peter said to her, "Tell me if you sold the land for such an amount." And she said, "Yes, for such an amount." But Peter said to her, "Why is it that you agreed to test the Spirit of the Lord? Listen! The feet of those who buried your husband are at the door, and they will carry you out." Instantly, she fell down at his feet and breathed her last. And when the young men entered, they found her dead and they carried her out and buried her beside her husband. And great fear came on the whole community and on all who heard these matters.

Ananias is a Greek form of the Hebrew name Hananiah, which means "God is gracious." His deceitful attempt at personal gain by cheating the community is in complete contrast to the generosity of Joseph Barnabas (4:36–37). Sapphira, whose Aramaic name means "beautiful" or "good," joins in the deception by her husband before she realizes what the consequences for him have been, and compounds her wickedness by lying about the sale of the land (5:8). Their joint act of dishonesty is depicted here as testing the Spirit of the Lord, and the results of that test are the punitive death of both of them. This deceit is the antithesis of the sharing of possessions that characterized the life of the new community as depicted in 4:32. Sharing in the fullest sense is the quality that is to characterize the newly defined people of God, including not only such spiritual factors as the belief in the resurrection of Christ and the indwelling of the Holy Spirit, but also such tangible features as the pooling of possessions. Failure to live up to all the dimensions of this new common life leads to divine punishment. The resulting death of this greedy and deceitful pair matches the outcome of the group process enjoined by Paul in 1 Cor. 5:1–5 of turning over to Satan "for the destruction of the flesh" an immoral member of the community, though in that case the issue was defiling the community by indulging in incest, and the sentence was to be agreed upon by the whole community. Just as those in the smaller group that heard of Ananias's death by divine judgment were filled with "fear" (5:5), so not only the whole community (*ekklesia*) but all those who heard of this second punitive action were overtaken by "great fear." Clearly the author of Acts wants both to attract participation in the community by his accounts of God's healing and transforming his people, and to issue solemn warnings of the dire consequences of exploiting the privileged life within this new people of God.

5:12–16: The Crowds Attracted in Jerusalem by the Apostles' Signs and Wonders

Through the hands of the apostles many signs and wonders took place among the people. And the entire single-minded community was in the Portico of Solomon. None of the others dared to join them, but the people held them in high esteem. There were added even more of those who trusted in the Lord — a multitude of men and women — with the result that the sick were carried out into the wide streets, and were placed on beds and pallets in order that when Peter passed, at least his shadow might be cast on some of them. And the crowd converged from the cities around Jerusalem, bringing the sick and those tormented by unclean spirits. All of them were healed.

The visible, tangible, and dramatic evidence of the power of God at work through the members of this new movement is apparent to the public in the healings and other wonderful acts that occur through the "hands of the apostles." The beneficiaries of these "signs" are not simply members of the group, but the "people" broadly speaking. United not just physically but with singleness of purpose (*omothumadon*),[44] the apostles gather once more in the temple's Portico of Solomon (3:12) in order to continue their work in the name of Jesus. The marvelous acts of healing and other manifestations of extraordinary power through the apostles have attracted much public interest, although there are those who have not made the commitment to the claims and convictions shared by the new "single-minded" community and hence are unwilling to identify themselves publicly with the group.

The place where the group gathers, the Portico of Solomon, is not only a monumental structure but is also of great strategic significance. Constructed by Herod the Great, this great colonnade, which was more than 2,000 feet long with columns nearly 40 feet high, extended the full length of the eastern side of the vast temple platform and overlooked the Kidron Valley and the Mount of Olives beyond. It was a favorite informal gathering place for worshipers and for those who wanted to declaim to the crowd their interpretations of the Jewish traditions, in a mode analogous to streetcorner preaching today. The area that it enclosed was the huge Court of the Gentiles, where non-Jews were permitted to come in order to see the temple complex, thought by modern scholars to have been the largest religious structure in the whole of the ancient world.[45] Here the preaching about Jesus and the subsequent discussions by the apostles were accessible to throngs, including both pious Jews and curious or seeking Gentiles.

The success of the movement is indicated by the increase in numbers, but also by the detail that the multitude of those who joined the group included both men *and* women. Access to the main sanctuary of the temple was from the Court of the Gentiles (which surrounded the more holy areas) through the Court of Women, which was as far as women were permitted to go. Beyond that were the Court of Israel (males only), the Court of the Priests, and Holy of Holies, where only the high priest could enter. In the new community, however, women seem to have received virtually equal status with men, as is indicated in the detail that the new adherents of the movement included "a multitude of men and women." Further contrast of this new community with the legal and ritual features of covenantal identity in the priestly tradition is offered by the condition of those who were brought from the towns surrounding Jerusalem to the apostles on the streets of Jerusalem: "the sick and those tormented by unclean spirits." By Jewish legal standards, such people would have been considered ritually impure, and hence untouchable. Yet the apostles reach out to them, physically and figuratively, with the result that "all of them were healed." The specific note that some sought to benefit from the healing power at work through the apostles by arranging to have the shadow of Peter fall on the ailing as he passed them in the streets differs from the intentional healings and exorcisms attributed to Jesus and the apostles, and more nearly resembles magic.[46] In any case, the healings and exorcisms are said to have taken place for *all* who came seeking help from the apostles and "trusting in the Lord."

5:17–26: Trials and Persecutions of the Apostles Begin

But the high priest arose, as well as all who were [allied] with him — who were the group called the Sadducees — and filled with zeal, they laid hands on the apostles and put them in the public prison. But during the night an angel of the Lord opened the doors of the jail, led them out, and said to them, "Go stand in the temple, and tell the people all the words of this life." When they had heard this, they went into the temple at dawn and began to teach. When the high priest arrived and those [allied] with him, he convened the council and the whole body of elders of the people of Israel, and sent to the prison to have them brought out. But when they arrived, they did not find them in prison, so they returned and gave a report, saying, "We found the prison locked with every precaution, and all the guards were in position by the doors. But when we opened up, we found no one inside." When the chief officer of the temple and the chief priests heard these reports, they were utterly at a loss as to what this might come to. Someone came and told them, "Look! These men whom you put in prison are standing in the temple and teaching the people." The chief officer and his assistants went off and brought them — with no violence, for they were afraid that the people would stone them.

As in Acts 4:1, the Sadducees are depicted as allies of the "high priest," although they are here referred to as a *hairesis*, which is usually translated "sect."[47] The Sadducees were by no means a fringe group during the time when Judaism was dominated by the temple and its priesthood, so it should not be understood in a pejorative sense here. The negative connotations of the term may be implicit when it is used in connection with the early Christians in 24:5,[48] 14, and 28:22, and whose leader, Paul, is scorned as a "plague," a provoker of "discord," and as one who reportedly tried "to desecrate the temple." The term in 5:12 — as in 4:1 — simply implies that the Sadducees are a distinctive group in Jerusalem at this time. The response of this priestly oriented coalition to what they regard as a desecration of the temple and to the repeated violations of ritual purity is to try to remove the perpetrators of this new movement out of the public scene by imprisoning them. The apostles were not quietly or secretly detained or placed under house arrest, as might be done with some distinguished persons who were suspects. Instead, they were placed in the public prison, along with other common criminals. There was no intention to accord them favorable treatment.

The divine support for the apostolic enterprise is dramatically evident, however, in their being set free and led out of the prison by an "angel of the Lord." The divine purpose and the implicit sanction for their enterprise are communicated by the angel: the apostles are to return to the "temple" where they are to resume proclaiming the "words of this life" through Jesus and demonstrating the power of renewal through him as they perform healings and exorcisms for the ailing ones who come to them there. Their work there resumed at the first possible moment: "at dawn."

The "high priest" convened his associates and the "whole body of elders," for which the Greek term *gerousia* is used, as it is in other Greek writings for various councils, including the Roman senate.[49] Unlike the senate in Rome, which consisted of former governmental officials and magistrates, the council in Jerusalem was composed of officers of by far the most significant cultural and financial enterprise in all of Palestine: the temple. Their aides and supporters appear to have constituted the membership of the council, and the fact that the Law of Moses provided the standards for operating the temple as well as for the lives of the Jewish people gave the council members a role analogous to that of the councils in more secular regions of the empire. It was in the jurisdiction of this council, based on the empire-wide policy of Rome, to examine and deal with violators of these local laws.

The actual limits of the council's control over the situation were dramatically evident, however, when the accused apostles were discovered not to be in the prison, even though it was still locked and the prison guards were still on duty and in place. The priestly leaders of the council were wholly unable to explain what had happened or to predict what the implications of this happening might be. Their loss of control was most dramatically evident when the report reached them that these apostles who had been incarcerated to halt their preaching activity in the temple courts had now returned and were carrying on their work of "teaching the people." The implication to the reader of Acts as to the reason for the council's inability to carry out its plan to halt the movement is clear: it is God who is at work fulfilling his plan through the apostles. This has taken place in spite of the official opposition of these leaders who, while members of the covenant people of Israel and managers of the world-renowned temple of the God of Israel, are functioning in this role they have accepted as allies and a tool of the Roman state. It is with apprehension and understandable caution that the council recalls for interrogation these men, who are seen as gaining a rapidly growing body of persuaded supporters. The Jews had the right to execute violators of their laws by stoning (Acts 7:58),[50] but what is seen here as feared by the council is a joint hostile action by a segment of the community against their official leadership as a result of the latter's attack on the leaders of this new group whose members regard the apostles as the agents and messengers of God (Acts 5:26).

5:27–39: The Examination of the Apostles by the Council

When they had brought them, they placed them before the council, and the high priest interrogated them, saying, "We gave you very strict orders that you were not to teach in this name, and look! You have filled Jerusalem with your teaching, and you want to put the blame for this man's blood on us." Peter gave answer, together with the apostles, and said, "It is necessary for us to obey God rather than humans. The God of our fathers raised from the dead Jesus, on whom you laid violent hands and hung on a tree. God exalted him at his right hand as Founder and Savior, in order to give to Israel repentance and forgiveness of sins. And we are all witnesses of these matters, as is the Holy Spirit which God has given to those who obey him."

When they heard this, they were infuriated and wanted to do away with them. But a certain Pharisee by the name of Gamaliel, who was a teacher of the Law honored by all the people, arose in the council and ordered that the men [apostles] be put outside for a short time. And he said to them, "Israelite men, be careful what you are about to do to these men. For before these days there arose Theudas, saying that he was somebody, and men numbering about four hundred joined up with him. But he was destroyed and all those who were persuaded by him were scattered and came to nothing. After him there arose Judas the Galilean during the period of the census and led some people to join him in a revolt. He also died, and all who had been persuaded by him were scattered. So now I tell you this: Keep your distance from these men and leave them alone. Because if this plan or this enterprise is of human origin, it will come to ruin. But if it comes from God, you will not be able to defeat them. You might be found to be God-opposers!"

After they are brought before the council quietly, the high priest reminds the apostles of their prior prohibition[51] to teach "in this name,"[52] which they have defied by having "filled Jerusalem with their teaching." Further, their teaching has sought to place the blame on the council for the death ("blood") of this one whose "name" they avoid mentioning. The apostles' response affirms once more that their claim concerning Jesus and what they teach about him are not their invention but are in fact a message about what the God of Israel has done and is continuing to do through him. Hence it is God's instructions and challenge to them which his true people must "obey," rather than the decree of this council. God's role in these events, according to what the apostles teach, was that he "raised Jesus from the dead." The council — not the Jewish people as a whole — is here denounced for having "laid violent hands" on Jesus and "hung [him] on a tree." In Luke's account of the trial of Jesus it is "the chief priests and the rulers of the people" who insisted that Pilate crucify Jesus, even though he did not find him guilty of violating Roman law (Luke 23:13–25). Although specifics are not offered in Deut. 21:22–23 about the mode of execution that resulted in the corpse of the condemned one remaining "hanging on a tree all night," the point is clear that the exposure of a dead body was regarded in the Law of Moses as an important message to the public concerning the seriousness of the culprit's misdeed, but if protracted, it would result in the ritual pollution of the land. Since the Roman method of crucifixion left the body of the condemned one exposed to public view elevated on a pole, it seems to have been regarded as a violation of the Mosaic law just cited, especially since the execution took place on the eve of the sabbath. Both Paul (Gal. 3:13) and 1 Peter (2:24) allude to the curse resulting from the exposed corpse of Jesus as part of the divine judgment on the sin of the leaders who executed him and that this divine judgment was operative in relation to the crucifixion of Jesus. This point of view is not developed here in Acts, but seems to be implicit in the charge against those who hanged Jesus "on a tree." In the Dead Sea Scroll *Commentary on Nahum* (4Q 169) there is reference to a wicked ruler ("a furious young lion") who practices revenge by hanging his opponents alive "on a tree" (2.12). This is the same imagery by which the author of Acts portrays the death of Jesus.

The apostles' claim is that God responded to the execution of Jesus by not merely raising him from the dead, but also by exalting him to the supreme place of cosmic honor: at God's "right hand." In ancient Israel, the place at the leader's right hand was the sign of unique favor and blessing, as in Jacob's special choice of Ephraim (Gen. 48:13–20). But it is also the symbol of special relationship with God: "The LORD says to my Lord, 'Sit at my right hand until I make your enemies your footstool'" (Ps. 110:1). The roles assigned to the exalted Christ are "Founder" (*archegos*) and "Savior" (*soter*). The first of these terms has a significantly different set of connotations in the Greek-speaking Jewish tradition from those it carried in the Greek philosophical literature. In the LXX, *archegos* is a recurrent term for the heads of the ancestral houses of Israel.[53] But in the Greek philosophical tradition, *archegos* is an abstract term for the originating power or cause of all things,[54] or in Heraclitus for the first cause which is origin of all that is. It is with these connotations that the word appears in the Letter to the Hebrews, which is powerfully influenced by the Platonic theory of the cosmic contrast between the eternal heavenly ideal and the ephemeral earthly copy (Hebrews 9–10). Christ is the eternal, perfect model (*archegos*) of the one who through obedience and sacrifice gains access and acceptance in the presence of God (Heb. 2:10). It is as a consequence of his archetypal role in obedience and faithfulness that he is now "seated at the right hand of the throne of God" (Heb. 12:2). Here in Acts 5:31 it is in a more traditionally Jewish role as

"Savior" that he leads God's people to repentance and provides for them "forgiveness of sins." The author of Acts strengthens his case for continuity and fulfillment between who Jesus is and what he has done on the one hand, and the hopes and promises of God to "Israel" on the other.

These claims in behalf of Jesus and the hopes for renewal of God's people are seen here as receiving both human and divine confirmation: the testimony of the apostles in these matters is reinforced by the powerful presence and active agent of God in the world: "the Holy Spirit." The Spirit was poured out on the new community in all of its ethnic diversity, as depicted in Acts 2:1–13, which as we have noted is perceived in Peter's sermon to have been the fulfillment of God's promise to ancient Israel (2:17–20 = Joel 3:1–5). What is happening is not the shattering of the hopes of ancient Israel, but the divinely instigated and empowered fulfillment of those hopes through Jesus. The one requirement for participation in the new community which God is calling into being through the apostles is obedience to his word. This claim is shockingly offensive to the core of official Jewish leadership who perceive their role as preserving the divinely instituted norms for worship and obedience to the God of Israel. These followers of Jesus not only bring a new agenda, with their claim to have the true understanding of God's purpose for his people, but their message also includes sharp criticism of the traditional way of understanding the norms for participation in the life of the covenant people. Compounding the controversy is the apostles' assertion that what they are teaching is the consequence of the work of the "Holy Spirit" in them and through them to others.

The response of the leaders of the council to this severe challenge to the traditional norms for obedience to the Law of Moses is understandable, and the intent to "do away with" these subversives is in conformity with the community leaders' rights according to that law, as noted above.[55] A solemn word of caution is uttered in the council[56] by *Gamaliel*, who is identified as (1) a *Pharisee* and (2) a teacher of the law (*didaskalos*).[57]

Excursus on the Pharisees

Contrary to the common modern use of "Pharisee" as a derogatory term for pious nitpickers who insist on strict conformity to rigid moral or procedural rules, the Pharisees began as a political group opposed to the Maccabean rulers during the century following their accession to rule of the Jews (165 B.C.E.) and their increasingly despotic tactics. When the Romans took control of the land in 63 B.C.E., the Pharisees made a major shift from the struggle for power to focus on the purity and mutual support of those who sought to live as the people of God in conformity to the Law of Moses as they understood it. This change is epitomized in the title of the early, important work of Jacob Neusner, *From Politics to Piety: The Emergence of Rabbinic Judaism.*[58] His hundreds of subsequent volumes enrich and confirm this picture, as is the case with a work directly relevant to our concerns, *Judaism in the Matrix of Christianity.*[59]

The group's self-designation as Pharisees (probably from the Hebrew word *parash*, which means "separate" or "distinguish") was chosen to emphasize the claim of the members that it enjoyed a special relationship with God, based on its obedience to the ritual, ethnic, and dietary codes of the Law. They met in homes or assembly rooms to examine the scriptures and to increase understanding and commitment to their understanding of God's will for his people. The group gatherings, the shared study of scripture, and their common devotion to purity served to unite them and to appeal to outsiders to make the commitment required to become part of this special pious community. Their twin aims in the study of the Law were to discern its relevance and to evoke obedience among their members. It is as a leader in such an enterprise that one must envision Gamaliel as a "teacher of the Law." It is on these issues of relevance of scripture and defining the identity of God's people that another Pharisee in Acts initially sought to destroy the Jesus movement, and then became one of its leaders: Paul (Acts 23:6–9, 26:5).[60]

•

Gamaliel, which means "reward of God," is a recurrent figure in Numbers 1–10. This leader of the tribe of Manasseh is a model of discipline and conformity to the requirements for offerings and proper order among the tribes. Jewish sources from the Roman period refer to others by that name as well. In addition to the role of Gamaliel as described here in Acts 5, and mentioned by Paul in Acts 22:3, there is a Gamaliel who has a significant place in the rabbinic traditions. As Jacob Neusner has shown through careful, perceptive analyses of those Gamaliel traditions, there were two individuals with this name: one in the mid-first century, sometimes referred to in these traditions as Gamaliel the Elder, and Gamaliel II, who had a leading role at Yavneh in the late first- and early second-century period when the rabbinic appropriation and adaptation of the Torah were beginning to take more systematic shape. Simon, the son of Gamaliel the Elder, is mentioned in Josephus's *Life* (189–203) as one who dissuaded the council in Jerusalem from confirming Josephus's leadership role in Galilee during the first Jewish revolt in 66–70 c.e. But Neusner despairs of sorting out which traditions should be assigned to each of these Gamaliels.[61] The respect in which the earlier Gamaliel is held by the Jewish leaders is implied when his "order" to have the apostles temporarily removed from the hearing is followed out.

Gamaliel's advice to the council against the execution of the apostles builds on historical analogies with troublemakers in the recent past whose enterprises were terminated by death apart from initiative by Jewish leaders. He mentions first Theudas as having launched a movement, "saying that he was somebody," and attracting "about four hundred" followers. His claim for himself and his objectives are not indicated in Acts, but Josephus reports that he claimed to be a prophet (*Ant.* 20.97-99), presumably in the tradition of Deut. 18:18–19. This text lies behind the expectation of an eschatological prophet who will appear with the messiahs of Aaron and Israel, according to the Dead Sea Rule of the Community (1 QS9), and is the basis for the questions raised in the Gospel of John whether Jesus is "the prophet" (John 1:21, 6:14, 7:40). Theudas claimed he would reenact the feat of Joshua in parting the waters of the Jordan. But Fadus the procurator sent cavalry to crush the movement, and Theudas was beheaded. The date Josephus assigned for Fadus's term of service is 45 c.e., which would be later than the probable date of the events described in Acts at the launching of the new community.

Equally difficult chronologically is the other uprising reported in Acts as having been led by "Judas the Galilean,"[62] since Josephus reports this man as joining the rebellion after Quirinius was made governor of Syria (*Ant.* 18.1-3), which took place in 6 c.e. and was followed by the "census" he ordered to be conducted. Yet Acts quotes Gamaliel as dating this uprising as having taken place *after* the revolt under Theudas. Scholarly efforts to explain away these chronological difficulties have not been successful.[63] It appears that the author of Acts was writing in the late first or early second century, and that the traditions he drew upon were not assigned sure dates. Gamaliel's conviction in the Acts account is clear: God works in human events to accomplish his purpose for his people, and does so in ways that bring destruction on those who oppose that purpose. What Gamaliel is calling for is to leave the administration of divine justice to God, lest misguided and irreversible actions by the Jewish leadership be found to have been contrary to God's plan for his people. If God is behind what the apostles are doing and proclaiming — as Acts wants to make clear he is — their determined and energetic effort will not be defeated, and those who try to do so will become "God-opposers."

5:40–42: The Apostles Beaten and Discharged

They were persuaded by him, and called in the apostles. After beating them, they ordered them not to speak in the name of Jesus, and released them. They went out with rejoicing from the presence of the council, because they had been considered worthy to experience dishonor for the name [of Jesus Christ]. Every day they were in the temple and in homes, never ceasing to teach and to proclaim the good news of Jesus as the Messiah.

The release of the apostles in response to the analysis of the situation by Gamaliel is preceded by their being flogged, which was a form of punishment permitted in the deuteronomic code (Deut. 25:1–3). Paul reports that he experienced "countless floggings" which brought him near death, that five times he underwent "forty lashes minus one" (which conformed to the limit imposed by the deuteronomic law), and three times was beaten with rods (2 Cor. 11:23–25). Once more the apostles are forbidden to "speak in the name of Jesus," as in 4:18, 5:28.

The basis of their joy as they left the "council" was not merely their release, but the conviction that the sufferings and trials they were undergoing were the consequence of their having been considered by God to be "worthy to experience dishonor for the name" of Jesus Christ. That motif appears later in Acts

(9:16, 15:26), and is a major theme in Paul's second letter to the Corinthians (2 Cor. 11:16–33). The settings in which the apostles continue to preach the "good news" that Jesus is the "Messiah" and to teach "every day" in the name of Jesus include the "temple" and private "homes," where the faithful gather, as they did in the early stages of the rabbinic movement.[64] They are pictured here as carrying on this work in direct violation of the decree of the council.

The Initial Shaping of the New Community (6:1–8:40)

6:1–7: The Seven Appointed by the Apostles to Serve

In these days when the disciples were becoming more numerous, there was a complaint of the Hellenists against the Hebrews, because their widows were overlooked in the daily distribution. And the twelve convened the whole community of the disciples and said, "It is not pleasing [to God] for us to leave the Word of God and wait on tables. So brothers, look for seven men of good reputation, full of the Spirit and of wisdom, whom we can assign to this necessary duty. But we shall devote ourselves to prayer and service of the word." This public message pleased the entire multitude, and they chose Stephen, a man full of faith and of the Holy Spirit, and Philip, and Prochorus, and Nicanor, and Timon, and Parmenas, and Nicolaus (a proselyte from Antioch). These they placed before the apostles, and after they prayed, they laid their hands upon them. And the word of God increased, and the number of the disciples in Jerusalem was multiplied greatly, and a great crowd of the priests embraced the faith.

The steady growth of the movement is seen here as having drawn into the membership Jews from two different cultural settings: those identified by language and sociocultural norms as "Hebrews," and those whose language and cultural orientation had been basically influenced by the aggressive process of the hellenistic rulers who in the second and first centuries B.C.E. sought to impose hellenistic language and culture on the conquered territories in the eastern Mediterranean world: the

"Hellenists." The impact of the hellenistic culture on the Jewish community in Palestine is evident in the names of the seven chosen for the service duties: all of them are Greek (Stephen, Philip, Prochorus, Nicanor, Timon, Parmenas, Nicolaus). Only the last-named is specifically said to be a *proselyte*,[1] which indicates that he was someone of non-Jewish origin who had earlier chosen to take his place within the Jewish community in "Antioch."

The necessity to effect this division of labor within the leadership of the new community between proclamation of the message and ministering to tangible community needs is said to have been caused by the inequality of the "distribution" — presumably of food and probably also of funds — to meet personal needs. This is, of course, linked with the problem of sharing "possessions and substance" described in 2:44–45. The special victims of this unfair practice were the "widows," support for whom was prescribed under the Law of Moses (Deut. 14:29) and by the prophets (Jer. 49:11) as well as in the psalms (Ps. 68:5, 146:9). The people of Israel as a whole had an obligation to care for widows, as well as for orphans and the homeless (Deut. 10:14–19, 24:17–22). The Gospel of Luke (7:11–17) pictures Jesus' special concern for widows. There is evidence in 1 Timothy, however, that in some situations within the early church "widows" were a distinctive group among the members, with requirements that they be listed among those who were to receive special support (1 Tim. 5:3–16). Whether or not that pattern of community grouping had yet developed in the Acts tradition is not clear.

The noun and verb used here for the distribution (*diakonia*) and for "wait on" (*diakonein*) suggest that more is at issue here than a sharp differentiation of modes of service within the community: preaching or menial assignments. The fact that Stephen was not only empowered to perform "signs and great wonders" (6:8), but that he also was "speaking" with "wisdom" by the "power" of the "Spirit" makes clear that the divinely given role of Stephen and his colleagues is by no means routine material service. After reporting the formal, ceremonial authority granted to this seven by the apostles through the laying on of "hands," Acts states only that the "word of God increased," as did the number of followers of the movement, but there is no explicit indication as to who was doing the preaching. The challenge to the ritual and cultic traditions of Israel by these preachers is so powerful that even "a great crowd of the priests" join the new community. It is indicative of the shift taking place in the movement that one can discern a change from perceiving "faith" as trust in God and in what he was doing through Jesus, to "*the* faith," meaning correct belief, which many of "the priests embraced."[2]

6:8–15: Stephen Taken before the Council

Stephen, full of grace and power, was doing wonders and great signs among the people, and certain ones of the group which is called "Libertines," and of the Cyrenians and the Alexandrines, and some from Cilicia and Asia rose up and debated with Stephen. And they lacked the power to withstand the wisdom and the Spirit by which he was speaking. Then they suborned men to say, "We heard this man speaking words of blasphemy against Moses and God." They aroused the people and the elders and the scribes. Then they appeared [suddenly], seized him violently, and led him to the council. They set up false witnesses who said, "This man never stops speaking words against this holy place and the law. For we heard him saying that this Jesus of Nazareth will destroy this place and will alter the customs which Moses passed on to us." As they gazed at him, all who were seated in the council saw that his face was like the face of an angel.

The designation of Stephen's continuing marvelous acts as "wonders and great signs" and the note that he did so because he was "full of grace and power" carry forward the theme of the author of Acts that the Jesus movement, as it is being furthered concurrently but in different ways by the apostles and by these hellenistic leaders, is the work of God, and not a merely human enterprise. A number of ancient Greek texts and versions add the detail that these "signs" were performed "through the name of Jesus Christ." The opposition to Stephen originates from a surprising source: a "group"[3] calling themselves the "Libertines" and composed of members from a wide geographical range: Cyrenaica and Alexandria on the northern coast of Africa, and from the provinces of Asia Minor. What they had in common is indicated by the name they chose for their group: "Libertines," which is transliterated from Latin, and was used to identify those liberated from slavery. Their places of origin indicate that they would have been Greek-speaking Jews, and hence an obvious audience for these deacons, the Greek-named messengers of the gospel. The fact that these freed Jewish slaves had migrated to Jerusalem indicates their strong commitment to the temple and to the mode of Jewish identity and practice associated with it, as set forth in the priestly traditions of the scriptures. Their inability to match the "wisdom" and "Spirit" with which Stephen spoke led them to an evil scheme of false testimony with the aim of bringing against him the wrath of the "people" as well as of two types of leaders — the "elders" and the "scribes" — representing respectively the official Jerusalem council and the self-appointed interpreters of the Law. Both these groups had much at stake in the challenge to temple and Torah raised by Stephen and the redefining of covenantal participation that he proclaimed in the name of Jesus. The suborned witnesses claim to have heard Stephen uttering "words of blasphemy," the substance of which they perceived to be contrary to the Law of "Moses" and to the purpose of "God" as it was understood by dominant Jewish tradition.

With this contrived testimony to support their case, they took Stephen to the "council," charging him with unceasing attacks against the temple and the Torah, and claiming that "Jesus" was going to "destroy" the former and radically "alter" the latter. In the prior volume (Luke 21:5–6), Luke reports Jesus' announcement of the destruction of the temple, although it is not to occur by his own action. The radical reinterpretation of the Law of "Moses" pervades the Gospel of Luke, but is especially evident in the Sermon on the Plain (Luke 6:20–49) and in Jesus' answer to the question from John the Baptist (Luke 7:18–35), where he identifies himself as a "glutton and a drunkard, a friend of tax-collectors and sinners" (7:34).[4] Additional indication of the divine support for Stephen and the movement is provided by God in the form of the angelic radiance of his face which is visible to the members of the "council," whether they are prepared to recognize it as such or not.

7:1–53: Stephen's Address to the Council

And the high priest said, "Are these things so?" And [Stephen] said, "You men who are brothers and fathers, listen! The God of Glory was seen by our father, Abraham, when he was in Mesopotamia, before he dwelt in Haran. And he said to him, 'Get away from your land and your kinfolk, away into the land which I shall show you' [Gen. 32:1]. Then he went out of the land of the Chaldeans and dwelt in Haran. From there — after his father died — he changed his residence to this land in which you are now dwelling, Yet [God] gave him no property in it, not even a foot of ground, but he promised to give it to him as a permanent possession and to his descendants after him [Gen. 16:1], even though he had no child. So God said to him that his posterity would dwell in an alien land belonging to others, and that they would enslave them and ill-treat them for four hundred years.[5] 'But I will bring judgment on the nation that enslaved them,' God said, 'and after that they will come out, and they shall be devoted to me in this place.'[6] And he gave to [the nation] a covenant of circumcision [Gen. 17:9–14, 21:4]. So he became the father of Isaac, and circumcised him on the eighth day, and Isaac [did the same] for Jacob, and Jacob [did so] for the twelve patriarchs.[7] And the patriarchs, since they were jealous of Joseph, sold him into Egypt [Gen. 37:12–28]. And God was with him and rescued him from all his afflictions. He gave him grace and wisdom in the opinion of Pharaoh, the king of Egypt: he placed him in charge of Egypt and of his entire household [Gen. 41:1–49]. A famine came on the whole of Egypt and Canaan, and the distress was great, so that our ancestors could not find sufficient food. When Jacob heard that there was grain in Egypt, he sent out our ancestors for the first time [Gen. 41:50–42:38]. On their second [visit] Joseph made himself known to his brothers, and the ethnic origin of Joseph became known to Pharaoh [Genesis 43–45]. So Joseph sent and summoned Jacob, his father, and the whole of his relatives, [numbering] seventy-five persons. Jacob went down to Egypt, but he himself died, as did all our ancestors [Gen. 46:1–49:28]. And they were transported back to Shechem and buried in the tomb that Abraham had purchased for a certain price in silver from the sons of Hamor in Shechem [Gen. 49:29–50:14].

"As the time which God promised to Abraham drew near, the people increased and [their number] in Egypt was multiplied, until a king rose up over Egypt who did not know Joseph [Exod. 1:8]. He took advantage of our nation by trickery and mistreated our fathers by making them abandon their children so that they would not survive [Exod. 1:15-22]. At this time Moses was born, and he was well-pleasing to God. He was reared for three months in his father's house, but when he was abandoned, the daughter of Pharaoh took him and brought him up as her own son [Exod. 2:1-10]. And Moses was educated in all the wisdom of the Egyptians; he was powerful in his words[8] and his actions.

"When he reached the age of forty years,[9] it arose in his heart to see [how matters were with] his brothers, the sons of Israel. When he saw one of them being mistreated, he retaliated and performed vengeance in behalf of the one who had been wronged by striking the Egyptian [Exod. 2:12]. He assumed that his brethren would understand that through his hand God was giving them deliverance, but they did not understand. On the following day he was seen by them as they were having a dispute, and he [sought to] reconcile them in order to restore peace, saying 'Men, you are my brothers. Why do you wrong one another?' The one who was doing wrong to his neighbor pushed him aside and said, 'Who set you up as ruler and adjudicator over us? You want to kill me in the same way that yesterday you killed the Egyptian, don't you?' [Exod. 2:14]. At this response, Moses fled and became a sojourner in Midian, where he fathered two sons.[10]

"After forty years passed, an angel appeared to him in the desert of Mt. Sinai in a flame of fire in a bush. When Moses saw this, he was amazed at the vision and came close to observe. And there came the voice of the Lord: 'I am the God of your fathers, the God of Abraham and Isaac and Jacob.' And Moses was trembling and did not dare to keep looking. And the Lord said to him, 'Take off your sandals from your feet, because the place on which you are standing is holy ground. I have indeed seen the mistreatment of my people in Egypt, and I have heard their groaning, and I have come down to set them free. And now, come! I shall send you to Egypt' [Exod. 3:1-12]. This Moses, whom they refused, saying, 'Who established you as leader and arbiter?' [Exod. 2:14], is the one that God sent as both leader and agent of rescue by the hand of the angel that appeared to him in the bush. He led them out, having performed wonders and signs in the Egyptian land and in the Red Sea and in the barren land for forty years.[11] This is the Moses who said to the people of Israel, 'God will raise up for you a prophet from your brothers, as [he raised] me' [Deut. 18:15]. It is this one who was in the community in the wilderness, with the angel who spoke to him on Mt. Sinai, together with our fathers. He received the living oracles to give to us. To him our fathers did not wish to be obedient, but repudiated him. And in their hearts they returned to Egypt, saying to Aaron, 'Make gods for us that will go before us, but as for this Moses who led us out of Egypt — we do not know what has happened to him!' [Exod. 32:1, 23].

"They made a calf in those days, and brought up to [this] idol an offering, and took delight in the products of their own hands [Exod. 32:1–6]. But God turned away and gave them over to worship the heavenly army of angels [Exod. 32:7–10], just as it is written in the book of the prophets: 'Didn't you offer me sacrifices and offerings in the desert for forty years, O house of Israel? And you raised up the tent of Moloch and the star of your god, Rompha [Rephan], the images which you made in order to worship them. And I will deport you beyond Babylon' [Amos 5:25–27].

"The tent of witness was [available] to our fathers in the barren land, just as the one who spoke to Moses gave him instructions to make it according to the model which he had seen [Exodus 26, 33:7–11]. Our fathers took it with them when they entered with Joshua and took possession of the [land] from the nations which God had expelled from the time of the arrival of our fathers and so it was until the time of David.[12] He found favor in the presence of God, and asked to establish [God's] dwelling place [2 Samuel 6–7] for the house of Jacob. And Solomon built a house for him [1 Kings 5–6]. Yet the Most High does not reside in places made by human hands, just as the prophet says:

Heaven is a throne for me,
And the earth is the footstool under my feet.
'What sort of house will you build for me?' says the Lord,

Or what is the place of rest for me?
Did not my hand make all these things? [Isa. 66:1–2]

"You stubborn people,[13] uncircumcised in your hearts and ears,[14] you always oppose the Holy Spirit! [Isa. 63:10]. Just as your fathers did, so do you! Which of the prophets did not your fathers persecute? They killed those who gave information beforehand of the coming of the Righteous One,[15] of whom you have now become betrayers and murderers. You are those who received the Law through instructions by angels [Exod. 3:2; Deut. 33:2], but have not kept it."

The central importance for the author of Acts of this speech by Stephen is apparent from the fact that it is by far the longest one in the entire book. The next longest is Peter's speech at Pentecost (2:14–36). The themes in Stephen's speech are multiple:

1. God's activity in behalf of his people and for the achievement of his purpose in their behalf is not limited to a single location: they must be prepared to change their situation when God calls them to do so, and his purpose will be revealed to them wherever he leads them.

2. The leaders of God's people, through whom God is at work to achieve his purpose, have undergone difficulty and suffered at the hands of hostile authorities.

3. Stephen repeatedly refers to the past history of God's activity in terms of what happened to "our" ancestors (7:2, 11, 12, 18, 38, 39, 44, 45). He is not adopting a stance over against the traditions of Israel.

4. God grants special wisdom and insight to those whom he has chosen to serve as leaders and liberators of his people (7:10, 22), although the self-appointed leaders do not always understand God's true message.

5. The chosen and empowered leader in the past has repeatedly been misunderstood and denounced by his own people (7:35).

The cumulative import of this speech is to show the hearers/readers that Stephen, Jesus, and the good news that is being proclaimed concerning him as God's agent for renewal of his people are by no means threatening or undermining the traditions of

Israel, but are instead the divinely empowered agents through whom God is fulfilling his purpose for the covenant people. The speech consists almost entirely of references to scripture rather than direct quotations,[16] but the overall effect is to document in detail how God's purpose for his people has been disclosed and achieved. The theological convictions are conveyed through the narrative of God's dealings with his people, rather than in a more abstract conceptual mode.

At several points the speech shows that it is basically Greek in its linguistic origins, rather than a translation of a semitic original. For example, "Mesopotamia" (7:2) is a pure Greek term ("middle of the river") which has no equivalent in Hebrew and is not used in the LXX. "Patriarch" (7:8–9) is likewise distinctively Greek, and is found only in the Greek versions of the later historical books of the LXX: 1 and 2 Chronicles and 4 Maccabees, in none of which is the translation exact.[17] Thus the linguistic and conceptual impact of hellenistic culture on Judaism and on this Christian author and his community is apparent throughout this speech, as it is in all of Acts.

The "God of glory" (7:2) is the deity who reveals his identity and his purpose to those who are chosen to be the instruments of the divine purpose for God's people. That purpose is not simply inferred in mystical form from the revelatory experiences of Abraham and Moses, but is explicitly conveyed in terms of instruction and promise: where to go and what to do (7:3, 30–34). This promise is not based on or embodied in territorial possession ("not even a foot of ground"), but rests solely on trusting God's word to his people (7:5). As the experience of Abraham, the founder of the covenant community shows, the "child" through whom the promise will be fulfilled is divinely provided, not an agent of merely human origin. Those "nations" or peoples who oppose the purpose of God or cause harm to his people will fall under divine judgment (7:7). God's own community must be willing to adopt practices that set them apart from the rest of alien, disobedient humanity. In this case, it was through the grace of God and his provision of a son, "Isaac," that the people of God began and flourished (7:8). The special place where God's relationship to his people will be experienced was to be in "this land," where Israel had dwelt after the exodus, and to which it had returned following the exile. Yet the divine purpose included the extended stay in Egypt for four hundred years, thereby demonstrating that God's purpose and support for his people are not restricted to a particular land. Obedience to God is to characterize his people no matter where they are living. The visible sign of commitment to the covenantal relationship between God and the people pictured in Torah as taking shape in the realm of history is, of course, "circumcision." It is a distinctively male rite, just as the identity and leadership of the covenant people are based on males, as in the case of the "twelve patriarchs" (7:8).

The first of the agents chosen by God to aid and preserve his people as they lived in a strange land in a time of grave difficulty was Joseph (7:9). Yet he was in Egypt because his own family resented him and sought to be rid of him by selling him as a slave to the Egyptians. It was with this rejected individual that God continued to be present and active, and on whom he bestowed wisdom that was so remarkable as to be recognized by the pagan ruler of Egypt (7:10). The analogy with the response to Jesus and his place in the divine plan for renewal of his people is clear, though never made explicit in Stephen's speech. Through the providence of God, Joseph was in Egypt and in a position of power to come to the aid of his kinsmen who had rejected him (7:11–14). Even the burial place for the "ancestors" was arranged for in advance in the form of the "tomb that Abraham purchased" at Machpelah (near Hebron), where Sarah was buried (Gen. 29:17–20). In Gen. 50:13, the tomb is said to have been bought by Abraham from Ephron the Hittite. In Acts 7:16, however, the site of the tomb is said to have been at "Shechem," and the former owners were "the sons of Hamor."[18] In Gen. 33:19–20 Jacob is said to have bought the plot in order to erect on it an altar to El-Elohe-Israel. Thus the author of Acts portrays Stephen as splicing together features of two different stories of the patriarchs, but his basic point is nonetheless clear: God's purpose triumphs over human differences in time and space, and may be fulfilled through the faithful intentions and commitments of his people.

Once again Stephen perceives what happened to Israel in Egypt as God at work to fulfill his covenantal promise to Abraham. Specific evidence for the divine action in history in order to bring to pass God's plan for his people is offered here in the story of the special role granted to Moses. The size of the Israelite community there is said to have "increased" significantly. The accession to power of a new "king," Rameses II, famed for his construction of a huge city that he named for himself on the eastern edge of the Nile delta, was followed by his plot to exterminate the Israelites. But the imperial decree to destroy the significantly increased number of Israelites by forcing the abandonment of all the males born among them had the reverse effect of bringing Moses into a place of unique favor in the center of power: the household of Pharaoh. His status as "well-pleasing to God"[19] has its human counterpart in a series of events: (1) the crucial period of his infancy in the Israelite household of his father (which would have included circumcision); (2) his rescue, adoption, and rearing by the daughter of Pharaoh "as her own son"; and (3) the opportunity afforded him for broad and deep education in "all the wisdom of the Egyptians." As will become evident during Paul's encounter with his learned examiners on the Areopagus in Athens (Acts 17), the author of Acts does not view disdainfully the wider wisdom of this world, although ultimate insight comes through direct disclosure by God to his chosen agent.

As a consequence of this combination of background, rearing, education, and challenging opportunity in the household of Pharaoh, Moses is here depicted as "powerful in his words and his actions." The picture of him in Exodus does not wholly fit this description of him in Acts. In Exod. 4:1–9 Moses performs three miracles: converting his staff into a snake, catching and curing himself of a dread disease, and changing water into blood. In the same chapter (4:10–16), however, he is seen as struggling with his lack of eloquence, and Aaron is appointed to articulate Moses' messages to the people. Philo of Alexandria, on the other hand, in his *Life of Moses*, describes Moses' commitment to temperance and self-control, how he sought to live for the soul alone rather than the body, and how "his words expressed his feelings, and his actions accorded with his words, so that speech and life were in harmony" (1.25–29). It is this same idealized model of Moses which is adopted by the author of Acts.

His decision in maturity was to investigate how things were going with his fellow Israelites. When he came to the help of one of his "brothers" and struck the Egyptian who was "mistreating" him, they did not recognize him as one of their group, nor did they perceive the potential for liberation of the whole of God's people through Moses. This misperception of him and his role in the purpose of God was repeated the next day when he sought to adjudicate a dispute between two Israelites and was scorned by them. Their rhetorical question as to who would have authorized him to serve as an authority and "adjudicator" over them had an answer which is not here articulated: it is God whose agent for leadership and for freedom and renewal of the covenant people Moses is. Mention of his having killed an "Egyptian" showed that his forceful action in coming to the aid of the mistreated Israelite was a matter of public knowledge, and so Moses took flight. His move to "Midian," the semite-populated district on the east side of the Gulf of Aqabah opposite Mount Sinai, was for an extended period of time, since he "fathered two sons" there: Gershom (Exod. 2:15–22) and Eliezer (Exod. 18:1-4). The name of his father-in-law is variously given as Reuel (Exod. 2:18), Jethro (3:1), and Hobab (Judg. 1:16). According to Exod. 3:1, it was from this region on the western bank of the Gulf of Aqabah that Moses led the flock of his father-in-law, and on the mountain there — Horeb in Exod. 3:1; Sinai in Exod. 19:1-21 — that God appeared to him. It is possible that this was regarded by the Midianites as "the mountain of God" (Exod. 3:1).

As in the Exodus account, Moses first sees the "angel" (Exod. 3:2) and then hears "the voice of the Lord" (Exod. 3:4), who identifies himself as the God of the patriarchs (Exod. 3:6) through whom the covenant with Israel was established. In Exodus 19 Yahweh appears to the whole of the people of Israel to establish the covenant, but the mountain is so holy that none of them except Moses is to ascend it or even to touch it (19:12). Quoting in a condensed version the account in Exod. 3:7-10 of God's instruction to Moses, the climax comes in the promise to "set free" the people — a message that he is return to Egypt and declare to them. Yet he is to be prepared to have to persuade the people that he is the agent of God, and to give an answer to their question earlier as to who authorized him to serve as their "leader and arbiter" (Exod. 2:14). The analogy with the rejection experienced by Jesus is clear: as God sent Moses to set his people free, so now Jesus — whom "God sent" — has encountered hostility just as Moses did. In spite of the initial disbelief that Moses faced, he was empowered by the "angel that appeared to him in the bush" — the visible and powerful presence of God — to carry out the divine plan of liberation for God's people. In the Luke-Acts tradition, the continuing presence and power of God in and through Jesus is the Holy Spirit, as is made explicit in the

distinctive Lukan version of Jesus' speech in the Nazareth synagogue, with the claim that his being "anointed" by the "Spirit of
the Lord" is enabling him to preach good news to the poor, to
heal and to "proclaim release" to those in bondage (Luke 4:16–
21). The combination of "wonders and signs" with the acts of
liberation performed by Moses is seen as directly analogous to
what God is doing through Jesus for his new people. The link
with Jesus is made even clearer in the quotation attributed to
Moses (Deut. 18:15), although the identification of Jesus as "the
prophet" that God will "raise up" as he raised up Moses for
ancient Israel remains implicit.

The analogy between Moses and Jesus continues in the contrast between the unique relationship with God that Moses had,
as evidenced by the "living oracles" that were given through him
for God's people, and the rejection accorded him and his message by the people. Under the perverted leadership of Aaron,
with his claim to be the priest of Yahweh, Israel's God, the
people turned from the worship of the true God to the "golden
calf" (Exod. 32:4), which they then acclaimed as the deity who
had liberated them from Egypt. Far from rebuking the people
for worshiping an object of human creation, Aaron — the religious leader of the people — sets up an altar and a program
of sacrifice and celebration to honor this idol, the "product of
their own hands" (Exod. 32:5–6; Acts 7:41). In the Exodus account these people are abandoned by God and are to pass under
fiery judgment (Exod. 32:9–10). Their subsequent behavior evidenced their devotion to false gods during their "forty years in
the desert," as the "prophets" attested. In the quotation from
Amos (5:25–27), however, the focus is shifted from the period of
the exodus to the eighth century B.C.E., when Israel's infidelity
to God is expected to result in the exile of the people "beyond
Damascus" (Amos 5:27). In the LXX, which is quoted (Amos
5:25–27) — and modified — in Acts 7:42–43, the exile is said to be
"beyond Babylon" (which occurred in the sixth century B.C.E.).
The Hebrew text names the gods worshiped by the disobedient
Israelites as Sakkuth and Kaiwan, although these terms may originally have referred to Saturn: Sakkuth the Steady One, and
Kaiwan, or *kayamanu*, so named because it was the slowest moving planet. The names were replaced in the LXX by "Moloch"
(from the semitic root meaning "king") and "Rephaim," the god
of the dead (sometimes used for the dead ancestors who were

venerated). Sacrifices to Moloch may have involved offering up one's own children (Lev. 20:1-5; 2 Kings 23:10). "Rephan" is probably a mistaken transliteration from the semitic *kywn*, since there is no other evidence for a deity by that name. The crucial point is clear: the deities that they worshiped they had "made" for themselves. It is this kind of fundamental replacement of God and his purpose for his people by objects and aims that they have themselves contrived which has resulted in divine judgment, as represented by the exile "beyond Babylon." The implication is that similar punishment will fall on those who turn from God and his revealed purpose for his people.

The "tent" that symbolized and embodied the presence of God with his people on the way to the promised land is most frequently called the "tent of assembly."[20] But both the tent and the ark of the covenant are designated by, or associated with, the term "witness,"[21] the implication being that the ark and its contents are a visible, tangible witness to the relationship that God has established with his people. It was constructed according to the divine "model" which had been disclosed to Moses in fulfillment of the promise reported in Exod. 25:8-9, the details of which are then given (25:10-30:10). It was the place where God met regularly with Moses "face to face" to give instructions for the people (Exod. 33:7-10). It continued to serve these functions for the people of Israel, and especially to bear witness to God's powerful presence among his people as they entered and settled in the land.[22] David gave concrete evidence of God's support for the nation when they took over Jerusalem as their new capital: he had the ark of the covenant brought into the "tent" in Jerusalem as "God's dwelling place" in "the house of Jacob" (2 Sam. 6:17-19). Yet God's covenant with David included the provision that not David, but one of his sons would "build a house for the name of Yahweh" (2 Sam. 7:13). The construction of this grand sanctuary by Solomon is described in 1 Kings 5-6. Yet Stephen goes on to quote Isa. 66:1-2 to make the point that God's sovereignty is over the whole universe, including both heaven and earth, and that it is therefore impossible to assign to God a "house" or a "place of rest," since God made everything.

This represents the climax of the entire speech, which has been indicating the variety of places and circumstances in which the presence and power of God were seen to be operative in the history of God's people. Stephen turns then to denounce the leaders, centered in the temple for their focus, values, and activities, as inwardly disqualified ("uncircumcised in your hearts") to share in the life of the covenant people, and as thinking and acting in opposition to the "Holy Spirit" (Isa. 63:10). Earlier, at the time of the restoration of the temple and its worship under Hezekiah, the people were warned not to emulate their ancestors who were "faithless to the Lord" and "stiff-necked" (2 Chron. 30:7–8). Elijah lamented to the Lord that the Israelites had "killed your prophets," and were seeking to kill him as well (1 Kings 19:10–14). At the time of the fall of Jerusalem in the reign of Zedekiah, the leading priests and the people as a whole are depicted in 2 Chron. 36:14–16 as "exceedingly unfaithful," as having "mocked his messengers, despised his words," and "scoffed at his prophets."

In Matt. 5:12 Jesus is reported as warning his disciples that they should expect hostile reaction similar to what was done by those who "persecuted the prophets." Hebrews 11:35 describes those messengers and agents of God who were "tortured, refused to accept release," suffered flogging, chains, and imprisonment, were stoned to death, or sawn in two, or killed by the sword.[23] It is appropriate to link the suffering of the faithful messengers of God with the death of "the Righteous One," as in the Suffering Servant passage (Isa. 52:13–53:12), where it is the Righteous One who sets man in right relationship with God (53:11). The same link of this title with suffering is found in Enoch 38:2 and 53:6, where the Righteous One appears prior to the eschatological judgment of the wicked and the vindication of the faithful. Here in Acts the wicked leaders are identified as "betrayers and murderers" of Jesus, whose rejection of him is matched by their infidelity to the Law of Moses, and reaches back to the period of the Judges.[24] Once again, there is insistence on the continuing validity of the Jewish tradition, extending back through Israel's history to the days of the prophets and even to the time of Moses and the receiving of the Law. Jesus is not the terminator of God's covenant with Israel, but its culmination.

7:54–8:1: The Stoning of Stephen

When they heard these things, they were infuriated in their hearts, and they gnashed their teeth against him. But being full

of the Holy Spirit, he gazed into heaven and saw the Glory of
God and Jesus standing at the right hand of God. And he said,
"Look! I am seeing the heavens opened and the Son of Man
standing at the right hand of God." But they shouted with a
loud voice, and stopping their ears, rushed together upon him.
They threw him out of the city and were stoning him, and the
witnesses put down their garments at the feet of the young
man named Saul. As they were stoning Stephen, he called
out saying, "Lord Jesus! Receive my spirit." Then getting on
his knees, he called out with a loud voice, "Lord, do not hold
this sin against them." And when he had said this, he went to
sleep. And Saul was fully supportive of killing him.

The members of the council were enraged by Stephen's indictment of them, but he has what might be called a trinitarian
vision: "full of the Holy Spirit," he is granted a vision of heaven
in which he sees Jesus "standing at the right hand of God." The
divine source that Stephen asserts for the movement and his
claim of a divine attestation of Jesus, whom the council had
earlier examined and rejected, are offensive to the authorities.
Stephen is said to have been "thrown out of the city and stoned."
This reaction and the tragic results fit well with this form of
execution as indicated in the Hebrew Bible. It was reserved for
those considered to be violators of the covenant between God
and his people, whether by their blasphemy (Lev. 24:14, 16, 23),
by their worshiping other gods (Lev. 20:2; Deut. 13:6–10; 17:2–
5), by violation of the sabbath law (Num. 15:32–36), or when
a son was regarded by his family as rebellious.[25] It is the community as a group that was to perform the execution, which
was carried out after two or three witnesses presented the evidence of the violation, then laid their hands on the accused
(Lev. 24:14) and threw the first stones. These would have been
large stones, heavy enough to crush and kill the accused. Then
stones were thrown by all the community (Deut. 17:7; Lev. 20:2).
The action was to take place outside the city (Lev. 24:13–23).
Rabbinic sources (second to the sixth centuries c.e.) describe
the condemned individual being thrown down from a ledge or
a tower, and if they did not die shortly, large stones would be
hurled down until the culprit was crushed. There is no concrete
evidence that such a procedure was actually employed in the
time of Jesus or at any subsequent time. The most significant

feature of this mode of execution is that it was performed by the community in the interests of preserving what it regarded as the legal basis for its identity and integrity. Stephen and his speech are regarded as threats to both these factors. Even more than the message and work of Peter and the other apostles, Stephen's words and actions are perceived here by the council as a threat to what they see as the standards governing participation in the covenant people. This man has not only advanced a radically different way of defining participation in the covenant people, but he has forcefully challenged the council's perception of the law and purpose of God for the covenant community, and has done so by his very different interpretation of their traditions about God's covenant with his people. The officials' determination to destroy him contrasts vividly with his prayer to God to forgive them.

What might seem to the first-time reader of Acts to be intrusive or irrelevant details — mention that those engaged in stoning Stephen placed their garments at the feet of "a young man named Saul," and that he supported their execution — serve, of course, as a skillful introduction of this person into the remainder of the book, with its overall narrative concerning one whose name is to be given major prominence: Paul. After he has been initially identified simply by the name of Saul — which is never found in Paul's letters with reference to himself — he is designated as the one who is leading the effort to "destroy" the "church" (7:3). In Acts he is referred to frequently as Saul[26] until he and Barnabas begin to carry out the mission to the wider gentile world for which they were chosen and sent by the church in Antioch (13:1–3), at which point his name is given as Paul. The shift of names that occurs in 13:9 marks the final point in Acts at which his semitic name is used. The details of the biography of Saul/Paul unfold in the subsequent narrative of Acts, including his conversion and initial preaching activity in Damascus (9:1–30; retold with some differences in detail in 22:3–21, 26:9–20), the launching of the mission to Gentiles, beginning in Cyprus and Asia Minor (13:1–14:27), his consultation with the council of the apostles in Jerusalem and his return to Antioch (15:1–40), the launching of the mission in Greece (16:1–18:17), his return to Antioch, Ephesus, and Jerusalem (18:18–21:27), his arrest and removal to Rome as one charged by the Romans (21:28–31). The initial mention of the name of Saul/Paul in

7:58 gives no clue to the central role that he is subsequently to fulfill.

8:2–3: Saul Ravages the Church

On that day there arose a great persecution against the church which was in Jerusalem, and they were all scattered throughout the districts of Judea and Samaria, except the apostles. Firmly committed men buried Stephen and made loud lamentation over him. But Saul was engaged in destroying the church: entering house after house and dragging off both men and women, he handed them over to prison.

Stephen's forceful challenge to the understanding by the Jewish leadership concerning the basis of its relationship with God evoked from the traditional leadership a forceful reaction, which is here depicted as led by Saul. The members of the new community fled, scattering throughout "Judea" and "Samaria." Judea was used in this period to refer to the land between the Jordan and Dead Sea on the east and the Mediterranean Sea to the west, and from the southern desert area below Hebron to some distance north of Jerusalem and Jericho. The coastal area farther north was under direct Roman control, but the district around Mount Gerizim and Mount Ebal and the valley in between (the Wadi Farah) were what constituted Samaria. The chief city of the district was Sebaste, formerly known as "Samaria," when it served as capital of the northern kingdom of Israel from the time of Omri (early ninth century B.C.E.) until it fell after a siege by the Assyrians in 721. In the Wadi Farah east of Samaria was Shechem, where God is reported to have met the patriarch Abraham (Gen. 12:6) and where Jacob, who bought a plot of ground there, erected an altar to God (Gen. 33:18–20), and where his body was buried after his death in Egypt (Josh. 23:32). Overlooking the valley in the time of Jesus was the temple erected on Mount Gerizim, where the Samaritans worshiped the God of the patriarchs in accord with their own version of the Law of Moses. Because they had their own priesthood and mode of worship, while claiming to have the authentic edition of the Law of Moses and to be the true heirs of the patriarchs as God's people, they were hated by the Jews, and associations with them were avoided. The refugees from the Jewish oppressors who fled there and to other parts of Judea thought they would be safe in such territory, since they now shared with the Samaritans a common enemy: the Jewish officials. In Jerusalem, there were not only the "apostles," but also some strongly "committed"[27] men who buried the martyr Stephen. Once again in Acts, the mistaken action of enemies of the good news against its messengers results in its wider outreach.

Meanwhile, "Saul" was seeking to "destroy" the "church," which is here seen as not yet identified by organization or a building, but as comprised of groups meeting in "houses." On the assumption by the authorities that these gatherings are composed of both "men and women" active in subverting the sociopolitical order by their undermining the ground and norms of Jewish covenantal identity, those seized by Saul and his co-workers are "imprisoned." Only the "apostles" remain in Jerusalem as the core of the new community.

8:4–25: The Good News in Samaria

Those who were dispersed went about preaching the word. Philip went down to a city of Samaria and preached the Messiah to them. And the crowds with one accord paid attention to the things that were said by Philip when they heard them and saw the signs which he was performing. For there were many who had unclean spirits which came out of them crying with a loud voice, and many who were paralyzed or crippled were healed. There came to be much joy in that city. A certain man by the name of Simon had formerly practiced magic in the city, and had astounded the people of Samaria, saying that he himself was someone great. They all paid attention to him from the least to the greatest, saying, "This person is the Power of God which is called great!" They paid attention to him, because for a considerable period of time he had astounded them by his magical acts. But when they believed Philip as he was telling them the good news concerning the kingdom of God and the name of Jesus Christ, the men and women were baptized. Even Simon himself believed, and after he was baptized, he attached himself to Philip. When he saw the signs and great deeds of power that took place, he was astounded.

When the apostles in Jerusalem heard that Samaria had received the message of God, they sent Peter and John to them, who came down and prayed for them so that they might receive the Holy Spirit, since it had not yet come down on any of them. They had been baptized only in the name of the Lord Jesus. Then they placed their hands on them and they received the Holy Spirit. When Simon saw that it was through the apostles' placing their hands that the Spirit was given, he put forth money, saying, "Give me this power, so that anyone on whom I place hands may receive the Holy Spirit." Peter said to him, "May your money be destroyed along with you, because you supposed that the gift of God could be acquired by money. There is for you no share in this matter, because your heart is not in right relation with God. So repent of this evil deed, and pray to the Lord so that this intention of your heart might be forgiven to you. For I perceive that you are in bitter gall and a bond of unrighteousness." Simon answered and said, "Pray to the Lord in my behalf, so that none of the things of which you spoke may befall me." And when they had given their testimony and spoken the word of the Lord, they returned to Jerusalem, preaching the good news in many villages of the Samaritans.

Once again, Acts points to a hostile action on the part of the authorities opposed to the Jesus movement which has a significant positive result. In this case, it is the spread of the good news to non-Jews. The flight from Jerusalem of "all" the new community, except its "apostolic" leaders, led to their preaching the gospel among the "Samaritans." The origins of this group are indicated in 2 Kings 17:24–28, which describes how the Samaritans were brought in as colonists by the Assyrians after they had expelled the northern tribes of Israel in 722 B.C.E. and how they were instructed by an Israelite priest. The Samaritans claimed, however, that when the worship of Yahweh which began in Shechem was set up by Joshua in Shiloh (Josh. 18:1), they had remained true to the original site, and followed the instruction of Moses (in their version of Torah) that the shrine of Yahweh should be built on Mount Gerizim. The opposition to rebuilding the temple in Jerusalem and the resultant delay following the return of the tribes of Judah from exile in Babylon around 400 B.C.E. (Ezra 4:1–24) were blamed on the Samaritans. By the first century B.C.E. the Samaritans seem to have had a modest temple on Mount Gerizim which was served by their own priesthood, and to have developed their own version of the Torah.[28] When, following the second Jewish revolt, the emperor Hadrian (117–138 C.E.) replaced the temple in Jerusalem with one to Zeus Hypsistos, however, he did the same on Mount Gerizim. For pious Jews in the first century C.E., there could not have been a more objectionable place than Samaria in which to offer the invitation to share in the life of God's people, as "Philip" did. For the author of Acts, it is significant that the first one to undertake an outreach to non-Israelites is someone with a Greek name, "Philip," from among those who were chosen by the apostles initially to care for the needs of the members of the Jerusalem community following the cultural tensions between the "Hebrews" and the "Hellenists" (6:1–6). The power of the message of what God was doing through Jesus for the renewal of his people was confirmed dramatically for the Samaritan "crowds" by the exorcisms and healings that were taking place among them in the name of Jesus.

Among those Samaritans attracted by the message was "Simon," who had achieved great fame as a "magician," and was acclaimed as "the Power of God which is called Great." The large numbers astounded by his extraordinary powers now turn to Philip and the "name of Jesus Christ," in which they are "baptized," although they do not receive the gift of the "Spirit." Simon himself "believes," is "baptized," and joins Philip and the huge group of converts. When "Peter and John" arrive from Jerusalem to confirm what has taken place among these non-Jews in their response to the message about Jesus, the apostles' conveying of "power" through "placing their hands" on those who have trusted in the name of Jesus seems to have reawakened his urges and motives as a magician. Accordingly, he seeks to purchase the power evident through the apostles, which he is told must be regarded as solely "the gift of God." His desire and his strategy to achieve this power evoke from Peter the warning that he has no "share" in this divine activity, and he is warned that his relationship with God is not right, but that he is bound up with bitterness and "unrighteousness." He pleads with the apostles to pray for his deliverance from divine punishment, but there is no further indication in Acts of his future status. In Christian writers of the second century, however, he is a major villain. Instead of "the Power of God called great," he is known as "the Great Power" and is said to have developed (in collusion with a prostitute, Helen) a gnostic system in which they were worshiped as Zeus and Helena. Irenaeus denounces them as having led "profligate lives and practiced magical acts."[29] The apostles' confirmation of this outreach to non-Jews is evident in their activities in Samaria, and in the evangelism which they carry out in the Samaritan "villages" on their way back to Jerusalem. They have begun to put into practice the injunction given them by the risen Jesus to bear witness to him, not only in Jerusalem and Judea, but in "Samaria and to the end of the earth" (Acts 1:8).

8:26 – 40: Philip and the Ethiopian Eunuch

An angel of the Lord spoke to Philip, telling him, "Get up and go toward the south on the road that goes down from Jerusalem to Gaza," which is a desert road. He got up and went, and see! there was an Ethiopian man, a eunuch who was an official of Candace, the queen of the Ethiopians, and he was in charge of her entire treasury. He had been worshiping in Jerusalem, and as he was returning, was sitting in his chariot and reading the prophet Isaiah. The Spirit said to Philip, "Go ahead and join this chariot." So Philip ran up to him and heard him as he was reading Isaiah the prophet, and said, "Do you understand the things you are reading?" And he said, "How should I be able to, unless someone instructs me?" He urged Philip to come up and sit with him. The portion of scripture that he was reading was this:

> As a sheep led to the slaughter or a lamb in the presence
>   of the shearer is silent, so he did not open his mouth.
> In his humiliation justice was taken from him.
> Who can describe his descent?
> For his life was taken up from the earth. [Isa. 53:7 – 8]

The eunuch responded to Philip and said, "I beg of you, concerning whom does the prophet say this? About himself or someone else?" Then Philip opened his mouth and, beginning from this scripture, he told him the good news about Jesus.

As they were going along the road, they came upon some water, and the eunuch said, "Look at the water! What is to prevent me from being baptized?" And he ordered the chariot to stop, and they both went down into the water — Philip and the eunuch — and he baptized him. When they came out of the water, the Spirit of the Lord carried off Philip, and the eunuch no longer saw him. So he continued on his way rejoicing. Philip was found at Azotus; as he was passing through, he was preaching the good news in all the cities until he reached Caesarea.

The next phase in the Acts description of the spread of the good news and hence of the new community across the world once again involves an individual who represents those on the periphery of the Jewish covenant people: an "Ethiopian eunuch." Likewise the physical direction, "toward the south," indicates movement from the center in Jerusalem, and the barren territory through which this "desert road" passes en route through "Gaza" to Egypt is symbolic of the unpromising nature — humanly speaking — of the enterprise, but it also echoes the prophetic promise in Isa. 40:3 that it is in the desert that the future "way of the Lord" will be prepared.[30]

The ethnic origin of the Ethiopian, combined with his official role as treasurer for the Ethiopian queen and his having been castrated, make him a most unlikely candidate for participation in the people of God as traditionally understood. Eunuchs presided over the royal harems in the Persian courts and served in major administrative roles,[31] but in Israel they were prohibited from entering assemblies of God's people on the grounds of inherent ritual impurity (Deut. 23:1). The authority of this Ethiopian is indicated (*dynastes*) but not his specific role in the court of "Candace," which was her title rather than her name (and probably meant "queen mother"). The realm of the Ethiopian rulers was in Meroe, along the Nile in what is now Sudan, rather than in present-day Ethiopia.

In every aspect of his background and role, this man would have been an outsider in terms of covenantal identity based on the Torah. Yet he is pictured as returning from Jerusalem, where he had been "worshiping." The depth of his interest in the religion of Israel is confirmed by his reading "Isaiah the prophet" as he is riding back through the desert, and he is obviously

reading aloud. As in the witness of the apostles from the beginning (2:4, 33, 40; 4:8; 6:3, 10; 7:55), it is the "Spirit" of God
at work to accomplish the divine purpose that impels Philip to
join the Ethiopian even before he can know or hear what he is
reading. On hearing the Suffering Servant passage from Isaiah
(8:32–33 = Isa. 53:7–8) and in response to the Ethiopian's acknowledgment that he does not understand its meaning or even
of whom the author is speaking ("About himself or someone
else?"), Philip builds on the scripture to bring to this outsider
"the good news about Jesus." In so doing, he is furthering the
work of the apostles in using the scriptures to bring to earnest
seekers from whatever background an understanding of the nature and meaning of what God is doing through Jesus Christ.
Earlier instances of this christological method appear in 2:34
(the exaltation/resurrection of Jesus; Ps. 110:1), in 3:22 (the ultimate prophet raised up by God; Deut. 18:15–20), and 4:11 (Jesus
as the rejected stone; Ps. 118:22).

As soon as water is available, the eunuch asks to be "baptized,"
using what seems to have been a technical term, *koluei* (8:37),
which appeared in the form of a question among early Christians. Their leaders were asking in one way or another, "Is there
any reason that this person should not be baptized, and thus
accepted as a member of the new community?" This is the issue stated explicitly in Acts 10:47, and the crucial term, *koluei*,
is linked there with the Spirit and baptism in 11:17. The joyous Ethiopian, in spite of his ritually unacceptable being, origin,
and occupation, continues on his way. Philip extends his outreach into new non-Jewish territory as he begins a journey up
the seacoast, where major centers of Greco-Roman culture were
located, reaching from "Azotus" (Ashdod) in the south, to "Caesarea," the major port city built by Herod nearly sixty miles to
the north. It is in this city named for the head of the Roman
Empire that the conversion of a Roman military officer, Cornelius, and the confirmation of this by the Holy Spirit are to be
recounted in Acts 10:1–48. But first the story is told of the conversion of the chief antagonist of the church's outreach to the
wider Roman world, who becomes its chief agent: Paul (9:1–19).

Chapter Three

The World Mission of the New Community: Launching and Confirmation (9:1–15:41)

9:1–19a: The Conversion of Saul

But Saul, still breathing out murderous threats against the disciples of the Lord, went to the high priest and requested from him letters to the synagogues in Damascus, so that if he found any who were of the Way, both men and women, he might bring them to Jerusalem as prisoners. It happened that as he was going and was approaching Damascus, unexpectedly a light from heaven shown around him. When he had fallen to the ground, he heard a voice saying to him, "Saul, Saul! Why are you persecuting me?" He said, "Who are you, sir?" He said, "I am Jesus whom you are persecuting. But get up and go into the city, and it will be told to you what it is necessary for you to do." The men who were traveling with him stood speechless, since they were hearing the voice but seeing no one. Saul arose from the ground, but when he opened his eyes, he was seeing nothing. They led him by the hand into Damascus, and for three days he saw nothing, and neither ate nor drank.

There was in Damascus a certain disciple by the name of Ananias, and the Lord said to him in a vision, "Ananias!" And he said, "Here I am, Lord." The Lord said to him, "Get up and go to the Street Called Straight, and in the house of Judas, seek out someone named Saul of Tarsus. For see, he is praying. He has seen a man by the name of Ananias come and lay his hands on him, so that he might regain his sight." But Ananias answered, "Lord, I have heard from many people about this man, how many evil things he has done to the saints who are in Jerusalem. And he has come here with authority from the high priests to put in fetters all who are calling on your name." But the Lord said to him, "Go! For this man is an instrument chosen by me to carry my name before Gentiles and kings, and before the sons of Israel. For I will show him what things he must suffer for the sake of my name." So Ananias went and entered the house, and after having placed his hands upon him, he said, "Brother Saul, the Lord sent me — Jesus, who was seen by you on the road by which you were coming — so that you might regain your sight and be filled with the Holy Spirit." And immediately something like scales fell from his eyes, and he regained his sight. He arose and was baptized, and after having taken food, he was strengthened.

9:1-2

The fierce efforts of Paul to destroy the new community of Christ in Jerusalem (8:1-3) are now to be extended to "Damascus." His targets are both "men and women," whose guilt in his eyes rests on their having committed themselves to "the Way." In the biblical tradition as a whole, there is a rich and diverse range of ways in which the term "way" is used. In the Law, the psalms, and the prophets, "the way of the Lord" is perceived in terms of living in conformity to the Law of Moses (examples include Exod. 18:20, 32:8; Deut. 5:33, 26:17; Pss. 18:21, 51:13, 103:7, 119:1; Isa. 42:24, 58:2).

In the wisdom and prophetic traditions, there are seen to be two ways open from which humans must choose: the way to life and peace (Ps. 16:11; Prov. 3:17; 10:17, 29; Jer. 21:8), and the way of death (Prov. 7:27, 16:25; Isa. 59:7-9). To live in obedience to God is to follow the way of the Lord (Isa. 40:3; Mal. 3:1). Elsewhere in the New Testament, Jesus is called "the Way" (John 14:4-6), and is said to be the one who opened "the new and living way" to the presence of God (Heb. 10:20). But only in Acts is the movement that Jesus launched designated as "the Way" (9:2; 19:9, 23; 22:4; 24:14, 22). The Jewish authorities in Jerusalem are said by Paul to have regarded "the Way" as a sect, or heretical group (*hairesis*; 22:14). In 18:25-26, however, the whole message concerning Jesus is referred to as "the way of the Lord" and "the way of God."

Excursus on the Historical Base of the Conversion of Paul in Acts

Three historical questions are raised by this account: (1) Did the Jerusalem-based high priest have such authority to deputize someone to seize and bring to Jerusalem deviants from official Judaism? (2) Was there so soon after the movement began in Jerusalem a visible, active community of the followers of Christ in a major gentile city as far away as Damascus? (3) How does this account match with the references to Damascus and Paul's conversion that appear in his letters?

1. Did the high priest have the authority over Jews in the Dispersion? When Archelaus was deposed by Augustus as ethnarch of Judea, Samaria, and Idumea in 6 C.E., this section of the province of Syria became an aristocracy, in which high priests were entrusted with the leadership of the Jewish people. The council (referred to in the New Testament as *synedrion* or *boule*)[1] was a political institution, authorized by the Romans to deal with local matters in accord with indigenous law. It was composed of the rich and powerful within the Jewish community, and was presided over by the high priest, who was appointed by the Roman authorities. The council decisions were subject to review by the governor of Judea, but final power rested in the hands of the Syrian provincial governor.[2] Only those who could be relied on to pursue policies approved by Rome were allowed to serve on the council. The Jews were guaranteed the sanctity of the temple,[3] as well as exemption from participation in the imperial cult, although the latter concession was challenged by Gaius and later by Nero. The functional legal code for Jewish communities was that of the Jewish tradition, and the council had the power to enforce it, although capital punishment could be carried out only by consultation with the Roman authorities.[4] To deal with various crises, the Syrian legate from time to time intervened directly in the control of the Palestinian districts: Varus in the reign of Augustus sent two legions to put down the revolt following the death of Herod; Vitellius absorbed the tetrarchy of Philip into the province of Syria in 34, and also deprived Pilate of his office when the latter massacred Samaritans on Mount Gerizim;[5] Petronius intervened when Agrippa I tried to organize a coalition of regional vassal kings, and when he began to re-fortify Jerusalem in 41–44 C.E., and arranged instead for Judea

to be put back under a procurator. Petronius also delayed obeying the imperial order of Gaius Caligula (37–41 C.E.) to have a statue of himself erected in the Jerusalem temple until it was rescinded. Thus the religious and political activities of Judea were formally under the control of the puppet ruler or the Roman procurator, but supervision and control were exercised by the legate in charge of the whole province of Syria, of which Judea was but a part. This evidence points to the possibility that someone authorized by the Jerusalem council — in this case, "Saul" — would have had the right to carry out its decisions in other parts of the Syrian province — in this case, Damascus.

2. Could there have been a community of the followers of Jesus in Damascus so soon after the crucifixion of Jesus? The cities of Syria, Galilee, and the East Jordan territory that later came to be designated as the Decapolis were the result of aggressive efforts by the Seleucid rulers of Syria to impose hellenistic culture on Palestine. Some of the cities were given new Greek names, such as Philadelphia (Ammon), Seleucis (Abila), and Scythopolis (Beth Shan), while others retained their traditional names. The specific designation of ten cities implicit in the name Decapolis varied over the years. When Pompey invaded the region and took control for Rome, the cities were rebuilt along thoroughly Greco-Roman lines, and served as centers of Greek culture, evident in the architecture, theaters, hippodromes, and the worship of Greco-Roman divinities. In his *Life* Josephus noted especially that there were large numbers of Jews in one of these cities: *Damascus*.[6] The short period of time between the crucifixion of Jesus and the conversion of Paul — probably about one year[7] — indicates the rapid spread of the Jesus movement to that city. Further, there is significant evidence from the gospel tradition that Jesus and his followers visited the cities of the Decapolis (Mark 5:70, 7:31; Matt. 4:25), including Gerasa (Mark 5:2), and Tyre and Sidon (7:24), as well as contact with the Syrophoenician woman (7:26). Thus the rapid spread of the gospel to Jews and Gentiles in predominantly hellenistic cities such as Damascus is clearly indicated in the oldest Jesus tradition. Paul's own testimony (Gal. 1:13–17) reports his having gone to Damascus with the intention of destroying the movement. Clearly it was not only present there, but was sufficiently effective and visible as to evoke concern and hostile reaction on the part of those like Paul the Pharisee, who wanted to preserve

the ritual and legal purity of the people of God based on the Law of Moses.

3. How does the Acts account match with the references to Damascus and to Paul's conversion that appear in his letters? Initially, in Paul's own account of his conversion (Gal. 1:15–17) there is no mention of Damascus, except the fact that after his stay in "Arabia"[8] he "returned again" there. The length of his stay in Arabia is not indicated, but he remained in Damascus for "three years" before going up to Jerusalem to confer with "Cephas" and "James, the Lord's brother." In 2 Cor. 11:32–33 Paul reports briefly on his escape from the effort of the "ethnarch" under King Aretas to seize him by being lowered through a window in the city wall.[9] Almost certainly Damascus did not at this time serve as the capital of the Nabatean kingdom (as it had until the city and region were conquered by Pompey for the Romans in 65 B.C.E.), but it is possible that an agent of Aretas — an "ethnarch" — was located there to look after resident Nabateans in what was now either under Nabatean control or an independent city-state on the model of or related to the Decapolis. One possible explanation for the ethnarch's determination to arrest Paul is that his preaching and teaching activity during the period of his stay in "Arabia" had led to severe conflict among the Nabateans, and the effort was now being made to arrest this troublemaker and put him out of operation. Paul was lowered over the wall in a rope-plaited basket and escaped, as had Joshua from Jericho with the help of Rahab,[10] and as David did with the help of his wife Michal (1 Sam. 19:11–12). This incident in the life of Paul seems to have occurred some time after his conversion, however, if it took place following his return from his stay in "Arabia" (Gal. 1:17). All that he reports about his conversion experience in the autobiographical sketch in Gal. 1:13–17 is that the God who had set him apart since he was in his mother's womb had called him through his grace and was pleased "to reveal his Son in me,"[11] which for him was a divine commissioning, not merely a subjective experience. Missing from the succinct reference to this encounter in Galatians 1 are any of the details offered in the vivid Acts narrative (9:1–19), which is repeated with some variants in 22:4–16 and 26:9–18.

9:3–9

In the Acts account, even before Saul has had any direct confrontation with the members of the new community in Damascus, he is stopped in his journey to that city by a heavenly "light" and voice. This recalls the divine encounters experienced by leaders in the formation, development, and judgment of God's historic people Israel: Jacob, with the promise of growth of the people in Egypt (Gen. 46:23–34); Moses, with the promise of the covenant (Exod. 3:2–6); Samuel, with the promise of establishment of the monarchy (1 Sam. 3:2–10); and the warning to Isaiah of judgment on the disobedient people (Isa. 6:1–13). In the Acts narrative, the divine hand is evident further in the judgment that falls on Saul and in the agent through whom his ailment is cured. Ironically, Saul's blindness is a consequence of the "light from heaven," which leads initially to his falling prostrate before the divine presence. Then comes the voice and message of the unidentified speaker that launch the process by which Saul will be transformed. In contrast to the indirect report from Paul in Gal. 1:12–16 ("[God] was pleased to reveal his son to me [or in me]"), Acts 9:4–5 reports a direct address to him by the risen Christ accusing him of persecuting "Jesus," even though Jesus is officially dead, executed by the Roman authorities. The link is only implicit between Paul's efforts to exterminate the Jesus movement and this message that he is continuing to "persecute" Jesus. Neither his companions nor Paul can comprehend the message and its import, but the former collaborate with the instruction by leading him into "Damascus," where his blindness continues, and he abstains from eating or drinking, or is unable to do so.

The details of this conversion experience of Saul are different from the very brief reference to it in Paul's letters. In Gal. 1:15–17 we read simply that God "was pleased to reveal his Son to me." The phrase *en emoi*, as noted above, could refer to a purely inward experience: "in me." This revelation also seems to differ considerably from the later heavenly transport and vision of Paul reported by him in 2 Cor. 12:2–4. This Acts account is not incompatible with Paul's, however, even though it offers unique details of the nature of his encounter with the risen Christ, when he is told that his efforts to destroy the new movement have resulted in the persecution, not merely of the leaders of the new

community, but specifically of Jesus (9:4-5). No instruction by
or about Jesus is offered here to Paul, but he is told that those in
the Damascus community will tell him what "it is necessary" for
him to do in carrying out the divine purpose for and through
him. But initially, the blindness he experiences is symbolic of
his lack of understanding concerning the task to which God is
calling him. Details of this conversion are also offered in the
subsequent accounts given by Paul in Acts 22:6-16 and 26:12-23
(see below).

9:10-19a

Among those targeted for destruction by Paul in Damascus had
been "Ananias," whom God moves to seek out and commission
Saul. The name Ananias derives from the Hebrew, Hananiah,
which means "Yahweh is merciful." He is described in a later
report of Paul's conversion (Acts 22:6-16) as "a devout man by
the standard of the Law," and hence was clearly Jewish in origin and commitment. But now he is designated as a "disciple,"
and hence as one of the Jesus-follower group that Saul was going
to Damascus to destroy (9:1). This man is not pictured as one
of Jesus' original disciples, however, since it is only by hearsay
that he knows of Paul's having persecuted God's "saints who are
in Jerusalem." The term *hagioi* with reference to the church is
frequent in Paul, and to a lesser degree in the Deutero-Pauline
letters,[12] but "disciples" is never used in that literature. Curiously, it is only here (Acts 9:13) and in references to the new
community in other cities in Palestine — Lydda (9:32) and Joppa
(9:41), as well as Paul's reference to his persecution of the Jerusalem community (Acts 26:10) — that "saints" appears in Acts as
a designation for members of the new community.

Excursus on Disciples in Acts

In the Gospel of Luke, references to the "disciples" are frequent.
Luke reproduces those in his Markan[13] and Q (6:40) sources, but
he often adds the term as well.[14] In the distinctively Lukan material within the Gospel of Luke, the term also appears frequently:
healing the widow's son at Nain (7:11); the instruction to the
disciples to seat the crowd at the feeding of the five thousand
(9:14); Jesus' response to the proposal to call down fire on the
Samaritan villages (9:54); the blessedness of the disciples (10:23);

the request to be taught how to pray (11:1); the advice to be free of anxiety (12:22); the need to hate one's family in order to become a disciple (14:26); the parable of the Unjust Steward (16:1); the instruction about the day of the Son of Man (17:22). And in two texts Luke notes that there was a large number of Jesus' disciples: 6:17, 19:37, where it is specified, "the entire multitude of the disciples." Obviously, this is not used by Luke as a term for the "twelve."

What is evident in this material is that for Luke, *mathetes* is a term with dual significance: it refers to the inner circle of Jesus' followers, but in Acts it is used for the great crowds that were drawn to Jesus and his message. In Luke 6:13, however, where Luke is drawing on Mark, he not only adds the term "disciples" with reference to the twelve, as Matthew does (10:1), but he further specifies that Jesus "named" them "apostles." This distinction is even more clearly evident throughout Acts, where *mathetes* is used as a general term for those who have joined the new community. In 6:1 is noted the increasing number of the "disciples," who are then referred to as the entire body of believers in Jerusalem — *to plethos ton matheton* — in distinction from the "twelve," whose symbolic number was carefully preserved according to 1:12–26, where the choice of Judas's successor is depicted.

Saul/Paul in 9:1–2 is seen as seeking to destroy "the disciples of the Lord," and in 9:26, in spite of their incredulity about him, following his conversion he "tried to join the disciples," rather than the apostles, to whom he was presented by Barnabas (9:27). Clearly, "disciples" is a standard term in Acts for the community of followers of Christ: in Joppa (9:38), Antioch (11:26), Antioch-in-Pisidia (13:52), Lystra (14:20 and 16:1), Derbe (14:22), Ephesus (19:1, 8–9), and Tyre (21:4). Further, in the apostolic pronouncement about the issue of obligation of non-Jews in the community to observe the Law of Moses, Peter makes a sharp distinction between "us" (apostles) and "the disciples" (15:10). A term unique in the New Testament but akin to *mathetes* — *mathetria* — is used in 9:36 for a woman in Joppa who is among the members, that is, disciples of the Lord. The importance of women in Acts is further indicated by the report that in Philippi the first conversion was that of an affluent businesswoman, "Lydia," who was baptized along with her entire household, and whose home became the residence for Paul and his companion(s) (16:11–15). We shall note below (9:31) the expansion in Acts of the use of *ekklesia* from its original reference to the whole community of believers in Jerusalem (5:11; 8:1, 3) to mean the church more broadly. But clearly, "disciples" is one of the favorite designations in Acts for the new people of God, and not merely a title for the original core of the followers of Jesus.

•

The Lord's instructions to Ananias in the "vision" are explicit as to the street, house, and the identity of the one who, in spite of his own initial anxieties and reluctance, he is to seek out: Saul/ Paul. Although in hellenistic times Damascus was eclipsed by Antioch-on-the-Orontes as the major city in Syria, it became the dominant city in Syria when it was under Seleucid, then Ptolemaic control, and after the death of Cleopatra in 30 B.C.E. it came directly under Roman rule. The city was built in geometric style in the Greco-Roman period, with a grid of streets at right angles, forming regular plots 300 by 150 feet. The main east-west street, about 50 feet wide, is probably what is referred to as the "Street Called Straight," where "Saul of Tarsus" was to be found in the "house of Judas." Ananias's response to the Lord Jesus' instruction is to recall the record of Paul's attempted destruction of the new community in Jerusalem, and the authority this man now has from the Jerusalem authorities to repeat such actions in Damascus. But the divine response is to inform Ananias that God has a unique role for Paul to fulfill: he is to be God's "instrument" to carry the gospel to "Gentiles," to earthly rulers ("kings"), and to the people of Israel. But further, this one who appears to Ananias as a threat to the community is himself destined to suffer greatly for the "name" of Jesus. After entering the house where Paul is, he places his "hands" on the sightless Paul, whose vision is restored, and informs him that he will be filled with the "Holy Spirit." As in the time of Moses God effects deliverance through the "hand" of the angels (7:35) and of certain of his people (7:25), so now Ananias's hand is likewise the divine tool for the bestowal of the Holy Spirit as was the hand of Peter for the gift of the Spirit (8:17), as well as for healing (3:7, 9:40–41). The outward sign of Paul's acceptance into the community and of his acceptance of his new identity takes place in the rite of baptism.

9:19b–22: Paul Preaches in Damascus

> He was for some days with the disciples in Damascus, and im-
> mediately he began preaching Jesus in the synagogues: "This
> man is the Son of God." All who heard were astounded, and
> said, "Isn't this the one who made havoc in Jerusalem of those
> who were calling on this name? And see, he has come to this
> place in order to take before the high priests those he has
> bound." But Saul instead was increasing in strength, and con-
> founded the Jews who were residing in Damascus, confirming
> that this man was the Messiah.

Saul's association with the "disciples" in Damascus is concurrent
with his preaching activity in the Jewish gatherings in Damascus. His message that Jesus is "the Son of God" amazes the
Jewish community, who had heard of Saul's persecution of the
new community in Jerusalem and his authorization from the
"high priests"[15] there to seize those in Damascus rallying around
the "name" of Jesus. But his effectiveness is seen as continuing to
build, as evidenced by his ability to "confirm" to the Jews in this
city that Jesus is indeed "the Messiah" expected in their tradition. The author of Acts is continuing to build his case that Paul
and the gentile mission to which he is soon to turn with such
astounding effectiveness is not in conflict with the messianic
hopes of Israelite tradition, but is instead its divinely intended
consummation. This is consonant with the theme in Paul's Letter to the Romans that the gospel is to be proclaimed first to the
Jews, and then to the Gentiles (Rom. 1:16), since God shows no
ethnic partiality (Rom. 2:11).

9:23–30: Saul Escapes to Jerusalem

> When a considerable number of days had passed, the Jews
> plotted to destroy him. But their plot became known to Saul.
> They were keeping watch at the gates day and night so that
> they might destroy him. But his disciples let him down from
> the wall at night, lowering him in a basket. When he arrived
> in Jerusalem, he tried to join the disciples, but all were afraid
> of him, since they did not believe that he was a disciple. But
> Barnabas took hold of him and led him to the apostles, and

> recounted to them how he [Paul] had seen the Lord on the
> road and that he [Jesus] spoke to him, and how in Damas-
> cus he had spoken fearlessly in the name of Jesus. So he
> [Paul] was with them in Jerusalem, going in and out, speaking
> fearlessly with the Hellenists, who were attempting to destroy
> him. When the brethren realized this, they took him down to
> Caesarea, and sent him off to Tarsus.

The ironic dimension in Acts continues here when Saul, who had
come to Damascus to destroy the Jesus movement there, is now
the target of the Jewish leaders determined to "destroy" him.
Their tactic is to lie in wait for him at the city "gates" in order
to seize him as he enters or leaves. As noted above, the clever
scheme that enables him to avoid seizure by those intent on
killing him — over the city wall — recalls the escapes of Joshua
and David. But whereas in Paul's own account of the incident
(2 Cor. 11:32–33) his escape was from the Nabatean ethnarch,
here in Acts it is the Jewish leaders who plot against him.[16] There
could have been a coalition among Paul's opponents, or — far less
likely — there could have been two such escapes. But the author
of Acts wants to put the responsibility for the hostile reaction to
Paul on the leaders of the Jewish community there, as he does
on similar leaders of Jewish groups in other cities, and especially
in Jerusalem (Acts 21, 23).

Saul's arrival in Jerusalem is met with profound suspicion
and fear on the part of the "disciples" there, who refuse to
give credence to his claim to have joined their movement. It
is only through the intervention of "Barnabas," who reports to
the apostles Saul's encounter with the Lord near Damascus and
his effective preaching "in the name of Jesus," that he finds
acceptance in the Jerusalem community of the disciples. Free
association with them follows, as does his vigorous preaching activity. Curiously, the chief opposition to Saul and his preaching
comes not from those identified with the semitic traditions of
Judaism, but from the "Hellenists." In 6:1 they are mentioned as
a distinct segment of the membership of the new community in
Jerusalem, and their names as given in 6:5 are all Greek, including one who is designated a "proselyte from Antioch." The term
as used in relation to the Jewish community as a whole has been
variously understood as meaning simply that "Hellenists" were
Greek-speaking Jews or that they were proselytes who had cho-

sen to become part of the Jewish community.[17] The latter seems more likely, and is consonant with the notion that those who had chosen to become members of God's people Israel would be especially sensitive about efforts like that of Paul to open participation in the new covenant community without any of the ritual requirements which the "Hellenists" had chosen to undergo when they became part of the people Israel. On the basis of Paul's origins in a major hellenistic center, Tarsus, and his skill in Greek and hellenistic literary and conceptual modes,[18] he is prepared to debate with the Hellenists. But their response is to seek to "destroy" him, and so the members of the new community — here designated as the "brethren" — conduct him safely to the port city of "Caesarea" Maritima,[19] from which he sails off toward his home town of "Tarsus." Later, following his arrest in the temple (21:27-36), Paul describes how, following his conversion, he had left Jerusalem after his first visit there on the grounds of a vision and a voice that urged him to leave Jerusalem hastily and assured him that he was being sent "far away to the Gentiles" (22:17-21).

Excursus on Brethren

Another frequently used term in Acts for the new community is *adelphoi*, "brethren." In several passages in Acts, the term appears with reference to Israel or the Jewish community in apostolic times: 3:22; 7:23-26, 37; 22:5; 28:21. But throughout the book it is primarily a designation for groups of followers of Jesus, first in Jerusalem (1:15, 9:30, 11:1, 12:17, 15:22-23, 21:17), and then for the local groups in various cities: Joppa (9:30); Antioch (11:29; 15:1, 32, 36); Iconium (14:2 and 16:2); Lystra (16:2); Philippi (16:40); Thessalonica (17:6, 10, 14); Corinth (18:18); Ephesus (18:27); Ptolemais (21:7); and finally in Puteoli and Rome (28:14-15). Women figure importantly in the communities of faith in Acts, especially Lydia (16:11-15) and Priscilla (18:2, 18, 26), so the membership was not exclusively male. But Acts uses only the masculine term *adelphos*, and not the feminine equivalent *adelphe*, which is found in the letters of Paul (Rom. 16:1; Philemon 2; 1 Cor. 7:15, 9:5). But in spite of the masculine preferential, the familial and organic relationships within the community are implicit in the use of "brethren" as a designation of the new people of God.

•

Paul's destination, "Tarsus," is mentioned here for the first time, but it is only in later autobiographical sketches in Acts that the reader learns what his associations with that city were (11:35, 22:3).

9:31: Summary of the State of the Church

The church throughout the whole of Judea and Galilee and Samaria experienced peace. Being built up and walking in the fear of the Lord and with the encouragement of the Holy Spirit, [the church] increased in numbers.

Most of the action described up to this point in Acts has taken place in Judea. But important as Galilee is in the gospel tradition, including Luke, it has not been previously mentioned in Acts, although there are specific indications of the Galilean connection of Peter and the other apostles (Acts 1:11, 2:7). The impact of the gospel on Samaria has been sketched in 8:1–14. The way of life in which the new community is to "walk" builds on both the legal and wisdom traditions of Israel. In the Old Testament "fear" involves loving and serving God in obedience to "all his ways" (Deut. 10:12), and obeying all his commandments (Eccles. 12:13). It must be taught to children from earliest days (Prov. 1:7, 5:7; Ps. 34:11). Paul contrasts the life of fear lived by those who see themselves bound to the Law of Moses with the freedom for those who through Christ have become children of God (Rom. 8:15). Yet he also warns the Philippians that they must allow God to work out his way in their lives "with fear and trembling." The transforming power at work in their lives is that of the Holy Spirit, who is active within them to produce the will and the results of a life of obedience (Phil 2:12–13). Living in "the fear of the Lord," the community is said to have continued to "increase in numbers."

9:32–43: Healings by Peter

It happened that as Peter was traveling about among them all, he went down also to the saints who were living in Lydda. He

found there a man named Aeneas, who had been confined
to his bed for eight years, and was paralyzed. And Peter said
to him, "Aeneas, Jesus Christ is healing you. Get up and make
your own [bed]." And he got up immediately. All those who
resided in Lydda and Sharon who saw him — these were the
ones who turned to the Lord.

Peter is pictured here as a prototype for an itinerant episcopacy.
His role was presumably to encourage the local congregations
and to check on the appropriateness of their faith and practice.
His itinerary apparently included *all* the territory mentioned in
9:31 (Judea, Galilee, Samaria), but the highlight here is on "Lydda," at the intersection of a major north-south coastal road
with the main road down from Jerusalem to the port city of
Joppa. The community here is identified by the term "saints."[20]
The paralytic, long confined to his bed, and apparently a member of the new community, is informed by Peter that the one
who is healing him is "Jesus Christ." His ability to stand erect is
proof to all the inhabitants of Lydda and the fertile coastal plain
of "Sharon" (on which the city is built) who see him in his recovered state that this is the work of "the Lord." And this is the
one in whom they put their "trust." The fact that this one who is
healed is named "Aeneas" —the mythical hero of Troy and Rome,
as in Virgil's *Aeneid* —does not imply that he was not Jewish. In
the long lists of decrees reproduced by Josephus to demonstrate
the positive relations between the Romans and the Jews in the
second century B.C.E., an envoy dispatched to Rome by the high
priest Hyrcanus was "Aeneas, son of Antipater." Indeed most of
the names in this list of Jewish representatives to the Romans are
of Greek origin, indicating the extent and depth of penetration
of Jewish life by hellenistic language and culture.

This event and the restoration to life of Dorcas which follows serve not only to widen the outreach of the gospel, but
also to demonstrate to the reader of Acts that God is indeed
at work through Peter. Thereby the author implies divine support for the conversion (through Peter) of a Roman military
officer, Cornelius, which is soon to be described in detail (10:1–
48) and which serves as a model for the subsequent outreach
of the gospel messengers described in the rest of Acts. The cultural mix within Judaism in this period is further demonstrated
by the pair of names of the woman disciples,[21] "Tabitha" and

"Dorcas," which are respectively the Aramaic and Greek words for "gazelle." The incident takes place at "Joppa," an important seaport on the Mediterranean from as early as the seventeenth century B.C.E., as shown by excavations, and as mentioned in the report of Solomon's bringing timber from Lebanon to build the temple (2 Chron. 2:16), and in the story of Jonah's fleeing from the Lord by ship to Tarshish (Jonah 1:3). Around 100 B.C.E. Joppa (or Jaffa) became once again the major port for Judea, though it was to be replaced in that role by Caesarea, one of Herod's major building projects (see the excursus on Caesarea, p. 130).

Tabitha had become a model of early Christian piety, with her abundance of "good works" and her "acts of charity" = *eleemosune*. The latter term is used elsewhere in the New Testament only in passages unique to Matthew (6:2, 3, 4) and Luke (11:41, 12:33), but is not part of the Q material as such.[22] Clearly the term is hellenistic, although the appeal to be generous to the poor is also a motif in the deuteronomic law (Deut. 24:12–13, 17, 19–21). After her death, her body is washed and laid out in "the upper space,"[23] which recalls what was done with the corpse of the son of the widow of Zarepath in the story of Elijah (1 Kings 17:19). Old Testament law gives no clear indication of practices for preparing bodies for burial, but the interment was to take place on the day of death (Deut. 21:23). Archaeological finds show that personal belongings were often buried along with the corpse, including weapons, rings, and lamps. When Peter arrives, the mourners have already gathered, since the burial would be expected to take place soon. The most obvious group of those lamenting her passing are "widows," which may here be a designation for a special group within the membership of the community.[24] The appeal to Peter to come "without delay" is consonant with the practice of same-day burial. After requiring all the mourners to leave, Peter prays and summons her by her Aramaic name, "Tabitha," to get up, which she does.[25] His extended hand is not to effect her restoration to life, as in the earlier healing story (3:7), but is the symbol of her reunion with the community, identified here as "saints and widows," to whom he presented her "alive." The news of this event spread throughout "Joppa," and impelled many to "trust in the Lord." Peter's host during his extended stay there is also named Simon, though his occupation is not a fisherman but a "tanner." In rabbinic tradition, tanners were considered to be unclean, since they dealt with bloody and ritually impure animals. Peter's break with purity laws is anticipated in the Acts narrative by his decision to reside for an extended period in such an environment.

10:1–48: Peter and Cornelius, the Roman Centurion: Gentiles Respond to the Good News

In Caesarea there was a man named Cornelius, who was a centurion of what was called the Italian Cohort. He was a devout man, who with all his household feared God, who made many charitable contributions to the people, and who prayed to God constantly. About the ninth hour of the day in a vision he saw vividly an angel of God which came in to him and said to him, "Cornelius!" He stared at him and became terrified and said, "What is it, sir?" And he said to him, "Your prayers and your charitable acts have gone up before God as a memorial offering. And now send some men to Joppa and summon a certain Simon, who is called Peter. He is a guest with a certain Simon, a tanner, who occupies a house by the sea." When the angel speaking to him left, he called two of his domestic servants and a devout soldier, who was among those who waited on him. And after explaining to them everything, he sent them off to Joppa.

On the next day, as they were on their way and approaching the city, Peter went up on the roof around the sixth hour to pray. He became hungry, and was wishing for something to eat. As they were preparing it, a trance came over him and he saw the heaven opened and an object like a huge sheet lowered to the earth by its four corners. In it were all kinds of four-footed animals, reptiles of the earth and birds of the air. And there came a voice to him, "Arise, Peter! Kill and eat!" But Peter said, "By no means, Lord, because at no time did I ever eat anything that is profane or unclean." Again, the second time the voice came to him, "What God has cleansed, you must not treat as profane." This happened three times, and immediately the object was taken up into heaven.

While Peter was greatly perplexed in his own mind as to what the vision which he had seen might mean — note this carefully! — the men sent by Cornelius, having located by inquiry the house of Simon, stood at the gate. They called out and asked if Simon, who was called Peter, was lodging there. While Peter was pondering concerning the vision, the Spirit said to him, "See! Three men are seeking you. Get up and go down, and go with them — with no deliberating! — because I have sent them." Peter went down to the men and said, "See! I am the one you are seeking. What is the reason for which you have come here?" They said, "Cornelius, a centurion, a righteous man and one who fears God, attested by the whole nation of the Jews, was directed by a holy angel to send for you to come to his house and to hear the message from you." So after he issued them an invitation, they stayed with him. The next day he got up and went off with them, and some of the brothers from Joppa went with him.

On the following day they entered Caesarea. Cornelius met him, fell down, and prostrated himself at his feet. Peter raised him up and said to him, "Get up! I also am human." And as he conversed with him, he went in and found many gathered together. He said to them, "You understand that it is not lawful for a Jewish person to associate with, or even to approach, someone of another ethnic group. But God has shown me that I cannot say that any human is common or unclean. For this reason I raised no objection when I was sent for. So then I want to learn what the reason is that you sent for me."

Cornelius said, "Four days ago, about this time, I was praying the three o'clock prayer in my house, and look! — there was a man in front of me in shining clothing, and he said, 'Your prayer has been listened to, and your acts of almsgiving have been recounted in the presence of God. So send to Joppa and invite Simon who is called Peter. He is staying as a guest in the house of Simon, a tanner near the sea.' So immediately I sent for you. And you reacted commendably, and have come. So now we are all here in the presence of God to hear all the things in which you have been instructed by the Lord."

And Peter opened his mouth and said, "In truth, I grasp that God is not one who shows partiality, but in every ethnic group the one who fears him and performs righteousness is acceptable to him. You know the message which he sent to the people of Israel, proclaiming the good news of peace through Jesus Christ — this one who is Lord of all — the word which went through the whole of Judea, beginning from Galilee, after the baptism which John proclaimed, how God anointed

Jesus of Nazareth with the Holy Spirit and power; how he went from place to place doing good works and healing all those who were overpowered by the devil, because God was with him. And we are witnesses of all the things that he did in the region of the Jews and Jerusalem. They did away with him, hanging him on a tree, but God raised him on the third day, and made it possible for him to become visible, not to all the people, but to us who had eaten and drunk with him after he arose from the dead. And he instructed us to preach to the people and to testify that he is the one appointed by God as judge of the living and the dead. To him all the prophets give testimony that all who trust in his name receive forgiveness of sins."

While Peter was still saying these words, the Holy Spirit fell on all those who were hearing his message. And those of the circumcision who were believers who had come with Peter were astounded, because also upon the Gentiles the gift of the Holy Spirit was poured out. For they were hearing them speaking in tongues and telling the greatness of God. Then Peter responded, "Is anyone ready to forbid water so that these may not be baptized who have received the Holy Spirit as we have?" And he gave orders for them to be baptized in the name of Jesus Christ. Then they asked him to stay for some days.

10:1-2

The proclamation of the good news in "Caesarea" had begun through Philip, who visited the southern coastal city of "Azotus" and then "Caesarea" (8:40). Now it is continued and the bringing of the good news to Gentiles is given divine approval there through Peter, to whom messengers were sent by the "centurion" named "Cornelius." His official position in the Roman military was that of "centurion," whose unit was the "Italian cohort," which in an undated inscription is reported to have been stationed in the province of Syria, which would include Palestine.[26]

Excursus on Centurion

In the Roman army the centurion was a lower-ranking officer in charge of 100 men, called a "centuria." A "legion" consisted of 4,000 to 6,000 men, who were grouped into ten cohorts, of which the six centuria and three maniples were subunits. The commanders of the legion were "legates," under whom were six tribunes or chiliarchs (commanding 1,000). There were 59 centuria to a legion, in addition to one legion which had 120. Those who served in these legions were of two types: legionary soldiers, who were Roman citizens, and auxiliary troops. Some soldiers were *alae* (cavalry), and the rest were *cohortes*, or *speirai* (infantry). The names of the army units often indicated the part of the empire from which they had been recruited: for example, Ascalonitani (Ascalon); Dacica (Dacia); Syriaca (Syria). They had to be free-born, and noncitizens would receive citizenship at retirement from service. Since Syria was regarded by the emperors from Augustus on as the essential powerbase of the region, several legions were stationed there, and the support of client-kings or ethnarchs was sought. Additional troops were sent into Syria in times of crisis, as is abundantly documented in literature and inscriptions from this period. The military base for the Romans in Judea was Caesarea, not Jerusalem. The soldiers were recruited from Syria and Sebaste (Samaria), as well as from the area around Caesarea itself. It is likely that Cornelius was retired — at which time he would have become a Roman citizen — and was living at the center of Roman power for the area: Caesarea.

•

This city of "Caesarea" was designated as "Maritima" to differentiate it from Caesarea Philippi, which was located in Upper Galilee at the sources of the Jordan (Mark 8:27) and was the site of a shrine to the Greco-Roman god Pan. The governors and military leaders were based primarily in Caesarea Maritima, and therefore it was appropriate that there the first action of the Jewish revolutionaries against Roman rule took place in 66 C.E. What is here described in Acts is the first direct outreach of the new community to members of the gentile social and political culture that dominated the world: the conversion of a Roman military officer.

Excursus on Caesarea

After Herod was confirmed as king of Judea by the emperor Augustus in 37 B.C.E., he was given authority over the area along the Mediterranean coast just south of the province of Syria and well north of Joppa. He decided to build a port city on the Mediterranean coast to serve three major objectives: (1) to provide the world with tangible, dramatic evidence that he was a leader in the Roman tradition, (2) to ingratiate himself with the sizable segment of population in the region who were not oriented toward Jewish culture and religion, and (3) to provide a major, efficient port for commerce with the wider Mediterranean world, and especially for shipping elsewhere the rich produce of the nearby coastal plain of Sharon. Building on the site of a port known as Strato's Tower, which was begun in the fourth century B.C.E. and significantly developed in the second century B.C.E., Herod expanded and greatly improved the port itself, including an outer and an inner harbor. The city that he built had a theater, a hippodrome, and temples to Roman gods, as well as well-developed water and sewer systems and a monumental tower marking the entrance to the harbor. The most notable of these sacred buildings was a great temple of Augustus and Roma, which overlooked the harbor. Following the death of Herod in 4 B.C.E. and the brief reign of his son, Archelaus (4 B.C.E.–6 C.E.), the region was designated a Roman province, the capital of which was at Caesarea. This was thus the official seat of the Roman governor, and significantly is the first place reported in Acts where the new community of followers of Jesus was expanded to include someone whose identity and status were within the culture and society of the Roman Empire: Cornelius.

Details of the city have been known from descriptions in Josephus,[27] but excavations in the last third of the present century, including underwater exploration of the harbor, confirmed the grand picture offered by Josephus of Herod's monument to the Caesar. Surveys of the results of earlier excavations at this site are offered by Lee J. Levine and E. Netzer, and by R. L. Hohlfelder. Recently published, however, is a huge volume on the subject, *Caesarea Maritima: Retrospective after Two Millennia*, edited by Avner Raban and Kenneth G. Holum.[28] Part 1 presents analyses of "Ancient Harbors: Geomorphological Challenge and Technological Response." In part 2 are comparisons of Caesarea with other ancient harbors, including the challenges to construction met and overcome by the builders of Herod's harbor there, and the evidence from pottery of the commercial and cultural orientation of the city toward the Aegean and the Western Ro-

man world. Part 3 gives details of "Caesarea's City Plan and
Urban Architecture," including the amphitheater, the temple of
Roma and Augustus built by Herod, and the warehouses and
granaries. It also traces the evolution of the city from the first
to the sixth century C.E.: from a civilian city adjacent to the
royal artificial harbor, to the political and economic center of
Judea as seat of the Roman procurators, and its subsequent en-
largement. Part 4 describes the Promontory Palace, which was
adjacent to the amphitheater, thereby combining political power
and public spectacle as the palace shifted in function from royal
residence to praetorium for the resident Roman authority. In
part 5 are described the sculptures found there, which include
merely decorative features, as well as representations of deities
and evidence of the Caesar cult. Part 7 shows how inscriptions
found there provide clues to ancient relationships, negotiations,
and experience in the life of the city, including the leadership
of the synagogues, the inscriptions which date from the fourth
to the sixth century C.E. Other inscriptions illumine the later
centuries of Arab control. The Christian and talmudic literature documents the importance of the city in the second and
subsequent centuries in part 8, "The Jewish and Christian Communities: Society and Thought." Part 9 traces the influence of
Origen and Eusebius during the period of Christian dominance,
while part 10 shows the importance of this city for the whole region of the province of Palestina in the Byzantine period. Part 11
indicates the still-debated issues in the archaeology and history
of Caesarea, based on architectural and numismatic evidence.
Part 12 sketches the importance of excavations at this site carried out by amateurs and professionals, and highlights the great
importance of underwater exploration carried out in the harbor.
The result of this research and these publications is a unique
contribution to historical knowledge of an important ancient site
on the basis of archaeological evidence.

•

The description of Cornelius is revealing concerning the social
dynamic and cultural diversity of Judaism in first-century Palestine. It is possible that he is depicted here as a Jew, although
as such he would have had problems obeying the Law of Moses
while in the military.[29] The terms used in Acts to describe his religious outlook and activities suggest rather that he is one drawn

to the God of the Jews, one whose manner of life displays forms of Jewish religiosity: his personal piety (*eusebes*), his "fearing God," and his "charitable contributions," which seem to have been made to the wider society (*to lao*). Further, this commitment is not merely personal but extends to "all his household." The term "proselyte" is not used here with reference to him, but there is no mistaking him to be in the full sense a God-fearer, the term which is explicitly applied to him (*phoboumenos ton theon;* 10:2).

Excursus on Proselytes and God-Fearers

"Proselyte" is a distinctively Jewish term, which is used in the LXX to translate *ger:* a resident alien (Exod. 20:10, 22:21, 23:9). That is, they are non-Israelites who are permanent residents in the land, either because their ancestors remain from before the Israelite conquest of the land, or because war (2 Sam. 4:3) or famine (Ruth 1:1) or some catastrophe forced them to leave their own native territory. They are to be treated with kindness, and may join in the worship of Yahweh (Num. 15:14–16), and are to be instructed in the Law of Moses (Deut. 31:2). The prophets were concerned that they be treated with justice by the people of Israel (Jer. 22:3; Ezek. 22:7, 29) and declared that these people would have a share in the land when it was to be renewed by God (Ezek. 47:21–23). Philo affirmed that proselytes had equal status with birthright Jews (*Special Laws* 1.51–53; *Virtues* 102–4). Although Josephus does not use the term *proselytos*, he does mention non-Jews who decide to live "in accord with our laws" (*Ag. Ap.* 2.123), and describes in great detail how Helena, queen of Adiabene (in northern Mesopotamia), and her son Izates "changed the manner of their life into the practices of the Jews." Izates's wives were instructed how to worship God according to Jewish custom, and he adopted the Law for himself, including circumcision. Helena visited Jerusalem in time of famine during the reign of Claudius (41–54 C.E.) and made generous provision of money and food for the Jews there (*Ant.* 20:17–53). In *Against Apion* (2.179–80, 281–83) Josephus notes that the Jewish mode of worship had spread to every city and nation, and that the generosity of those who worship God (*sebomenon ton theon*) is now evident from even Asia and Europe (*Ant.* 14.110).

In Acts proselytes are mentioned as those who, together with

Jews, had gathered in Jerusalem on the Day of Pentecost from all parts of the known world (2:9–11). Nicolaus, a proselyte from Antioch, was among those chosen to assist the apostles (*diakonein;* 6:3–5). In 13:43 proselytes described as "devout" (*sebomenon*) join "many of the Jews" in following Paul and Barnabas. In Luke-Acts a kindred term used with reference to devout Jews is *eulabeis:* Simeon, who blessed Jesus in the temple (Luke 2:25); those gathered in Jerusalem at Pentecost from all over the world (2:5); and those who buried Stephen (8:2).

Considerable light has been shed on the subject of Gentiles affiliated with the Jewish community by the recent discovery of an inscription at Aphrodisias in the Caria district of Asia Minor honoring the donors to the local synagogue. A late second- or very early third-century date for the tablet recording the names is indicated by the fact that the list of affiliates of the local Jewish community includes the special designation of some as citizens, which after 212 C.E. became the status of nearly all the inhabitants of the Roman Empire.[30] Sixty-nine are listed as Jews, but fifty-two are designated as *theoseboi.* Nine were members of the city council (*boule*), and the occupation of many is indicated. It seems that the God-fearers participated in the prayer and study activities of the synagogue, as well as in the charitable work of the community.[31] It is possible that God-fearers were free of the obligation to obey not only the Jewish circumcision law, but also those affecting occupations and even sabbath observance, since a Roman military officer (such as Cornelius, the centurion) could not have set aside his army obligations in order to obey the sabbath. It is also possible that they were bound instead by the so-called Noahic commandments listed in rabbinic sources as binding on pagans who would live in a future Jewish state. One such list prohibits idolatry, incest, murder, profaning the name of God, robbery, and eating meat cut from living animals.[32] Other lists of requirements binding on non-Jews are offered in the Letter of Aristeas, 4 Maccabees, and the Testaments of the Twelve Patriarchs. It is possible that the earliest mention of God-fearers is in the LXX of 2 Chron. 5:6, where three groups affiliated with the people of God are differentiated: Israel, *hoi episynegmenoi* (the proselytes), and the *phoboumenoi* (the God-fearers). This pattern of diverse gentile modes of association with and participation in the life of the Jewish community is also evident in Sardis, where Gentiles of substance were attracted to and made substantial contributions to the Jewish community, whose impressive synagogue building has been excavated.[33] Although this evidence comes from sites in Asia Minor which date from a century or more later than Acts, it seems to confirm the basic pattern of Gentiles who were impressed by and — with some qualifications — participated in the worship life and social activities of Jewish communities in the Roman period.

Although at the time Acts was written there seems not to have been universally agreed-upon terminology to identify Gentiles of this persuasion, there are phrases that clearly indicate individuals who publicly identify in some way with the God of Israel and Jewish tradition. Cornelius is pictured as one who is "devout" and "fears God" (10:2). This description is matched by the messengers' depiction of him as "a righteous man and one who fears God" (*phoboumenos ton theon*) (10:22). In Peter's address he declares that "in every ethnic group the one who fears [God] and performs righteousness" finds acceptance with God (10:35). The same terminology appears in Paul's speech to the synagogue in Antioch-in-Pisidia (13:16), but farther on in that same address Paul is reported as joining two modes of identity of those who are recipients of the good news of salvation: "sons of the family of Abraham" and "those among you who fear God." Both groups are indicated by Paul as those to whom has been sent this message (13:26). Following Paul's speech another distinction is bridged: the term "those who fear God" (*sebomenon*) is applied to "proselytes." On the other hand, those incited against Paul and Barnabas include "the prominent devout [*sebomenas*] women" as well as "the leading men of the city" (13:50). Near Philippi, Paul's first convert in Europe is "Lydia," who is "one who worshiped God" (*sebomene*) (16:14), and in Thessalonica, those persuaded by Paul and Silas are identified as "a great number of devout [*sebomenon*] Greeks and not a few of the leading women" (17:4). In Corinth, among the "Jews and Greeks" converted by Paul is "Titius Justus," who is one "who worshiped God [*sebomenou*]" in a synagogue, and then invited the newly formed group to meet in his house next door (18:7). Clearly for the author of Acts these terms are not general references to piety among Gentiles but point instead to those drawn to the life and faith of the Jewish community, who have not, however, made the step of gaining complete identity on such ritual grounds as circumcision, which would place them in the category of "proselytes."

10:3–8

The initial message that prepares for what is to bring about a major step in the expansion of the new community comes through a vivid "vision" experienced by Cornelius, this Roman military figure who has been drawn in conviction and commitment to the Jewish perception of God and his people. Terror-stricken at the appearance of the "angel of God," Cornelius's response to being addressed by name is to ask what is happening. His designation of his visitor as *Kurie* is ambiguous and deferential, although it seems to be merely a form of polite address to an authoritative figure, rather than his using the Greek equivalent of "Yahweh," the God of Israel. Yet it is this God from whom the message comes, and to whom his own prayers and "memorial offerings" in the form of charitable acts have ascended. The instruction of the angelic messenger concerns two Simons: one whose nickname is Peter, and one who is a "tanner" serving as host to the former at his house in "Joppa," some thirty-five miles southward from Caesarea along the seacoast. As noted above, since tanners had to work with animal skins, they were involved with ritually impure and aesthetically revolting items, and seem to have been consigned by society in general, but especially by ritually observant Jews, to peripheral places of residence and business. This is indicated here by Simon's house "by the sea," which would likely have been an area of commercial activity, not an elegant residential section as might be assumed today. The messengers sent to Joppa include two "domestic servants" and one of Cornelius's military aides who shared his piety, and to them he describes what is apparently happening to him in the form of divine communication.

10:9–16

Meanwhile, the divine communication is going on in Joppa as well, where Peter is about to conclude his noontime prayers in order to have his midday meal. Praying on the "roof" was convenient and appropriate, since the nearly flat mud and thatch roofs constructed in this period were easily accessible and served multiple purposes — as storage space or guest quarters, for example. They also gave ready access to God, since prayers were perceived

to mount up to God like incense or smoke from sacrificial offerings (Ps. 141:2). In older Jewish tradition, prayers were to be
offered morning and evening (Pss. 5:3, 65:8, 88:13), but the pattern of prayers thrice daily is also evident (Ps. 55:17; Dan 6:10).
In the "trance" — or literally, ecstasy (*ekstasis*) — that came on
Peter, he saw some kind of a container resembling a "huge sheet"
being lowered to earth from heaven, containing all kinds of animal life, which recalls the charge to Noah about taking every
kind of animal into the ark (Gen. 6:19–20). The universal implication of this vision and the subsequent command about eating
such ritually unclean items is made explicit in Peter's objection
on the grounds of ritual purity to the order to "Kill and eat!"
What is at issue for the author of Acts is not which of these
innumerable creatures may be eaten in observance of the purity laws that differentiate clean (Lev. 11:1–23) and unclean (Lev.
11:24–44). What is at stake is the basic concept of ritual purity,
which is highlighted and commanded in Lev. 11:45–47. Peter's
reaction of refusal fits the latter injunction, but God's decree implies that all is now ritually clean, and nothing is to be treated as
"profane." So radical is this notion that its message in the form
of the vision is repeated three times, and the heavenly origin of
this insight is confirmed by the sheet and its contents returning
to "heaven." The lesson to be taught to the puzzled Peter will be
conveyed to him in two stages (10:17–33) and then by him to the
eager listeners in the house of Cornelius (10:34–43), and will be
confirmed finally in the same way that the worldwide mission
of the apostles was announced through him as fulfillment of the
prophetic promise (Acts 2:17–20 = Joel 3:1–5): by the outpouring
of the Holy Spirit (10:44–48; cf. 2:4, 14–21).

10:17-23a

The messengers from Cornelius arrive to invite Peter to return
with them, as "directed by a holy angel," before Peter has been
able to understand the import of the vision he has seen. The author of Acts directly urges the reader to discern the dynamics of
this interweaving of divine action and human agency by insert-
ing *idou*, which could be paraphrased, "Pay close attention!" The
"Spirit" continues to direct Peter by informing him of the arrival
of the messengers and by instructing him that he is to respond
by accompanying them on their return back to Cornelius. Their
persistence had found the house of Simon the tanner and then

"Simon, who was called Peter," his guest. These details show that the Spirit is at work in concrete ways, and operates with precision.

In response to Peter's inquiry as to who has sent these messengers and why, he learns about the identity and qualifications of this one to whom Peter should speak: (1) Cornelius is a Roman military officer; (2) he is "righteous and one who fears God"; (3) his integrity and morality are "attested by the whole Jewish nation." Hence Peter cannot dismiss Cornelius as an immoral pagan, unworthy of his attention or concern. (4) An "angel" has directed Cornelius to send for Peter — not for just any possible member of the new community — inviting him to come "to his house" and convey the message from God. This invitation raises implicitly the issue of ritual restrictions against Jews entering gentile households, which will be addressed explicitly after Peter arrives (10:28). But the breakdown of this ritual law with such potent social and ethnic implications is already indicated when Peter invites these non-Jews to stay as guests with him in the house of Simon the tanner, and they accept the invitation. The issue of participation in the new community across ethnic and ritual barriers is already being addressed before it is directly articulated by Peter.

10:23b-33

The crucial event in the house of Cornelius at which the universal access to the good news about Jesus is affirmed (10:34–43) is not to be a private exchange between Peter and Cornelius. Rather, both of them are accompanied during this encounter by colleagues, who can hear and testify to the event and its import: Peter by members of the new community in Joppa, and Cornelius by a large crowd, including "relatives and close friends," who have gathered at his invitation. Instead of treating in a demeaning or condescending way this Gentile who has invited him, Peter rejects his deferential act of prostration, affirming unconditionally their shared humanity. Confronted by the crowd of inquirers, however, Peter does acknowledge that his very presence in a ritually impure household among a gathering of Gentiles is in violation of Jewish purity laws. Although the rabbinic perceptions of these ritual requirements can be found only in material from Mishnah and Talmud, which must be dated in its preserved form to the second through the sixth century C.E., first-century C.E. or earlier documentation of these rigid standards within at least one segment of Judaism is provided by the most basic of all the Qumran materials, the Rule of the Community:

> No man of the men of the Community of the Covenant, who strays from any one of the ordinances deliberately may touch the pure food of the men of holiness nor know any of their counsel.... Indeed every man of them who transgresses a word of the Torah of Moses deliberately or through negligence, shall be banished from the Council of the Community and never come back again.[34]

This Jewish community defines itself as "a house of holiness for Aaron" and "a community of the Holy Ones," and its members' property is "not to be merged with the property of men of deceit who have not cleansed their way by separating themselves from deceit and walking with the perfect of the Way." Issues of knowledge of God and righteous behavior are to be argued only with "the chosen of the Way" (1 QS 9.17–18). The fact that the issues raised in this foundation document from Qumran correspond precisely with those highlighted in Acts — relationships with those not obedient to the Torah, the sharing of property, the designation of the true community as "the Way" — make clear that the author of Acts is dealing with matters very much alive in Judaism in the mid-first century C.E. The insistence on avoidance of unclean food or of "profaning the holy covenant" (1 Macc. 1:62–63) was the fundamental principle invoked by Mattathias and his sons in launching the Maccabean revolt. Although the specific detail of association with non-Jews is not referred to in the Rule of the Community, the insistence on maintenance of contact only with those who follow the purity laws as rigorously interpreted at Qumran shows how crucial the issue posed by Peter was for many first-century Jews, and how radical was the response that he finally gave. The sole ground of Peter's basic shift on the ritual purity issue was the divine disclosure to him that he should not designate any human being (*anthropon*) as "common [*koinon*] or unclean." It is precisely this term, *koinos*, which is linked in 1 Macc. 1:47–49 with "unclean" (*akatharton*) and in 1:63 with profanation of the "holy covenant." The radical instruction that Peter says he has received from God is that he is to attach these terms for ritual and covenantal exclusion to no human being. Conversely, the prerequisites for acceptability with God are fearing God (*phoboumenos*) and performing "righteousness." Obviously, Cornelius meets both these requirements, so the prerequisites are established for declaring to him the good news. His fearing God is evident (1) in his conformity to the pattern of prayer at the ninth hour, in keeping with traditional Jewish piety, and has been confirmed (2) by the one from God that appeared to him (in 10:3, an angel, or messenger; here, described as a male human [*aner*]) with the assurance that his prayer has been "listened to," and that his "acts of almsgiving" —which qualify him as a "righteous man" (10:22)—have been recounted "in the presence of God." Cornelius is now ready to hear from Peter "all the things in which you have been instructed by the Lord."

10:34–43

Peter's address in the house of Cornelius begins with the enunciation of a basic principle that is a central motif throughout Luke and Acts: God shows no partiality to any single ethnic group. Instead, the invitation to share in the life of his people extends across all humanly defined social lines, both those derived from tradition and those imposed by cultural developments, as in the history of Israel and the Jewish people. The divine purpose is to achieve reconciliation, not only between God and humanity, but among diverse and often hostile sociocultural distinctions imposed by humans. The word of reconciliation of humans with God — "peace through Jesus Christ" — has been addressed initially to God's people, "Israel," through Jesus the Messiah (*Christos*), whose office and role in the purpose of God are here defined by Peter. The clearest analogy to the affirmation that Jesus is "Lord of all" is in the pseudepigraphic work, the Testament of Moses (4:2), where God's role includes ruling the world, designating the chosen people, and entering into covenant with them.[35] Jesus' unique relation to God is here seen as functional rather than ontological — in terms of divine essence — as in later credal formulations. The word was proclaimed throughout Judea, but it began in Galilee subsequent to Jesus' baptism by John, which figures so prominently in the Gospel of Luke, where the role of John is linked explicitly and in detail with the promise of God concerning the renewal of his people.[36] In what follows Peter succinctly summarizes the role of Jesus as it is presented in the Gospel of Luke.

Jesus' designation as *Christos* rests on the fact that God anointed (*echrisen*) him "with the Holy Spirit and with power." That anointing is detailed in the gospel tradition only in Luke 4:16–30, where the agenda of Jesus — "to preach good news to the poor, to proclaim release to the captives, recovery of sight to the blind, liberty for the oppressed" — is seen to be the consequence of the coming of the Spirit of the Lord upon him and empowering him (*echrisen me*), in fulfillment of the prophetic promise in Isa. 61:1-2, 6. Once again it is clear that the christology of Luke-Acts is set forth in functional rather than titular or conceptual terms. Those functions include "doing good works," "healing all those who were overpowered by the devil" — activities that are detailed throughout the Gospel of Luke. Further, in Luke alone Jesus is quoted as saying that precedent was set by the ancient prophets Elijah and Elisha to extend these healing benefits to those outside the traditional boundaries of Israel (Luke 4:25–27) — whence the significance of healing to "all who were overpowered." The secret of these extraordinary powers of human liberation and renewal was that "God was with him."[37] The most important function of the apostles is that they saw at first hand — as "witnesses" — the great works that God was accomplishing through Jesus and heard his message about the renewal of God's people. His activities took place throughout the "region" populated by Jews, and culminated in his final work in the holy city of "Jerusalem" itself. Their testimony rests on their direct observation of him and his work for God, rather than merely on abstract religious concepts. The identity of those who "did away with" Jesus is not specified here, although in 2:22-23 the charge of having crucified Jesus is addressed to the "men of Israel." The portrayal of his execution as "hanging him on a tree" (10:39) matches the reference by Paul to Jesus having become a curse for his people by undergoing the horror of being "hanged on a tree" (Gal. 3:13),[38] which refers to hanging (probably by a noose) rather than crucifixion, which was a mode of execution developed by the Persians and later practiced by Greeks and Romans. Josephus considered it to be "the most pitiable of deaths," and describes how those Jews about to be crucified pleaded to be put to death by another mode (*Wars* 7.203). The similarity between the suspended body of a criminal

hanged on a tree and one nailed to a cross enabled the earliest Christians to link the death of Jesus to a scriptural text. In
the same way, the tradition that "God raised" Jesus from the
dead "on the third day" was perceived to be "according to the
scriptures" (1 Cor. 15:4) by reference to the prophetic promise
of God's renewal of his people "on the third day" (Hos. 6:2).
This encounter with the risen Christ was not a private matter
or the experience of isolated individuals, but neither was it a
wholly public event. Rather, it took place for a special group
with a distinct responsibility: God handpicked them in advance
as "witnesses," because they had had direct experience of Jesus
raised from the dead in a concrete, tangible mode, as they
shared bread and wine with him subsequent to his death and
resurrection. An important feature here is the claim that the
encounter with the risen Lord was not a misty, mystical vision
but that it took place in the context of physical, social human
existence.

The message that these witnesses of the resurrection of Jesus
are to proclaim is here presented with two major emphases: Jesus
as the eschatological judge of all humanity;[39] and the promise of
forgiveness of sins for those who trust in his authority and accept identity in his "name." This message is not an innovation;
rather, it is to be understood as the fulfillment of what has been
proclaimed by the prophets, as in Isa. 53:10–12. The credibility of these claims concerning Jesus is said to be confirmed by
a configuration of witnesses: the apostles' observation of Jesus'
healings and exorcisms; God's having raised him from the dead;
the experience of the risen Christ by the apostles, whom God has
chosen to bear testimony to all humanity. Jesus' role as "judge
of the living and the dead" corresponds to that of the eschatological judge in Jewish apocalyptic writings, but also in later
Stoic writers such as Cicero and Seneca, who expected a day
of judgment in which all humans, living and dead, would be
held morally accountable for their moral behavior and rewarded
or punished accordingly.[40] What is distinctive in the Christian
claim set forth here and in other New Testament writings, in
contrast to the Stoic discussion of the matter, is that Jesus will be
the divine instrument of universal judgment, and that "forgiveness" is granted now, rather than being a hoped-for possibility
in the day of judgment.

10:44 –48

The proof that admission of non-Israelites to the new community is intended by God is given through the event that results from Peter's sermon to his gentile hearers: "the Holy Spirit fell on them all." This accords with the prophecy of Joel 3:1–5 quoted in Peter's Pentecost address (2:17). The birthright ("circumcised") Jews in the community were "astounded," and the proof that the Spirit has in fact come upon these hearers is twofold: the charismatic gift of "speaking in tongues" and the ecstatic praise of God which they utter. The initial coming of the Spirit at Pentecost was evident in the ability of those in the crowd to hear the message in their own language (2:6), but now the phenomenon of charismatic speech attested elsewhere in the New Testament is indicated here.[41] According to Paul, this gift of ecstatic speech should be linked with the gift of interpretation of tongues in order for the import of the work of the Spirit to reach the other members of the community. His advice to those with the gift of speaking in tongues was that a charismatic utterance should be followed by an interpretation: if there is no one to interpret, let each of them keep silence (1 Cor. 14:27–28). Here in Acts, however, the ecstatic manifestation in the form of their praise of God is seen as in itself sufficient to demonstrate that it is God's Spirit that is now at work among these gentile converts. The community's acceptance of them is then to be given public demonstration through their being baptized "in the name of Jesus Christ," as was the case with the three thousand baptized on the Day of Pentecost (2:38 –41). As noted above,[42] the use of the term *koluo* here (10:47) seems to derive from a formula used when candidates for membership in the new community were about to be baptized. It parallels the use of the word in the gospel tradition, where it occurs in connection with children coming to Jesus,[43] and may also be a technical term concerning admission to the new community. The presence and power of the Spirit on these Gentiles provides the confirmation of the proposed action, and they are baptized. The "several days" that Peter remained among them would have been an occasion for both fellowship and instruction.

11:1–18: Peter's Report to the Church in Jerusalem

The apostles and the brothers who were throughout Judea heard that the Gentiles had received the word of God. When Peter went up to Jerusalem, those of the circumcision took issue with him, saying, "Why did you go and associate with men who still have the foreskin, and join them in eating?" Peter began explaining to them systematically, saying, "I was in the city of Joppa praying, and in an ecstasy I saw a vision: an object like a huge sheet being let down from heaven by the four corners, and it came right to me. I was examining it carefully and saw quadrupeds of the earth and wild animals and reptiles and birds of the air. I listened and a voice was saying to me, 'Get up, Peter! Kill and eat!' But I said, 'By no means, Lord, because at no time did a common or an unclean thing enter my mouth.' And the voice responded to me a second time from heaven, 'The things that God has cleansed, you must not consider common!' This happened a third time, and everything was taken up again into heaven. And immediately at the house in which I was there appeared three men who had been sent from Caesarea to me, and the Spirit told me to go with them. And these six brothers also went with me, and we entered the house of the man. He reported to us how he had seen the angel standing in his house and saying, 'Send to Joppa and summon Simon, who is called Peter. He will speak to you the words by which you and your entire household may be saved.'

"As I was beginning to speak, the Holy Spirit fell upon them as it also [did] on us at the beginning. I remembered the word of the Lord, how he said, 'John baptized with water, but you shall be baptized by the Holy Spirit.' Since God gave to them the same gift as to us when we trusted in the Lord Jesus Christ, who was I to stand in God's way?" When they heard these things, they were silenced and glorified God, saying, "So then even to the Gentiles God has granted repentance [which leads] to life."

Up to this point in the Acts narrative, the apostles — with the exception of Peter — have remained in Jerusalem, although Philip (one of the seven; 6:5–6) had ventured forth with the gospel to Samaria (8:4–8) and south toward Gaza, where he encountered and converted the Ethiopian eunuch, and north toward the gentile center of power, Caesarea (8:26–40). The apostles, however, have remained geographically and ethnically based in Jerusalem. Stephen's denial that the Jerusalem temple or any physical structure was the special place of God's dwelling on earth (7:48–49) had led to his execution (7:54–58). The apostles alone had remained in Jerusalem following the outbreak of persecution of the new community (8:1). Accordingly, the report to the Jerusalem-based apostles that "Gentiles" had also "received the word of God" was problematical for their understanding of their mission and threatening in terms of the likely response from the official Jewish leadership to such a revolutionary program.

The issue was posed for Peter by that group within the new community which continued to insist that members should observe Torah, as symbolized by the law that required circumcision for those who seek participation in the covenant community — whether it was traditional Israel or the community of the new people which was taking shape in the name of Jesus. In response to his critics Peter explains why he visited and ate with the "uncircumcised," in violation of Jewish law and tradition. He recounts his thrice-repeated heavenly vision: the voice from heaven ordering him repeatedly not to classify as "common" or ritually unclean what "God has cleansed," and the return to heaven of the sheet filled with the diversity of creatures. Further evidence of the divine origin of these events is offered by the arrival of the visitors with their report of the vision and instruction received by Cornelius. The point is made emphatically: it is God who is the agent at work in this vision and hence in the epoch-making action that Peter has been ordered to carry out. That this development is not an aberrancy on the part of Peter is confirmed by the presence with him in Caesarea of "six brothers," who as witnesses can support Peter's testimony of the unprecedented event that has taken place there. Further, it is by the Spirit that this understanding of the events is made clear, and that the confirmation of the acceptance of these believing Gentiles into the new community is demonstrated when the Spirit "fell upon them," just as it had on the apostles (Acts 2:4, 18, 33, 38). To these "Gentiles" God has granted what he gave to the apostles and to their Jewish followers: the possibility of adopting a basic change of mind and perspective — "repentance" — which has enabled them to share in the new "life" within the new people of God.

11:19–30: The Church in Antioch

Now those who had been dispersed because of the persecution that occurred on account of Stephen went as far as
Phoenicia and Cyprus and Antioch, speaking the message to
no one except Jews. But there were certain of them, Cypriotes
and Cyrenians, who were talking to the Hellenists, giving the
good news of the Lord Jesus. And the hand of the Lord was
with them: a great number who believed turned to the Lord.
The message concerning them reached the ears of the church
which was in Jerusalem, and they sent off Barnabas to travel
to Antioch. When he arrived and saw the grace which was
from God, he rejoiced and exhorted them all to remain true
to the Lord with devotion of heart. So he went off to Tarsus to
seek out Saul. When he had found him, he took him to Antioch. It came about that they met with the church for a whole
year and taught a large crowd, and that for the first time the
disciples were designated as Christians.

In those days prophets came down from Jerusalem to An-
tioch. One of them named Agabus arose and foretold by the
Spirit that there was about to be a great famine over the whole
inhabited world. This took place in the [reign of] Claudius.
Each one of the disciples determined — each according to his
[financial] ability — to send aid to the brothers who lived in
Judea. They did this, sending it to the elders by means of
Barnabas and Saul.

11:19–26a

The verb (*diasparentes*) describing the dispersion resulting from
the persecution recounted in 8:1 (*diasparesan*) — from which
"Dispersion" and "Diaspora" derive — combines the image of the
scattering of the Jews from the time of the exile in the sixth century B.C.E. with the report of the scattering of "all ... except the
apostles." The areas mentioned — Phoenicia, Cyprus, Antioch —
are not so far from Palestine as the earlier dispersion had led
some Jews to flee and take up residence, but the cross-cultural
features in these districts are evident and central for the overall thesis of the author of Acts, as is the suitability of Hellenists
who had been associated with Stephen (6:1) to launch this wider
mission. Ironically, it is Saul/Paul, from the major hellenistic
city of Tarsus and earlier a target of the Hellenists in Jerusalem

(9:29), who is to have the major role in launching this determined outreach to the gentile world. Initially, however, these dispersed bearers of the good news in the three hellenistic centers address audiences that are exclusively Jewish, which serves to underscore the central importance for the author of Acts of continuity with the Jewish tradition of God's people. A further irony is evident in that among those scattered as a result of the persecution following the execution of Stephen there were some believers originally from Cyprus and Cyrene who, unlike the Cyrenians and Alexandrians that "disputed with Stephen" and consequently plotted successfully to kill him (6:8-14), now begin to preach to "Greeks"[44] the good news about Jesus. The earlier combining of Alexandrians and Cyrenians is consonant with the wide and deep impact of Greek language and culture on the coast of North Africa under the Ptolemies, including the Jews of the Dispersion in residence there. So deeply persuaded by the good news about Jesus were these Diaspora Jews that they traveled a considerable distance to Antioch-on-the-Orontes in Syria for the purpose of seeking to convince Gentiles there concerning the "Lord Jesus." God's support of this enterprise ("the hand of the Lord") was evident in the large numbers who "believed" their message, and hence "turned to the Lord."

On hearing of this outreach to non-Jews and of the many who had come to trust in Jesus as "Lord," the Jerusalem leadership sent "Barnabas" to check out what was happening in Antioch. This city, which around 300 B.C.E. was founded by the hellenistic ruler Seleucus I and named for his father, was located on the fertile banks of the Orontes River in northwest Syria. It became the third largest city in the Roman Empire and a major center of cultural and economic exchange. In the early Roman period Jewish mercenaries were a significant factor in the army and were granted political rights. Herod sought to ingratiate himself with the rulers and people of Antioch by paving with marble the main street of the city.[45] The emperor Caligula (37-41 C.E.) and his successors tried to coerce the Jews there into offering sacrifices to the pagan gods, but Titus resisted pressure to persecute or destroy the Jewish community there following the failure of the Jewish revolt in Jerusalem (66-70 C.E.), though he did take to Antioch some of the sacred items (cherubim) from the temple.[46]

It was in Antioch — according to this passage in Acts, as well as in the letters of Paul — that the issue came to a head as to whether Gentiles who joined the new community were bound to obey all or even part of the Mosaic ritual requirements, especially on dietary matters and circumcision. Barnabas's observation of the transforming power of God's "grace" among the new converts brought him joy, and led him to engage in instruction for them to remain faithful in their new commitment to Jesus as "Lord." Obviously, what was needed was nurturing these newcomers to the community of faith: the best-qualified candidate to carry out this vital task was Saul, who had returned to his hometown, Tarsus, whose training had been in both hellenistic culture there and in Jewish legal tradition in Jerusalem.

Excursus on Tarsus

Tarsus was a prehistoric settlement on the plain of Cilicia in southeast Asia Minor which became a fortified town as early as the third millennium B.C.E., and was a significant city under Hittite rule in the second millennium. The name probably derives from a local deity worshiped there. It was destroyed by the Sea Peoples about 1200 B.C.E., but Greeks began settling there after this catastrophe, and it continued to be inhabited by a mix of indigenous people and Greeks. In addition to the benefits of the fertile plain on which it was located, the main trade routes between Syria and the West passed through it, and a major seaport was provided at a nearby lagoon where the River Cydnus, which flowed through the city, emptied into the Mediterranean. After being conquered by the Assyrians and then by the Persians in the fifth century B.C.E., Alexander saved the city from destruction in 333, and it continued under Seleucid control and cultural influence until the Romans took over in 67 B.C.E. and made it the capital of the province of Cilicia. Under Augustus, Tarsus became a free city, but the only documentation for locals becoming Roman citizens concerns discharged soldiers, rather than hereditary citizenship, although the latter is a likely result of the imperial favor to the city. Strabo (14.673–74) attests to the fame of the city as an intellectual center, and notes especially that the local people were the chief participants in scholarly inquiry and instruction. The dominant philosophy was Stoicism, and among the famed philosophers from there were Zeno, Antipater, and Athenodorus, who was a teacher of Augustus and who effectively exposed the dishonesty of an administrator appointed by

Anthony. It was in Tarsus that the latter met Cleopatra, who — dressed as Aphrodite — sailed up the Cydnus to meet him. Only in Acts is there mention of Tarsus as the hometown of Saul/ Paul, but it is plausible to accept this tradition as credible, in view of the obvious facility of Paul in Greek, his consistent use of the LXX rather than the Hebrew Bible, and his effective and accurate use of Stoic philosophical terminology and concepts in his letters. Examples of the former are evident in the technical philosophical moral terms he includes among the fruits of the Spirit (Gal. 5:22–23)[47] and the latter in the central importance of natural law and conscience in his argument in Rom. 2:14–15. This Stoic approach to morality would have been a staple in the intellectual life of Tarsus.

11:26b

The author of Acts makes the point that Paul's activities among the gentile churches, as here in Antioch, did not occur on his own initiative, but as a result of explicit instruction and hands-on activity by the apostles and their designated agent, "Barnabas." This extended instructional work was a joint operation of the two: an apostolic agent and the one specially fitted to meet the objective of instruction of the new predominantly gentile community in Antioch. The clear image that emerges here of the activity in this new movement is not an exclusive or even primary emphasis on evangelism, but rather on the essential task of instruction of those who have come out of non-Jewish traditions to share in the life of the new people of the covenant. It is worth noting that the designation assigned to the members here is "disciples," which obviously derives from the term used for the followers of Jesus in the gospel tradition, but which now serves for the whole range of membership. This word, *mathetes* (literally "learners"), matches well with the emphasis here on instruction that they receive. But a new designation does appear for the first time in the title now applied to the members, *Christianoi*. It is impossible to determine with certainty the origins of this term, but the fact that it is used in a derogatory sense by the Roman historian Tacitus[48] may indicate that it originated among opponents rather than among adherents of the movement. Suetonius, in his *Life of Claudius* (25.4), notes that the Jewish community had been split apart "at the instigation of Chrestos," which is clearly a mistake for what would have been an uncommon term among Gentiles: *Christos*. Yet his use of this mistaken term implies that *Christos*, rather than Jesus, was the familiar name associated with the movement. In the other sources, the title *Christos* has clearly been mistaken for a personal name, and the movement came to be scornfully named for him. Its widespread use by the end of the first century is well attested in Pliny's correspondence with the emperor Trajan (98–117), in which "Christian" is used frequently and unambiguously to refer to members of the movement launched by Jesus.[49] Elsewhere in the New Testament, the term appears in only two other places: (1) in Acts (26:28), where it is a derogatory term on the lips of the scornful King Agrippa, and (2) in 1 Peter 4:16, where it is linked with the persecution that the members of the movement must be prepared to undergo. Although the text of Acts 11:26 does not make clear who has begun to call or "designate" the movement members as "Christians," the force of *chrematizo* in Acts 11:26 appears to be derogatory, and the inference is that this designation of them was not chosen by members of the new community out of loyalty to Jesus as the Christ but by their scornful and hostile opponents.[50]

11:27–30

The role of the prophets as pictured here is primarily that of foretelling what is to occur — in this case, the worldwide "famine." This is reported to have occurred in the "reign of Claudius" (41–54 C.E.), although the precise date is difficult to determine: either 45 or 46 C.E.[51] Josephus's account implies that the drastic food shortage was local to Judea, rather than worldwide. The role of "prophets" in Acts ranges from (1) the historic messengers of God to his people Israel[52] to (2) the messengers sent by the leadership of the Jerusalem community to groups of followers of Jesus in other parts of the world (11:27–28, 21:10–11), to (3) prophets as early leaders of the new community (13:1, 15:32), and (4) to Jesus as the ultimate prophet promised through Moses (3:22–23, 7:37). Acts 7:52 implies that there was a continuing function of prophets in the period intermediate between the time of the classical prophets of Israel and Judah and the prophets in the new movement.

The message of the prophets from Jerusalem concerning the famine there evokes the generous response of the Antioch community, who commission "Barnabas and Saul" to take the contribution to the primal community in Jerusalem. Their visit to Jerusalem is not commented on in Acts, but combined with the mention of their return in 12:25 serves to bracket the account of the divine action that punishes those, like Herod Agrippa I, who seek in vain to halt the outreach of the good news through the apostles (12:1-24).

12:1-17: James Killed and Peter Imprisoned

About that time King Herod laid violent hands on some of those from the church. He killed with a sword James, the brother of John. When he saw that this was pleasing to the Jewish [leaders], he went to seize Peter also. This was during the [festival] days of the Unleavened Bread. After he had seized him, he put him in prison and turned him over to four squads of soldiers to guard him [from escaping], with the desire to bring him before the people after the Passover. So then Peter was kept in prison, but prayer to God for him was made continually by the church.

12:1-5

"Herod the king," known as Herod Antipas, was made tetrarch of Galilee and Perea following the death of this father, Herod the Great, and reigned from 4 B.C.E. to 39 C.E. He is the ruler most frequently mentioned in the gospels in relation to Jesus and John the Baptist. Labeled "that fox" in Luke 13:31-32, he was infamous for having taken as his wife Herodias, who was his niece and married to his half-brother. It was this Herod who had imprisoned and executed John the Baptist (Luke 3:19-20, 9:7-9), and who is reported to have had a role in the trial of Jesus according to Luke (23:6-16) and Acts (4:27). In 18 C.E. he built on the shore of the Sea of Galilee a capital for his domain — a fully developed Greco-Roman city, which he named Tiberias, in honor of the emperor Tiberius (reigned 14-37 C.E.). To ingratiate himself with the Jewish leadership he had put to death "James the brother of John," and imprisoned "Peter." His first victim was "James," the son of Zebedee[53] and brother of John,[54] the pair that Jesus called to be among the twelve.[55] In reporting this event in his *Ecclesiastical History* (2.7) Eusebius quotes a story from the *Hypotyposes* of Clement of Alexandria in which

the guard who brought James to court was so moved by his con-
fession of faith in Jesus that he publicly acknowledged himself to
be a Christian, with the result that both of them were beheaded
at the same time.

Herod Antipas's attack was obviously launched against the
leadership of "the church," which here designates the Jerusalem
community, although elsewhere in Acts *ekklesia* refers to local
congregations,[56] clusters of congregations in various regions,[57] a
municipal assembly in Ephesus (19:32, 39), and the people of Israel in the desert (7:38). But it is not used in Acts to designate the
entirety of God's new people, as in the Deutero-Pauline letters.[58]
These attacks on the new community took place during the "Festival of the Unleavened Bread," which was linked with the Passover,
and was one of three annual festivals in which all males in Israel were to participate at the central sanctuary in Jerusalem.[59]
The other two were the Feast of Weeks, which was celebrated
as the harvest began (Exod. 23:16, 34:22; Num. 28:26–31) and
the Feast of Booths, which marked its close (Exod. 23:16; Lev.
23:33–36; Deut. 16:13–18). This festival had come to be linked
with Passover (12:4) in a blend of historical recollection and celebration of the agricultural cycle. Thus the time of Herod's attack
on the leadership of the church is an added element in the combination by the author of Acts of explicit and implicit location of
these early Christian events in the historic context of the life of
God's people, Israel. The interval of seven days between the pair
of feasts was to be the period of imprisonment of "Peter," with
four squads of four soldiers each to keep him in custody during
the four military watches of six hours each. The "Passover" as a
celebration of Israel's historic escape from Egyptian enslavement
would be an appropriate time for Antipas to display and destroy
publicly this leader of a troublesome movement within Judaism.
The counterforce that would shatter this publicity scheme is evident in the continuing petitions to God on Peter's behalf by the
members of the new people of God, "the church."

12:6–17: Peter Freed from Prison

> When Herod was about to bring him out, that very night Peter
> was sleeping, bound with chains between two soldiers, and
> two sentinels were at the door guarding the prison. And look!
> An angel of the Lord came and stood, and a light shown in
> the cell. He nudged Peter in the side and raised him up, say-

ing, "Get up quickly!" And the chains fell away from his hands. The angel said to him, "Put on your clothes and your sandals." He did this, and [the angel] said to him, "Wrap your mantle around you and follow me." And he went out and followed [the angel], but he did not know that what was happening through the angel was real; instead, he supposed that he was seeing a vision. After they had passed by the first guard and the second guard, they came to the iron gate which led into the city. It opened automatically, and after they went out, they proceeded through one street. And suddenly, the angel went away from him. Peter came to himself and said, "Now I know in truth that the Lord has sent his angel and has set me free from the hand of Herod and from all the expectations of the people of the Jews." When he perceived this, he went to the house of Mary, the mother of John (who was also called Mark), where there were a considerable number gathered and praying. When he knocked at the entrance to the gateway, a servant girl by the name of Rhoda came in response. But when she recognized Peter's voice, in her joy she did not open the door, but ran in to report that Peter was standing at the gate. They said to her, "You are crazy!" But she was firm in claiming that it was so. They said, "It is his angel," but Peter continued knocking. When they opened and saw him, they were astounded. Giving them a sign for silence with his hand, he recounted to them how the Lord had led him out of the prison, and said, "Tell these things to James and the brethren." And going out, he went to another place.

Once more the author of Acts demonstrates the convergence of human decisions and divine action. Herod's decision to bring Peter out of prison for condemnation and execution following the conclusion of the feast coincides with God's action through the angel to set Peter free. Although the guards were on duty, there is no hint in the narrative that they saw the "angel of the Lord" which had come to liberate Peter from prison. Even when Peter sees this celestial visitor, he assumes that it is purely a vision, although the physical contact with the angel is depicted as occurring in multiple form: the radiant light, the nudge in the side, the miraculous release from the chains, the instructions about dressing to go outside, and climactically the opening of the "iron gate" which gave access to the city. It is only with the disappearance of the angel that he understands that what has happened is in the realm of physical, earthly experience rather than merely a vision. The hostile plans of "Herod" and of the "people" opposing the movement have been completely thwarted by this divine action. What is essential is for Peter to report and to demonstrate to the new community in Jerusalem what God has done.

A significant number of members have assembled and are praying in a private house belonging to "Mary, the mother of John (who was also called Mark)." The implication is that this was a well-known gathering place for the movement, since it is there that Peter goes promptly upon his release from prison. "Mark," also known as John, figures significantly in the Acts narrative (1) as the companion of Barnabas and Saul when they took the Jerusalem community's relief contribution to Antioch (Acts 12:25) and (2) when he abandoned them during their missionary journey to Cyprus and Asia Minor (13:4-14). (3) He is seen as a divisive factor between Paul and Barnabas when a subsequent mission is contemplated (15:36-40). Mark's association with Barnabas is also attested in Col. 4:10, where he is identified as Barnabas's "cousin." In the Deutero-Pauline writing 2 Tim. 4:11, Paul is reported as welcoming Mark's joining him as an aide, and in 1 Peter 5:13 the author quotes Peter as calling Mark his "son." Whether these references are all to the same person is impossible to determine, but the implication of this account in Acts is that this young man named Mark was a participant in the new community from a very early time.

The miraculous nature of Peter's escape from prison is heightened — ironically — by the disbelief of those gathered at Mary's house, who dismiss her claim about Peter as madness. The "servant girl named Rhoda," whose joyous recognition of Peter by his voice failed to convince the others until they finally responded to his persistent knocking, is an example of the inclusiveness of the new community: she is a woman and a servant. The group's astonishment at his release is countered by Peter's report of how "the Lord" had enabled him to escape from prison. This divine sanction of Peter is to serve as further confirmation to the traditionalist leaders of the new community ("those of the circumcision") that Peter and the outreach to the Gentiles which he had launched in the house of Cornelius the centurion (10:1-48) were supported by God. It is especially

important that "James," the brother of Jesus and leader of the
apostles, should be informed of this additional evidence for divine sanction of Peter as missionary to the Gentiles. This role
for Peter is recalled here when he leaves Jerusalem and goes to
the place where the dramatic new outreach to non-Israelites had
taken place: "Caesarea."[60] Before going there, however, he leaves
the gathering at the house of Mary and goes to "another place,"
which is not specified but, as is implied by to the narrative, must
have been a village near Jerusalem.

12:18–24: Herod's Opposition and Death

When day came, there was no small disturbance among the
soldiers as to what had happened to Peter. Herod sought for
him and could not find him. He interrogated the sentries, and
ordered them to be executed. Then he went down from Judea
and remained in Caesarea. He was very angry with the Tyrians and the Sidonians, and they came to him with singleness
of purpose, and after having persuaded Vlastos, the king's
chamberlain, they sought peace, because their region was dependent on the royal district for food. On a set day Herod
clothed himself in royal apparel, sat at the tribunal, and gave
them a public address. The people shouted aloud, "A voice
of a god, not of a human!" Immediately an angel of the Lord
struck him down, on account of his not giving glory to God.
And he became eaten by worms and breathed his last. But the
word of God flourished and grew.

Peter's being concealed from the authorities was important, as
is shown by the report that once again his life was threatened
when "Herod" — that is, Herod Agrippa I — sought to seize and
execute him. The soldiers were perplexed by his escape, and the
inability of some of them to locate him resulted in their interrogation and execution. Herod is clearly intent on destroying Peter,
on the assumption that to do so will bring to an end this strange,
unparalleled, and expanding movement in the name of the executed Jesus of Nazareth. Frustrated by his failure to carry out his
punitive plan, he ordered the execution of some of those who
were the prime instruments for maintenance of Roman order,
but who had failed to hold on to the one whom Herod regarded

as the primary local threat to Roman authority: Peter. Thereupon he retreated to "Caesarea," the seat of control of the region by the Roman Empire,[61] and there he "remained." In these dramatic incidents the divine support for the new movement is effectively contrasted with the frustrated efforts by agents of the empire to halt its spread to the wider Roman world.

Excursus on Herod Agrippa I

Herod Agrippa I, the grandson of Herod the Great, was born in 10 B.C.E., the son of Aristobolus and Bernice. At age six he was sent to Rome with his mother as a guarantee of Herod's fidelity to Roman authority. Herod as a youth was educated and brought up with Claudius, the future emperor (41–54 C.E.) and Drusus, the son of the emperor Tiberius (14–37 C.E.), but was especially friendly with Gaius Caligula, the notorious emperor from 37–41 C.E. When he returned to Palestine, he was impoverished because of his spendthrift ways, and had to borrow money from rich relatives, but was given the rule of the territory north of the Sea of Galilee, which was adjacent to the traditional land of the "Tyrians and Sidonians." When Claudius became emperor in 41, he made Agrippa king of Judea and Samaria, thus naming him ruler over the extensive territory that had comprised the realm of his grandfather Herod the Great. Agrippa also succeeded in having Claudius decree that Jews everywhere in the Roman world were to be permitted to live in accord with their own laws, and were not to be coerced into conformity with local customs.[62] Agrippa was able to ingratiate himself with the Jewish religious leaders and many of the people in his realm. It was apparently in this connection that he took violent actions against the leaders of the incipient Christian movement. He was, however, reprimanded by the governor of Syria for convening regional monarchs and indigenous leaders, since this could be interpreted as fostering rebellion against Roman rule. At a festival in Caesarea Maritima he made a dramatic appearance in glistening garb as the sun arose, and was acclaimed as a god and hence immortal by those whom he had placed in power. Thereupon a horned owl appeared and warned him of his impending death, which recalled an earlier experience when he had been enchained by the Romans and an owl had assured him of release but predicted that following his exaltation and honors it would return to warn him of his impending death. After five days of horrendous pain, he died in 44 C.E., which was an occasion for great rejoicing by the populace and for actions to defame him.[63] Subsequently in 50 C.E., his son, Agrippa II, was made ruler of the district north of Galilee, and was able to ingratiate himself with the Jews more broadly by funding elaborate improvement of public areas in Jerusalem.

●

The occasion for Herod's anger with "the Tyrians and Sidonians" is not known, nor are any details of the identity of "Vlastos, the king's chamberlain," through whom the dispute was settled. The title of the latter, *koiton*, derives from the word for "bed" (*koite*), and was the designation for the servant in charge of a bed-chamber, and hence someone who would presumably have had an intimate relationship with the royal family. When the deputation of Tyrians and Sidonians came to Agrippa in Caesarea, the splendor of his appearance and his "address" to them elicited from them — whether honestly or for tactical reasons cannot be determined — an acclaim of him as a "god." His refusal to decline this honor in deference to the God of Israel was punished by sickness and death. The circumstances and details here in Acts 12 are different from those in Josephus, but the end result of divine punishment is comparable. Once more the author of Acts sounds his dramatic theme about God's direct actions in human history to achieve his purpose for his people and to thwart the hostile efforts of their enemies.

The observation concerning the flourishing and growth of "the word of God" carries forward the earlier reports as to how the message about Jesus has continued to reach farther and farther into the Roman world, starting in Jerusalem through the original apostles (6:2) and the "seven" (6:7), advancing to Samaria (8:14), to Gentiles (11:1), to Asia Minor (13:5, 7), and to Europe (17:13, 18:11).

12:25–13:12: The Continuing Spread of the Good News

Barnabas and Saul returned from[64] Jerusalem to Antioch when they had fulfilled their ministry, bringing with them John,

who was called Mark. In the church which was in Antioch
there were prophets and teachers: Barnabas, Simeon (who
was called Niger), Lucius of Cyrene, Manaen (a close friend
of Herod the tetrarch), and Saul. While they were engaged in
worship of the Lord and in fasting, the Holy Spirit said, "Ap-
point for me Barnabas and Saul for the work to which I have
summoned them." Then after fasting and praying, they placed
their hands on them and sent them off.

Therefore, having been sent out by the Holy Spirit, they
went down to Seleucia, and from there they sailed off to
Cyprus. When they came to Salamis, they proclaimed the
word of God in the synagogues of the Jews. They had John as
an assistant. When they had gone through the entire island as
far as Paphos, they found a certain magician who was a Jewish false prophet by the name of Bar-Jesus. He was with the
proconsul, Sergius Paulus, who was seeking to hear the word
of God. But Elymas the magician — for that is the meaning of
his name — argued against them, trying to divert the proconsul
from the faith. But Saul — who is also named Paul — being filled
with the Holy Spirit, looked at him intently and said, "Son of
the devil, you are full of every deceit and every fraud, the enemy of all righteousness! Will you not cease from perverting
the ways of the Lord's piety? See! Now the hand of the Lord
is upon you, and you shall be blind, not even seeing the sun
for a time." Instantly mistiness and darkness fell on him, and
he went seeking those who might lead him by hand. When
the proconsul saw what had happened, he believed, because
he was astounded at the teaching of the Lord.

12:25–13:3

With the completion of the famine relief visit to Jerusalem,
"Barnabas and Saul" return to Antioch, accompanied by a new
co-worker, "John, who was called Mark." The identity and role
of Mark as depicted in Acts and reflected elsewhere in the New
Testament are considered above in the notes on 12:12. Verse 25
serves as a transition typical of the style of Acts, and resumes
the strand of narrative that halted at 11:30.

The founding of the new community in Antioch through the
preaching of the gospel to "Greeks" has only recently been described in Acts (11:19–26), but it is already depicted here as
having members with special roles — "prophets and teachers" —

who are the instruments of the Spirit to guide the "church" there in designating a new role for Barnabas and Saul. These co-workers are identified as — in addition to Barnabas — "Simeon who was called Niger," "Lucius of Cyrene," and "Manaen." The linking of someone whose nickname was "Niger," which means "black," with someone from "Cyrene" clearly implies that both of them were from Africa. Already those who are by no means Palestinian Jews are not only members of the community, but have been assigned leadership roles. Similarly surprising is the mention of "Manaen" as a leader in the church, since he is identified as a "close friend" of "Herod the tetrarch" (= the recently deceased Herod Antipas). The social and cultural range of those moving into leadership roles is striking. This quartet of leaders in Antioch are said to be moved by the "Spirit" as they are engaged in two rather formal dimensions of the community life: "worship of the Lord and fasting." The term used for worship, *leitourgeo*, is used throughout the LXX with reference to cultic and formal worship of God. There is here in Acts no qualifying adjective linked with worship, as there is by Paul in the phrase "spiritual worship" (*ten logikein latreian*) in Rom. 12:1. Rather, the implication in 13:2 is that this community is adopting formal structures not only for its leadership, but also for its corporate worship. Similarly, "fasting" appears only in this pericope in Acts, and never in the letters of Paul.[65] Its importance is emphasized by the fact that the practice is reportedly repeated in connection with the prayers of the group concerning the commissioning of Barnabas and Saul, which is followed by the formal laying on of "hands" and sending them off on the mission aimed expressly at those outside the arena of Syria-Palestine.

13:4–12

Confirmation of the divine origin of this venture is given when it is reported that the effective agency for sending Saul, Barnabas, and Mark was the "Holy Spirit," rather than the Antiochene leadership of the movement. Their departure for "Cyprus" was from the obvious point: "Seleucia," the port of Antioch, which lies down the Orontes about fifteen miles and about five miles from the mouth of the river. Their first goal was "Cyprus," an island about sixty miles west of the Syrian coast and about the same distance south of Asia Minor. It measures some 140 miles in length east to west, and is around 40 miles in width. It was famous for the copper produced there, and its name is the source of that English word. Jews were there as early as the third century B.C.E. (1 Macc. 15:23; 2 Macc. 12:2) and had become a visible segment of the population by the time the Romans took over the island in the mid-first century B.C.E. A major reason for launching the mission there was that this was the native land of Barnabas, who was born into the Jewish cultic heritage: "a Levite" (Acts 4:36).

The bearers of the good news traveled across the island from the chief city and major eastern port, "Salamis," to "Paphos" at the western end, the capital of the province and famed for its temple of Aphrodite, the fertility goddess. In Salamis were the obvious first targets of their mission: the "synagogues of the Jews," where their message was proclaimed initially. "John Mark" is identified as an "assistant" (*hyperetes*), without specifying his role(s), but it is significant that in Luke 1:2 it is precisely those who were eyewitnesses and *hyperetai* of the word upon whom the evangelist claims to have relied in compiling his "narrative of the things which have been achieved among us" by God through Jesus. After passing through the entire length of the island, it is in "Paphos" that we first learn of diabolical opposition. The evil agent is identified by the Aramaic name of "Bar-Jesus," by ethnic origins as a "Jew," and by role as a "magician" and a "false prophet." Later (v. 8) he is assigned another name, "Elymas," which sounds semitic, but for which no meaning or parallel occurrence is known. It clearly does *not* mean "magician." One possibility for resolving this puzzle is to follow the Greek manuscript tradition, which reads "Etoimas" here, since this may refer to the Cyprian Jew, "Atomos," described by Josephus as a magician (*Ant.* 20.142).

Excursus on Magic and Magicians

The term "magic" derives from the *magoi*, representatives of a dualistic Persian religious tradition that penetrated the eastern Mediterranean world in the hellenistic period and continued in altered form to exert powerful influence in the Roman world. Assuming that cosmic history involved conflict between the powers of good and those of evil, the magicians were the agents with the wisdom and techniques to bring their followers under the beneficent powers and to achieve the defeat of their evil enemies, human and superhuman. There was strong emphasis on the abilities of the magicians to cause harm to one's opponents. The specific religious features of the tradition were eclipsed by the attention given to the recipes, incantations, and techniques by which the desired ends were achieved, whether beneficial or punitive. As magicians exploited their capabilities for personal gain,[66] and as skepticism mounted concerning their actual accomplishments, *magos* came to be replaced by or linked with *goes* = fraud or charlatan. The hope for cosmic triumph of a divine purpose for humanity or the world — as in the Jewish and early Christian expectations of the triumph of God's purpose for his people — was eclipsed by the eagerness for immediate attainment of specific, personal ends.

•

The ascent of the new movement into the upper levels of Roman society and culture is dramatically evident when Sergius Paulus, the "proconsul," summoned before him Barnabas and Saul in order to hear their message, and is further confirmed when he is identified as a "man of good sense." Attempts to link him with proconsuls with similar names found in Roman inscriptions are inconclusive, or clearly refer to other individuals.[67]

Excursus on Roman Governors and Provincial Administration

For administrative purposes the Roman Empire was divided into provinces, of which there were nearly fifty by the first third of the second century C.E. Each of the provinces was placed under a governor, who was either chosen by lot from the senators (heads of wealthy, prestigious families, with extensive lands) or appointed by the emperor from the equestrians (men of wealth, but lacking lands and prestige). The former were designated proconsuls (in Greek, *anthypatos*) and were placed in charge of a larger province, usually for a period of about three years, while the latter were called procurators and presided over smaller provinces or units within a larger province. In the first century C.E., Palestine was part of the larger province of Syria, presided over by a proconsul, with Galilee under a puppet king (the Herodian dynasty), but Judea was administered by a series of procurators, of whom Pilate is the best known. In the New Testament the procurator is referred to simply as a "leader" (*hegemon*), which is usually translated as "governor" (Matt. 27:2–27, 28:14; Luke 20:20). The tribunes, who were in charge of auxiliary military forces in the provinces, were called in Greek *chiliarchoi*, implying that there were a thousand soldiers under them, although the actual number was six hundred. The *centurion* was the officer in charge of each subunit of a hundred soldiers. The judicial administration of the provinces and their subunits was assigned to praetors, or in Greek *strategoi*, who adjudicated cases between citizens or involving foreigners (Luke 22:4, 52; Acts 4:1; 5:24, 26). The prime example in Acts of the function of a *strategos* is in connection with the seizure, imprisonment, and escape of Paul and Silas in Philippi (Acts 16:20–38).

•

Surprisingly but significantly, what the proconsul wanted to hear was the message that was spreading across the Greco-Roman world, geographically, ethnically, and culturally: the "word of God" (12:24). Bar-Jesus/Elymas, who seems to have been a kind of advisor-in-residence to Sergius Paulus, endeavored to "divert the proconsul" from a believing response to the message — that is, "from the faith." Here, as in other texts in Acts, the primary connotation of the term *pistis* is belief in the content of what is proclaimed about Jesus,[68] and hence "the faith," rather than focusing on the quality of trust in God or the divine promise.[69] The response of Saul, identifying Elymas as a diabolical agent, a complete "fraud," an opponent of God's plan to set things right in the world by trying to pervert God's message to humanity and thereby to thwart the way of true "piety" that the good news is fostering, concludes with an invocation of divine punishment upon him that results in his being struck blind. Once more, the author of Acts employs vivid irony, in that the magician's effort to obscure the "word" that the Cypriot proconsul wanted to hear brings about his own blindness and thereby enhances astonished belief on the part of the Roman official. The explicit shift in name from the semitic "Saul" to the hellenistic "Paul" at this point likewise matches the change in the identity of the false prophet from the semitic and ironic name "Bar-Jesus," "son of Jesus," or "son of salvation," to his designation as "Elymas," the magician.[70] This name does not "mean" magician, but appears to have been his choice of name for his function in that role.

13:13-52: The Good News Proclaimed and Believed in Asia Minor

After Paul and those with him set sail from Paphos, they came to Perga in Pamphylia. But John left them and returned to Jerusalem. The others went through Perga and arrived at Pisidian Antioch. On the sabbath day they went to the synagogue and sat down. After the reading of the law and the prophets, the leaders of the synagogue sent to them, saying, "Brother men, if you have some word of exhortation for the people, Speak!" Paul stood and motioning to them with his hand began saying:

"Israelite men and those who fear God, listen! The God of this people Israel chose our fathers and exalted this people during their sojourn in the Egyptian land, and with uplifted arm[71] he led them out of it. And for a period of about forty years he put up with them in the desert. Having overpowered seven nations in the land of Canaan, he gave them this land as an inheritance for about 450 years. After that, he gave them judges until [the time of] Samuel the prophet. Then they asked for a king, and God gave them Saul, son of Kish, a man from the tribe of Benjamin, for forty years. And after having removed him, he raised up David as king for them, to whom he also bore witness, 'I have found David, the son of Jesse, to be a man after my own heart, who will do everything according to my will.'[72] From the offspring of this man God has — in accord with his promise — brought to Israel a savior, Jesus. Before his arrival, John was proclaiming the baptism of repentance to the entire people of Israel. As John was completing his career, he kept saying, 'What do you suppose that I am? I am not he, but see, there is coming after me one, the sandals of whose feet I am not worthy to loosen.'

"Brother men, sons of the family of Abraham, and those among you who fear God, to us the message of this salvation has been sent forth. For those who reside in Jerusalem and their rulers did not recognize this man, and the voices of the prophets which are read every sabbath they fulfilled in condemning him. Since they could find no legal ground for putting him to death, they requested Pilate to do away with him. And when they had fulfilled all the things that were written concerning him, they took him down from the tree and placed him in a tomb. But God raised him from the dead. Over a period of many days he was seen by those who had come up with him from Galilee to Jerusalem, who are now witnesses concerning him to the [covenant] people. And we announce to you the good news that the promise which was made to the fathers God has fulfilled for us, their children, having raised Jesus, just as it is written in the second psalm, 'You are my son: I have begotten you today.' Because he raised him from the dead, no longer to be turned over to corruption, therefore he said, 'I shall give you the holy and sure things of David' [Isa. 55:3]. For this reason, he says in another place, 'I will not grant that my holy one see corruption' [Ps. 16:10]. For after David had rendered service to the counsel of God in his own generation, he fell asleep and joined his ancestors, and saw corruption. But the one that God raised up did not see corruption. Let it be known to you, therefore, men and brothers, that through this one forgiveness of sins is proclaimed. And from all the things for which you could not find renewed relationship through the Law of Moses, by this one all who trust in him are set in right relationship. So beware that there will not befall you what was said by the prophets, 'Look out! You who are contemptuous, be amazed and perish! Because I am going to perform a work in your days, a work which you will not put your trust in, even if someone told you about it in detail.' "

As they were going out the people were making an appeal that these words would be spoken to them on the next sabbath. When the meeting broke up, many of the Jews and devout converts followed Paul and Barnabas, who after having talked with them, urged them to remain with the grace of God. When the sabbath came, nearly the whole city gathered to hear the word of the Lord. When the Jews saw the crowds, they were filled with envy and contradicted the things said by Paul, defaming him. But speaking fearlessly, Paul and Barnabas said, "It was necessary for the word of God to be spoken to you first. Since you reject it and consider yourselves not to be worthy of eternal life, see! We are turning to the Gentiles. For the Lord has given us orders concerning this: 'I have established you as a light to the nations, in order that you might be the [instruments] for salvation to the end of the earth' " [Isa. 49:6].

When the Gentiles heard [this], they rejoiced and glorified the word of the Lord. And those who were destined for eternal life believed. The word of the Lord spread throughout the entire region. But the Jews aroused the prominent devout women and the leading men of the city, and stirred up persecution against Paul and Barnabas, and threw them out of their district. But they shook off the dust from their feet against them, and went to Iconium. And the disciples were filled with joy and the Holy Spirit.

13:13–15

Sailing northwest from Paphos on the island of Crete, Paul and his associates reached the southern coast of Asia Minor in the district known as Pamphylia at the city of "Perga." Located about seven miles upstream from the mouth of the River Cestrus, the city was founded by Greeks following the Trojan War (probably twelfth century B.C.E.) and achieved continuing successful relations with the Romans through one of its major families (Plancius), a member of which became a proconsul under Vespasian and another became a senator under Hadrian. Remains dating back to the third century B.C.E. include a huge theater, a stadium, aqueducts, baths, and gymnasia — in short, a fully developed Greco-Roman city. The district of Pamphylia, located between the Taurus mountains and the seacoast, was about eighty miles long and thirty miles wide. Controlled by the Seleucids in the hellenistic period, it was taken over by the Romans in 189 B.C.E., and became part of the province of Cilicia, which extended along the coast to the east. Both inscriptional and literary evidence show that there was a sizable Jewish population in Pamphylia from at least the second century B.C.E.[73] Acts 2:10 reports Jews from there present in Jerusalem at Pentecost. But there is no indication at this point in Acts of evangelistic activity by Paul in Perga or of contact with the Jewish community there, although on the subsequent journey through Pamphylia the "word was spoken" there (14:24–25).

The reason for the departure of John Mark and his return to Jerusalem is not stated, but the fact that Paul's subsequent refusal to have John Mark resume his role as a companion of him and Barnabas (15:37–40) comes just after the apostolic pronouncement that eliminated ritual obligations for gentile converts may mean that Mark's conservative stance on this issue was the cause of the earlier division implied here. Certainly the Acts narrative begins precisely at this point to show dramatically how the opening to Gentiles for participation in God's new people and the basing of this enterprise on an appeal for liberation from the requirements of the Law of Moses are deeply offensive to those who adhere to the traditional legal and ritual requirements for covenantal participation. The opportunity to explain the new perception of God's plan for his people is extended to Paul and his associates on the sabbath in the synagogue, where Paul accepts the invitation to offer a "word of exhortation."

On leaving Perga, Paul and Barnabas are reported to have moved on northward into the province of Pisidia, the chief city of which was named Antioch, like Antioch-on-the-Orontes in Syria (Acts 11:19–30).

Excursus on Antioch-in-Pisidia

Pisidian Antioch in central Turkey was founded in the third century B.C.E. by one of the Seleucid kings named Antiochus (I or II) but flourished after it was established as a Roman colony under Augustus, in connection with his founding of the central Anatolian province of Galatia in 25 B.C.E. In the early decades of the first century C.E. distinguished Romans were resident there, including relatives of the future emperors Tiberias and Nero. In the center of the city was built a temple and an impressive colonnade and square that formed a major center for the imperial cult.[74] Members of Antiochene families served in important military and administrative positions in the empire, and were among the first from the eastern part of the empire to gain places in the Roman senate. Paul's well-documented activity there serves as an important model for Christianity's penetration of the Roman Empire, culminating in his coming to Rome and his expected hearing before the emperor. It is significant that in Antioch Paul explicitly asserts that the purpose of God for his people includes the participation of Gentiles as well as Jews in the new community (13:46–47). His address to the synagogue reaches its climax in the affirmation that "all who trust" in Jesus — regardless of ethnic or ritual status — can share in the "right relationship" that characterizes God's new people (13:39).

13:16 –41

In Paul's speech the author of Acts makes the point emphatically that this new mode of defining God's people is by no means a novelty, nor is it contrary to the Jewish heritage. Rather, it is grounded in the scriptural traditions of Israel, as is apparent (1) in the context of Paul's speech, which is an invited address in the synagogue following the formal "reading of the Law and the prophets," and (2) in its content, with its sketching the history of Israel from the patriarchs' sojourn in Egypt through God's establishment of the monarchy (Saul and David) under the aegis of the "prophet," and culminating in Jesus, the "savior" whom God has now brought to "Israel." The divine initiative in these developments is further confirmed by the quotation of scriptures in which God speaks in the first person: "I have found...after my own heart...everything according to my will." This is a composite of scriptural phrases from Ps. 89:20, 1 Sam. 13:14, and Isa. 44:28.[75] It is "God" who has "brought to Israel a savior," who "raised [Jesus] from the dead," and thereupon acclaimed him as his "Son" and as a "holy one," who has kept him from "corruption" in death, and who has granted him "the holy and sure things" that were promised to David, as declared by the prophet (Isa. 55:3). Far from this message constituting a replacement or denial of the promises made to Moses, David, and the prophets, it is the historical demonstration of their fulfillment by God through Jesus. The specific mode of Jesus' execution — being hung on a "tree" (cf. Acts 5:30) — as well as his being placed in a tomb soon after his death were likewise in accord with the scripture, which announced that one hung on a tree was cursed and that his body should be removed the same day and buried, so as to avoid defiling the land (Deut. 21:22–23). Similarly, in Gal. 3:13 Paul notes that Christ freed his people from the curse of the law by becoming a curse through "hanging on a tree."[76] The clinching feature of the argument here in Acts is that it is God who acted in behalf of Jesus to effect a triumph over death, whereby he did not experience the "corruption" that is universally the consequence of human death. The significance of this unique event of Jesus' resurrection goes far beyond his own personal destiny, however, since it effects the liberation of all who trust in him: sins are forgiven, and freedom is granted

in a manner never possible through conformity to the requirements of the Law of Moses. Having made his case, Paul then
warns the scoffers and the unpersuaded that, as the prophet
Habakkuk foresaw, even when this great work of God has been
accomplished and has been explained to them "in detail," there
will be those who refuse to give it credence, and the consequence of their hostile reaction will be that they will suffer
precisely the fate that Jesus escaped and over which he tri-
umphed for the benefit of his people: they will "perish." The
doubters fail to enter "right relationship" with God because
they reject the very one through whom God has made it possible: Jesus. It is precisely this sad destiny that is sure to be that
of those who refuse the message of and about Jesus, and they
are here denounced as not merely dubious but as "contemptuous" of God's good news to them. They are astonished by what
they have heard about what God has done through Jesus, but
remain unconvinced. Even painstaking explanation of this message based on what was promised through the prophets and has
now been fulfilled through Jesus leaves a segment of the hearers
unpersuaded.

13:42–47

In spite of the fierce hostility to the message about Jesus on
the part of the local Jewish leaders, the people as a whole are
fascinated by it, and urge Paul and his associates to amplify
this message to them on the following sabbath when the synagogue would convene. But not content to wait a week, "many"
of the hearers — including both "Jews and devout converts" —
pursue Paul and Barnabas, who recognize that these earnest
seekers are those who have already been persuaded by the message about Jesus and have experienced "the grace of God." The
phrase "devout converts" combines two of the terms used in
the literature of this period with reference to Gentiles who associate themselves with or become members of the covenant of
Israel: *sebomenoi proselytoi*.[77] On the "next sabbath" nearly the
entire population of the city turned out to hear the "word of
God" — the phrase that has been central in the Acts account
of the spread of the good news about Jesus in spite of the official opposition, both political and religious: 12:24, 13:7, and
now in 13:46. There the turning to the Gentiles is announced as
a central feature of apostolic strategy, and is confirmed by the

quotation from Isa. 49:6 which is seen in process of fulfillment as the light of the gospel reaches out "to the nations" and its geographical spread extends to "the end of the earth," echoing the prediction and precise wording of the risen Jesus, according to Acts 1:8.

13:48–52

The response to the gentile mission and to the announcement of the apostolic policy in support of it is sharply divided in Antioch: The Gentiles "rejoice," and their "glorifying of the word of the Lord" (a phrase found only here in the Bible) stands in stark contrast to the Jewish leaders' rejection of this message (13:46). The faithful reaction consists in the honoring of the good news and perceiving in it and through it the powerful presence of God which in the tradition of Israel was thought to be present in the "cloud of glory" within the Holy of Holies.[78] Here the radiance of the divine presence has become apparent in the "word" concerning Jesus and is discerned by those prepared to receive it in faith. The forces that are operative are not merely human decisionmaking but the divine purpose for his people, who are here designated as those "destined for eternal life" by the will and purpose of God. The immediate result of the proclamation of the gospel and its acceptance in faith in this major city of Asia Minor is that this "word" is "spread" throughout the entire region, presumably by the hearers rather than by the apostles alone. The Jewish leaders' hostile reaction to Paul and Barnabas is supported by (1) leading women who were drawn to the Jewish tradition and its claims to offer right relationship with God (*sebomenas*) — which is in contrast to the male group (*sebomenoi*) who were drawn to Paul's claims about Jesus (13:43) — and (2) by the men who were the foremost civic leaders — presumably with no affiliation with or interest in the local synagogue but concerned about avoiding conflict in the city. The consequence of this coalition of opposition was "persecution" of the two messengers of the good news and their departure from the district. The identity and location of "the disciples" mentioned in 13:52 is not clear, but presumably it means that there was joy and experience of the Holy Spirit among those who had entered the new community in Pisidian Antioch, even though Paul and Barnabas had been forced to flee.

14:1–7: The Good News in Iconium

It happened in Iconium that they entered together into the meeting of the Jews and that they spoke to them in such a way that a great number of the Jews and Greeks believed. But the unpersuaded Jews stirred up and poisoned the minds of the Gentiles against the brothers [and sisters]. Yet they continued for a considerable time, expressing themselves fearlessly concerning the Lord, who bore testimony to the message of his grace, granting signs and wonders to take place through their hands. A large number of those in the city were divided: there were those who [sided] with the Jews and those who [sided] with the apostles. When there was a surge among the Gentiles and the Jews, together with their leaders, to abuse and stone them, they became aware of it and fled to the Lycaonian cities, Lystra and Derbe and the region around them. There they were proclaiming the good news.

Once more the author makes the ironic point that the efforts of the God-opposing powers, which here take the form of "persecution," while leading to the expulsion of the apostles from this region, do not by any means terminate their mission, but rather result in the extension of it to the wider central section of Asia Minor, and specifically to the important city of "Iconium." Located in central Asia Minor, this city was north of Cilicia, south of Galatia, and between Phrygia on the west and Cappadocia on the east. It was settled as early as 2000 B.C.E., and then apparently by migrants from Thrace or Macedonia when the Hittite rule of the area occurred around 1200 B.C.E., so the people there became culturally and linguistically Indo-European. In the third century B.C.E. some twenty thousand Gauls, together with their families, crossed over from Greece and settled in central Asia Minor, where they became the dominant group, and established what became known as Galatia. Over the years however, various rulers from adjacent regions dominated the area, until in 25 B.C.E. the Romans took control, and assigned to the whole region the official name: the province of Galatia. In that province was Iconium (modern Konya), an important city situated on a lofty, quite fertile plateau. During the Greek and Roman periods Iconium was linked with various provinces and other cities: Phrygia, Lycaonia, Derbe, and Lystra. It was a prosperous center for regional agriculture, and was located on the major east-west trade routes from Syria and eastern Asia Minor to the Aegean. In 25 B.C.E. it became part of the empire, and under the emperor Hadrian (117–38 C.E.) was made a Roman colony. It is mentioned in 2 Tim. 3:11 as one of the places where Paul had been persecuted, along with Antioch and Lystra. It seems likely that the churches in these cities mentioned in Acts were the ones addressed by Paul in his Letter to the Galatians.[79]

In keeping with Paul's typical strategy, as depicted in Acts, he and Barnabas went to a synagogal gathering in Iconium comprised of both "Jews and Greeks." The response of faith on the part of "a great number" of both types of hearers evoked a fiercely hostile reaction on the part of those in the Jewish community who remained "unpersuaded" by the message. The tactic of the latter opponents is said to have been aimed at totally discrediting the gospel in the minds of the "Gentiles," rather than among their fellow Jews. This implies that the Gentiles were the primary focus of these newly arrived messengers of the good news, and the strategy of the opponents was not merely to combat the apostolic claims but to persuade the Gentiles that the movement as a whole was subversive and that its leaders should be destroyed. The success of this tactic is evident in the "abuse" and "stoning"[80] that the "apostles" suffer, and the divided condition of the populace on this issue. At the same time, the "signs and wonders" performed by Paul and the others persuaded many of both Jews and Gentiles, who saw in these extraordinary capabilities of the apostles evidence of divine support. The violence of the hostile reaction was so great, however, that the apostles are reported to have moved on to two cities south and east of Iconium in the district of "Lycaonia":[81] "Lystra" and "Derbe." Once more, the antipathy toward the good news has resulted in its further spread.

14:8–20a: The Good News in Lystra

In Lystra there sat a man unable to use his feet. Lame from his mother's womb, he had never walked about. He heard Paul speaking, who — looking intently at him and seeing that he had faith to be healed — said in a loud voice, "Stand up on your feet, erect!" And he sprang up and began walking. When the crowds saw what Paul had done, they lifted their voice in Lycaonian, saying, "Resembling humans, the gods have come down to us." They called Barnabas Zeus, and Paul [they called] Hermes, since he was the leader who brought the message. The priest of Zeus, whose temple was just outside the city, brought bulls and wreaths to the city gates and, together with the people, wanted to offer sacrifices. When the apostles Barnabas and Paul heard this, they tore their garments and jumped out into the crowd, shouting, "Men! Why are you doing these things? We also are humans, of the same nature as you, we who bring you the good news, that you should turn from these useless things to the living God, 'who made the heaven and the earth and the sea and all things that are in them' [Exod. 20:11; Ps. 146:6]. In the generations which have passed, he permitted all the nations to go their own ways. But he did not leave himself without a witness, since he did good things, giving you rains from heaven and fruitful seasons, filling your hearts with food and gladness." When they had said these things, they could scarcely restrain the crowds from offering sacrifices to them. Jews arrived from Antioch and Iconium. Having persuaded the people, they stoned Paul and dragged him out of the city, assuming that he had died. But when the disciples gathered around him, he got up and went into the city.

Lystra, located about twenty-five miles south of Iconium, was settled by Roman military veterans in the time of Augustus (37 B.C.E.–14 C.E.), and the impact of their residence there is evident in the predominance of Latin rather than Greek inscriptions that have been found in the vicinity. Even the civic officials and council had Latin titles there. The military element in the city served to protect the Romans from attacks on the Via Sebaste (the main east-west trade route) and from potential invaders based in the Taurus mountains to the south. Yet the Acts account shows that the indigenous Greek language and culture seem to have flourished there in spite of the Roman military presence. Archaeological items discovered in Lystra include a statuette of Hermes and a bird of Zeus, which show the appropriateness of the divine identity assigned to these miracle-workers, Paul and Barnabas, as well as a sculptured relief portraying these gods:

"round-faced and solemn, with long hair and flowing beards, a searching gaze, and the right hand held prominently across the chest."[82] The widespread assumption in the Greco-Roman world indicated here is that those who perform extraordinary public actions are the gods in human form. This section of Acts matches well the narratives included in pagan romances of this period, such as Chariton's *Callirhoe*.[83] What evoked the popular response in the local vernacular — acclaiming these visitors as gods — as narrated here was the public evidence that the life-long invalid was healed through the word spoken by Paul, and it was this that led to the assumption that he was indeed the messenger of the gods: "Hermes." Also persuaded of the divine nature of these visitors was the "priest of Zeus," whose temple lay outside the city gates. Hence, he made ready to offer in that place the appropriate sacrifices to the gods now in their midst. It is when the report of this priestly action reaches the ears of Paul and Barnabas that their vehement public protest begins. The detail of the priest's bringing "bulls and wreaths" fits the description of the procedure by Lucian of Samosata in *On Sacrifices* 12, according to which the sacrificial animal was decked with wreaths as it was brought for ceremonial offering. The Greek verb used in describing the reaction of the apostles in tearing their "garments" — *diarregnuein* — is used in the LXX in the vast majority of cases in the pentateuchal and early historical writings of the Bible in connection with tearing garments as a sign of public sorrow or contrition.[84] This is made explicit in the prophets (Jer. 36:24) and especially in Joel 2:13, where the visible act of rending the clothing is not so important as the rending of the heart. The same terminology is used in the *Paraleipomena of Jeremiah*.[85] Thus this reaction of the apostles to the unwanted popular acclaim is a model of traditional Jewish piety, though it is performed in a context dominated by Greco-Roman religious tradition.

Paul's speech, which aims at discouraging and showing the inappropriateness of the priestly and popular interpretation of the healing, compounds rather than resolves the issue. He begins by flatly denying that he or Barnabas possesses anything other than purely human qualities, and then presses his hearers to abandon belief in or reliance upon any "useless" objects that may be masquerading as divine and hence receiving worship. Instead they are to turn to the one supreme God, who is the source of life and of everything that is in the universe. Here he quotes a synthesis of Exod. 20:11 and Ps. 146:6, and then goes on to affirm the freedom God has granted to all people down through the successive "generations" of human history, as well as the way in which the sovereign order of nature and the divine providence supply physical sustenance and inner happiness to human beings. These affirmations could be documented from scripture, but they also have counterparts in Stoic philosophy. This emphasis on the divine order in the universe and in human existence is compatible with pagan piety that constitutes a blend of natural law with the imagery of traditional Greco-Roman religions. As a result, Paul's speech has an impact directly opposite to his intention to offer a critique to those seeking to honor the two of them as divine: the hearers are now fully persuaded that these two are in fact the gods present with them and are the more eager to worship them. The Jewish leaders who have followed the apostles from the two cities where they have previously had a significant public impact now are able to counter the convictions of the people. Acting in accord with Jewish law concerning punishment of violators of the covenant, Paul was assaulted with stones and left for dead. But his life is preserved, as is the core of the new community—here already styled "disciples," as in Pisidian Antioch (13:52)—who come to see his battered condition and with whom he then returns into the city. The opposition to the new movement is fierce, but in spite of it, the new people of God continues to grow, the appeal to those reared in the Greco-Roman tradition is potent, and even the hostile efforts of the opposition serve only to pave the way for the wider spread of the message.

14:20b–28: Through the Cities of Eastern Asia Minor and the Return to Antioch-in-Syria

The next day he went off with Barnabas to Derbe. When they had declared the good news to that city and made a considerable number of disciples, they returned to Lystra and Iconium and to Antioch, strengthening the souls of the disciples, exhorting them to continue in the faith and [warning] that it is necessary to enter the kingdom of God through many painful experiences. And having installed elders for them in each church, and having prayed for them with fasting, they entrusted them to the Lord in whom they believed.

Having passed through Pisidia, they came into Pamphylia, and when they had spoken the word in Perga, they went down to Attalia. From there they sailed off to Antioch [in Syria], where they had been entrusted to the grace of God for the work which they had completed. When they arrived and convened the church, they declared all the things that God had done with them, and that he had opened the door of faith to the Gentiles. They stayed with the disciples no little time.

"Derbe," to which Paul and Barnabas went from Lystra, was also in Lycaonia some sixty miles to the east, and was located on a main highway that led down from the Anatolian Plateau to the seacoast at Seleucia about sixty miles west of Tarsus. This area was incorporated into the Roman province of Galatia in 25 B.C.E. The precise location has been debated, but the most likely site is at a place now called Kerti Huyuk, where an inscription was found dedicated to the council and people of Derbe. It was the home of Gaius, who became a companion of Paul on his journey to Ephesus and later to Macedonia and Greece (Acts 19:29, 20:4). Their proclamation of the good news was effective in this city, resulting in the addition of a "considerable number of disciples." Gaius is not mentioned here, but appears in the subsequent narrative as noted above. On returning to the other previously evangelized cities in the Galatian region — "Lystra, Iconium, and Antioch" — major formal features of the emergent church are evident: the "strengthening" of the disciples; the appeal to them to persist or endure "in the faith," thereby implying a distinct system of beliefs; the warning that the decision for membership in the new community awaiting the "kingdom of God" inevitably involves persecution and "painful experiences"; the installation of leaders ("elders") in the community; the guidance of the members into the practices of "prayer and fasting"; the commitment of the members to the "Lord" in whom they have placed their trust. Here is presented a compact but detailed picture of life in the new people of God, dealing with moral and credal features, warnings about persecution, and organization of church leadership, worship, and community life.

Retracing their steps through the region to the southwest of Galatia — "Pisidia" and "Pamphylia" (13:13) — the apostles now speak "the word" concerning Christ in "Perga" (where there was no indication earlier of preaching activity; 13:14), and then proceed to its port city, "Attalia," not previously mentioned in Acts. Founded by and named for Attalus II, king of Pergamum (159–138 B.C.E.), it was taken by the Romans in 79 B.C.E. and served as a settlement for army veterans. It was well fortified, surrounded by a wall and a moat. It was from this harbor that Paul and his associates set sail for Antioch-on-the-Orontes in Syria, from which this mission to the Gentiles had been launched (13:3) and the first phase of which was now "completed." The report to the church in Antioch confirmed that indeed the "door of faith" had been opened to the Gentiles, and that in impressive numbers, they had entered the new community. What had taken place was not impulsive or a radical departure from the norm, but is here identified as what "God had done with them." These specially chosen and endowed messengers extend their stay with the "disciples" in Antioch. The confirmation of the wisdom of the Antiochene community in commissioning them to carry out this pioneering work is now complete.

15:1–35: The Issue of the Legal Requirements for Gentile Converts Decided by the Apostolic Council in Jerusalem

Certain people who came down from Judea were teaching the brothers that unless you are circumcised according to the custom which is from Moses you are not able to be saved. After there took place no little dispute and debate with them on the part of Paul and Barnabas, they designated Paul and Barnabas and certain others from among them to go up to Jerusalem to the apostles and elders concerning this issue. So being sent forth by the church, they went through Phoenicia and Samaria, telling in detail about the conversion of the Gentiles. They provided great joy for all the brethren. And when they arrived in Jerusalem, they were received favorably by the church, the apostles and the elders, and they reported all the things which God had done with them. But certain ones from the sect of the Pharisees who had believed rose up, saying, "It is necessary to circumcise them and instruct them to keep the Law of Moses."

The apostles and elders gathered together to see about this subject. After much debate took place, Peter arose and said to them, "Men and brothers, you know that from the earliest days God chose among you that by my mouth the Gentiles should hear the message of the good news and believe. And the God who knows the human heart gave attestation to them, having given them the Holy Spirit just as he did to us. And he made no differentiation between us and them, having cleansed their hearts by faith. Now then, why do you put God to the test by placing a yoke on the neck of the disciples which neither our fathers nor we have the capacity to bear? But we believe that it is through the grace of the Lord Jesus that they will be saved by the same means [as we are]." The whole multitude was silent and kept listening to Barnabas and Paul as they were expounding concerning the signs and wonders which God did through them among the Gentiles.

After they were silent, James responded, saying, "Men and brothers, hear me! Symeon has reported how God first saw to it that he would form among the Gentiles a people for his name. And with this, the words of the prophets are in harmony, as it is written,

'After these things I shall return, and I shall rebuild the
    dwelling place of David, which has fallen.
And I shall rebuild the parts that have been destroyed,
and I shall restore it,
In order that the rest of humanity may search for the
    Lord,
And all the nations which invoke my name upon them'
    [Amos 9:11–12],

says the Lord, who has been making these things known from earliest times. For this reason, my opinion is that we should not cause difficulties for those of the Gentiles who turn to God, but that we should instruct them by letter that they should keep away from the polluted things offered to idols, and from what is strangled and from blood. For from ancient generations, Moses has had in every city those who proclaim him, since he has been read every sabbath in the synagogues."

Then it seemed good to the apostles and leaders, together with the whole community, to choose men from among them and to send them to Antioch with Paul and Barnabas: Judah, who was called Barsabbas, and Silas, leading men from among the brethren, having written [a letter to be carried] by them:

"The members, [including] both the apostles and the elders, to the members who are in Antioch and Syria and Cilicia, greetings! Since we heard that certain ones who went from among us have upset you with speeches and troubled your souls, even though we gave them no such instructions, it seemed good to us, having become of one mind, to choose men and send them to you, together with our beloved Barnabas and Paul — men who have risked their lives in behalf of the name of our Lord Jesus Christ. Therefore we have sent off to you Judah and Silas, and they will declare these same things to you through direct speech. For it seemed good to the Holy Spirit and to us not to place any greater burden upon you than these essential things: to abstain from things sacrificed to idols and from unchastity and from things strangled and from blood. If you keep yourselves free from these things, you will be doing well. Be well!"

After they were sent off, they went down to Antioch, and when the large number [of believers] had gathered together, they handed over the letter. When they read it, they rejoiced over the encouragement. Judah and Silas, who were themselves prophets, through an extended message encouraged and strengthened the brothers [and sisters]. After they had been active for some time, they were sent away in peace from the brothers [and sisters] to those who had sent them. Paul and Barnabas stayed on in Antioch, teaching and proclaiming the message of good news of the Lord, together with many others.

It is fitting that the new community in Antioch-in-Syria, which had commissioned Barnabas and Paul to carry out the mission to the Gentiles, would be the setting in which the issue of ritual criteria for participation in the people of God would be raised. Those who confront the community with the issue through their "teaching" are visitors from "Judea." Their insistence on circumcision for all male members of the community is completely understandable among those reared in the Jewish tradition or those who had chosen to become part of that group by submission to this ritual requirement, which in the Pentateuch is dated back to Abraham (Gen. 17:9-14) and is explicitly demanded in the Law of Moses (Lev. 12:3). Further, there was a requirement in this law that if any non-Israelite ("alien") who lives in the land wants to join in celebrating the Passover, he and all the males in his family are to undergo circumcision (Exod. 12:47-49). After fierce debate between proponents of this regulation for circumcising those who volunteer to join the community and Paul and Barnabas, plus their supporters, the church decides to refer the issue to the leadership in Jerusalem. Those to be asked for a formal ruling on the matter are "the apostles and elders," which would involve a representative and responsible group: the former chosen by Jesus, and the latter selected by the members. Those who are to convey the question to them are not only "Paul and Barnabas," but also certain unnamed members of the Antioch community, who would serve not only as representatives of possibly a different point of view than these two agents of outreach to Gentiles, but would also function as authorized intermediaries between the Antiochene and the Jerusalem groups. En route to Jerusalem, they take the opportunity to report to the new communities in Phoenicia and Samaria. In Phoenicia the refugees from the persecution that followed controversy aroused by Stephen (8:1, 11:19) — which, ironically, had been promoted by Saul (8:3) — had limited to Jews their proclamation of the good news about Jesus.

Philip's evangelism in Samaria (8:4-6), followed by the bestowal of the Spirit on the converts through Peter and John (8:14-16), took place among a people who conformed to their own version of the Law of Moses, which included circumcision as a universal requirement for males. For both groups, therefore, the detailed report of "the conversion of the Gentiles" would have come as a surprise, but it was an occasion for "great joy" for all the members of the new community. Similarly, the initial and widespread response of the members of the Jerusalem community to a similar report by the delegates from Antioch is favorable. The primary actor in this revolutionary development is declared to be "God" who "had done all these things" through Paul and Barnabas.[86] One segment of the new community, whose members had come from "the sect of the Pharisees," was fiercely opposed to this policy of not demanding observance of ritual requirements for admission to the people of God.[87] These members of the new community from a Pharisaic background insisted on "circumcision" and on instruction that would train the new members to "keep the Law of Moses." The issue has now been sharply focused: Is conformity to the legal traditions of Israel to be required of those who seek admission to the new community? It is especially important for those, like the wave of new converts in the cities of Asia Minor, who have come to faith in Jesus without having been reared or taught to observe the Mosaic law. The resolution of this issue will determine whether the new movement remains one of the options within the then-current Jewish traditions, or whether it will set out on its own distinctive path.

The author of Acts highlights the importance of this question by locating the discussion and resultant decrees within the context of the apostolic council in Jerusalem. The authority of the decisions reached by the council is emphasized by the fact that the two pronouncements are uttered by the leader of the original group of disciples, who was also the pioneer on outreach to Gentiles — that is, Peter — and then confirmed and specified by the new leader of the Jerusalem-based apostles — that is, James. Peter's argument that there is to be no "yoke" of the law "placed on the neck" of the gentile "disciples" builds on the divine action and confirmation evident in his call to proclaim the gospel to a Roman centurion (Acts 10) and in the subsequent outpouring of the "Holy Spirit" on the gentile believers. This divine confirmation of Gentiles as members took place completely apart from any imposition of ritual or other legal requirements, and rested instead wholly on "the grace of our Lord Jesus." The purity of God's people is declared not to be the consequence of their conformity to the requirements of the law, but of God's having cleansed their "hearts" — that is, transformed their wills — by their "faith" in Jesus as God's agent of human renewal. Peter had earlier learned the lesson through his experience with Cornelius the centurion that he was not to label anyone as "unclean" (Acts 10:28). Further evidence of God's confirmation of the policy of inclusiveness for the new community has been provided by the "signs and wonders" that Paul and Barnabas had been enabled to perform "among the Gentiles." The policy of admitting Gentiles without requiring them to meet ritual or legal obligations has now been demonstrably sanctioned by God and formally affirmed by the apostles.

James's rationale builds on the prophetic promises to explain that it is essential to the plan of God that his "people" should include those "from among the Gentiles." The scripture quoted is a composite, primarily from Amos, but with features from Jeremiah and Isaiah.[88] What is happening in the emergence of this new ethnically inclusive community is not a novel enterprise but is depicted in imagery of a major feature of ancient Israel as God's people: the temple is the place where God dwells among his people. The "house of David" is not David's ancient residence but is to be seen as the people of God among whom God dwells and is active. This divine presence and power were embodied in the temple, which David had intended to build but which his son, Solomon, actually constructed. David's house is also the dynasty through which God's rule is effective in the world, which was launched through David and his descendants (2 Samuel 7). Although not alluded to in Acts, historically the monarchy of Israel had come to an end, in spite of the efforts of the Maccabees to restore it. The current Herodian dynasty had no links with David or even with Jewish ancestors, but consisted of a string of client kings of Idumean origin. Ironically, it was Herod who rebuilt the temple of God, wholly apart from the Davidic connections. What is now happening through Jesus and the apostles is the creation of a wholly new dwelling place of God: this is the new community, which is constituted in continuity with God's promises to Israel, but in which participation is open to people from among "all the nations." The "name" to be invoked in order to qualify for a place in this new people is the name of Jesus Christ. His quotation from Isaiah ends with the declaration that this insight is not a novelty, but is what God has been making known to his people "from earliest times" (Isa. 45:21). This conclusion is wholly concurrent with that of Peter, sketched earlier.

A significant and complicating additional feature comes, however, in the conclusion of his speech, when James specifies the three items from which the gentile converts are to abstain: "polluted things offered to idols," "what is strangled," and "blood." The contrast has often been noted between these ritual prohibitions and the opinion rendered by James, Cephas, and John for non-Jews who join the new community after the issue of circumcising gentile converts was raised (Gal. 2:1–5): no requirements were added (2:6), but Paul and Barnabas were told that they — and presumably their gentile converts — should "remember the poor" (Gal. 2:9–10).[89] Some manuscripts of Acts[90] omit the phrase, *kai tou pniktou* ("and from what is strangled"), which led some interpreters to assume that the earlier text of Acts did not deal with ritual issues at all, but with matters religious (idolatry) and moral (unchastity and shedding of blood: i.e., murder).[91]

Other scholars have sought to link these requirements with those stipulated in the rabbinic tractate *Sanhedrin,* where the seven commands given to Noah and his sons are perceived to be binding on all humanity: obedience to law, abstinence from blasphemy, idolatry, incestuous marriage, blood, robbery, and meat from an animal still alive. Apart from the late date of this tractate (second to the sixth century C.E.), a much clearer link is evident in Leviticus 17–18, where rules are laid down for how Israelites as well as aliens resident in the land are to behave on precisely the subjects addressed in Acts 15:20: eating meat offered to idols (Lev. 17:8–9); partaking of blood (17:10); eating meat that was not properly slaughtered (17:15); and having intercourse with close kin (17:15). It seems clear, therefore, that Acts seeks to portray James and the Jerusalem apostles as adopting a position that is a compromise between the law-free invitation for gentile participation that one finds in the letters of Paul and a position that transfers to new gentile converts the basic rules binding on non-Israelites resident in the land as formulated in the final version of the Pentateuch. These are set forth in Leviticus 17–18, where the precepts are seen to be binding on both Israelites and on "aliens" resident in the land. The prohibitions include eating meat offered to idols (Lev. 17:8–9), partaking of blood (17:10–14) or of strangled animals (17:15), as well as having intercourse with those who are close of kin (18:6–13). That intent is confirmed in Acts by James's final statement that the contents and requirements of the Law of Moses are common knowledge to all who have attended synagogue sessions on the sabbath and heard these principles read. They are to be conformed to by proselytes, God-fearers, and even by seriously inquiring Gentiles. It is from such a clientele that the non-Jewish members of the new community were being drawn, and it is these legal obligations that they are to be called upon to observe.

Once the apostolic policy had been formulated, it was important to have it conveyed by a fully qualified set of representatives: two delegates supported by the "whole" Jerusalem "community" to accompany Paul and Barnabas on their return to Antioch. The representatives are the otherwise unknown "Judah" (whose name "Barsabbas" may mean "son of the sabbath," or "born on the sabbath") and "Silas," who is likely the Silvanus mentioned in the letters of Paul (1 Thess. 1:1; 2 Cor. 1:19) as a companion and co-worker, along with Timothy. These were not merely messengers from the apostolic group in Jerusalem: they are described as "leading men" in that community. The message is not be conveyed orally, which might result in conscious or unconscious modifications, but in "written" form.

The support group for this communication is a combination of the (1) apostolic leadership, (2) respected members to whom responsibility had been assigned ("the elders"), and (3) the membership as a whole (literally, "the brethren"). Those addressed in the letter are members of the new people of God who are of "gentile" origin, living in the three major areas in which Paul and Barnabas had carried out their evangelistic activities with such marked effectiveness: "Antioch, Syria, and Cilicia," although in fact the good news had evoked the response of faith among Gentiles in Galatia and other regions of south-central Asia Minor as well. The aberrancy of the more radically law-oriented Jerusalem-based troublemakers who had insisted that gentile converts must keep the whole law and that the males must undergo circumcision is not only denounced by this letter, but it is countered by the unanimous apostolic opinion ("of one mind") to reduce greatly the obligations to be placed on those who enter the new community from outside of Judaism. This decision is to be confirmed by both the written communication and the oral testimony ("direct speech") of these emissaries of the Jerusalem community.

Furthermore, essential to the authority of these principles is the affirmation that support for this policy decision is derived from the "Holy Spirit." The four items listed above—and derived from Leviticus—are explicitly stated as to be avoided by gentile believers. If the latter conform to these moral and ritual prohibitions, their way of life will be adjudged healthy and admirable by the standards of the Jerusalem community and its leaders. Once the message has been communicated to the large group of

Antiochene believers who have gathered to hear it read, they are filled with joy and feel supported in their common life together. Judah and Silas are seen to employ their prophetic gifts in order to provide "encouragement" and instruction for the members of this new community. After an extended visit, they are sent off in an atmosphere of "peace" now that the inner conflict and fierce differences regarding ritual obligations have been overcome. In the continuing efforts of Paul and Barnabas in instruction and preaching there they were apparently joined by "many others," whose identity is not disclosed but whose approach was presumably compatible with that of these two. The basic strategy of evangelism among Gentiles and the rules for acceptance of them into the new community have been established and confirmed by this apostolic pronouncement. It is substantively different from Paul's claim that the Jerusalem-based apostles placed no legal requirements on gentile converts (Gal 2:1-10), but seems to reflect a subsequent compromise position on this issue as the Gentiles were being instructed in the Jewish scriptures and felt a necessity to define more concretely the requirements for membership in the new community.

15:36 – 41: Paul and Barnabas Part Ways

> After some days Paul said to Barnabas, "Let's go back, so that we might check on the brothers [and sisters] in every city in which we have preached the word of the Lord, [to see] how they are faring." Barnabas was wanting to take with them John, who was also called Mark. But Paul did not think it suitable to take along with them someone who had departed from them in Pamphylia and did not go along with them in their work. A sharp disagreement arose, with the result that they separated from each other: Barnabas took along Mark, and sailed off to Cyprus. But Paul selected Silas and left, having been entrusted by the brothers [and sisters] to the grace of the Lord. He went through Syria and Cilicia, strengthening the communities.

From the base in Antioch, Paul proposes that he and Barnabas revisit the communities they had established in Asia Minor by proclaiming "the word of the Lord" there (13:13-14:28), in order to see how the members there are coming along in the life of the new community. They disagree, however, on the proposal to take "Mark" with them. Just as no reason is given in 13:13 why he had left them earlier "in Pamphylia" to return to Jerusalem, so there is no principle articulated here on the basis of which Paul refuses to agree to have him accompany them now. Nor is there any hint as to why this "disagreement" should have led to a radical split between the two, with "Barnabas" going off to "Cyprus," accompanied by Mark, presumably to visit the communities that had been established on that island when Paul and the other two (13:4–5) first launched their mission there. Instead of Mark, Paul chooses "Silas," one of the two apostolic emissaries from Jerusalem, to accompany him on his return visit to the churches in Asia Minor. The cities they visit are initially those where Paul had worked earlier in the southeastern part of Asia Minor: "Syria and Cilicia."

Excursus on Silas/Silvanus

"Silvanus" is the Latin equivalent or substitute for "Silas," which seems to be of semitic origin. He was one of the two "leading" men commissioned by the Jerusalem community to convey their letter to the community in Antioch (15:22). Their prominence among the Jerusalem believers was such as to enhance the authority of the apostolic decision transmitted in the letter (15:23–29). Like Mark, Silas was a member of the Jerusalem group, whose constituency was predominantly of Jewish origin and orientation, although there may have been proselytes among them as well. It was important, therefore, that a leading figure from the Jewish community, who was persuaded of the importance of including non-Jews in the membership of the new community, would now accompany Paul on his wider mission to Gentiles in Asia Minor. His journey with Paul leads to their imprisonment in Philippi (16:19–29), and to the evocation of a hostile reaction on the part of the Jewish leaders in Thessalonica and Beroea (17:4, 10). Their direct collaboration ends for a time when Paul goes to Athens, while Silas and Timothy remain in Beroea, but the latter two then join him in Corinth (18:5). Silvanus is associated with Paul in the introductory sections of his letters to the Thessalonians and the Corinthians,[92] but also with Peter in 1 Peter 5:12, where he carries out the role of *amanuensis* or letter-bearer for Peter.

Chapter Four ⎯⎯⎯⎯⎯⎯⎯⎯⎯⎯⎯⎯⎯⎯⎯⎯⎯

The Outreach to the Greek World (16:1–20:38)

16:1–5: Paul and Silas Set Out with Timothy

He also reached Derbe and Lystra, and see! A disciple was there by the name of Timothy, son of a Jewish believer, but his father was Greek. He was attested by the brethren in Lystra and Iconium. Paul wanted him to go on with him, so he took him and circumcised him on account of the Jews who were in those places, because they all knew that his father was Greek. As they were going through the cities, they transmitted to them for their observance the ordinances which had been determined by the apostles and leaders in Jerusalem. The churches were strengthened in the faith, and they increased in number daily.

The account of Paul's earlier visits to Lystra and Derbe is in 14:1–23. Notes above offer details concerning these cities and the events described as having taken place there through Paul and Barnabas. In Lystra the community continued to expand after Paul's departure, and now included "Timothy" and his "mother," who is "Jewish," but is married to a Gentile ("Greek"). Paul, because he wanted "Timothy" to assist him in his itinerant mission, has him "circumcised" in order to be sure he would find acceptance among Jews of these cities who were prospective members of the new community, but whose tradition would lead them to think that because Timothy's father was a Gentile he could not be considered as part of God's people. At the same time, the decisions reached by the apostolic and other leaders of the Jerusalem community were passed on as precedents and norms to be observed by the new communities in south-central Asia Minor. Clearly these standards set by the church in Jerusalem, rather than being the outcome of spontaneity or merely random innovations, are intended to provide the norms for the common life of the new communities. The result of the adoption of these rules and procedures is that the "communities" there are made stronger "in the faith," and continue to grow in numbers. The apostolic decisions and patterns of behavior are here seen as normative for the new communities emerging in Asia Minor.

Excursus on Timothy

Timothy's lack of circumcision, which was viewed by Paul as a handicap to the potential effectiveness of his mission among Jews and proselytes, was remedied by Paul's initiative in having him circumcised, according to this account in Acts. Remarkable is the special relationship Timothy enjoyed with Paul, as reflected not only in Acts, but also in the letters of Paul and in the Deutero-Pauline literature (1 and 2 Timothy). In Acts he is pictured as carrying on the work begun by Paul in Beroea (together with Silas; 17:14-15), as joining Paul in his activities in Corinth (18:5), and as being sent (with Erastus) from Ephesus to Macedonia to continue the work begun in that region. It is with representatives of the churches of Macedonia (Sopater of Beroea, Aristarchus and Secundus of Thessalonica; Acts 20:4) that Timothy accompanies Paul on his final visit to Macedonia. In the letters of Paul, Timothy is repeatedly identified as the co-sender (1 Thess. 1:1; 2 Cor. 1:1; 2 Thess. 1:1; Phil. 1:1; Philemon 1).[1] Paul refers to him in terms that imply special, intimate, familial relationship: as "brother" (1 Thess. 3:2; 2 Cor. 1:1; Philemon 1) but also as his "child" (1 Cor. 4:17). He is identified as a fellow-worker with Paul in 1 Thess. 3:2 and Rom. 16:21, and the special relationship between them is highlighted in Phil. 2:20-22. Indeed 1 Thess. 2:6 may indicate that Paul included him among the apostles. The Acts picture of Timothy as the special emissary of Paul is likewise reflected in Paul's letters: commissioned by Paul to establish the Thessalonians in their faith, and as the one who reports on their condition (1 Thess. 3:2, 6); sent to Corinth to confirm the members of the community in the way Paul had taught them about Christ (1 Cor. 4:17), including the continuation of Paul's work in proclaiming the gospel in that city (2 Cor. 1:19); sent to Philippi to aid the community there (Phil. 2:19). It is compatible with the evidence for this special relationship between Timothy and Paul that the two later letters that build on this distinctive link between them were created: 1 and 2 Timothy. Surprising, however, is the report in Acts that Timothy's mother and grandmother were believers, which suggests that Timothy may have been converted within an already Christian family rather than by Paul or one of his contemporaries. It could mean that three generations of Timothy's family were converted at about the same time.

16:6–10: Paul and Timothy in Asia Minor

They went through the district of Phrygia and Galatia, since they had been prevented by the Holy Spirit from speaking the message in [the province of] Asia. When they had come opposite Mysia, they tried to go into Bithynia, and the Spirit of Jesus did not permit them. So passing by Mysia, they went down to Troas. During the night, a vision was seen by Paul: a Macedonian man, who was standing and imploring him, saying, "Come over to Macedonia, and come to our aid!" As soon as he had seen the vision, we sought to go over to Macedonia, having come to the conclusion that God had called us to proclaim the good news to them.

Traveling northwest through the provinces of "Phrygia," "Galatia," and "Asia," in the direction of the Hellespont, the narrow strip of water that separates Asia Minor from Thrace on the mainland of Europe, the two emissaries of the good news are prohibited from entering the province to the north on the coast of the Black Sea: "Bithynia" and Pontus. There is no indication in the text as to the form that the Holy Spirit's prevention took, but it should be noted that the churches in that region (as well as those in the provinces farther east in Asia Minor, Pontus and Cappadocia) mentioned in the New Testament are linked with the name of Peter (1 Peter 1:1) and the members are referred to there as "exiles of the Dispersion." These details may mean that the good news had already been declared in that region by Peter or other apostolic representatives whose orientation was more strictly in the Jewish legal tradition, and who therefore identified Peter as their primary link with the apostolic circle. For Paul to have gone there, or at least for the author of Acts to have depicted him as going there, might have been understood as his being in competition, or even in basic disagreement, with other apostles. It is the "Holy Spirit" who is credited here with avoiding this kind of division or conflict, while affirming the validity of Paul's outreach to the wider Greco-Roman populace.

The route of Paul and Timothy is said to have bypassed "Mysia," the province adjacent to "Bithynia," proceeding to "Troas." Ancient Troy or Ilium was only a village when Alexander the Great took over the region, and the new city he built a dozen miles to the south, Alexandria Troas, eclipsed the earlier settlement and became a major highway terminal and port giving access by the shortest route from Asia Minor to the northern parts of Greece (especially Thrace and Macedonia) and the islands of the northern Aegean (Lemnos, Lesbos, and Samothrace). The emperor Augustus had established a Roman colony at Alexandria Troas, which flourished as a port and as a vital center of hellenistic tradition, and then readily adapted to Roman culture. It was there that Paul had a vision of a man from "Macedonia," on the mainland of Europe, calling him for help. This call was understood by him as coming from God, and authorizing the extension of the geographical and cultural territory in which the good news was to be proclaimed. Once again, the innovative outreach is not based on an impulse originating within Paul, but is perceived as being of divine origin and sanction. The shift to narrative in the first-person plural (16:10–17) suggests that an associate of Paul from western Asia Minor joined him for this phase of his mission journey, and the subsequent we-passages imply that the companion continued with him to Rome.

Excursus on the We-Passages in Acts

As has long been noted in studies of Acts, there are four sections of Acts in which the narrative shifts from the third person to first-person plural: 16:10–17, 20:5–15, 21:1–18, and 27:1–28:16.[2] In each of these we-passages, there is mention of places and persons who are associated with the vicinity of Troas and Ephesus in west-central and northwest Asia Minor and with Macedonia and cities in northeastern Greece, especially Thessalonica. For example, Aristarchus, who appears in the last of the we-sections as a companion of Paul on his journey to Rome is identified as "a Macedonian from Thessalonica" and "a companion of Paul" (Acts 19:29, 27:2). In Col. 4:10–11 and Philemon 24, Aristarchus is said to be with Paul at the time these letters are being written. Since it is in such passages (Col. 4:14; Philemon 24) that Luke is also identified as a companion and fellow-worker (*synergos*) of Paul, some scholars have concluded that the we-passages are by Luke, who has been traditionally considered to be the author of Luke and Acts, and thus are not derived from an independent source. This view is adopted by Martin Hengel in *Acts and the History of Earliest Christianity*.[3] A more cautious set of conclusions about this material is offered by Stanley E. Porter in his essay, " 'We' and 'I' Passages in Luke-Acts."[4] He concludes that the we-sections constitute a separate and distinct literary source used by the author, which focused primarily on travel, but was not excerpted from the author's own notes, diary, or travelogue. The author of Acts has simply quoted this source without altering it, he concludes. Its author could have been an eyewitness, or the text could be the product of some earlier compilation, but he thinks it unlikely that these passages derive from the author's own source. Nevertheless, Porter thinks that the author of Acts seems to have considered this we-source to be reliable, including details of what happened when Paul was not present, and hence essential for the overall picture. He does not think that its origins or distinctive theological perspective can be determined. Similarly, Susan M. Praeder, in "The Problem of First-Person Narration in Acts,"[5] rejects (1) the link some scholars have proposed between these we-passages and the style of sea voyages in hellenistic romances, since some of them are written in the third person, and (2) the notion that the author is pretending or claiming to have been a traveling companion of Paul. Instead, it is probable that a first-person source has been used, and these traces of it provide evidence for the redactional process by which the author of Acts produced this work. These proposals, which focus on the literary process, rather than on conjectures about authorship, are highly plausible.

16:11–15: Lydia: The First Convert in Europe

Putting out to sea from Troas, we took a direct route to Samothrace, and on the next day to Neapolis, and from there to
Philippi, which is a city in the first district of Macedonia, and
a [Roman] military colony. We spent several days in this city,
and on the sabbath day we went outside the city gate by the
river, where we supposed that there was a place of prayer.
Sitting down, we talked with the women who had gathered.
A certain woman by the name of Lydia listened. She was a
dealer in purple from the city of Thyatira, and was one who
worshiped God. The Lord opened her heart so that she paid
attention to the things which were spoken by Paul. When she
was baptized, with her household, she urged us, saying, "If you
have judged me to be trusting in the Lord, enter my house and
stay." And she prevailed upon us.

The route followed by the ship led west from "Troas" across
the northern Aegean Sea, past Samothrace, and on to "Neapolis"
in "Macedonia." "Samothrace," a small island off the northern
coast of Greece is mountainous, famed as the center for the
worship of the twin fertility gods, the Cabiri. The highest peak
on the island, which is about a mile high, served as an important landmark for ships sailing from the ports of northern
Greece toward the Hellespont (the channel separating Europe
and Asia Minor) or between Troas and such ports in Greece as
"Neapolis," the port city about ten miles from "Philippi." The
northern shore of Samothrace provided a place of safety from
the prevailing southeasterly winds in the region, and it is likely
that the ship carrying Paul spent the night there on its journey
to "Philippi." "Macedonia" was a district of prime importance
in Greco-Roman history, since its most renowned monarch,
Philip II, was the father of Alexander the Great, the one who
launched the project of bringing Greece, Asia Minor, and most
of the Middle East under the political and cultural influence of
Hellenism. Philip took control of a town named Krenides,[6] and
renamed the city in honor of himself. In 30 b.c.e. when Octavian
(later to be known as Augustus) defeated Anthony in the battle
of Actium, he based several hundred Roman soldiers there and
renamed the region Colonia Julia Augusta Philippensis in honor
of his daughter. The province reached from the mountains in

the north to the seacoast at Neapolis. Across it ran perhaps the most important commercial highway in the eastern part of the Roman Empire: the Via Egnatia, which crossed the Balkans from the Adriatic Sea to the Bosphorus, thereby linking Rome with Asia Minor and the Orient. Macedonia extended west to the Adriatic; Thrace was the province to the east, reaching to the Black Sea as well as the Aegean. When the Romans first took over the region in 167 B.C.E., it was divided into four districts, although under Tiberius and Gaius these were combined into a single imperial province until 44 C.E., when it was again divided. Although there has been much debate concerning the original text at this point,[7] it is likely that the author is describing Philippi as the (major) city in the "first district of Macedonia." Thessalonica was the largest city and at least later on was the capital of the united province, but Philippi was clearly the important center of its own district. In addition to the military colonists brought in by the Romans, Macedonia was the residence and commercial base for entrepreneurs from Asia Minor, as exemplified by "Lydia," the "dealer in purple from the city of Thyatira," near Pergamum in the province of Asia, who is identified as "one who worshiped God."[8] Although she is a Gentile, a woman, and not fully a member of the Jewish community, she is faithful in taking part in the activities at the *proseuche*, which Philo indicates were places for gatherings of pious Jews, such as those throughout the city of Alexandria.[9] Only here in all of Acts (16:13) is there an explicit reference to the "place of prayer." Significantly, it is located "outside the city gate," which reinforces the image of Judaism and its proponents as peripheral to Greco-Roman society as a whole. Its location "by the river" made water accessible for libations or cleansing. Lydia's occupation as a seller of "purple" suggests that she was a woman of some wealth, since purple dye, which was made from a kind of shellfish (murex), was expensive, and accordingly was used chiefly by those of eminent power or prestige in the Roman society. The cost and prestige of purple garments is apparent in Dan. 5:7 and 1 Macc. 10:20, and removal of such a robe was a sign of debasement (2 Macc. 4:38). In the Lukan parable, the contrast between the rich man and Lazarus is succinctly set forth in the detail that the former was dressed in purple (Luke 16:19–31). The mocking acclaim of Jesus as king of the Jews is epitomized in the purple robe that the soldiers placed on him (Mark 15:17).

The crucial factor in Lydia's coming to trust in Jesus was that "the Lord opened her heart," rather than merely the persuasive power of Paul's teaching. Here again the author emphasizes the divine sanction for the inclusiveness of the new community. Lydia's inner convictions were given outward, public expression by her accepting baptism, which was easily arranged since the "place of prayer" was on the riverbank. Yet its proximity to the "city gate" implies that neither the meeting nor the consequent public act of baptism was covert, but rather that both were open to public scrutiny. The essential pious action of hospitality on the part of gentile seekers associated with the Jewish community there toward the leaders of the new movement[10] is now apparent in the invitation offered to Paul and his companion and accepted by them to reside in her "house" — which presumably was reasonably commodious. The crucial factor in this change in Lydia and in the new base of operations for Paul and his colleagues among those who are birthright Jews is that Lydia is now recognized to be "trusting in the Lord," and hence a believer in Jesus as the Messiah and agent for renewal of God's people. It is of this inclusive new people that Lydia has become a prime example.

16:16–40: Paul and Silas in Prison at Philippi

It happened that as we were going into the place of prayer that we met a female slave who had a spirit of divination and who, through her giving oracles, brought much profit to her masters. She followed Paul and us, calling out and saying, "These men are servants of the Most High God, and they proclaim to you a way of salvation." This she did for many days. But Paul was greatly disturbed, and turned and said to the spirit, "I order you in the name of Jesus Christ to come out of her." And it came out in that very hour. When her masters saw that their hope of profit had departed, they laid hold of Paul and Silas, and dragged them into the marketplace in the presence of the authorities. And when they had brought them to the chief magistrates, they said, "These men, who are throwing our city into confusion, are Jews. They are promulgating practices which are not lawful for us who are Romans to accept or to perform." The crowd joined in the attack against them, and the magistrates tore their clothes from them and commanded that they be beaten with rods. When they had inflicted many blows upon them, they threw them into prison, giving orders to the keeper of the prison to keep them securely. Having received such an order, he threw them into the inner prison, and fastened their feet in the stocks.

But about midnight, as Paul and Silas were praying and singing hymns to God and the prisoners were listening to them, suddenly there was a great earthquake, so that the foundations of the prison were moved to and fro. Instantly all the doors were opened and the fetters of all of them were loosened. When the keeper of the prison awakened and saw that the doors of the prison were opened, he drew his sword and was about to do away with himself, assuming that all the prisoners had run away. But in a loud voice Paul called out, "Do not do yourself any harm, for we are all here!" After asking for lights, he leapt in and became tremulous, and fell at the feet of Paul and Silas. After leading them out, he said to them, "Sirs, what is it necessary for me to do in order to be saved?" They said, "Put your trust in the Lord Jesus, and you shall be saved and your household." And they spoke the word of the Lord to him, together with all those in his house. And having taken them with him that hour of the night and washed their wounds, he himself was baptized at once, as were all those who were with him. Having taken them to his house, he prepared the table for them, and rejoiced with his entire household that he had trusted in God.

When day came, the chief magistrates sent the lictors saying, "Release those men." The keeper of the prison reported these words to Paul: "The chief magistrates sent orders that you should be let go. Now, therefore, come out and depart in peace." But Paul said to them, "Having bound us publicly without a trial, men who are Roman citizens, they threw us into prison. Are they now throwing us out secretly? No! Let them come themselves and lead us out." The lictors reported these words to the chief magistrates, and they were fearful when they heard that they were Roman citizens. They came and tried to conciliate them, and after leading them out, they asked them to leave the city. After they went out of the prison, they went to the [home of] Lydia. When they had seen the brothers [and sisters] and encouraged them, they departed.

16:16–24

Here the narrative of Acts continues briefly in the first-person plural: through verse 17. Striking is the correspondence between the insights and utterances produced by the "spirit of divination" and the disclosures through the Holy Spirit, but even more remarkable is the utterance of the woman who possessed this divinatory spirit, in which she linked Paul and the others with "the Most High God" and declared that the apostolic message concerned "a way of salvation." Both this designation of the supreme God and the hope for salvation through deliverance from evil, sickness, and death were common features of the Greco-Roman world, and this woman is depicted as having at least a partially correct insight as to the source and the intent of the apostolic message. "Divination" was a widespread phenomenon in the Greco-Roman world, and was much discussed by philosophers of that period. The text reads literally that "a certain servant girl had a pythonic spirit," and it said that she brought "much profit" to her owners by "giving oracles [*manteuomene*]." Three essays by the philosopher Plutarch (46–120 C.E.) demonstrate the ways in which divination was regarded by intellectuals in the latter first and early second century C.E. — the probable time when Luke-Acts was written. What is clear in these essays is that the wisdom of God is believed to be conveyed to seeking humans by means of diviners, especially through prophetesses affiliated with the shrine of Apollo at Delphi, where the snake, "python," was the sign and symbol of the divine presence. The enslaved diviner, whose activity was mantic, is depicted as one of the agents possessing the pythonic spirit of divination, which Paul subsequently expelled. Scholarly efforts that try to depict her oracular powers as ventriloquism[11] miss the point of this passage in Acts and of the wider Greco-Roman phenomenon of divination. Plutarch himself denounces such an interpretation of divination as "simple and childish."

Excursus on Divination

In his discourse "On the 'E' at Delphi" Plutarch applies to god precisely the terms also used in Acts: "mantic" and "pythian" (385B). God is seen as no less a philosopher than a mantic, but for those who are only beginning to learn about the divine, he is a "pythian." Plutarch quotes one Ammonius as asserting that "since philosophy embraces inquiry, wonder, and doubt, it seems natural that most of the things related to the god should have been hidden away in riddles, and should require some account of their purpose, and an explanation of their cause" (385C). Clarification of these issues comes through the diviners, an essential process that aids and informs philosophical analysis.

The letter "E" at the Delphic oracle is perceived as standing for the conjunction *ei,* "if," which is an essential feature of human decisionmaking (e.g., if one is to marry, or to travel) but, more important, it is the function of "if" in the dialectical process that brings one into perception of oneself, of the divine, and of the nature of the cosmos in abstract terms (386–87). "E" also functions as the equivalent of the number 5, which is the number of the human senses, as well as of the principles of the universe set forth by Plato (in *The Sophist*) and in Pythagorean cosmology (387–88). But most important, *ei,* understood as "Thou art," affirms the existence and accessibility of the god.

In the second essay, "Why Does Pythia Not Now Give Oracles in Verse?" the details of oracular communication are spelled out more fully. The verbal messages are not composed by the god, but from the god comes the initial impulse which then is given expression according to the innate capacity of each prophetess. Hers are the voice, the phrasing, and the meter, but the god provides the fantasies and puts light in her soul to illuminate the future — for that is what inspiration (*enthusiasmos*) is (397B–C). Presented as a quotation from Serapion, the Athenian poet, it is asserted, "We ought not to fight against the god, nor to remove, along with his prophecy, his providence and godhead, but to seek fresh solutions for apparent contradictions, and never to surrender the reverent belief of our ancestors" (402E). The quality of the messages transmitted by the Pythian oracle is characterized thus: "The language of the Pythia illustrates what mathematicians mean by calling a straight line the shortest distance between two points: it makes no bend or curve, no doubling or ambiguity, but lies straight toward truth...and it has never been found to be wrong" (408F–409G).

In the last of these three essays, "On the Cessation of the Oracles," the spokesman, Ammonius, asserts that the soul does not achieve mantic power when it passes out of the body, but since "all things come into being at the same time — all actions, words, and feelings" — the soul is able to recall and preserve things in the past through *mneme* (memory, or calling to mind), just as it is able to "grasp and invest with appearance and being that which is not present," on into the future. "Memory is the ability to hear things to which the ear is deaf and to see things to which the eye is blind," and thus it is able to anticipate things to come, to "confront the future and attach itself thereto" (432A–D). Thus the Pythian oracle was perceived as possessing and able to communicate insights about ultimate reality, past, present, or future. The correspondence between these divinatory features and the insights or disclosures that come through the Spirit in the biblical tradition are evident, and help to account for the relatively rapid spread of the Jesus movement in the wider Roman world.

•

What the author of Acts is seeking to convey to the reader is that this slave girl who has prostituted her divinatory capacities for the benefit of her owners is nevertheless communicating the truth concerning the apostles: they are indeed "servants of the Most High God," and the message they proclaim is indeed the "way of salvation." The identity of God or the details of his salvific mode are not stated by her, but the ultimate sovereignty of this deity and the human transformation and renewal that he is effecting are affirmed. Her persistent repetition of this perception, exploited as she is by her owners, is an unwelcome kind of advertising that Paul finds deeply troubling. Accordingly, he does not deny what she affirms, but exorcizes the "spirit" that has possessed her, and does so by appealing to the crucial factor that was omitted from her declaration about the apostles' role: "the name of Jesus Christ." The effectiveness of this appeal does not persuade her owners, whose chief concern is that she has now lost her capacity to bring them income through the divinatory fees they had been gaining through her, and so they bring charges against the apostles before the civic "authorities." There is no title indicated for these officials (*archontes*), but in the next verse the term *strategoi* is used. Some interpreters of Acts have considered this term to be equivalent to the Roman title *praetor*, which was used to designate the Roman magistrates who helped consuls in the administration of justice. The initial appeal of a plaintiff was made to the *praetor*, who would pass the case on to a judge if he was convinced of the substance of the accusation. On the other hand, if the plaintiff was of humble origins or low in status within the community (*humiliores* rather than *honestiores*), the *praetor* could simply discriminate against the weaker party and dismiss the case.[12] If this equation of *strategos* with *praetor* is correct, however, it is curious that the text refers to such an officer in the plural (*strategoi*). Since the "magistrates" do not assign the case to a judge, but instead take direct action, it is likely that they were officials of lesser rank in the civic administration.

The details of the counterattack by the owners of the slave girl are multiple: (1) the apostles are charged with disturbing the peace by causing confusion among the populace; (2) the accusers rightly recognize the basic orientation of the apostles in the Jewish tradition, and seek to exploit anti-semitic sentiments among the leaders and the people; (3) they charge them with "promulgating practices" that are illicit for Romans. The latter are neither specified nor documented, but the crowd "joined in the attack" — up to this point, in the form of accusations only. It is the "magistrates" themselves who initiate the punishment of these troublemakers by ripping off their clothing[13] and giving orders for them to be severely beaten and then to be fettered in prison, with special orders for them to be kept "securely" incarcerated. The jailer follows his instructions, and the prisoners are "securely" immobilized with "their feet in stocks." These details demonstrate to the reader the falsity and the emptiness of the charges that are being brought against the messengers of the good news, but they also show dramatically that the solution to the problems and persecution that they experience rests with God and not merely with human ingenuity.

16:25–34

The dramatic transformation of those whose trust in Jesus as the Christ has brought them into membership in God's new people is powerfully evident in the next stage of this story. Instead of becoming discouraged or embittered by the fierce opposition and consequent punishment they have experienced, Paul and Silas are still awake at "midnight," engaged in "praying and singing hymns," thereby bearing testimony to God and to the audience composed of their fellow-prisoners concerning their confidence that God's purpose is being worked out through them. The credibility of this trust and the dramatic divine basis

for it are given cosmic support in the "great earthquake" that occurs, which results in the freeing of all the prisoners, not merely
of the apostles.

The symbolic significance of this is powerful: the God of
whom Paul and Silas speak is not a deity whose sphere of action
is limited to his own special devotees, but who has the potential to liberate all humanity. The solidarity of the entire group
in the benefits of this experience is evident in that none of them
exploits this divine act of release by fleeing from the prison. But
there is in this narrative the astonishing feature of deliverance
for the prison keeper as well, whom Paul keeps from suicide and
whose subsequent question to Paul and Silas uses a term that
carries a meaning in the Christian context of which the jailer is
not initially aware. These men who the previous day had been
brusquely sentenced to prison, treated by the magistrates as *humiliores*, are now addressed by the jailer with the term of esteem
and social stature, *Kurioi* ("sirs")! Presumably, when he asks what
he must do in order to be "saved," he is interested in finding out
from these two prisoners how he might escape punishment from
his own superiors for having failed to maintain the security of
the prison, or from this divine power that has literally shaken
the foundations of his establishment and challenged his official
authority. The apostles' answer uses his term in a very different
and far more positive way, calling for him to "trust in the Lord
[*kurios*] Jesus," and thereby to be "saved" — that is, to be made
whole, to be renewed and placed in right relationship with God.
This promise — "the word of the Lord" — is explained to the jailer
and to his entire "household," all of whom join through faith
and the rite of "baptism" to take their places in the new community, just as was the case with Lydia (16:15). Confirmation of
the new relationship is provided by the shared meal and by the
common joy of all who through the earnest seeking of the jailer
have now come to trust in God.

16:35–40

Apparently in reaction to the supernatural consequences of having jailed Paul and Silas, the magistrates send their agents,
the "lictors,"[14] to set them free and to urge them to "depart
in peace." Rather than rejoice in this offer of liberation, Paul
protests against the violation of Roman law and due process
which had led to their being condemned without proper trial,

beaten in public, imprisoned, and now to their being expelled
from prison "secretly." All this has been taking place in spite of
the fact that he and Silas are "Roman citizens," an item that Paul
does not mention in his letters.

Excursus on Roman Citizenship

A central social concept and phenomenon which the Romans
took over and adapted from the Greeks of the hellenistic period was that of the city (*polis*, which in Latin became *civitas*),
often carrying the connotation of city-state, rather than simply
the urban center itself. In addition to Rome itself and the Italian cities — especially those south of the Po which constituted
the Latin League — there were two types of *civitates:* (1) those
cities where the basic culture was not Roman or dominated by
Romans, which were called *civitates peregrinae* (foreign cities),
but with which the Roman senate established a treaty relationship; (2) those cities dominated by Romans, often through large
settlements of Romans in their districts, which the senate might
raise to higher status by designating them as *municipia* or *coloniae*. The grant of citizenship was a privilege of the emperor,
and there seems to have been no need for confirmation by the
senate. On being designated a citizen, one took two first names
(*praenomen* and *nomen*) in honor of one's benefactor — such
as Claudius — while retaining one's original single name (*cognomen*). A select group of the indigenous leaders in the *coloniae*
would be designated as Roman citizens, while other residents
were called *incolae* (resident aliens). Non-Romans who had administrative roles in the community (such as ex-magistrates)
were called *contributi*, and had the possibility of becoming
citizens. As momentum for this process increased, *civitates peregrinae* (foreign cities) were converted into *municipia* or *coloniae*,
and the number of citizens increased markedly throughout the
empire. Citizenship was granted even to slaves who had been
manumitted by citizens, as well as to military veterans and their
sons. The names of the new citizens were kept on official lists
in their resident cities and were originally inscribed on metal
plaques on the walls of public buildings on the Capitoline in
Rome, although these plaques were subsequently melted down
and destroyed. Citizens often served as members of the civic
councils; chosen from the wealthy in the community, they were

appointed for life. They dominated local affairs and played central roles in administrative as well as in regional law-and-order matters, including both passing and enforcing local legislation.[15] But possession of citizenship was not considered essential for access to the ranks of the privileged. In the eastern empire, citizenship was more sparsely distributed than in the west, and was given to individuals and families, rather than to cities or certain ruling elites. In much of the empire all the members of the Roman city councils were citizens, but this was not so in the east until the reign of the emperor Caracalla (211–17 C.E.).

•

Although there is no evidence outside of Acts for this claim that Paul and Silas were Roman citizens, the fact that they are both reported as having two names — Paul/Saul; Silas/Silvanus[16] — is at least compatible with this claim of citizenship. How or why they received this designation is not even hinted at, but the claim made here increases the relevance of Acts for its first generation of readers, who would have been facing the severe tensions between obedience to the community of faith in which they had taken their place and the demands or limitations being imposed on them by the increasingly hostile imperial powers. That issue will be confronted directly beginning with Acts 22:25–29. Here there is only a report of an apology by the officials, who spend some time with "Lydia," visit the other members of the community ("brothers and sisters") and leave.

17:1–9: Success and Conflict in Thessalonica

After they had traveled through Amphipolis and Apollonia, they came to Thessalonica, where there was a synagogue of the Jews. As was the custom for Paul, he went into them and on three sabbaths he debated with them from the scriptures, explaining and demonstrating that it was necessary for the Messiah to suffer and to rise from the dead, and that "this Jesus, whom I now proclaim to you, is the Messiah." And some of them were persuaded and joined up with Paul and Silas, including a great number of devout Greeks, and not a few of the leading women. But the Jews were jealous, and bringing together certain evil men from the rabble, they assembled a

mob, threw the city into an uproar, and attacking the house
of Jason, they tried to bring them out to the people. When
they could not find them, they dragged off Jason and certain
of the brethren to the politarchs, shouting, "These men who
have turned humankind upside down have also come here. Jason has received them, and all of them are behaving contrary
to the decrees of Caesar, saying that there is a different king:
Jesus." It disturbed the crowd and the civic authorities[17] when
they heard these things, and after taking security from Jason
and the rest [of the community], they let them go.

Farther west in Macedonia on the Via Egnatia was "Amphipolis," a few miles inland from the point where the River Strymon
empties into the Aegean. The fact that the river looped around
this military post and commercial center positioned on a hill
gave the city its name, which means "around," or "on both sides
of the city." It was famed for fine textiles produced there and
for nearby gold and silver mines. "Apollonia," named for the
Greek god, Apollo, was also on the Via Egnatia, located just about
halfway between Amphipolis and "Thessalonica."

Excursus on Thessalonica

Although ancient temple fragments suggest that there was an
earlier city on the site, the dominant remains of Thessalonica,
located on the Via Egnatia in Macedonia, include items that
date back to the early hellenistic period. The city was founded
in 316 B.C.E. by successors of Alexander the Great and named
in honor of the last survivor of his royal family, Thessalonike.
There is abundant evidence that a sanctuary dedicated to Egyptian deities flourished there over an extended period, a scale
model of which was constructed following modern excavations
of the site. Both the architectural features and the evidences of
worship of various deities disclose a mixture of hellenistic and
Roman — as well as Egyptian and Greek — elements. Remains of
statues found there include heads of Isis and Sarapis, Dionysus
and Aphrodite. In the Roman period the city played an important role as refuge and support base for those engaged in the
struggle for achieving the primary leadership in the emergent
empire. These figures included Cicero, Pompey, Brutus, Cassius,
Anthony, and finally Octavian (Augustus). Evidence of local par-

ticipation in the cult of the emperor is provided by inscriptions concerning the temple of Caesar and a "priest of Roma" (the personified and divinized city), as well as by a statue of what appears to be a deified Augustus. The latter dates from the reign of Gaius Caligula (37–41 C.E.), and would have been evident when Paul was there. Dominant in this city was the devotion to the civic and the imperial deities, as well as to the traditional gods and goddesses, but inscriptions dating from as early as the first century C.E. indicate that there was also a disposition there to honor the deity believed to be beyond all the others: the Most High God (*theos hypsistos*). Some archaeological finds linked with the Egyptian Osiris may indicate that Thessalonica was not only a place where this god was worshiped, but also a center for promulgation of the cult of this deity.[18] The bearing of this cultural context on the work of Paul as evident in his letters to the Thessalonians is a subject of intense scholarly debate.[19]

•

Paul's earlier life and the extensive involvement he had in the Jewish communities of the Diaspora are essential factors in the strategy and effectiveness of his engagement with this "synagogue" community and its leaders in Thessalonica. His strategy involves "debate" concerning such issues as the identity of Jesus and his role in the purpose of God for the renewal of his people, and this kind of argument has its primary basis in his appeal to the "scriptures." Paul's exposition of them enables him not only to show the links of Jesus with these texts, but also to demonstrate that the cruel "suffering" and death that Jesus experienced have taken place, not as signs of divine punishment of someone who was a deviant from God's purpose, but wholly in fulfillment of scripture. Beyond these perceptions about the place of Jesus' crucifixion in the divine purpose of God is the declaration that equally in accord with the scriptures is Jesus' having been raised from the dead. It is the crucified, risen Jesus whom Paul now declares to his Jewish hearers, and to the Gentiles taking part in the life of the Jewish community, to be indeed the "Messiah": the chosen and anointed agent of God for the renewal of his people. Those hearers — and presumably, discussants — who respond in faith to Paul's claims about Jesus include "some Jews," but are preponderantly "devout Greeks."[20] Also, among those who "joined up" with the new movement are "not a few of the leading women," which recalls the experience of Paul in Philippi, where his first convert in Europe was a prosperous gentile business woman (16:11ff.). The importance of the new movement's attraction for upper-class women is evident in the letters of Paul, as well as in Acts.[21] Those Jews who were unpersuaded by Paul's arguments about Jesus as the Messiah are not only "jealous," but seek to develop a core of violent opponents and to construct a case against this movement as a threat to Roman authority and civic order. "Jason," the host to Paul and his colleagues, was their first target, since he appeared to be the chief supporter of what the opponents wanted to depict as an insurrectionist movement. These antagonists endeavor to intensify the impact of their case by having "certain evil men from the rabble" join their public demonstration. Both the character and the low social level of these supporters of the opposition would intensify the dramatic nature of the civic crisis that the enemies of Paul are seeking to conjure up for the local authorities, here designated as *politarchs*.[22]

The opponents' first line of attack is an effort to seize Paul and the others in the place where it is assumed they are staying: the "house of Jason." No further details about Jason are offered here, but in spite of his name being so common in that period, it is possible that he is the same Jason whose greetings are extended by Paul to the church in Rome (Rom. 16:21). Since Paul and the others are not in the house of Jason, it is likely that the latter offered his house as the place where the "synagogue" convened, rather than as only living accommodations for these visitors who brought the claim that Jesus was the "Messiah." The setting for this gathering of the new community in a relatively spacious private home matches the development that can be traced in general for the synagogue in the first century C.E. The charges that are brought against Paul and the movement he represents, though articulated by the local Jewish leaders, are not religious issues. While seeking to distance this group from traditional Judaism, which was accredited and given special status by Roman law,[23] their accusations are of a strictly political nature: Paul and his group are charged with violation of the "decrees of Caesar" and of designating a monarch other than Caesar: Jesus. This strategy of the opposition culminates in the Acts account of Paul's being accused before the Roman authorities in

Palestine and then sent to Rome for a hearing before Caesar (Acts 22:22–28:16).

Excursus on the House Church

Two recent studies of the evolution of the *ekklesia* from a meeting to a formal edifice are those of L. Michael White, *Building God's House in the Roman World*, and of Bradley Blue in *The Book of Acts in Its Graeco-Roman Setting*.[24] White's study includes analyses of synagogues, while Blue's is limited to churches, on the unsound assumption that the first-century synagogues were already formal, identifiable public structures.[25] The evidence points rather to the parallel development of church and synagogue from informal gatherings in the first century C.E. to the beginnings of formal public structures in the second and subsequent centuries, as White's analysis indicates. Blue's study is important, however, for his detailed examination of the evidence from the New Testament, and especially from Acts, for the settings of the early Christian gatherings that he depicts, but especially for his having brought together the evidence in the form of reconstructions based on archaeological excavations of buildings used by Christians as gathering places. The sites analyzed cover the period from the later first century to the fourth century. What is clear from this evidence is that the locus for the Christian community underwent considerable evolution in this period, and that the excavated results (combined with literary references) show four stages in the development of the church's base in buildings: (1) the house church; (2) adaptation of the interior of the house to serve the needs of the congregation (*domus ecclesiae*); (3) the erection of a sizable building to accommodate the growing congregation and its various needs (*aula ecclesiae*); (4) the basilica: the formal and elaborate structures built subsequent to the imperial support of Christianity from the time of Constantine onward. In Acts the only social and architectural structure evident as the gathering place of the members of the new community is, of course, the private house, that is, the house church. The antecedents of this phenomenon — or perhaps the evidence for its having developed by the later first century — appear in the gospel tradition. In Mark 14:12–16 the disciples are instructed to check with the *oikodespotes*, the master of the house, to confirm that a guest room (*kataluma*)[26] is ready for Jesus and that preparations have been made for the eating of the Passover in a "large upper room [*anagaion*], furnished and ready" (Mark 14:15). This description of the room is repeated in Luke 22:12, which reinforces the picture of this final meal of Jesus before his crucifixion as taking place in a spacious house belonging to a person of considerable substance. The dwelling places of members of the lower classes in the Roman world were called *insulae*, and consisted of a small room or two as a unit in a larger residential structure complex (analogous to modern apartment buildings), often with shops or workplaces on the lower floors. The house of the wealthier individual was called a *domus*, and consisted of a central courtyard accessible from the street by a gate, with sizable rooms opening off the court and one or more large rooms on the ground or second floor where extended families and guests could gather to eat and enjoy socialization. In addition, there would be several sleeping rooms, some of which would be available for short- or long-term guests. An analysis of the remains of residences in ancient Rome and Ostia shows that only 3 percent of the population lived in a *domus*.[27] That some of the earliest followers of Jesus were from the upper class is clearly indicated in Acts 1:13, where the disciples return to Jerusalem from witnessing the ascension of Jesus and take up residence (*katamenontes*) in upper-level quarters, which are called a *hyperoon*.[28] That is the term used in 9:37-39, when Tabitha, famed for her "good works and acts of charity," died and her body was placed on display in "the upper level." Her affluence is further indicated by the apparently numerous "garments and tunics" that she had made. The social function and the spacious facility of the *hyperoon* are made explicit in 20:9, where the community in Troas is gathered (*synegmenon*) to break bread in what is clearly a large structure, since the meeting is in a *hyperoon* on the "third floor." This is indicated when the young man who fell asleep and slipped out the window, plunging to the ground, is restored to life by Paul and the two return to the lofty upper room where the crowd has assembled. Similarly, in the earlier report of the experience of Peter at the house of Cornelius in Caesarea (10:1-48), this God-fearer has gathered a considerable crowd of "his relatives and close friends" who were "many in number" (10:24, 27). The issue discussed by Peter is not concerned with individual religious convictions, but the basis for shared life of the covenant community, and specifically with the inclusion of those ritually and ethnically excluded by traditional Jewish standards (10:28). That Peter was not merely paying a brief visit is clear from the detail that he stayed "several days" (10:48). In addition to Cornelius's prestige as a Roman army officer, this centurion is famed for his "charitable acts" — once more an indication of wealth among the members of the new community. The pattern of hospitality experienced by Paul on his travels confirms this picture in Acts of a strand of economic substance among the first generation of believers: Lydia (16:15); Aquila and Priscilla (18:1-3); Jason (17:5); the Philippian jailer (16:31-34); in Troas (20:6); in Tyre (21:4); in Caesarea (21:8ff.), and Mnason of Cyprus in Jerusalem, who is described as one of the disciples "from the beginning [*archaio mathete*]," which confirms the picture in Acts of the new community as having from the outset a significant base among the wealthy (21:16).[29]

•

Failing to find the bearers of this message in the house of Jason, the organized opposition "dragged" him together with some of those who had been persuaded by the good news about Jesus — "certain of the brethren" — before the "civic authorities." They depict these captives and the movement with which they are now identified as revolutionary: (1) they are overturning the established social and moral patterns that have come to characterize the human race; (2) their actions are in defiance of the "decrees of Caesar," which demanded that all those subject to Rome acknowledge the divinity of the emperor; (3) they claim that there is another monarch: their founder, "Jesus." All three of these accusations are indeed accurate implications of what the apostles are claiming about Jesus, but they also could be perceived by outsiders or opponents as threats to Roman law and order, and therefore those promulgating these teachings could be regarded as subject to harsh but just punishment by the "civic authorities." Nevertheless, in the dramatic development of the Acts story of the spread of the good news throughout the Roman world, the time for formal confrontation between the empire and the messengers of Christ has not yet come: it will take place in Rome itself, with hearings before Roman officials which will include formulation of the issues. For now, however, the authorities are content to take some "security" or bond from the local supporters of the apostles, as a guarantee that their disturbance of the peace will not continue, or perhaps simply that Jason would no longer serve as their host.

17:10–15: Paul and Silas in Beroea

> The brethren immediately sent Paul and Silas away by night to Beroea. When they reached there, they went into the synagogue of the Jews. These Jews were more high-minded than those in Thessalonica, and received the message with all good will, examining the scriptures daily to see if these things were so. As a result, many of them believed — not a few of both prominent men and women. But when the Jews of Thessalonica learned that the word of God was being preached by Paul in Beroea, they came there, arousing and stirring up the crowds. Then immediately the brethren sent off Paul toward the sea, but Silas and Timothy stayed there. Those who took Paul led him as far as Athens and, carrying with them his command to Silas and Timothy to come to him as quickly as possible, they left.

Even though those in Thessalonica who received in faith the message concerning Jesus included a considerable number of "leading women," the community as a whole is referred to by the author of Acts as "the brethren," which in spite of its masculine bias connotes an organic community or family of faith, rather than merely an aggregation of individuals. The next place of witness and encounter, "Beroea," is some fifty miles away from Thessalonica, on the route that leads south from Macedonia, past Mount Olympus through Thessaly, and down the coast toward Athens. As in Thessalonica, Paul's initial effort in Beroea is in the assembly of the Jews there. His hearers, however, are less contentious and more "high-minded," with the result that they not only listened to his message — here again designated as the "word of God"[30] — but were persuaded by it, including a significant number of prominent women and men. The penetration of the good news is not only ethnic as it is accepted among those of non-Jewish birth, but it is here also depicted as reaching sociologically and economically into the upper strata of Greco-Roman society. Those who came down from Thessalonica to cause trouble succeed in doing so, making similar charges of disturbance of the peace and Roman order, and eliciting support from the "crowds." Once again, the group of newly persuaded supporters decides that the only safe thing to do is to send off Paul as the one whose message was the chief source of trouble. "Silas and Timothy" remain, however, presumably in order to give further instruction to the newly formed community there. As guides and protectors, some from the community lead Paul south across Thessaly into Achaia, and on to Athens. The district of Achaia was so named because of a tribe of eastern people called Achaians who occupied this region in the thirteenth century B.C.E. They came to dominate the whole of Greece, which accordingly became known as the Achaian League until the Romans took over in the mid-second century B.C.E. Achaia thereafter was the designation for the southern half of the Greek peninsula; its chief cities were Athens and Corinth.

Excursus on Athens

Throughout the Greco-Roman period, Athens was renowned throughout the world as a center of art and philosophy. The most striking feature of the city is a great hill of rock that towers more than 500 feet above the city. On it was built in the fifth century B.C.E. a temple of Athens, the virgin goddess (*parthenos*), which is still known as the Parthenon. Subsequently, other shrines to other deities were also erected on this sacred mount, and below were temples of Asclepius, the god of healing, a theater dedicated to Dionysus, and a vast temple of Olympian Zeus, whose primary dwelling was on Mount Olympus far north of Athens. The temple of Zeus, one of the largest in the ancient world, was begun in the sixth century B.C.E., but was not completed until the second century C.E., in the reign of the emperor Hadrian. Of major significance in the city was the great *agora*, the public marketplace, which dated from the Greek period but was greatly enlarged by the early Roman emperors. Likewise famed and carefully reconstructed in modern times was the stone-pillared portico, the Stoa of Attalos. Adjacent to it was the Stoa of Zeus Eleutheros, which some scholars think was the regional center for the imperial cult. Other public buildings included the *bouleterion,* where the city council of five hundred convened, and the Odeum (or music hall), and later a library. An important feature, and an indication of the intellectual sophistication of Athens, was the great marble structure in the center of the city on the outside of which was a famous sundial, and within which was probably a water clock. Near the foot of the Acropolis was a lesser hill (about 350 feet high) dedicated to Ares, the god of war, whose Roman name was Mars. On this hill convened the smaller but powerful council of the Areopagus, which supervised judicial and political aspects of the city, as well as such public social features as education and religion. Some scholars doubt that the council was formally in session when Paul is reported as making a speech on this hill, but they assume that he used the prestige and the crucial role of this site in the life of the city as the arena in which to make his appeal to those who heard him there. In any case, the symbolism of the Areopagus as the primary place in Acts for intellectual encounter between the good news about Jesus and the Greco-Roman world is potent.

17:16–34: Paul in Athens

While Paul was awaiting them in Athens, his spirit was deeply troubled within him when he saw that the city was dominated by idolatry. Then he debated in the synagogue with the Jews and worshipers, and in the marketplace every day with those who chanced to be there. Certain of the Epicurean and Stoic philosophers engaged him, and some were saying, "What does this seed-picker want to say?" Others said, "He seems to be a proclaimer of strange divinities," because he was preaching Jesus and the resurrection. After having taken hold of him, they led him to the Areopagus, saying, "Could we know what this new teaching is that you are asserting? For you are presenting in our hearing certain things which are strange. Therefore we want to know something about what these things claim to be." All the Athenians and the foreign temporary residents spent their leisure in nothing but speaking or hearing some novelty.

So Paul stood in the midst of the Areopagus and said, "Athenian people, I observe that in every way you are most religious. As I was going along and observing your objects of worship, I found an altar on which is written, 'To an unknown god.' Therefore the one whom you worship without knowing I proclaim to you. The God who made the ordered world and all the things that are in it does not dwell in sanctuaries made by human hands, nor is he served by human hands, as though he were in need of something. He gives to everyone life and breath and everything. He made from one [original] being every nation of humans to dwell upon the entire face of the earth, having assigned the predetermined time periods and the boundaries of their dwelling place, so that they would seek God, if indeed they might grope for him and find him. And he really is not far from each one of us. For in him we live and move and are. Certain of your poets have said,

'Of him we are indeed offspring.'

"Since we are offspring of God, we ought not to suppose that the Deity is like gold or silver or stone, an image formed by the skill and imagination of a human. God looked beyond the times of ignorance, but now he instructs all humans everywhere to change their minds, because he has set a day in which he is going to judge with justice the whole inhabited world by a man whom he has designated, having provided assurance to everyone by having him raised from the dead." When they heard of the resurrection of the dead, some sneered, but some said, "We will hear from you again concerning this." Certain men joined him and believed, among whom were Dionysius the Areopagite and a woman by the name of Damaris, as well as others with them.

The central section of Athens was dominated by impressive edifices erected in honor of the traditional Greek deities: Athena, Ares, Olympian Zeus, Dionysus, Asclepius, including the Parthenon and the Areopagus (see excursus on Athens, p. 209 above). There was no avoiding the dominant role of idolatry in the first-century C.E. culture of Athens, and Paul is reported as being deeply "troubled" by this feature of the renowned city. The religious and intellectual challenges there also included engagement with the birthright "Jews" and Gentile seekers who joined them as "worshipers."[31] In the public gathering places such as the Stoa of Attalos he encounters proponents of popular philosophy of this period: "Epicureans and Stoics." The name of the latter derived from their practice of addressing the populace in such civic centers as these great public porticoes in Athens, called *Stoa*, where shopping and informal gatherings took place. Both these schools of philosophy were accessible to thoughtful people at large, not merely to refined, professional intellectuals, and both involved a way of life, rather than simply an abstract conceptual scheme.

Excursus on Epicurean and Stoic Philosophy

The fifth-century B.C.E. philosopher Democritus perceived the universe as having been produced by spontaneous interaction between what he called the full and the empty elements in the universe, the All. The flowing together of contiguous bodies whirling around in a vortex produced the earth and the other heavenly bodies: the sun, moon, and stars, with the earth at the center. This world stuff was perceived as divine and is, in essence, fire. The personal gods and goddesses of religion are personifications of natural phenomena and moral qualities. But there are also divine, anthropomorphic beings in the world, which account for human dreams, intuitions, and intimations of the future. Human life originated from mud, but the soul is the result of the clustering of atoms of fire, which give rise to human life and consciousness, and the loss of which results in death. Human consciousness is affected by the effluence of atoms from material objects, which impact the sense organs, but reason enables humans to see beyond sensory perceptions (which are always unreliable) and to discern ultimate reality. Images that reach the soul directly, rather than through the sense organs, enable the mind to perceive the otherwise unseen structure of reality. The highest goal of humans is the avoidance of pain and the experience of joy, which is not to be equated with sensual pleasure but with the enduring and gratifying contemplation of noble and true reality.

Building on this tradition, Epicurus (fourth century B.C.E.), whose writings survive only in fragments, developed a system of thought and a concept of human life akin in some ways to that of Democritus. This way of thinking is symbolized by his famous garden in Athens, where he lived and thought and taught. His concept of reality and of human destiny were taken up by Lucretius in the first century B.C.E., whose best-known writing, *On the Nature of Things*, was published by Cicero, the important Roman agent and advisor (106–43 B.C.E.). The goal of life is seen to be pleasure, but this must be defined and qualified by reason in order to avoid ultimate pain. True pleasure leads to comfort and serenity, which is not merely a promise for the future, but is accessible immediately to all who use will and wisdom to seek it. Those who cultivate this approach to life are protected from what is harsh and uncomfortable, and they find instead friends who joyfully share with them this mode of living. One must avoid politics or seeking public acclaim, living instead in the "garden of pleasure" developed by Epicurus, free from anxieties fostered by religions with their doctrines of divine judgment and their promotion of fear concerning death. Death is only endless sleep, and is as natural as life. Humans are free, and what divine beings there are in the world are unable to interfere with human life. Humans are to live by natural right or law, which leads to an exchange of positive attitudes and actions, and to a desire for self-preservation as well as common welfare.

The Stoic school of thought took its name from the Painted Colonnade (*Stoa Poikile*) in Athens where the philosopher Zeno (336–264 B.C.E.) taught for some twenty years. Unlike the Epicureans, Zeno declared that one should accept with courage and indifference the vicissitudes and painful experiences of life. The ruling principle of life is to live according to reason in independence of the human and social forces that are contrary to it. One must have the strength of mind and will to triumph over these negative aspects of human experience: the commitment must be total, and only those who are wise by Stoic standards can attain it. This can be gained by discerning the cosmic reason or mind (*logos*) which pervades and orders the universe. Later Stoics came to discern a divine purpose at work in human history, which would lead to the reward of the righteous and punishment of the wicked. Such a view of historical reality and human responsibility was adopted by some leading figures in the emergent Roman Empire, including Cicero (106–43 B.C.E.) and Seneca (4 B.C.E.–65 C.E.), both of whom served as advisors to the top Roman leaders. In his treatise *On the Nature of the Gods*, Cicero pictures the movement of the world as cyclical, which culminates in the "great year," when the heavenly bodies complete their prescribed course and return to their primal positions. In parallel with this cosmic cycle is the movement of human history, insights into which are given by the gods through oracles, auguries, dreams, and portents. The wise will see the developing course of history and be on guard to avoid inherent dangers. In his essay *On Divination*, Cicero develops this theme, commending the senate for its consultation of the Sibylline Oracles, and encouraging his contemporaries to avail themselves of knowledge of the cosmic plan known to the gods but discernible to earnest seekers. In the middle of the first century c.e., Seneca in his *On Providence* affirmed the universality of the divine order, and asserted that the difficulties humans experience are part of the process of divine discipline: "God hardens, reviews and disciplines those whom he approves, whom he loves."[32] In his letter *To Marcia on the Death of Her Son* he describes how the world renews itself over and over within the bounds of time, with cyclic conflagrations and renewal of the creation. The stars and all the fiery matter of the world will be caught up in a cosmic fire, and the souls of the blessed will be purged in this fire but then renewed to resume their place in the new order. This is in harmony with the Stoic cosmology which affirmed that there is a world-soul that permeates the universe, sustaining it and renewing it through the fire and cyclical renewal through which it passes.[33]

•

For his hearers in Athens, one of the most puzzling features of Paul's presentation of his point of view was his seeming invocation of an unusual pair of divinities: "Jesus and the resurrection." To the uninformed this probably sounded like a new set of male and female deities, since *Iesous* was obviously masculine, and *anastasis* was feminine. The analogies this combination would bring to mind would have been such divine pairs as Isis and Osiris, or Venus and Adonis. Paul's hearers wanted more information about these divinities, although they were initially inclined to dismiss them as inconsequential notions being peddled by a *spermologos*, who picks up scraps and is concerned with worthless items. It appears that Paul was taken to the "Areopagus" by the philosophers rather than by law-enforcement officers, and that there he was asked to clarify the subject matter of his "teaching." As noted above, there has been scholarly disagreement on the question whether "Areopagus" here refers simply to the hill where the council gathered or to the council itself.[34] It is most probable, however, that the author of Acts is picturing Paul as confronting the cultural and intellectual overseers at the center of the intellectual world, Athens, just as the book ends (Acts 28) with Paul about to confront the political and military center of the Roman world in his appeal to

Caesar. In his address to those on the Areopagus Paul begins with an ambivalent compliment when he commends his hearers because they are "most religious." The terms *deisidaimon* and *deisidaimonia* sometimes carry negative connotations ("superstition"), but in Philo and Josephus they are used with reference to religious convictions in a neutral or positive sense, though not exclusively so. Josephus, for example notes that it was their "deep religious convictions" that caused the Jews to stop defending themselves on the sabbath (*Ant.* 12.5–6), and elsewhere he writes of those with "religious commitments" (*deisidaimonias strateias, Ant.* 14.228). Philo, in setting forth the "conception and birth pangs of the virtues," appeals to those with "religious convictions" to "stop concentrating on their own and let themselves be transformed."[35]

It would be foolish and self-defeating to report Paul as launching his religious apology in this setting with an insulting remark about the Athenians as being "very superstitious." Instead, he is pictured as seeking to affirm elements of their tradition, which are consonant with his own. His first tactic is to employ a play on a word which he had found on a public inscription: *Agnosto theo.* Instead of worshiping an unspecified and hence unknown (*agnostos*) god, he declares that their tradition—and here he builds on the Stoic concept of the divine (as traced in the excursus on Epicurean and Stoic Philosophy)—affirms much that he would assert concerning God, who created and orders the world, who is sovereign over "heaven and earth," who is not located in humanly made "sanctuaries," who is in no way dependent upon human resources, and who has given life to "everything" and to people from "every nation" throughout the earth, and who orders the periods of time and the "boundaries" of human habitation. His argument is based on a paraphrase of Isa. 42:5, and pairs God's past act of creation with his present activity in the bestowal of "life and breath" on all humanity. The details of this declaration concerning the divine immanence and cosmic order have antecedents in various parts of the Jewish scriptures,[36] as well as counterparts in popular Stoic philosophy. God has done this in order that humans might "grope for him and find him." It is this God who is the true God, even though this inscription implies that he is unknown. He is the source and locus of life for everyone, and is accessible for those who truly "grope for him" and thus are able to "find him." This divine immanence is succinctly expressed in a line — "In him we live and move and are" —for which no source has been found,[37] so it may well have been merely a popular philosophical saying that Paul is here reported as quoting. The direct quote, "Of him we are indeed offspring," is from *Phaenomena* by Aratus of Soli (315–240 B.C.E.), and resembles the declaration in the *Hymn to Zeus* by Cleanthes (301–232 B.C.E.), where the god is directly addressed as kin of humans. Accordingly, no one should identify the deity with a physical object or representation, such as an idol, since such things are the product of human "skill and imagination." Scorn of idols and the folly of those who worship them are expressed vividly in the prophetic and wisdom tradition of Israel (especially Isa. 44:9–20 and Wisd. 13:10–19).

Resuming the argument based on the term for the "unknown" (*agnosto*) in the inscription, Paul declares that the epoch of "ignorance" (*agnoias*) has now come to a close as a result of God's disclosure of his purpose for humanity through Jesus. God has "looked beyond" this era of unknowing to the new era in which humanity will be judged "with justice" by the ultimate agent whom he has designated to serve as the "judge" of the whole human race (10:42). God's approval of this "man"[38] and of the results of this new divine initiative have been publicly and historically demonstrated by God's having "raised him from the dead." The appeal to recognize and participate in what God has done is universal: to "all humans everywhere." The theoretical notions of an archetypal human and of a coming divine judgment on humanity were familiar features in the Greek philosophical tradition, with elements of the Platonic and Stoic schools. But to base this claim on belief that God has "raised" someone "from the dead" was considered preposterous by some,[39] but led others to request additional information. Among those who were moved by Paul's address to identify with the new community was "Dionysius," a member of the prestigious Athenian council of the Areopagus. His name derived from one of the most sensational of the Greek deities, famed in this period as the god of wine and fertility, whose devotees formed cult groups that engaged in ecstatic, mystical activities through which they sought to gain identity with the god, transformation of their present existence, and participation in a life beyond death. Neither the name nor the role nor the identity of "Damaris" is attested elsewhere, but mention of her here shows that in the new community neither the traditional Greek nor Jewish norms that suppressed the public role of women were operative any longer.

18:1–17: Paul in Corinth

After these things he departed from Athens and went to Corinth. And he found a certain Jew by the name of Aquila — from Pontus by birth, but recently come from Rome with his wife Priscilla, because Claudius had decreed that all Jews were to depart from Rome. [Paul] went to them, and because they practiced a similar trade, he stayed with them and worked, for by trade they were tentmakers. He conducted discussion in the synagogue on every sabbath, and persuaded both Jews and Greeks.

When Silas and Timothy came down from Thessalonica, Paul was absorbed in preaching, bearing witness to the Jews that Jesus was the Messiah. Since they opposed him and uttered blasphemies, he shook out his garments and said to them, "Your blood is on your head! I am free [of responsibility]. From now on I am going to the Gentiles." Shifting from there, he entered the house of someone named Titius Justus, who was a worshiper of God whose house was adjacent to the synagogue. Crispus, the synagogue leader, trusted in the Lord, with his entire household. Many of the Corinthians, when they heard, believed and were baptized. By means of a vision in the night, the Lord said to Paul, "Do not be afraid, but speak and do not stop, because I am with you and no one shall attack you so as to cause you harm, for in this city there are many who belong to me." He stayed for a year and six months, teaching the word of God among them.

When Gallio was proconsul[40] of Achaia, the Jews made a concerted attack on Paul and took him before the tribunal, saying, "This man is persuading the people to worship God contrary to the law." As Paul was about to open his mouth, Gallio said to the Jews, "If it were something concerning a crime or unscrupulousness, O Jews, there would be a reason that I should bear with you. But since it is a matter of disputes concerning a subject and names and the law which are yours, you see to it yourselves. I do not wish to be an arbitrator of these things." And he drove them away from the tribunal. They all seized Sosthenes, the synagogue ruler, and beat him before the tribunal, but none of these things was of any concern to Gallio.

18:1–11: Paul's Effectiveness in Corinth

The city of Corinth is important, not only for the narrative in Acts, but also because among the residents of this city were the recipients of two of Paul's preserved letters — 1 and 2 Corinthians[41] — and because these letters provide considerable evidence about the sociocultural developments of churches in the wider Roman world.

Excursus on Corinth

Located about seventy miles west of Athens, Corinth is situated on the narrow isthmus that links the Peleponnesus with the main part of Greece. It was founded in the tenth century B.C.E., by 400 B.C.E. had a population of about 100,000, and in the first century C.E. was even larger. Destroyed by the Romans in 146 B.C.E., it was rebuilt by Julius Caesar, beginning in 44 B.C.E., and seems to have become the capital of the province of Achaia in 27 B.C.E. It was a cosmopolitan center, with its own two ports located on the east and west sides of the isthmus (Cenchrae and Lechaeum). To avoid the dangers of sailing around a perilous cape at the southern end of the Peleponnesus, a rock-hewn track was constructed across the peninsula in the sixth century B.C.E., on which ships were placed on platforms and dragged from one port to the other. The city and vicinity of Corinth have been excavated over the last hundred years by the American School of Classical Studies in Athens, with dramatic and detailed evidence produced concerning the structures and activities in the city. Located at the foot of the towering Acrocorinth (its summit about 1,500 feet above the fertile plain), the city was not only a lively mix of commercial and administrative enterprise, but also involved a variety of religions and culture.

Important culturally and economically for life in Corinth were the Isthmian Games, which dated back to the sixth century B.C.E., and included arts and music, as well as sports, which were based in a theater and a stadium. When the Romans restored the city, they populated it with freed slaves from various parts of the eastern Mediterranean, including Syria, Palestine, and Egypt, as well as former residents of Italy. Accordingly, many of the names linked with Corinth in the New Testament are of Latin rather than Greek origin. Ancient buildings and documents attest the diversity and vitality of religion in Corinth, although the reports by Strabo in his *Geography* and others that there were a thousand cult prostitutes at the temple of Aphrodite there are now regarded as unreliable tradition that may have derived from Corinth many centuries earlier. The deity worshiped in the grand Doric temple, dating from the sixth century B.C.E., is not known for certain, but may well have been Apollo.

Important and much visited by those from nearby and distant lands was the shrine of Asclepius, the god of healing, where in addition to the temple there were extensive facilities for lodging and clinics in which healing was effected. Not far to the east of Corinth was a center for the mystical cult of the goddess Demeter. A major element in religion in this city was a temple of Poseidon, the god of the sea. The Romans fostered there the cult of the emperor as divine, with a temple for that purpose in the main forum of the city. The presence of Jews in Corinth probably began as part of the resettlement of peoples there by the Romans in 46 B.C.E., and is attested by Philo in his *Embassy to Gaius* (281). The damaged inscription found there in modern times which probably read *"Synagoge ton Hebraion"* was not linked with any datable archaeological evidence, but on epigraphic grounds it seems to come from the late second century C.E. The account of the Jews in Acts 18 confirms the thesis that synagogues in the first century were meetings in homes, and that this practice was copied by the early Christians there and elsewhere. The shops found in the forum at Corinth are of the type that fits Paul's description of the workplace where he joined Aquila and Priscilla in tentmaking (18:3). Useful detailed descriptions of Corinth in this time are offered by J. Murphy-O'Connor in an article on Corinth in the *Anchor Bible Dictionary* and by Victor P. Furnish in his commentary, *II Corinthians.*[42]

•

First mentioned as those whom Paul met on arriving in Corinth are a pair with whom he had two important factors in common: they were Jews, and their occupation was that of "tentmakers," or leather-workers, which may have included preparing leather for use as tents.[43] "Aquila" was originally from "Pontus," the northern strip of Asia Minor bordering on the Black Sea which included Bithynia. In Acts 16:7 Paul is said to have been prevented from going through this region, although it is one of the areas where Peter reportedly addressed believers in Christ as "exiles of the Dispersion" (1 Peter 1:1) — which obviously builds on the Jewish tradition. "Aquila" and "Priscilla" — both of whom have Latin names — had recently come to Corinth from Rome as a result of the decree of "Claudius" expelling all Jews from the latter city, which occurred in the year 49/50 c.e. They became important co-workers with Paul, moving to Ephesus when Paul went there briefly (18:18–21), and carrying on a significant instructional role (18:26). Paul extends greetings from them in his first letter to the Corinthians (1 Cor. 16:19) and in his letter to the Romans commends them for the risk they took in his behalf (Rom. 16:3–4). Mention of them here implies that they had returned to Rome from Ephesus. Greetings are also sent to them in the Deutero-Pauline 2 Timothy (4:19), although there is no hint of their location.[44]

The brief description of Paul's relationship with this couple fits well the overall picture in Acts of his missionary strategy: he maintains his daily life by work and/or through the generosity of others, and when the Jews gather "on the sabbath," he is there among them making his case that "Jesus was the Messiah," addressing both Jews and gentile God-fearers or inquirers. The arrival of his former co-workers, "Silas and Timothy," from Macedonia (17:15) seems to intensify Paul's preaching activity, which in turn heightens the opposition toward his message from within the Jewish community. His response to the hostile reaction of the Jewish authorities, which his convictions about what God is doing through Jesus led him to regard as "blasphemies," is twofold: (1) the shaking of the "garments" is Paul's public act declaring his total separation from the way that these evil leaders have responded to Jesus; (2) his call for their "blood" to be on their own "heads" is a familiar motif in the historical books of scripture by which responsibility for violence and murder is laid on the evil perpetrator of the wicked action.[45] Significantly, this expression is also used in Matthew's bitterly critical picture of the Jewish leaders who perpetrated and took responsibility for the death of Jesus: "His blood be on us and our children" (Matt 27:25). The point in Acts is that Paul is "free of responsibility" to give primary attention to Jews as prospective members of the new community if they refuse to listen, and that he is now shifting his efforts to gentile inquirers. This shift of the primary focus of his mission from Jews to Gentiles is affirmed here as in 13:46, 22:21, 26:17–18, and 28:28. Yet it is crucial to the theme throughout Acts that what God is doing through Jesus and the new community is in continuity with the promises to God's people in the Jewish scriptures.

Accordingly, Paul continues to reach out and to have some success in persuading Jews concerning Jesus as "Lord," including the "leader of the synagogue" and "his entire household."[46] The implication of the change of locus for Paul's mission from the synagogue to the house next door is that both Jewish and early Christian groups were meeting in private residences that had sufficient space for public gatherings. The host for the new gathering, who has a pure Latin name, "Titius Justus," had been participating in the synagogue as a "worshiper of God," rather than as a proselyte, until he was persuaded by Paul's message about Jesus as the Messiah. He is obviously not the Titus who was associated with Paul in Antioch (Gal. 2:2) and who accompanied him on his second official visit to the leaders of the new community in Jerusalem. Those persuaded by Paul's message include not only "many Corinthians" of unspecified religious or ethnic background, but even the "synagogue leader, Crispus." His trust in the Lord was matched by that of his entire household, all of whom are then formally united with the new community through baptism. Encouraged by a vision in which the "Lord" Jesus appeared to him in the night, assuring him of protection from opponents and of the numerous members of the new community there, Paul is reported as remaining for a year and a half, during which he offers instruction in "the word of God." This seems to refer not only to his "teaching" the scriptures but also to his showing the correlation between the scriptures and the message of Jesus, which is now to be perceived to be "the word of God" to his new people.

18:12-17: Paul Encounters Jewish Opposition in Corinth

Junius "Gallio" Annaenus was the brother of L. Annaenus Seneca, who was important as a politician and author in the mid-first century C.E. The emperor Claudius (41–54 C.E.) appointed Gallio as proconsul of Achaia, with his administrative base in Corinth. An inscription found at Delphi indicates that he served in this capacity in 51 or 52, which provides a firm date for Paul's first stay in Corinth. In his *Life of Claudius* Suetonius reports Claudius's expulsion of the Jews from Rome in the ninth year of his reign, which would have been in 49. This case is a prime example of one in which the Roman judge must decide whether the unusual charge that has been brought is appropriate for his court of law. Gallio decided that it was a matter internal to Jewish law and practice, and was not subject to Roman jurisprudence.[47] Later in Acts, charges of disturbing the peace are brought in Ephesus (19:40) and in Caesarea (24:5), but Gallio insists that the conflict here is intra-Jewish. The ambiguity of the accusation is a central factor here and in the remainder of Acts: Paul's action allegedly "contrary to the law" involves only "disputes" within the realm of Jewish law, not infractions of Roman law. It is not clear whether Sosthenes, a leader of the Jewish community, was beaten by gentile onlookers or by his own people in their frustration at their failure to terminate the mission activity of Paul. In either case, Gallio simply ignored this spontaneous outburst of unofficial punishment. Excavations in Corinth have recovered the *bema* (tribunal) at which this incident is depicted as having occurred.[48] What is described here in Acts is an important feature in the overall case that the author is building to show that this new movement is based on the Jewish scriptures and traditions, so that it is not contrary to them and hence not subject to jurisdiction by Roman civil authorities. Rather, it should be regarded as legitimate on the basis of Roman legal recognition of Judaism. Above all it is not revolutionary in terms of threatening the Roman order — an issue that will occupy center stage for the last chapters of Acts (21–28). The effective outreach of the good news about Jesus to those beyond the Jewish community and the nonrevolutionary import of this message are both affirmed implicitly in the person of one of Paul's converts, whom he mentions as joining in the greetings to the church in Rome from the local community — almost certainly Corinth: Erastus, the city treasurer (Rom. 16:23).

18:18–23: Paul Returns to Antioch and Asia Minor

After remaining for some additional days, Paul bade farewell to the brothers [and sisters] and sailed off for Syria. With him were Priscilla and Aquila. At Cenchrae he cut off his hair, because he had made a vow. When they arrived at Ephesus, he left them. But he himself, after going into a synagogue, debated with the Jews. When they kept asking him to remain a longer time, he did not give his consent, but as he was bidding them farewell he said, "I shall return to you again, if God is willing." And he set sail from Ephesus. When he got off [the ship] at Caesarea, he went up and greeted the church, and then went on to Antioch. After spending some time there, he departed, passing through the Galatian region and Phrygia region, strengthening all the disciples.

The high mobility of the more prosperous members of the new community is indicated in the next move of "Priscilla and Aquila": accompanying Paul to "Antioch" and then to "Ephesus" (18:26), and subsequently returning to Rome (Rom. 16:3). As noted above, the repeated occurrence of this woman's name ahead of that of her husband may indicate her superior leadership role in the community. Another indication of Paul's continuing personal identification with his Jewish tradition is offered in the detail of his cutting off his "hair" prior to the ship's departure for Antioch in "Syria" from the eastern port of Corinth, "Cenchrae." The only explanation offered for this haircutting is that Paul had a "vow."[49] The most likely type of vow undertaken here by him is that of the Nazirites, which means "separatists": those consecrated to the Lord (Num. 6:1–3). A major sign of this commitment was to have the head shaved, following which the hair was not to be cut so long as one lived (Num. 6:5, 18).[50] The larger purpose of this ascetic action by Paul is not indicated directly in the text of Acts, but one may infer that it represents Paul's public declaration of his commitment to the Jewish tradition as he has come to understand it. The importance of this stance is evident in the activities of both Paul and Apollos as sketched in the remaining chapters of Acts. The details of Paul's itinerary are missing in this chapter, and although he and his companions set out for "Syria," the first city mentioned is "Ephesus," where his time and energy were spent "debating with the

Jews." There is no indication of the reason for Paul's refusal to remain there longer, but he promises to return, "if God is willing." That the work of God in Ephesus is most significant for the author of Acts is evident from the fact that the rest of Acts 18 and all of the next chapter are concerned with the events in this city. A compact account is first given of Paul's journey to Caesarea, where we are told that "he went up and greeted the church," which could have been in that city or in Jerusalem, but no details are offered for determining which it was. The implicit force of *anabas* ("went up") may be simply that he got out of the boat up on the land, but more likely it implies that he "went up" from the seacoast to the Judean hills where Jerusalem stands, although no account is offered of any exchange with the leaders of the new community in Jerusalem on this occasion. After returning to "Antioch," he retraces his earlier route through the central plateau of Asia Minor, including "Galatia and Phrygia." This time, however, he is not evangelizing but "strengthening the disciples."

18:24–28: Apollos Preaches and Teaches in Ephesus

A certain Jew by the name of Apollos — an Alexandrian by birth — arrived at Ephesus. He was a cultured man and effective in [the study of] the scriptures. He had been instructed in the way of the Lord and was burning with spiritual zeal. He was speaking and teaching accurately the things concerning Jesus, although he knew only the baptism of John. This man began to speak eloquently in the synagogue. When Priscilla and Aquila heard him, they took him aside and explained to him more accurately the way of God. When he wanted to cross over to Achaia, the brothers [and sisters] encouraged him and wrote to the disciples to receive him cordially. When he arrived, he was of great help to those who had believed through grace, because in public he refuted powerfully and completely the Jews, demonstrating by the scriptures that Jesus was the Messiah.

The vitality and diversity of the community in Ephesus are evident in the description of Apollos and his role there. He was born in Alexandria, where the vigorous intellectual life in the

Greco-Roman period powerfully influenced the Jewish community there, as is evident from the extensive works of Philo and from the tradition that the Septuagint was translated there.[51] Like Philo, Apollos had synthesized his involvement in that "culture" with the Jewish need to interpret the "scriptures," which for Philo involved allegorical and symbolic exegesis. Either while still resident in his native city or after moving to Ephesus, he had also been "instructed" in the "things concerning Jesus," which is here designated as "the Way of the Lord." As noted above, this phrase — which was used earlier in Jewish tradition with reference to the mode of life in accord with the Law of Moses — appears as a designation for the Jesus movement as a whole which Paul had been initially seeking to bring under judgment by the Jewish authorities in Jerusalem in order to destroy it (9:1-2). Apollos is said to have had accurate information about Jesus, but he did not understand the full import of baptism. Apparently he perceived only the preparatory role of this rite, without recognizing that the baptism in the name of Jesus brings the Holy Spirit, as John reportedly declared in the Q tradition drawn upon by Luke (3:16). The full import of this was conveyed to the community in Ephesus only after Paul's return there (19:1-7). The essential next phase of Apollos's instruction came through "Priscilla and Aquila." The immediate occasion and the subject matter of their additional teaching of Apollos is not specified here, but a plausible thesis is that he did not understand the factor that was so central for the writer of both Luke and Acts: the importance of the coming of the Holy Spirit. In Luke 4, shortly after the account of Jesus' receiving the Holy Spirit[52] at his baptism by John (3:22), from which he returns "full of the Holy Spirit" (4:1), he goes to Galilee "in the power of the Spirit" (4:14). Luke locates at this point in his narrative his expanded version of the story of Jesus' rejection at the synagogue in Nazareth (4:16-30), with its claim that the prophetic promise of one anointed by the Spirit of the Lord has been fulfilled. In the Acts narrative, it remains for Paul to return to Ephesus before the full significance of the coming of the Spirit is communicated to some of the "disciples" there. With the encouragement of the Ephesus community and with a letter of recommendation from them, Apollos shifts to "Achaia" his scripture-based program of "refutation" of Jewish counterclaims about Jesus' messiahship.

19:1–10: Paul at Ephesus

It happened that while Apollos was in Corinth, Paul went through the upper regions and came to Ephesus. He found there some disciples and said to them, "Did you receive the Holy Spirit when you believed?" But they said to him, "We did not even hear that there is a Holy Spirit!" He said, "For what purpose, then, were you baptized?" They said, "The baptism of John." Then Paul said, "John baptized with the baptism of repentance, telling the people that they should trust in the one who was to come after him: this one is Jesus." When they heard this, they were baptized in the name of the Lord Jesus. And after Paul placed his hands on them, the Holy Spirit came upon them and they began to speak in tongues and prophesied. All the men were about twelve in number.

After going into the synagogue, he kept speaking boldly, discussing and arguing convincingly concerning the kingdom of God. But since certain persons were stubborn and refused to believe, defaming the Way before the assembled crowd, he withdrew from them, took away the disciples, and carried on discussions in the lecture hall of Tyrannus. This went on for two years, with the result that all who resided in Asia heard the message of the Lord, Jews as well as Greeks.

Having crossed through the "upper regions" of Galatia and Phrygia, which were on the lofty plateau in central Asia Minor (18:23), Paul arrived in Ephesus, where the good news about Jesus had already been proclaimed — apparently not through the apostles, but through Jewish converts from Rome (Priscilla and Aquila; 8:19) and from Alexandria (Apollos; 18:24–25).

Excursus on Ephesus

With a population of more than 200,000, Ephesus at the end of the first century C.E. was either the third largest city in the Roman Empire (after Rome and Alexandria) or the fourth (after Antioch-on-the-Orontes). But it was recognized as outstanding in its cultural and intellectual importance for the contemporary world. This is epitomized in Philostratus's somewhat later description of Ephesus as

a city which took the basis of its people from the purest At-
tic source, and which grew in size beyond all other cities
of Ionia and Lydia, and stretched herself out to the sea,
outgrowing the land on which she is built, and is filled
with studious people, both philosophers and rhetoricians,
through whom the city is strong, not by her cavalry but by
the tens of thousands of her populace in whom she extols
wisdom.[53]

Ephesus was economically strong and developed significantly in
the Roman period because of its location at the point where
major routes from the Middle East and from the eastern and
southern provinces of Asia Minor reached the sea. Commerce
between these lands and the ports of Greece and Rome was
substantial. The adjoining valley of the Cayster River included
verdant fields for producing food. The basic layout of the city
was set during the reign of Augustus, but the most impressive
rebuilding and enhancement came in the second century during the reigns of Trajan and Hadrian.[54] A major factor in the
continuing prosperity of the city was the location there of the
temple of Artemis, the Greek name for what was likely the local version of the fertility goddess worshiped throughout Asia
Minor. She has been identified by some scholars with Cybele,
the Great Mother of the gods.[55] In Rome, however, Artemis was
known as Diana. She was believed to be the source of life in the
natural world, as well as the instrument of mystical renewal of
human life. Her sixth-century B.C.E. temple was destroyed, and
then replaced in the fourth century B.C.E. by a structure initi-
ated by Alexander the Great, which was subsequently expanded
and became so vast and splendid that it was regarded as one of
the Seven Wonders of the World, and over the subsequent centuries was visited by huge numbers of worshipers.[56] Statues of
the goddess have been found in Ephesus and elsewhere, in several of which she is pictured with bulbous appendages on her
chest, which may be either breasts or other symbols of fertility. The temple also served as a depository of wealth, much of
it gained from pious visitors, but also huge sums deposited for
safekeeping.[57] Called the Artemision and located north of what
became the main part of the city in Greco-Roman times, the
temple was at various times connected to the city center by different roads along which solemn processions moved honoring

the goddess. Another important temple was dedicated by Domitian in 89/90 C.E. to the *Sebastoi*, the Roman emperors of the Flavian dynasty,[58] thus indicating the major importance in this metropolis of the acknowledgment of the divinity of the emperor. Other major structures in the city were the theater, the civic agora, where the populace could gather, overlooked by the *bouleterion*, where the city council met, and the library of Celsus, where it is estimated that as many as ten thousand volumes were kept.

The rate of infant and childhood mortality in the ancient world was so high that urban centers did not grow in numbers by natural process of increase but by immigration of people from other lands and cultures. Accordingly, the dramatic growth of Ephesus in the Roman period was essential for the economic development of the city, but created social tensions through the influx of people from very different cultures. At the same time, many of the city officials named on public inscriptions are not of local origin, and the same is true of many benefactors whose names are publicly inscribed. Other references on these inscriptions are to resident Jewish groups.[59] The ethnic, religious, and cultural complexities of this great city are most evident.

•

The instruction of the members of the new community in Ephesus was already in progress, though with some serious limitations, which Paul feels he must address. He finds there some who were "disciples," but their instruction concerning the basis for their participation in the new community is sadly lacking, in that they are wholly ignorant of and have had no experience of the "Holy Spirit." Paul explains to them that, important as the work and message of "John the Baptist" were in the purpose of God, they were purely preparatory. The act of "repentance" to which John called people was the initial stage in their preparing themselves for the "one who was to come after him," who of course was "Jesus," in whose "name" they were now to be "baptized." In addition to carrying out the baptismal rite with the use of the essential formula, "in the name of the Lord Jesus," Paul also performs the rite that symbolizes and effects the transfer of divine power: the laying on of "hands." The efficacy of his actions is confirmed inwardly by the receipt of the "Spirit," and publicly by the manifestation of the Spirit through the gift of tongues, as is described as occurring on the Day of Pentecost (Acts 2:4) as well as by the prototypical event at the house of Cornelius when Gentiles first responded to the good news about Jesus and through baptism were linked with the new community (10:46).[60] There is no hint here of the distinction in function and value for the community which Paul makes between the gift of tongues and the gift of prophecy as respectively private divine communication and public upbuilding of the community (1 Cor. 14:1-5). Here both gifts are seen as confirmation of God's presence and power by the Spirit. The symbolism of the number of those renewed by the Spirit — "twelve" — is clear: they are sharing in the life of the new Israel, and in conformity to the number of the initial core of followers of Jesus. The description of this gap in the insights and experience of various members of the new community points up the acknowledgment by the author of Acts that the movement was by no means uniform in convictions and experience, but that the members need to bridge their differences and to engage in mutual support. In spite of the earlier declarations of Paul that he is shifting his focus from Jews to Gentiles (as in 13:46 and 18:6), Paul attends the meeting (*synagoge*) of the Jews in Ephesus, where over an extended period ("three months") he debates persuasively concerning how God is establishing his "kingdom" through Jesus. The results are impressive, in terms of both the large numbers of those who come to the debates and the intensity of the opposition and disbelief that the discussions evoke, as well as the long period of time ("two years") during which these vigorous discussions continue. When he withdraws from this series of controversial exchanges, the author tells us that the "message of the Lord" had permeated the entire region, reaching both Jews and Gentiles. Once more, the symbolic importance of this development is of great importance for the author of Acts: the message and the manifestations of its power to renew human lives have gone out initially in Jerusalem, the center of the Jewish tradition, in Athens, the center of the intellectual tradition of Greece, and now in Ephesus, a major center of Greco-Roman religiosity in both its personal and political dimensions. Still to come is the great confrontation that is to take place with the political powers, first in Jerusalem and vicinity, and ultimately in Rome.

19:11-20: Magic and Miracle

And God did extraordinary wonders through the hands of Paul, with the result that face-cloths and aprons were carried off from [contact with] his skin to those who were sick, and the illnesses left them and the evil spirits departed. And certain of the itinerant Jewish exorcists attempted to invoke the name of the Lord Jesus upon those who had evil spirits, saying, "I adjure you by the Jesus whom Paul preaches...!" There were seven sons of a certain high priest, Sceva, doing this. But the evil spirit responded and said to them, "I know Jesus and I am acquainted with Paul, but who are you?" And the man in whom was the evil spirit pounced on them, took control of them all, and overpowered them, so that they fled out of that house naked and wounded. This became known to all those who resided in Ephesus, both Jews and Greeks, and fear fell on all of them, and they glorified the name of the Lord Jesus. Many of those who had believed were coming and acknowledging and disclosing their practices. A number of those who had performed these magical acts assembled their books and burned them up in front of everyone. They counted up the value of them and found it was fifty thousand pieces of silver. Thus the word of the Lord grew mightily and became powerful.

Yet another mode of divine confirmation of the good news is provided through the "extraordinary wonders" which are done by "God," whose instrument is "the hands of Paul." The power of this divine activity is so great that the effort is made by many to take advantage of it, even though they do not share belief in the message that Paul is proclaiming. In keeping with the basic conviction in the Greco-Roman world that the power of magic rests on the use of effective techniques and formulae,[61] these nonbelievers want to benefit from the healing power that has been publicly demonstrated through Paul. Some are able to reap beneficial results in the form of healings and exorcisms simply through the transfer of power by means of cloths that had touched Paul and then were taken to those in need of healing. But ironically, seven "Jewish exorcists,"[62] sons of a "Jewish high priest," try to borrow Paul's spectacularly effective technique by invoking what they consider to be the powerful magic formula he had employed: the name of "Jesus." The esoteric knowledge necessary for performing exorcisms is highlighted by Josephus in his depiction of Solomon (*Ant.* 8.45–48), who is said to have prepared incantations and formulae by which demons could be expelled. The practice is described by him in detail as enduring through Jewish exorcists, who continued to employ the name and techniques transmitted by Solomon. There are no records of a Jewish high priest by this name, "Sceva," which is probably not an actual name but a variant of the Latin epithet, Scaeva, meaning "left-handed." Accordingly, the claim of the exorcists to be the son of a Jewish high priest by this name is in every way dubious, and may be intended as an indication of the falsity of their alleged family connection. But it is clear that exorcism was a feature of mainstream Judaism in the first century C.E. What is distinctive here is twofold: the declaration that the instrument of superior power in expelling "evil spirits" is "the name of the Lord Jesus"; and the evidence that this name can be invoked only by those whose identity is linked with this name. The violent reaction of the spirit-possessed man and the consequent wounding of those who seek to exploit the "name" show the peril of abuse of this power. With the irony characteristic of the author of Acts, this self-serving effort in exploitation of the "name" of Jesus on the part of the exorcists results in that name being "glorified" by the mass of Jewish and gentile populace in the city of Ephesus. But further, those performing exorcism and "magical" practices publicly "confess" their misdeeds and proceed to destroy the "books" that contain the magical formulas on which they have relied. The seriousness of the new commitment to Jesus by an unspecified "number" of these practitioners and their repudiation of their past actions are evident in their common act of destruction of these essential tools worth "fifty thousand pieces of silver," which is a huge sum regardless of the specific type of coin that is assumed in the narrative. The result of this mode of manifestation of divine power and purpose through the name of Jesus, in spite of the perverted efforts of some, is the dramatic increase in the might and power of "the word of the Lord."

19:21-41: The Riot at Ephesus

After these events took place, Paul determined in the Spirit
to pass through Macedonia and Achaia, and then go on to
Jerusalem, saying, "After I have been there, it is necessary for
me also to see Rome." Having sent into Macedonia two of his
assistants, Timothy and Erastus, he himself spent some more
time in Asia.

At that time there took place not a little disturbance concerning the Way. For a certain man by the name of Demetrius,
who was a silversmith making silver portable shrines of Artemis, promoted not a little profit for the craftsmen. Bringing
them together he said to those engaged in similar work, "Men,
you know that our earning a living is from this trade. We see
and hear that, not only in Ephesus but also in nearly all of
Asia, this Paul has persuaded and changed the minds of a
considerable crowd, saying that those things which are made
by hands are not really gods. This is a danger for us — not
only that our line of business may come into disrepute, but
also that the temple of the great goddess Artemis may be
considered as nothing and thus she may be deprived of her
magnificence, which is revered by the whole of Asia and the
inhabited world." When they heard this and became filled with
rage, they cried out saying, "Great is Artemis of the Ephesians!" And the whole city was full of tumult. They rushed
with one purpose into the theater, dragging with them Gaius
and Aristarchus, the Macedonians who were Paul's traveling
companions. Paul wanted to go in among the crowds, but
the disciples would not let him. Certain of the Asiarchs, who
were friendly toward him, sent to him and urged him not to let
himself be taken into the theater. Some shouted one thing or
another, for the assembly was confused, and the majority did
not know why they had been convened. Some joined in the
support of Alexander, whom the Jews put forward. Alexander
signaled with his hand, since he wanted to present his case
to the people. But when they realized that he was Jewish,
like one voice there kept coming from all of them for two
hours, "Great is Artemis of the Ephesians!" When the clerk
had quieted the crowd, he said, "Men of Ephesus, who among
humanity does not know that the city of Ephesus is temple-
keeper for the great Artemis and of the image which fell from

heaven? Since these things are not to be contradicted, it is necessary for you to be restrained and not to do anything rash. For you brought these men who are neither desecrators nor those who blaspheme our goddess. So if Demetrius and the craftsmen who are with him have a charge against any-one, the courts are in session and there are proconsuls: let them bring charges against one another. But if you are seeking something further, let it be decided in the regular assembly. For we are risking being charged with rioting today, since there is no charge which we are able to produce as a rationale for this seditious gathering." When he had said this, he dissolved the assembly.

The journey that the "Spirit" moves Paul to plan is wholly in keeping with the overall thesis of Acts as to the divine purpose in spreading the good news throughout the world. This is evi-dent from the designation of the cities of Jerusalem and Rome, which are, respectively, the center of authority and tradition for understanding the identity of the people of God, and the center for the political structure of the world. Paul is ultimately going to "Rome," though he must first return to "Jerusalem." But his planned route is also to take him through the center of Greek culture: "Macedonia and Achaia." His strategy of designating co-workers to prepare for his visits and to follow up on his mission activity — as when Silas and Timothy remained in Beroea (17:15) and Priscilla and Aquila preceded him to Ephesus (18:18) — is once more operative. In addition to "Timothy," who was Paul's agent in Corinth according to 1 Cor. 4:17, he here is reported as sending "Erastus" as well. The latter, not previously mentioned in Acts, has the same name as the city treasurer in Corinth who joined Paul in extending greetings to the church in Rome (Rom. 16:23).[63] If the same individual is assumed to be referred to in all of these texts, the author of Acts is once again making his point about the sociocultural breadth of the impact of the good news on the Roman world, since a man of such significance in a major city has become Paul's agent in developing the new communities.[64] The interface between the new movement and the culture — po-litical and religious — of the Greco-Roman world is dramatically demonstrated in this account, and especially in what follows.

The hostility that is seen as arising in Ephesus toward "the Way"[65] is economically based: the movement is perceived as a threat to the means of livelihood of those who make the popular images of the local goddess, Artemis. These were probably silver portable shrines of Artemis, the sale of which to pious visitors devoted to this goddess was a major factor in the local economy. None of these silver shrines has been found, but images of the goddess positioned in terra-cotta niches are well known, and a bilingual (Latin and Greek) inscription from Tarentum refers to an aedicule dedicated to Diana/Artemis.[66] Demetrius, whose business it was to make and sell these sacred objects, states his conviction about the impact that Paul's message about God and his dismissal of Artemis as divine are going to have, not only in "Ephesus" but throughout "nearly all of Asia." This term is probably intended to include the whole of what is now known as Asia Minor, since Acts has already reported his successful mission in the wider reaches of Asia Minor, rather than merely in the Roman province of Asia in the vicinity of Ephesus. Paul is denying the divinity of the sacred objects he and his colleagues earn their living by fashioning, and has discredited the chief local asset and source of pride: the "temple of the great goddess." As defamation of a major attraction that was bringing the devotees of Artemis and sightseers eager to see her great shrine, Paul's message is perceived as totally subversive. The ensuing "tumult" causes an uproar throughout the city, and the people crowd spontaneously into the great theater. The two terms that refer to this gathering are *demos* and *ekklesia;* the first indicates that it is open to the people as a whole, and the second that they have been called together (from *ek* + *kaleo*) in public assembly. In this period both words appear in literary and inscriptional sources throughout the Greco-Roman world as standard terms for describing (1) the populace and (2) its formal convocation for decisions affecting the common life. Since the people are not observing due process in condemning Paul, however, their actions are in violation of Roman law.

Excursus on Local Governmental Systems in the Roman Period

When the Romans took control of Greece and Asia Minor, beginning in the second century B.C.E., each free city was given the right to form a council and an assembly. The former was comprised of men of wealth and power in the district, while the assembly included all who possessed citizenship. These groups were charged with enacting legislation to establish and maintain order among the regional populace, and to elect magistrates to enforce the local laws. Issues that affected the maintenance of peace or that seemed to threaten Roman ultimate control were reserved for the Roman authorities. These might be the provincial leaders[67] or, in the event of a major challenge, the Roman senate and the principal ruler. From the outset, the tendency was developing to lessen the power of the assembly and to increase that of the council. Local leaders in cities and their surrounding district included "politarchs" (Acts 17:6)[68] and "Asiarchs" (Acts 19:31).

The major terms for the organizational structures of cities in the Roman period, especially in regions like Asia Minor dominated by Greek culture, are *boule, gerousia, synedrion.* The citizens as a whole, who constituted the assembly, are most commonly referred to in the Greco-Roman sources as the *demos* = "people" or with reference to the gathering of the citizens — a more elite group — for the purpose of reaching formal group decisions, as the *ekklesia* = "assembly." Both terms are used in Acts in connection with this feature of city life. It is before the spontaneously gathered "assembly" of the populace that the discussion about these alleged "blasphemers" takes place; but the "town clerk" declares that the ultimate decision about the punishment of these alleged violators of law and order must be addressed in the presence of the formally convened "assembly." Above all, he notes that there is a formal judicial process that relies on the "courts" and the local Roman officials, "the proconsuls," to render justice in such matters. They have not yet been appealed to, but the crowd is seeking to reach a decision of condemnation by an illegitimate popular conclave, which will open the participants to the charge of "rioting." Clearly, the author wants to make the basic point that the apostles represent a movement that has not been analyzed by due legal process and thus formally declared to be contrary to Roman law.

20:1–12: Paul's Return Visit to Greece

After the uproar quieted, Paul summoned the disciples, and after having exhorted them and bade them farewell, Paul departed to go to Macedonia. When he had passed through those districts and encouraged them with extended discourse, he arrived in Greece, where he spent three months. Since a plot against him was made by the Jews as he was about to take off for Syria, he came to a decision to return through Macedonia. Sopater of Beroea, son of Pyrrhus, accompanied him, and from the Thessalonians, Aristarchus and Secundus; Gaius from Derbe, and Timothy; the Asians were Tychicus and Trophimus. These went on before and were awaiting us at Troas, but we sailed from Philippi after the days of Unleavened Bread, and after five days came to them at Troas, where we remained for seven days.

On the first day of the week, as we were gathered for breaking bread, Paul led a discussion with them, since he was about to leave them on the next day, and he prolonged his speech until midnight. There were many lights in the upper chamber where we were assembled. A certain young man named Eutychus was sitting at the window. He fell into a deep sleep as Paul was continuing the discussion even longer, and having been overcome by sleep, he fell down from the third story and was picked up dead. But Paul went down, fell on him, embraced him and said, "Don't be distressed, because his life is in him." After [Paul] went up and broke bread and partook of it, he conversed with them for a considerable time, until dawn, and so he left. They led away the young man alive, and were greatly encouraged.

When the furor caused by the devotees of Artemis and the makers of her images subsided, Paul gave final encouragement and instruction to the "disciples" among the people of Ephesus who were allied with the new movement in the name of Jesus, and then departed. He crossed over the Aegean to his former areas of evangelism and instruction: first in the northern region, "Macedonia," and then in the central section of "Greece." The opposition that developed on the part of some "Jews" led him to set out for "Syria" by way of "Macedonia," accompanied by delegates from the new communities of followers in that region, including "Sopater of Beroea," two from "Thessalonica" ("Aristarchus" and "Secundus"); others accompanying him were from Asia Minor: "Gaius" from "Derbe"; "Timothy," whose city of origin is not here mentioned, but who was presumably from Lystra (Acts 16:1–3); "Tychicus and Trophimus" (whose names mean respectively, "lucky" and "healthy") are mentioned in the Deutero-Pauline writings as being sent by Paul to carry letters (Eph. 6:21; Col. 4:7) or as accompanying him on his travels (2 Tim. 4:12, 20; Titus 3:12). Trophimus, who is from Ephesus, became a major cause of hostile reaction to Paul in Jerusalem (21:27–29; see below). These companions sailed ahead and awaited Paul at "Troas" (see the notes at 16:11). Here the narrative resumes the first-person-plural style, which implies that an unnamed companion of Paul continued with him on the journey back to Jerusalem (20:4–16).

Paul's delaying his voyage by remaining in "Philippi" for the seven-day Feast of "Unleavened Bread" is an additional indication by the author of Acts that Paul did not make a radical break with the Jewish traditions in which he had been reared.[69] Yet his firm commitment to the Jesus tradition is also immediately evident in his sharing in the "breaking of bread" on the "first day of the week"—the new "breaking bread" celebration of community which replaces the traditional Passover, according to Jesus' interpretation of the shared bread and cup as the ground of the "new covenant" in the Lukan account of the Last Supper (Luke 22:15–20). The combination of an exceedingly extended address by Paul, the lateness of the hour, and the scarcity of oxygen as a consequence of the many lights in the "upper chamber" resulted in the falling asleep of the *young man*—ironically named "Good Luck" (*Eutychos*)!—and his plummeting out the window and down three stories to his death. Correctly confident that through physical contact the young man would be restored to life and only briefly interrupting his lengthy speech, Paul continued his participation in the eucharist and his exhortation of the community "until dawn." The members of the community were "greatly encouraged" by this dramatic manifestation of divine power through Paul, resulting in the triumph over human frailty and death.

20:13–16: Paul Continues His Journey toward Jerusalem

Proceeding to the ship, we journeyed toward Assos, having in mind to take Paul on board there. For this is what he had ordered, since he was himself intending to travel by land. When

he met us in Assos, we took him on board and came to
Mitylene. Sailing off from there, on the next day we arrived opposite Chios. On the following day we came near Samos, and
a day later we came to Miletus. For Paul had decided to sail
by Ephesus, so that he might not have to spend time in Asia.
He was hurrying so that if possible he might be in Jerusalem
on the Day of Pentecost.

The route taken by the ship as it sailed down the western coast of
Asia Minor began at Troas, and then went a short distance south
to "Assos," which Paul reached by land and where he boarded
the ship as it continued down to the island of Lesbos, where
it called at "Mitylene." Proceeding south it passed the island
of "Chios" and the entrance to the harbor of Ephesus (to the
east) as well as the island of "Samos," before stopping at "Miletus," the major city at the mouth of the Maeander River. It once
had four harbors, and three extensive market areas (*agora*), a
great council chamber (*bouleterion*), baths, stadium, and a theater, in which was found an inscription identifying a section
as the "place of the Jews and God-fearers."[70] Josephus attests an
appeal by a Roman official of the first century B.C.E. to the "magistrates, council and people" of Miletus to grant Jews there the
right to observe the sabbath and perform their traditional rites
(*Ant.* 14.244–46). Paul's avoidance of a stop at Ephesus was part
of his plan to assure his reaching Jerusalem prior to the next crucial date in the Jewish sacred calendar: "the Day of Pentecost."
Once again, Acts attests Paul's devotion to aspects of Jewish piety
and tradition.

20:17–38: Paul's Conference with the Ephesian Elders

From Miletus he sent to Ephesus and summoned the elders
of the church. When they were present with him, he said to
them, "You know how, from the first day that I set foot in
Asia, I was with you all the time, serving the Lord with all mod-
esty, and you know of the tears and testings which happened
to me through the plots of the Jews; how I held back not at
all from declaring to you the things that would be helpful, or
from teaching you publicly and in private houses, bearing witness to the Jews and Greeks concerning repentance toward

God and faith in our Lord Jesus. See! Now I am going to Jerusalem, bound by the Spirit, not knowing the things that will happen to me there; only that the Holy Spirit testifies to me in every city, saying that fetters and afflictions threaten me. But I do not take any account of my life as having value for myself, so long as I complete my course and the ministry which I received from the Lord Jesus to bear witness to the good news of the grace of God. See now! I know that all of you among whom I have gone about, preaching the kingdom, will no longer see my face. For I did not shrink from proclaiming the whole counsel of God to you. Take care of yourselves and of the whole flock in which the Holy Spirit has placed you as overseers to shepherd the church of God, which he gained through the blood of his Own. I know that after my departure there will come in among you savage wolves, not sparing the flock, and from among yourselves men will arise, speaking perverted things so as to pull away the disciples after them. Therefore, watch out! Remember that for three years, day and night, I did not stop warning each one with tears. And as things are now, I commend you to God and to the word of his grace, which is capable of building you up and giving you an inheritance among all those who are consecrated. I had no desire for the silver or gold or garments of anyone. You yourselves know that these very hands served my own needs and the needs of those who were with me. In every way I have demonstrated to you that it is necessary by laboring in this way to come to the aid of those who are powerless, and to remember the words of the Lord Jesus, that he said, 'It is more blessed to give than to receive.'" And when he had said these things, he went down on his knees and prayed with all of them. They all began to weep loudly and, falling on his neck, they kissed him, filled with pain most of all by the word he had spoken that they were not to see his face again. And they took him to the boat.

About thirty miles north of Miletus across the Maeander River was Ephesus, from which Paul sent and summoned the "elders" of the church, apparently assuming that he could more speedily deal with them there than with the community as a whole in their own city. Paul's words to them serve as an evaluative and interpretive summary of his activities from the beginning in the province of "Asia." This designation was used for the three regions — Mysia, Lydia, and Caria — through which rivers flow down from the Anatolian plateau, their valleys giving access to the interior of Anatolia and the districts to the east (Galatia, Pontus, Cappadocia). It is to Paul's activity in Ephesus, a major western city in Asia, that attention is given in this Acts passage and which serves as a model for Paul's entire apostolic career. His activity has been characterized by suffering, difficulties and humiliation that he has undergone (especially at the instigation of Jewish opponents), but this did not inhibit him from "declaring" the good news about Jesus or from "teaching" the members of the new community about the ground and import of their "faith." The locus of his activities included both public arenas and "private houses," which is where at this time both Jewish and nascent Christian groups gathered for worship and study. His hearers were both "Jews and Greeks," who were urged to change their understanding of God ("repentance") and come to trust in Jesus as God's agent of renewal ("faith").

Paul now senses that his return to Jerusalem, while undertaken by the guidance of the "Spirit," is to have most fearful and painful consequences for him, including imprisonment and punishment everywhere he goes. His concern is not for ease or extension of his life, but for completion of what he regards as the divine calling that he seeks to carry out. The major theme of his preaching and teaching, as well as the motivating force behind his dedicated, sacrificial mode of life he epitomizes as "the grace of God." He does not hesitate to proclaim the complete message ("whole counsel of God"), regardless of the controversy or hostility that it evokes. Both these elements are important for the overall aim of the author of Acts: (1) to make his case that the effective factor in the relationship that God is developing anew with his people is not their conformity to any specific set of legal obligations, but their primary reliance upon what has been provided for them through Jesus by "the grace of God"; (2) Paul's understanding of the divine purpose is not presented as based on selective features of the biblical tradition or of the Jesus tradition, but as encompassing "the whole counsel of God." Thereby he has discharged his responsibilities as the bearer of the message about Jesus as the ultimate agent of God for renewal of his people.

Paul then warns these leaders of the church that they should expect trying experiences, analogous to his own. They are responsible for their own spiritual condition, as well as for that of the community ("flock") in which they have been given leadership roles. This metaphor for the community is employed in the Lukan word of Jesus, "Do not be afraid, little flock" (Luke 12:32), where the share in the kingdom is God's gift to the community. Here the figure is extended by the designation of their leadership role as "overseers" (= *episkopoi*) who are to "shepherd" the people of God under their care, as well as by the image of their having been purchased or gained at a severe cost[71] and by the warning about the wild beasts ("savage wolves") that will attack them, as well as the severe conflicts and controversies that will develop within the group. The cost expended by God to obtain the "flock" was "the blood of his Own": the sacrificial death of Jesus as the unique son of God.

Excursus on the Blood of Jesus

Blood is perceived in the Old Testament tradition as the essence of life, as explicitly stated in Deut. 12:23: "Be sure you do not eat the blood [of a sacrificial animal], for the blood is the life." It was therefore perceived as the symbol and agency of the covenant relationship between God and his people, as when Moses responds to the commitment of the people as they are hearing the book of the covenant by sprinkling them with blood and declaring, "See the blood of the covenant that the Lord has made with you in accordance with all these words" (Exod. 24:7-8). The prophetic hope was that God would set his people free by means of the blood of the covenant (Zech. 9:11). Accordingly, the blood of Jesus is seen in the New Testament as the ground of the new covenant, which is made explicit in the gospel tradition in the accounts of the Last Supper (Mark 14:24; Luke 22:20): "This is the new covenant in my blood." The symbolism of this participatory act is further developed in the discourse on the Bread of Life in John 6:53-56, where the believers are instructed to "eat the flesh and drink the blood of the Son of Man." The symbol of the blood of Jesus figures prominently in Paul's understanding of the meaning of Jesus' death on the cross, as in Rom. 3:25: "God put forward Jesus as a sacrifice of atonement by his blood." In Rom. 5:9, God's new people are set in right relationship with him through the blood of Jesus. In Col. 1:20, God is said to "reconcile to himself all things...by making peace through the blood of his cross." In Hebrews Christ is seen to have "entered once for all into the Holy Place with his own blood" (9:12), and thus his people can "enter the sanctuary with confidence by the blood of Jesus" (10:19). In Rev. 5:9 Jesus is lauded because "you were slaughtered and by your blood you ransomed for God saints from every tribe, language and people and nation." Thus, while the agent is at times said to be God, and other times Jesus, it is the death of the latter — and specifically the shedding of his blood — which is seen throughout the New Testament as the instrument of liberation from sin and of establishment of the relationship that is the ground of the new covenant between God and his people.

●

The difficulties that will beset the new community are of both internal and external origin. The attacking "wolves" will come from outside, seeking to destroy the community, while those who claim to be members of the new people of God will promulgate false teachings and seek to lure members to follow their perverse ideas and standards of conduct. These sad developments should not be a surprise, since Paul had been issuing tearful warnings during the "three years" that he had been at work among them. There is a defense against these hostile and corrupting attacks, however: the presence of God and the power of his message of "grace" can enable them to withstand attacks from without and false teachings from within. By this means they can continue to lay claim to the "consecrated" status that has been given to them and to all who share the beliefs and the commitments that are essential to the tradition that Paul and his associates have communicated to them. Far from having exploited his authoritative role as the leader of the community for personal benefit, Paul not only sought no economic advantage for himself, but worked in menial ways in order to provide basic needs and support: for himself, for those who worked with him, as well as for the "powerless" among those affiliated with the community. The text to which he appeals as justifying this outlook and pattern of behavior — "It is more blessed to give than to receive" — is a feature of the Jesus tradition that is not preserved in the canonical gospels or in any apocryphal gospels. Scholars have long noted analogous sayings in ancient sources,

Jewish and Greek. The basic commendation of generosity rather than avarice is expressed in proverbial form in Sir. 4:31 and elaborated in Sir. 29:1–13, as it is in such early Christian documents as *Didache* 1.5, which builds on the gospel tradition (Luke 6:29–30), and *Shepherd of Hermas* (Mandate 2.4–6), which sets forth the generosity of God as the model for his people. The text from Acts 20:35 is paraphrased in 1 Clement 2.1. Matching convictions were reportedly expressed by such philosophers as Epicurus[72] and Seneca (*Letters* 51.17), and by the ancient monarchs such as Artaxerxes[73] and Ptolemy I.[74] Thucydides states that it was a norm for Persian rulers (II.97.4), and Xenophon said it applied to the dealings of the monarch with his subjects (*Cyropaedia* 2.97.4). The attribution of this saying to Jesus here is in accord with the aim of the author of Acts to demonstrate the compatibility of aspects of the teachings of Jesus and the apostles with insights articulated by Greek philosophers, as is most clearly evident in Paul's address to the Areopagus (Acts 17).

The profound emotions at the prospect of Paul's departure to certain suffering and death are depicted in imagery that corresponds to the language in which are depicted the reunion between Jacob and Esau (Gen. 33:4) and of Joseph with his brothers and subsequently with his father (Gen. 45:14–15, 46:29). Not only the Old Testament events but even the literary mode in which they are narrated serve as models for the narratives of Acts. Paul is here depicted as one firmly within the basic biblical tradition rather than — as his Jerusalem-based opponents will soon claim — one who is seeking to undermine the true basis of God's covenant with his people that has now been renewed through Jesus.

The Arrest of Paul and the Outreach to the Center of the Roman World (21:1–28:31)

21:1–16: Paul's Final Journey to Jerusalem

When we had set sail and departed from them, we went following a straight course to Cos, and on the next day to Rhodes, and from there to Patara. When we had found a ship crossing over to Phoenicia, we got on board and set off. After having passed within sight of Cyprus and leaving it on the left, we sailed to Syria and arrived at Tyre, for there the ship was to discharge its cargo. And having searched out the disciples, we remained there for seven days. Through the Spirit they told Paul not to go up to Jerusalem. When our days there were finished, we set out on our way, and they all — with wives and children — escorted us on our way until we were out of the city. Getting on our knees on the beach, we prayed and said farewell to one another. When we got on the ship, they returned to their own places. When we had completed the voyage from Tyre, we reached Ptolemais, and after having greeted the brethren, we stayed with them for one day. On the next day we left and reached Caesarea. After having entered the house of Philip the evangelist, who was one of the seven, we stayed with him. He had seven virgin daughters who prophesied. While we remained there for some days, a prophet by the name of Agabus came from Judea. He came to us, took Paul's belt, bound his own hands and feet with it, and said, "The Holy Spirit says these things: 'The man whose belt this is, the Jews in Jerusalem will bind and will turn over into the hands of the Gentiles.'" When we heard these things, we and the local people urged him not to go up to Jerusalem. Then Paul responded, "What are you doing, weeping and shattering my heart? For I am ready not only to be bound [in chains], but even to die in Jerusalem for the sake of the name of the Lord Jesus." Since he would not be persuaded, we stopped and said, "Let the will of the Lord be done." After these days we made preparations and went up to Jerusalem. And some of the disciples from Caesarea went with us, leading us to where we should lodge with a certain Mnason from Cyprus, an early disciple. When we had reached Jerusalem, the brethren received us cordially.

The third segment of Acts in the first-person-singular style runs from 21:1 to 16, continuing the implication that an unnamed associate of Paul from Greece or Asia Minor was with him when the elders came to him from Ephesus, and that this individual then continued with Paul on toward Jerusalem. The ship on which Paul and his companions were riding followed a traditional route, which was confirmed by the prevailing winds in this area from the northeast. Cos is a small island off the coast of Asia Minor, famed in antiquity for its wine and the purple dye produced there, as well as for its utility as a major port. Hot springs on the island were visited by those in search of healing, and it became a center for the cult of Asclepius, the god of healing. 1 Macc. 15:23 includes Cos in the list of places where there were significant Jewish communities for which the Roman decree of the later second century B.C.E. supported the rights of Jews. The next stopping point, the island of Rhodes, was famed for its healthy climate and as an esteemed intellectual center, where both Cicero and Caesar studied. The Romans denied the Rhodians control of their territories on the mainland of Asia Minor, but even so the island regained a degree of prosperity under the Romans. The final Asian stage in the journey was at Patara, the chief port of Lycia at the extreme southwestern part of Asia Minor. There they boarded a ship whose destination was Phoenicia, the traditional name of the coastal strip that is now known as Lebanon, south of Syria proper and north of Judea.

The route took them along the southern coast of Asia Minor and then south of the island of Cyprus (placing it on their left) until they reached their destination: Tyre.[1] This city was originally located on an island, which was connected with the mainland by a causeway built by Alexander the Great in order to capture Tyre. It was a busy port and commercial center, with important routes connecting it to Caesarea Philippi and Damascus to the east. The large number of Tyrian coins found in Upper Galilee indicates the economic importance of that city for the interior. The links between Tyre and Galilee are also implied in the synoptic gospel tradition, where Jesus is reported as going to those places (Mark 7:24–31), and from them draws hearers (Mark 3:8; Luke 6:17). Paul and his associates "searched out" the new community there, which seems to have been of some size and stability, since it included not only men, but also "women and children." After remaining in Tyre for "seven days," while the ship unloaded its "cargo" before sailing on to other coastal ports farther south, and in spite of the warning given "through the Spirit" that grave difficulties awaited Paul in Jerusalem, he and his companions were prayerfully sent on their way by the community. Christian communities already existed in the two other ports of call as well: (1) "Ptolemais," earlier (and currently) known as Acco, and later as Acre, but in hellenistic times it was renamed for Ptolemy, ruler of Egypt. It functioned as an important commercial shipping center for more than two millennia.[2] (2) "Caesarea" (Maritima)[3] was where Peter launched the first predominantly gentile community in the house of "Cornelius" (Acts 10:1–48), and where the chief leader of the new community was "Philip the evangelist." This is not the same as Philip the disciple, mentioned in the gospel tradition.[4] This Philip was one of the seven appointed initially to oversee the distribution of food to the members of the community in Jerusalem (Acts 6:1–6), but the appropriateness of his designation here as "the evangelist" is evident from the report earlier in Acts that he was the first to take the good news about Jesus to the Samaritans (Acts 8:4–13) and to the Ethiopian eunuch (8:26–40). Here he is in residence with his "seven virgin daughters" who had the gift of prophecy, and who thus provide evidence for the continuing presence of the Spirit within the new community, though whether their prophetic powers are intended here to be understood as ecstatic or predictive is not indicated. The predictive dimension of prophecy is explicit, however, in the symbolic act and pronouncement of "Agabus" (whose prophetic role and base in Jerusalem are mentioned earlier in Acts 11:28–29), which warn about the persecution Paul is to experience in Jerusalem. The binding of himself with Paul's "belt" is the explicit sign that Paul will be seized by the Jews in Jerusalem, but instead of their punishing him by their customary mode (stoning), he will be handed over to the Gentiles. What will be essential is that the charge of a violation of Jewish laws by Paul will be converted into an allegation of his having broken Roman law and thereby subject to the Roman mode of condemnation and punishment. Paul is distressed by the sad mood in which these predictions are uttered, but is neither surprised nor deterred by them. Instead, he announces his readiness to suffer and die in order to further the cause to which he is committed in "the name of the Lord Jesus."[5] The confrontation between human power and divine purpose is soon to culminate in Jerusalem, involving both the Jewish leadership that will denounce him and the Roman authorities who will take him into custody. That purpose will be fostered, not frustrated, by these actions of the authorities, so Paul commits himself to go up to Jerusalem in order that "the will of the Lord" might be done. Paul is guided to his lodging place in Jerusalem by "disciples from Caesarea." The host is one "Mnason," identified only as "from Cyprus," which could imply that he was associated with another Cypriote, Barnabas, who was an early member of the new community in Jerusalem (Acts 4:36).[6] Or he could have been one of those converted by the Hellenists, who were commissioned by the apostles and produced such spectacular results from their evangelism based in Jerusalem (6:7). This would qualify him for the description as an "early disciple," and would explain the tension implicit between Paul and his associates having been received "cordially" by only some of "the brethren." There were others in the Christian community in Jerusalem who continued to be oriented toward the Law of Moses, however, and hence were so severely critical of his flexible position about the degree to which this Law was binding on gentile converts. This becomes a major issue in the next section (21:17–26).

21:17–26: Paul's Report to the Leaders of
the New Community in Jerusalem

On the next day Paul went in with us to James, and all the
leaders were present. After having greeted them, he recounted
in detail the things that God did among the Gentiles through
his ministry. On hearing this, they glorified God and said to
him, "You see, brother, how many thousands there are among
the Jews who have believed, and all of them continue to be
zealous for the Law. They have been instructed concerning
you that you teach all the Jews who are among the Gentiles
the abandonment of Moses, saying that they are not to circumcise their children or to live by the [legal] customs. What
is this? They will doubtless hear that you have come. So do
what I am saying to you: there are four men who have taken a
vow upon themselves. Take them and become purified along
with them; pay for their expenses in order that they might
have the head shaved. And so everyone will know that the
things that have been reported about you are nothing, but
rather that you yourself follow the principles by keeping the
Law. Concerning the Gentiles who have believed, we have
communicated our opinions that they should keep themselves
from idolatry, from what is strangled, and from fornication."
Then Paul took along the men and on the following day, after he was purified with them, he went into the temple, giving
public notice of the fulfillment of the days of purification, at
which time the offering would be presented in behalf of each
one of them.

After having established the base for their lodging with the presumably Gentile-oriented Christians from Caesarea (8:16), Paul
and the representatives of the communities in Asia Minor and
Greece who had accompanied him on his return journey to Jerusalem, and who are designated here as "us," go as a delegation
to "James and all the elders." The latter are the leaders of the
more Torah-oriented Jerusalem community, who had made the
earlier decision, reported in 15:13–29, as to the minimal ritual
requirements that were to be observed by gentile Christians,
and which are repeated here (21:25): abstinence from "idolatry, from what is strangled, and from fornication." They report
the continuing devotion to the Law of Moses on the part of

"many thousands" of Jews who have joined the new community, but they also repeat the accusation that has been brought against Paul: that he encourages all the Jews who are believers in Christ and reside among Gentiles to abandon the Law of "Moses," including the circumcision of their children and living by the "customs" associated with the Law. Here and in Acts 15, the author of Acts describes Paul as more open to compromise on the issue of obligations to the Law of Moses on the part of members of the new community than he portrays himself in Gal. 2:15–21, where he articulates the radical distinction between being set right with God by faith in Christ and by the Law. Indeed, here in Acts 21 the proposal of James and his associates is that Paul support financially and follow the example of four men who have taken on themselves a radical rite of purification — very likely the Nazirite vow. This practice sketched in Numbers 6 involved abstinence from wine and shaving the hair, followed by allowing the hair to grow uncut. Provisions were made if the purified one should become defiled, as by touching a dead body, and details were offered for the final sacrificial act that culminated the consecration process. A version of this rite is the procedure depicted by Josephus as performed by Bernice, the sister of Herod Agrippa, in reaction to the slaughter of Jews by the Roman governor, Florus. The rite is said by Josephus to require abstaining from wine and shaving the head for thirty days prior to offering sacrifices (*Wars* 2.313-14). The thesis of James and his colleagues is that if Paul was to participate in this kind of ascetic rite, the charge by his opponents that he ignored the Law and its provisions for purity would be dramatically refuted. Following James's repetition of the minimal legal requirements said to be binding on gentile members of the new community, Paul follows the suggestion, sharing in the purification process for himself and the other four, including paying the necessary fees for them, for which he gives public notice in the "temple," with a promise that the rite will culminate in the appropriate sacrifices. The period chosen for purification, however, is not thirty days, but seven (21:27). The intent of Acts to portray Paul as obedient to the purification modes of identity for God's people is given major support through the recounting of this incident.

21:27–36: The Accusations against Paul before the Jerusalem Authorities

When the seven days were about to be completed, the Jews from Asia who had seen him in the temple stirred up the whole crowd. They laid hands on him, crying out, "Israelite men, give us your help! This is the man who is everywhere teaching against the people, the law and this place. Further, he brought Greeks into the temple, and desecrated this holy place." Because they had previously seen Trophimus the Ephesian in the city with him, they assumed that Paul had taken him into the temple. The whole city was aroused, and a mob of the people formed. Laying hold of Paul, they dragged him out of the temple, and immediately the gates were closed. Since they were trying to kill him, a report went up to the tribune of the cohort that the whole of Jerusalem was in an uproar. Immediately he took soldiers and centurions and hurried down to them. When they saw the tribune and the soldiers, they stopped beating Paul. Then the tribune came up and apprehended him, and ordered that he be bound with two chains. He inquired as to who he was and what he had done. Certain ones in the crowd shouted one thing or another, and because he was unable to know anything for certain as a result of the confusion, he ordered that he be taken up into the headquarters. When he got to the stairs, it turned out that he was carried by the soldiers, because of the violence of the crowd, for the throng of people were crying out, "Away with him!"

Ironically, as Paul's period of ritual commitment was in process, "Jews from Asia" recognized him as being the chief instrument of the message concerning Jesus and the redefining of the people of God. Hence they launched a fierce public attack against him, accusing him of violation of three fundamental features of Jewish tradition: (1) the identity of the "people" of God; (2) adherence to the requirements of the "Law" of Moses; and (3) sanctity of the temple, the sacred "place" where God was believed to dwell among his people. The climax of his alleged violations was said to be his having brought non-Jews — "Greeks" — into the "holy place." As mentioned earlier, the boundaries of the Court of the Gentiles, beyond which non-Jews were not permitted to go, were marked by inscribed warnings, one of which has survived and reads:

> Let no foreigner [*allogene*] enter within the screen and enclosure surrounding the sanctuary [*to hieron*]. Whoever is taken so doing will be the cause of his own death, which will follow.[7]

The charge that Paul had violated the sanctity of the temple is seen by the author of Acts to be false, based as it is on an inference from his having brought to Jerusalem "Trophimus," one of his gentile convert companions from Ephesus (20:4). This accusation is accepted as fact by the crowd, however, who gives credence to the claim that Paul is undermining the integrity of "Israel," the people of God. What Paul is pictured throughout Acts as doing is redefining the "people" and making new claims and offering radically new interpretations of the "law." He is not quoted in Acts as voicing one of the most radical propositions attributed to Jesus in the gospel tradition, including the Gospel of Luke: that the temple will come to an end, and that its function as the locus of God's presence with his people will no longer be valid (Luke 21:5–7). Instead, Paul is here charged with violating the holiness of the temple by bringing in those who by birth and ritual condition are unqualified to enter this sacred precinct. The reaction of the incited "mob" is to seize Paul and expel him from the temple's precincts, with the intent to "kill" him. Ironically, the one who comes to Paul's aid is an agent of the Roman Empire: the "tribune of the cohort," who was informed that "confusion" had taken over the whole of the city. Since the maintenance of peace and order was the primary role of the military contingents stationed throughout the empire, this disturbance warranted sending down soldiers into the temple area where the trouble had begun.

Excursus on the Roman Army in Judea

The major center for Roman troops based in Judea was in Caesarea,[8] but those stationed in Jerusalem were positioned in the Tower of Antonia, which was built on the ridge directly north of the temple area. The official residence of the local Roman authority and the locus of the military and administrative authority were both at the praetorium. This was the case in both Jerusalem (Mark 15:16; Matt 27:27; John 19:9) and Caesarea (Acts 23:35). In Jerusalem, from the tower one could look down into the courtyards of the temple, and there was direct access by the military from the fortress into the outer temple courts when it was necessary for them to intervene and repress disturbances or attempts to display power. The troops were mainly of Syrian origin, recruited in areas of predominantly non-Jewish inhabitants, such as those from the hellenistic-dominated region of Caesarea and the adjacent coastal cities, or from Sebaste (the Greco-Roman name for Samaria), which was the center for the semitic group that had developed on Mount Gerizim its own temple and priesthood, in direct competition to the one in Jerusalem. The troops located in Judea also included those of Italian origin, as indicated in Acts 10:1. Accordingly, one can infer that these soldiers were not disposed to be sympathetic or supportive of the local Jewish populace in times of tension and controversy. (See the excursus on Centurion in chapter 3, p. 129.)

•

Since it was impossible to obtain an ordered, official judicial presentation of the charges against Paul in the midst of the mob, the "tribune" had Paul taken "in chains" up the "stairs" that connected the temple area to the military "tower." The irony is continued in the contrast between (1) the throng incited by the pious Jews from Asia and hence calling for Paul's death and (2) the Roman "soldiers" who assure him that his case will be justly heard and dealt with by the Roman authority, the "tribune." The action of taking Paul in custody by binding him "with two chains" (as Peter was earlier; 12:6) was regarded in the early Roman Empire as primarily a way of guaranteeing the presence of an accused person at a proper trial, rather than as simply a mode of punishment. Modes of detention ranged from protective custody under military or civilian authority to entrusting the accused to someone who served as surety for guarding and retaining him.[9] Paul's coreligionists threaten his life; the Romans offer him formal protection.

21:37–22:21: Paul's Initial Defense in Jerusalem

As Paul was being led up into the headquarters, he said to the tribune, "Is it permitted for me to say something to you?" He said, "Do you know Greek? So then you are not the Egyptian who in recent days started an uprising and led out into the desert four thousand men of the Assassins?"[10] Paul said, "Instead, I am a Jewish man from Tarsus in Cilicia, a citizen of a not insignificant city. Please allow me to speak to the people!" When he had given him permission, Paul stood on steps, made a sign to the people with his hand, and when there was a general silence, he addressed them, speaking in the Hebrew dialect: "Men who are brothers and fathers, hear me now in my defense before you." When they heard that he was addressing them in the Hebrew language, they became even more quiet. And he said, "I am a Jewish man, born in Tarsus in Cilicia, but trained in this city, educated at the feet of Gamaliel according to the strict interpretation of the ancestral law, and as zealous toward God as all of you are to this day. I persecuted this Way to death, binding and handing over to prison both men and women, as the high priest and the whole council of elders attest. Having received from them letters to the brethren in Damascus, I went there to bring to Jerusalem those who were there in bonds, so that they might be punished.

"It happened that while I was on the way and approaching Damascus, toward midday suddenly a great light out of heaven shone around me, and I fell to the ground and heard a voice saying to me, 'Saul, Saul! Why are you persecuting me?' And I answered, 'Who are you, sir?' He said to me, 'I am Jesus of Nazareth, whom you are persecuting.' Those who were with me saw the light, but they did not hear the voice that was speaking to me. And I said, 'Sir, what shall I do?' And the Lord said to me, 'Arise, go into Damascus, and there it will be told to you concerning all the things which have been appointed for you to do.' And since I was unable to see because of the brilliance of the light, I was led by hand by those who were with me and came to Damascus.

"A certain Ananias, a devout man by the standards of the law, well-attested by all the Jewish residents, came and stood by me and said, 'Brother Saul, regain your sight!' And at that same moment I regained my sight [and saw him].[11] He said, 'The God of our fathers predestined you to know his will, to see the Righteous One, and to hear a voice from his mouth, because you will be a witness to him for all humans concerning what you have seen and heard. And now, why do you delay? Get up, be baptized to wash away your sins, calling on his name.'

"After I had returned to Jerusalem and was praying in the temple, I went into a trance and saw him saying to me, 'Hurry! Get out of Jerusalem quickly, because they will not accept from you testimony about me.' And I said, 'Lord, these people know that I was imprisoning and beating in the synagogues those who were trusting in you, and that when the blood of Stephen the witness was poured out, I also was standing there and giving approval, and keeping the garments of those who were murdering him.' And he said to me, 'Leave, because I shall be sending you far away to the Gentiles.'"

21:37-22:5: Paul Begins His Defense and Autobiography

Paul's security was assured by his being taken up the staircase that led into the military headquarters of the Romans in the tower beside the temple. In earlier linguistic usage, *parembole* was the ordinary term for a military camp, but it came to be used more broadly for any facility where military officers and troops were based. Before he was removed from the public gathering in the temple courts, however, Paul addressed the chief officer (*chiliarchos*) in Greek and disabused him of his assumption that he was "the Egyptian" revolutionary. Who this person was is not historically certain, but Josephus reports in his *Antiquities* (20.169–72) the coming to Jerusalem of a self-styled Egyptian prophet early in the reign of Nero (54–68 C.E.). He called the people to the Mount of Olives, predicting that at his words the walls of Jerusalem which spread out below would fall and the Jews could regain full control of the city. He reportedly had brought his troops to the city through the desert, apparently in reenactment of the exodus of ancient Israel. The parallel account in Josephus's *Wars* (2.261–63) indicates that there were thirty thousand whom he had deceived into following him. His effort to take over the city failed, and from the violent retaliation of the Roman troops only a few of the revolutionaries escaped. Drawing on Josephus, Eusebius reports this same incident as part of his depiction of the surge of nationalism among the Jews in Palestine in the reign of Nero (*Eccl. Hist.* 2.21). Paul's differentiation of the Jesus movement from the nationalistic groups is another important feature of the aim of the author of Acts to show that Christianity, while critical of the Jewish leadership, was not an anti-Roman enterprise. Paul identifies himself as a "Jew," but also indicates that he is from a prominent center of Greco-Roman culture, "Tarsus in Cilicia,"[12] and that he is a "citizen."[13] These claims serve to give him status in the mind of the Roman official, but his speaking to the Jewish crowd in "Hebrew dialect" — which would of course have been Aramaic — captures their attention, and he now proceeds to establish his Jewish credentials.

Although Paul was born to a Jewish Diaspora family resident in a prestigious Greco-Roman city, his orientation and in-depth training in the Jewish tradition are here depicted as having taken place in Jerusalem under a leading figure in the early stages of what was to develop into rabbinic Judaism: "Gamaliel."[14] He has already appeared in Acts 5:34–39 as a cautious and conciliatory figure, who urges that the Jewish leaders wait and see whether or not this new movement which they seek to destroy survives and thereby demonstrates that it has divine approval. Here, however, Paul identifies him as one who taught "a strict interpretation of the law." Whether this characterization of Gamaliel is accurate cannot be determined on the basis of the little and late evidence that has been preserved about him in the later rabbinic tradition. But what is essential for the argument of Acts is to show Paul's devotion to the integrity of the people of God and his substantial training in the Pharisaic tradition (5:34), as Paul subsequently affirms (23:6), and as he noted in his Letter to the Philippians (3:5).[15] Historically speaking, the Pharisees by their concentration on personal purity along ritual and dietary lines prepared Jews for adjustment and accommodation to the radically altered situation that confronted them following the destruction of the temple, when sacrifices and the priestly functions enjoined in the Law could no longer be carried out. From this perspective their interpretation was not strict in the sense of literal and total conformity.[16] But Paul here is not debating legal issues; instead, he is making the point of his deep devotion to the Jewish tradition and his commitment to its relevance for his own people. Commending his antagonists for their zeal toward

God, he shows how his persecution of the new "Way" linked
with Jesus provided public evidence of his own devotion to the
tradition. Although there is no such claim in Paul's letters, he
here asserts that he had gained a reputation among the Jewish
leaders in Jerusalem, including the "high priest" and the entire
"council of elders,"[17] with whom he cooperated in bringing to
"prison" those allied with the new movement. Then the council had acted to assist his work of crushing this movement by
providing supporting letters addressed to the Jewish community
in "Damascus," in order to bring to Jerusalem for "punishment"
those who were departing from the tradition and urging others
to do so, thereby violating the dominant ethnic and ritual definition of the people of God. There is no clear Roman documentary
evidence that the council of Jews in Jerusalem had formal authority for such punitive action beyond its own district, but the
prestige of the council would surely have influenced Jews elsewhere to cooperate in achieving the shared goal of destroying
this subversive movement.

22:6–21: Paul Describes His Encounter with Jesus and His Commissioning by Him

This second account of Paul's conversion near Damascus parallels the original description in 9:1-19, but with some additions
and minor differences. Here the time is "noon" and the light
from heaven is "great," and his companions see the light but do
not hear the voice, in contrast to 9:7 where they hear the voice
but do not see the light. Other features are added in the third
account of his conversion in 26:9–20 (see below).

Although Ananias is the one through whom the sight of the
blinded Paul is restored (as in 9:10–18), there is here no account
of Ananias having a parallel vision informing him of the role
that God has assigned to Paul, as is the case in 9:9–16. Emphatic
here as evidence that the agent behind what happened to and
through Paul is the God of Israel are three factors: (1) the one
who commissioned Paul is "the God of our fathers"; (2) the
one whom he was enabled to see in the vision is designated as
"the Righteous One"; and (3) this is the one through whom the
authorization came for his wider mission. Proof of the validity
of these claims was provided by Paul's having "regained" his
"sight," as well as by his hearing "the voice." The range of Paul's
mission, which in 9:15 is to include "Gentiles, kings, and sons of

Israel," is here stated more broadly: to "all humans."[18] Also distinctive here is the instruction given by Ananias, which reflects what had clearly become standard practice for those joining the new community: entrance to the new community is to be demonstrated publicly by participation in the rite of "baptism," understood as "washing away sins," and calling on the "name" of Jesus Christ. Also unique here is the account of Paul's vision of Christ in Jerusalem, which resulted in his commissioning to go to the Gentiles. The details are again important for the apologetic aims of the author of Acts by documenting the depth and intensity of Paul's former commitment to the integrity of the community of Israel as it was commonly perceived. It was this which had led him to "imprison" and "beat" those who were joining the new community, and to share in the execution of those such as "Stephen" (22:20), who were viewed as threats to the ethnic and ritual purity of God's people. The commissioning of Paul by Jesus to go to the "Gentiles" is not reported in the original account of his conversion in Acts 9, but its import here (22:17-21) resembles that of the vision of Peter described in Acts 10:9-16. The two linked features of this commissioning of Paul are that he is to go to the "Gentiles," and that he is to be prepared to go "far away." The specifics of the mission to the Gentiles are indicated more fully in Paul's account of his conversion in Acts 26:17-18, where they are described in his initial vision rather than in a subsequent encounter with Christ as here.

22:22-29: Paul Declares His Roman Citizenship

Up until this statement they listened to him. Then they raised their voice[s] saying, "Take this one away from the earth, for it is not right for him to live!" As they were shouting and waving their garments and throwing dust into the air, the tribune gave the order for him to be brought to headquarters, and said that he should be examined by scourging, so that they might know thereby the reason that they shouted in this way against him. But as they were stretching him out with thongs [for beating], Paul said to the centurion who was standing by, "Is it lawful for you to scourge a man who is a Roman [citizen] and has not been properly tried?" When the centurion heard this, he went to the tribune and informed him, saying, "What are you about to do? For this man is a Roman [citizen]!" So the tribune came and said to him, "Tell me, are you a Roman [citizen]?" And he said, "Yes." The tribune responded, "I purchased this citizenship for a great amount of money." But Paul said, "I was even born [a citizen]." Instantly those who were about to examine him [by scourging] gave up, and the tribune was fearful when he realized that he was a Roman [citizen] and that he had impounded him.

What triggered the demand of the crowd of Paul's opponents that he be put to death was his claim that an agent of God (Jesus) had instructed him to invite Gentiles to join the people of God. The leaders of the traditionally defined covenant people saw Paul as a threat to the integrity of their community, as they defined it in terms of ethnic and ritual purity. Their hostility was vividly demonstrated by their "waving garments and throwing dust in the air." The earlier reports in Luke-Acts of shaking dust off the feet as testimony to the unrepentant attitude of a city or people (Luke 9:5, 10:11; Acts 13:51) represent a symbolic action which declared that those who reject the message and its messengers must accept the consequences of divine judgment. Here, however, these actions are intended as a public sign of lament, similar to the import of earlier events in the biblical writings: the condition of a wretched individual (Job 2:12), or a leader who has recently died (2 Sam. 1:2); a sad event in the history of God's people (the capture of the ark by the Philistines; 1 Sam. 4:12); a grievous misdeed (the rape of Tamar; 2 Sam. 13:19); the disastrous condition of Jerusalem (1 Macc. 3:47) and the temple (1 Macc. 4:39) as the Maccabees began to seize control of the land from the Seleucids. In that tradition, Paul's opponents decry what they see as his program to violate the purity and integrity of the covenant people, and they demonstrate this deep concern by their waved garments and the dust thrown in the air.

The tribune, whose responsibility was to preserve order and to punish those who threatened Roman control of the land and people, sought to avoid unwarranted mob action motivated by Jewish religious concerns, and gave orders that Paul be brought into the "headquarters," where the Roman troops were based. If Paul could be shown to have violated the sanctity of the temple by bringing into the sacred courts someone who was neither a Jew nor a proselyte, then he would be subject to the juris-

diction of the Jewish council (see below; 23:30), whose authority
on such matters was recognized by the Romans. The pressing
prior question for the tribune, therefore, was whether Paul was
guilty of violating a civil law, and hence under Roman jurisdiction, or an indigenous Jewish law, for which he could be
punished by the Jerusalem council. The initial proposal of the
tribune was for Paul to be scourged. This could have been a
severe mode of testing in order to determine if the charges of
insurrection or disturbing the peace were well founded. Or it
could have been intended as simply a cruel form of punishment,
on the assumption that he had indeed violated the Jewish law
by taking a ritually impure person into the inner courts of the
temple. The Roman practice of scourging and imprisoning bel-
ligerent disturbers of the peace is reported by Josephus (*Wars*
2.266) as having taken place in a dispute between Jews and Syrians in Caesarea. Indeed in the Roman colonies, arrest, beating,
and imprisonment of noncitizens were common ways of han-
dling noncitizens accused of legal violations.[19] Likewise, Roman
confirmation of the right of Jewish authorities to execute those
who entered this sacred temple area is reported by Josephus in a
statement attributed to Titus.[20] But even before the tribune can
decide whether the accused should be punished for disturbing
the peace (and hence in his own jurisdiction) or for violating
the sacred precincts (and hence in the jurisdiction of the Jewish
council), Paul has complicated the process by informing the centurion that he is a Roman citizen (see the excursus on Roman
Citizenship, p. 200).

In the eastern part of the empire, citizenship was more
sparsely represented than in the west, and was granted to individuals or to families rather than to ruling elites or to specially
favored cities as a whole. But since Josephus reports in detail
the several actions of the Roman senate confirming the right of
Jewish citizens in the cities of Asia Minor to be excused from
military service, and to carry out sabbath observance and group
worship, it is clear that for Jews to have received citizenship was
not an uncommon feature of the empire.[21] In much of the empire, all members of the city or regional councils were citizens,
but citizenship was probably not a requirement for council participation in the east.[22] For the centurion and then the "tribune"
to find that this accused Jew in Jerusalem was a Roman citizen
was a great shock, especially since the tribune had been obliged

to pay "a great amount of money" in order to become a citizen. The bribe would have been paid to the imperial secretariat or to a provincial administrative official in order to have one's name added to the list of candidates for citizenship.[23] It is not clear whether or not citizens carried with them a certificate of their status; the certification would be in the records at the place of their official residence. Dio Cassius reports that during the reign of Claudius (41–54 C.E.) citizenship could be obtained by the payment of "large sums" of money (*Roman History* 60.17.5), and it was presumably in this period that the tribune had obtained his citizenship. Yet Dio also reports that Tiberius (14–37 C.E.) had a hostile attitude toward Jews, who were making many converts, and for a time banned most of them from Rome, and then sought to prohibit them from gathering for meetings (57.18.6). By the time of Claudius (41–54 C.E.), Jews were so numerous in Rome that it would have caused a major disturbance to expel them, so instead he allowed them to continue their traditional lifestyle, while prohibiting them from holding meetings (40.6.6). Claudius also withdrew the citizenship of an envoy from the province of Lycia in Asia Minor because he failed to understand Latin (40.17.6), although Latin and Greek were the official languages of the empire in the mid-first century, as noted by Suetonius (*Life of Claudius* 42.1). With the hostile attitude toward Jews on the part of Tiberius and Claudius, it is understandable why the tribune would be astounded to hear that Paul and his father had become citizens, presumably during their reigns. The tribune was now faced with a major dilemma: Roman authorities were well aware of the importance of maintaining the safety and legal rights of citizens in their territory, and there would be serious consequences if citizens were given the same harsh treatment as aliens.[24] To have seized and bound a citizen without prior investigation or convincing evidence of a civil charge against him was a major violation of citizen rights, and hence the tribune was justly "fearful."

22:30–23:11: The Hearing before the Jerusalem Council

On the next day, since he wanted to know the firm basis on which the charges had been brought against him by the Jews, [the tribune] released him [from his bonds] and ordered the chief priests and the whole council to convene. He led Paul down [from the tower] and placed him before them. Looking intently at the council, Paul said, "Brother men, with complete good conscience I have lived my life in obedience to God until this day." The high priest, Ananias, gave orders to those standing by him to strike him on the mouth. Then Paul said to him, "God is about to strike you, you whitewashed wall! Are you sitting to judge me according to the law, and yet contrary to the law, you command that I be struck?" Those who were standing by said, "Are you reviling the high priest of God?" And Paul said, "I did not know, brothers, that he is the high priest; for it is written, 'You shall not speak ill of a leader of the people.'" [Exod. 22:27]

When Paul realized that the one part were Sadducees and the other were Pharisees, he called out in the council, "Brother men, I am a Pharisee, a son of Pharisees. I am being examined with respect to hope and resurrection of the dead." When he had said this, there came a discord between the Pharisees and the Sadducees, and the crowd was split. For the Sadducees say that there is no resurrection, nor angel nor spirit, but the Pharisees affirm them all. There came a great outcry, and certain of the scribes and the party of the Pharisees arose and contended sharply, saying, "We find nothing wrong in this man. What if a spirit or an angel spoke to him?" When the discord became total, the tribune was afraid that Paul would be ripped apart by them, so he ordered the troops to go down and snatch him from their midst, in order to conduct him to the headquarters. On the next night the Lord appeared to him and said, "Have courage, for as you testified concerning me in Jerusalem, thus you must also bear witness in Rome."

The tribune's first effort to resolve the question concerning the allegation of Paul's violation of the law —whether it was contrary to Jewish or Roman law —led him to order the "council to convene" and examine Paul formally. The council,[25] composed of the Jewish leaders among both the priests and the wider Jerusalem community, is pictured as presided over by the high priest, "Ananias."

He was appointed to that post by Herod of Chalcis, the

brother of Agrippa I, whom Claudius rewarded for his help in gaining the imperial post by making him king of the territory of Herod the Great in 41 C.E. When Agrippa died in 44, Claudius appointed a procurator, Cumanus, in Judea. The governor of Syria, Quadratus, responded to a power struggle between the Jews and the Samaritans by sending off to Rome Ananias, as well as Cumanus (the procurator) and Jonathan (the former high priest), together with other Jews and Samaritans accused of fostering the conflict, for interrogation by the emperor Claudius. Agrippa II, who had lived in Rome at the court of Claudius until around 50 C.E., interceded successfully in behalf of the Jews, who were released, but the Samaritan leaders were killed. Cumanus was sent into exile, and Felix was sent off as procurator of Judea. Ananias remained loyal to King Agrippa when the royal establishment was under siege by the Jewish revolutionaries and was seized and executed by them.[26] Clearly Ananias was a component of the ruling coalition of Roman military and Jewish priestly authorities.

Paul's opening line in his defense before the council involved a form of address, "Brother men," which implied for himself full membership in the people of God, as well as an explicit claim to having been completely obedient to God. The confirming feature to which he refers here is one drawn from hellenistic tradition: "in all good conscience." This term, central for Stoic ethics, is a major feature of Paul's argument in the Letter to the Romans, where he argues that the natural law is at work within human hearts among people who have no access to the Law of Moses but who have moral testimony within and therefore moral obligations through their conscience (2:14–16).[27] Josephus similarly links conscience, obedience to the law, and the promise of life beyond death (*Ag. Ap.* 2.218). Paul's claim here to total obedience is for the ritually and legally oriented high priest grossly false, and he orders a public punitive action against him. Hitting Paul in the mouth symbolizes Ananias's conviction that he has spoken a total untruth. Paul turns the image back on the high priest by combining features of the law and the prophets: it is God who will do the striking of those who are truly disobedient (Deut. 18:20–22), and Ananias is linked by Paul with the false prophets who smear with the whitewash of moral pretense the structures (walls) that are to about to fall under divine judgment. He continues his attack on the high priest by rejecting the charge that he has broken the law, and hence he denounces as unjust the order for him to be struck. This is an "unjust judgment," such as is denounced in Lev. 19:15. Those present inform Paul that the subject of his verbal counterattack is the "high priest," and he declares his ignorance of his identity, confessing the wrongness of his prior denunciation of him, since one in that office is a "leader of the people" (Lev. 19:28). He does not, however, accept the validity of the high priest's fierce rejection of his testimony concerning his obedience to God.

Instead, Paul shifts his tactics by taking advantage of a basic split within the Jewish leadership over the belief in the "resurrection of the dead," which was affirmed by the Pharisees and denied by the Sadducees. He declares his identity with the Pharisees and his acceptance of their belief in "resurrection," "angels," and "spirit."

Excursus on Belief in the Resurrection

The distinctive belief of the Pharisees in the resurrection of the dead is not affirmed in the Law of Moses. It appears in several of the prophets as an image of the renewal of the covenant people rather than as hope of survival beyond death for individuals. A few persons are reported to have been restored to life by the prophets Elijah and Elisha (1 Kings 17:17-24; 2 Kings 4:8-27, 13:20-21). Enoch (Gen. 5:24) and Elijah (2 Kings 2:1-15) were spared the experience of death and taken up directly to be with God. God was thought to reward the faithful by giving them long lives (Job 42:17), and when the creation was renewed, his people would live to great age again as in the time before the flood (Isa. 65:20). Some of the prophets used the image of being raised from the dead to depict the renewal of God's people as a whole (Hosea 6:1-3; Ezek. 37:1-14; Isa. 26:19). Only in Dan. 12:1-3 is there an explicit promise that beyond the suffering and death which God's people are experiencing will come a new everlasting life for those who have been faithful, when they will shine like the stars forever. Other Jewish writers in the centuries before the Common Era declared that the souls of the righteous would live on (Wisd. 3:1-9, 5:15-16) and that the powers of evil would be defeated (5:17-23). In 1 Enoch the righteous are promised life in a new age under the care of the Lord of Spirits and ruled by the Chosen One of God (1 Enoch 37-71). They will live as body and soul, flooded with light, sitting on thrones in the presence of God (1 Enoch 108). The discovery of Enoch among the Dead Sea Scrolls provides firm testimony to the vitality of the belief in the resurrection among Palestinian Jews in the first century C.E.

Josephus reports that the Pharisees believe that souls have the power to survive death, and that "the good souls receive an easy passage to a new life," while the Sadducees think that the soul perishes with the body (*Ant.* 18.14-15). Josephus's own view is that the soul is a part of the divine reality which takes up residence in the human body, and that when the faithful die, their souls are given a "most holy place in heaven." When the "revolution of the ages" takes place, these righteous souls "return to find in chaste bodies a new habitation" (*Wars* 3.372-75). The similarity between this view and that of Paul in 1 Cor. 15:35-54 is clear.

Belief in the resurrection is, of course, central for the Book of Acts, which begins with the report of the appearance of the risen Lord to the apostles; it is highlighted in Peter's speech at Pentecost (2:32-34) and in the house of Cornelius (10:40-41), as well as by Paul in his speech at Antioch-in-Pisidia (13:30-37) and in Athens before the Areopagites (17:18, 31). The belief in the resurrection of Jesus is basic to all of Paul's accounts of his conversion which is seen to have occurred through his encounter with the risen Christ.

•

Although the dramatic event that demonstrates that Jesus is God's agent for the renewal of his people is the resurrection, it is the outpouring of the Spirit that launches the apostles' mission, and then guides and empowers the messengers throughout Acts.[28] Similarly, angels are essential agents in the mission of the church and the guidance of its messengers.[29] More is involved in Paul's appeal to the Pharisaic views that he and the new movement share than mere partisanship: what is essential is that these beliefs of the followers of Jesus are also major features of what the Jews believed who were to become the dominant segment of those within the rabbinic tradition after the failure of the priestly and nationalist blocs. The Sadducees, who rejected these views, were probably a group that arose in the priestly families, tracing their origin to Zadok, the high priest

in the time of David and Solomon.[30] Josephus describes them
as one of the major groups in Judaism from the time of the
Maccabees, whose distinctive teachings denied the providence
of God and stressed the human choice of good or evil and responsibility for the consequences (*Wars* 2.165; *Ant.* 13.173). He
also asserts that the Sadducees considered to be binding on
God's people only those laws that are written down in scripture (*Ant.* 13.297). On the question of human fate, they taught
that the soul perishes with the body (*Ant.* 18.16). It is likely
that their group dominated the priesthood, which would account for their disappearance from the historical scene after
the destruction of the temple in 70 C.E. It was this catastrophe
that also marked the time of the Pharisaic rise to dominance
in Judaism and the launching of what was to become the rabbinic movement, which produced the Talmud and Mishnah.
Writing some time after the failure of the first Jewish revolt
(66–70 C.E.), the author of Acts wants to reinforce the claim
of Christians that their beliefs are in line with major aspects
of Jewish tradition, as represented by doctrines shared with the
triumphant Pharisees. This struggle for dominance is mirrored
in the account of the conflict between Pharisees and Sadducees
precipitated instantly by Paul's remarks. And the validity of
his teaching from the Jewish standpoint is confirmed by the
Pharisees' pronouncement of his innocence, as well as by their
rhetorical question that perhaps "a spirit or an angel" is speaking
through him.

The fierce discord leads the tribune to assure Paul that his case
will be fairly heard in a context free of these intra-Jewish debates
by having him removed from the territory and the jurisdiction
of the Jewish "council." Clearly the charges that Paul had violated Jewish law and was therefore subject to execution by the
council were not confirmed. Instead, the charges and the jurisdiction now shift back to the Roman legal system. That these
events, as well as what is to follow, are the outworking of the
providence and purpose of God is seen to be confirmed through
the subsequent vision in which the "Lord" promises Paul that
he is to have opportunity to repeat his "witness" in the world
center of political power: "Rome."

23:12–22: The Conspiracy to Murder Paul

When day came, the Jews made a conspiracy under oath, say-ing that they would neither eat nor drink until they had killed Paul. There were more than forty who formed this conspiracy. They went to the chief priests and the leaders and said, "By an oath we have bound ourselves to taste nothing until we have killed Paul. So now you, together with the council, report the charge to the tribune so that he will bring him down to you, as though you were going to investigate more exactly the things concerning him. But before he comes near, we are ready to kill him."

Now the son of Paul's sister, having heard of the ambush, went over and entered the headquarters, and told Paul. Paul called one of the centurions and said, "Take this young man to the tribune, because he has something to tell him." So he took him and led him to the tribune and said, "The prisoner, Paul, called me to bring this young man to you, because he has something to say to you." Taking him by the hand and with-drawing in private, the tribune inquired, "What is it that you have to report to me?" And he said, "The Jews have agreed to ask you to bring Paul down to the council tomorrow, as though they were going to investigate matters concerning him more exactly. But do not be persuaded by them, for more than forty men are lying in ambush, who have taken an oath not to eat or drink until they have killed him. And now they are ready, awaiting the agreement from you." The tribune sent off the young man, after instructing him, "Do not disclose to anyone that you have revealed these things to me."

The initiative to kill Paul came from an otherwise unidentified group of "more than forty Jews," who are bound by an oath to kill Paul as soon as possible. Their plan was to have the "coun-cil" notify the tribune that they had a specific charge against Paul which would presumably lie within their jurisdiction, and which they now wanted to "investigate" more fully. There is no indication of the charge, but it would presumably have been re-lated to his alleged violation of the sanctuary in order for their council to be the appropriate locus of the inquiry. The pro-posal is reported in Acts as only a ruse to expose Paul to those committed to assassinating him. The lives of the conspirators are at risk because of their refusal to eat or drink until their scheme is carried out. Clearly the plan is not to reopen the case against Paul but to murder him once he is out of the military headquarters.

There is no prior mention in Acts of Paul's having relatives in Jerusalem, and none in his letters, but the reference to his "sister" and her "son" adds subtle support for the important aim of Acts to show that Paul's deep roots are within the Jewish tradition. That the young man had access to his imprisoned uncle fits well the tradition of Greco-Roman writers that Christians in prison could receive visits and support from family and friends, as is recounted in detail by Lucian in *The Passing of Peregrinus* (11-13), where Proteus (Peregrinus) was showered with visits, food, and gifts by visitors — some from great distances — during the period of his identification with Christianity. When Paul learns of the plot, he has the support of the military officer to get the secret message to the tribune, who receives the young man most cordially. On hearing of the murderous scheme, the tribune orders the messenger not to reveal it to anyone. Once more, the author of Acts depicts the Roman officials as humane, fair, honest, and concerned for true justice. It is the priestly oligarchy and their supporters who are the ones seeking to subvert due legal process.

23:23–35: The Plot Circumvented: Roman Justice Prevails

Then he summoned two of the centurions and said, "Make ready two hundred soldiers to go with seventy horsemen and two hundred bowmen at the third hour of the night. And provide mounts so that Paul may ride, so that he may be transferred safely to Felix, the governor." He wrote a letter which had this form:

"Claudius Lysias, to his excellency, governor Felix:
      Greeting! Since this man had been seized by the Jews and was about to be killed by them, when I came upon them with the troop of soldiers, I rescued him, having learned that he was a Roman [citizen]. Since I wanted to know the charge that they were bringing against him,

> I took him down to their council. I found that he was
> being accused about questions concerning their law, but
> that they had no charge [against him] deserving death
> or imprisonment. When it was revealed to me that there
> would be a plot against the man, I immediately sent him
> to you, having given orders to the accusers to state to
> you the things they have against him."

So then the soldiers, in accord with how they had been instructed, escorted Paul and led him by night to Antipatris. On
the next day, leaving the horsemen to accompany him, they
returned to the headquarters. When they arrived at Caesarea
and handed over the letter to the governor, they also turned
Paul over to him. Having read the letter and asked Paul from
what province he was, and having learned that it was Cilicia,
he said, "I will give you a hearing when your accusers are
also here." He gave orders that he should be guarded in the
praetorium of Herod.

The military corps ordered by the tribune to safeguard Paul's
transfer to Felix, the governor in Caesarea,[31] is of impressive
size and strength, including as it does foot-soldiers, cavalry,
and other light-armed forces, perhaps bowmen.[32] The number
of troops varies in the different manuscript traditions, with the
so-called Neutral text asserting that there were 470, thereby
underscoring the seriousness of the issue confronted by the tribune and the Roman officials. The important factor is that the
Roman official is here depicted as guaranteeing the safety and
legal rights of Paul the Roman citizen. Their departure from
Jerusalem at the "third hour of the night" (nine o'clock in the
evening) would have made it impossible for Paul's would-be
attackers to achieve their goal.

For the first time in this narrative, the name of the tribune
based in Jerusalem is given: "Claudius Lysias." His cognomen,
"Lysias," and the detail that he had had to pay for his citizenship status make clear that he was not of Roman birth. That his
nomen was Claudius may indicate that his acquisition of citizenship was recent: during the reign of Claudius, which began in 41
C.E. and ended in 54. The governor based in Caesarea was "Felix," the brother of Pallas, who was a freed slave and a favorite
of the emperor Claudius. Tacitus, the Roman historian, characterized him as having the power of a king and the mind of a

slave.[33] Felix was appointed by Claudius in 52 C.E. as procurator over Judea, Samaria, Galilee, and Perea,[34] and continued in that capacity under Nero (reigned 54–68 C.E.). He is described by Josephus as having put down numerous Jewish insurrectionist efforts, including one fostered by the Egyptian prophet who announced the doom of Jerusalem, one by a group who — like the Dead Sea community — went out on the edge of the desert to await divine intervention in their behalf, and one by Jews who battled the Syrians resident in Caesarea for control of the city.[35] Given his fierce hostility toward Jewish nationalists, one might expect Felix to have been keen on discovering any such features in the career and aspirations of Paul, a Jew accused as a disturber of the peace. The tribune's letter to Felix summarizes what had occurred, however, repeating a major motif in Acts: that the accusations made against Paul in the Jerusalem "council" had to do solely with matters of their law, and that neither by their law nor by Roman law was there any charge brought against him that required his "death or imprisonment." The scheme of the Jewish leaders to bypass the legal process and kill Paul had been discovered, and was now being thwarted by his being sent to the jurisdiction of the governor. There any charges to be brought against him might be heard in accord with due process and in a situation where the life of the accused would not be in jeopardy from attackers. The huge contingent of military took Paul as far as "Antipatris,"[36] a strategic military point located on the edge of the Judean Hills northwest of Jerusalem, about halfway along the fifty-mile route that led to Caesarea up the Mediterranean coast. Accompanied only by the cavalry, Paul was escorted from there to "Caesarea," the seat of the Roman governor of the region.[37] When the letter from the tribune was delivered to the governor, he inquired of Paul which "province" he was from. Since it was "Cilicia," located in southeastern Asia Minor, it was not in the governor's jurisdiction, but the accusers were from the governor's province, and so he decided to hear the case. Meanwhile, Paul is kept for his own safety in the "praetorium" that "Herod" had built in Caesarea,[38] and which continued to serve as the official base for the Roman-authorized official, Felix, as it did earlier for Herod, the puppet king. Here Paul was guarded until the appearance before the governor of his accusers from Jerusalem.

24:1–23: Paul's Defense before Felix, the Governor

Five days later the high priest, Ananias, came down with certain elders and an attorney, a certain Tertullus. They laid out for the governor their charges against Paul. When he was summoned, Tertullus began to make his accusations, saying, "Since we have achieved peace through you, and since reforms for this nation have come to pass through your foresight, we accept this in every way and in every place with all gratitude, most excellent Felix. But in order not to waste your time, I urge you in your graciousness to hear us briefly. For we have found this man to be a plague, provoking discord among all the Jews throughout the inhabited world, and a ringleader of the sect of the Nazarenes. He even attempted to desecrate the temple, but we prevented him. When you interrogate him yourself, you will be able to understand all the things of which we accuse him." The Jews also joined in the accusation, asserting that all these things were so.

When the governor had nodded to Paul to speak, he responded: "Since I know that for many years you have been a judge over this nation, I cheerfully offer as a defense the things concerning myself. As you are able to ascertain, it is not more than twelve days since I went up to worship in Jerusalem. And they did not find me in the temple debating with anyone or causing the convergence of a crowd, either in the temple or in meetings or elsewhere in the city. Nor are they able to present evidence concerning the things of which they now accuse me. I admit to you this, that according to the Way — which they call a sect — I worship the God of our forefathers, trusting in everything that is in accord with the law and all those things that are written in the prophets, having a hope in God which these very people accept: that there is going to be a resurrection of the righteous and the unrighteous. In connection with this, I also do my best to have a blameless conscience before God and humans in every matter. After many years I have come, presenting to my people alms and offerings. As I was involved with these matters, they found me in the temple purified, [causing] neither a crowd nor a disturbance. But certain Jews from Asia — they should be present before you and make any accusations they may have against me, or let them say what transgression they found when I was standing before the council. There was this one statement which I shouted out as I was standing among them: 'It is concerning the resurrection of the dead that I am being tried before you this day.' "

Since he knew quite accurately the things concerning the Way, Felix adjourned them, having said, "When Lysias the tribune comes down, I shall decide your case." He instructed the centurion to retain him in custody, but with some freedom, and not to hinder his associates from rendering service to him.

Ananias was accompanied by "certain elders," presumably members of the council in Jerusalem, and by a legal spokesman named Tertullus. It is not likely that he was Jewish, but his rhetorical style and his knowledge of Roman law are the essential features of his role. His initial thrust was to flatter the governor and to express "gratitude" for the status and procedures by which the Roman authorities had brought "peace" and stability for the Jewish people resident in their land. It is here said to have been accepted by the people totally throughout their territory: "in every way and in every place." In contrast to this grateful conformity to Roman rule on the part of the Jewish residents there has come Paul, here characterized as a "plague" undermining the peaceful state of this people. The "discord" he has produced spread among Jews throughout the "inhabited world." Although obviously Paul's missionary activities have not covered the whole of the Greco-Roman world, the disruption he has caused is widespread and rapidly expanding. It is not seen here as merely a matter of religious differences among Jews but as threatening Roman law and order throughout the empire by its fiercely divisive claims and message. Paul's role is designated by Tertullus as "ringleader of the sect of the Nazarenes." For the Romans, Judaism is a licit form of religion, but Tertullus wants to show that this new movement is divisive and is undermining law and order, specifically by the desecration of the "temple," the functions of which were major factors in the social and economic stability of the land, and the leadership of which through the high priest was confirmed by Roman authority. The special features of the "Nazarenes" are not indicated here,[39] but calling them a "sect" (*hairesis*) forcefully implies that the movement is divisive and deviant from the state-approved operation of the Jewish religion and its leaders. Tertullus does not detail any of the issues, but seeks to show that Paul and his supporters are basic threats to the stability and peace of the empire and its subject people. His point of view is affirmed as accurate by the Jewish leaders. Their public concurrence with his analysis confirms the impression that he is not a Jew but that he articulates their concerns and viewpoint concerning this disruptive movement here seen as headed by Paul.

Paul's line of defense in response to this portrayal of him as a subverter of the legal religious movement, Judaism, begins with flattery of the governor paralleling that of Tertullus in its intent. His portrayal of himself, however, is totally contradictory to the charges made against him. He pictures himself as having come to Jerusalem as a pious worshiper, and as one devoted to the ancestral God of Israel, in full obedience to both the "Law" and the "prophets." He did not engage in controversy when he took part in the meetings, nor did he draw together crowds to whom he promoted divisive views. He sees himself rather as a representative of one of the options within the Jewish tradition, which he calls "the Way," the beliefs of which include a "hope" which Jews on the whole accept: the belief in a future judgment at which God will call to account all people, "righteous and unrighteous." Paul has expressed this expectation repeatedly in Acts, and the links between this belief and popular Stoic philosophy have been noted above.[40] He then makes the ironic note that the very ones who want to portray him as a violator of the Law and the Jewish tradition include those who share his belief in the resurrection, which he here refers to as "a hope in God which these very people accept." These would be the Pharisees, although they are not here directly named. He goes on to affirm the fidelity with which he obeys his "conscience," which (as noted above) is also an element taken over by some Jews and early Christians from Stoic philosophy, and which figures importantly in Paul's argument about moral responsibility among Gentiles who do not have access to the Law of Moses but have the divine law written on their hearts, as their conscience attests (Rom. 2:1–16).[41]

Further, Paul was indeed conforming to standards of Jewish piety: presenting "alms and offerings" in the temple, and he was there in a "purified" condition. He had not assembled a crowd of those who would violate the purity of the temple nor launched any kind of disturbance, which gives the clear implication that his opponents were the instigators of the trouble and were responsible for the tumultuous crowd that had gathered in the temple courts. They, not Paul, are the true disturbers of the peace. They have made no formal accusation against him, and have come up with no specific violation during his hearing before the council. The statement that had triggered the hostile uprising against him had been his affirmation in public of a basic Pharisaic belief, which was rejected by other Jews, and especially by the priestly linked Sadducees.[42] The conflict that has erupted is not between Jews and their critics or opponents, but an intra-Jewish debate over belief in the "resurrection" or denial of it. Paul's argument is that there is no substance to the charges either that he is a radical violator of Jewish law, or that he is guilty of infraction of Roman law. Clearly, those addressed here are by no means merely the participants at this hearing in Caesarea, but the readers of Acts who may have suspicions or have heard allegations of law-breaking about this new movement on either Jewish or Roman grounds.

Felix is not convinced by those who have brought charges against Paul, but postpones final action on the case until Lysias comes down from Jerusalem to give his official report as tribune. Meanwhile, Felix takes care that Paul, as a Roman citizen, is assigned to the guardianship of a "centurion," with the provision that he can live in relative "freedom," and that his "associates" may have access to him in order to care for his needs. The clear implication in this account is that agents of the empire are providing justice and even protection for Paul, rather than their being persuaded by unfounded charges that he is an agent threatening the order of society maintained by imperial authority.

24:24–27: The Treatment of Paul during His Two-Year Imprisonment in Caesarea

After some days Felix appeared in public with Drusilla, his wife, who was Jewish. He summoned Paul and heard him speak about the faith in Jesus Christ. As he was discussing justice, self-control, and the judgment that is to come, Felix became fearful and responded, "For the time being, go away. When the time is opportune, I shall summon you." At the same time he was hoping that money might be given to him by Paul, so he summoned him very frequently and conversed with him. But when two years had passed, Felix had a successor: Porcius Festus, and wishing to bestow a favor on the Jews, Felix assigned Paul to be imprisoned.

Felix's wife, Drusilla, had important connections along two lines. Her father was Herod Agrippa I, grandson of Herod the Great and ruler of Palestine from 41–44 C.E. At her birth in 37 C.E., she was named for Julia Drusilla, the sister of the emperor, Gaius Caligula (reigned 37–41 C.E.), and was a Roman citizen by birth. Josephus reports that "she surpassed all other women in beauty" (*Ant.* 20.141), and hence "Felix," whom Claudius (41–54 C.E.) appointed as governor of Palestine (52–60 C.E.),[43] engaged a magician to entice her to abandon her husband and marry him in violation of Jewish law. She did so, and reportedly died with him when Mount Vesuvius erupted in 79 C.E.

Felix's repeated attempts to extract a bribe from Paul extended without success over a period of "two years," at which time he was replaced as governor by "Porcius Festus." Felix's final act was a belated effort to ingratiate himself with the Jewish leadership: he gave orders for Paul to be "imprisoned" (literally, "bound"), rather than as earlier being kept in custody with some freedom of movement and access (24:23).

Excursus on Roman Modes of Legal Custody

In his comprehensive analysis of modes of custody in Roman judicial practice, Brian Rapske notes the three major types: (1) protecting the accused prior to appearance in court; (2) coercive effort to force the recalcitrant to obey the authorities; (3) awaiting sentencing. The types of imprisonment included the following settings: death cell, quarry prison, enchainment, military custody, location in a private house, or release on one's own recognizance. It is not clear whether Paul's arrest was punitive or protective. Imprisonment was protracted in the case of noncitizens, slaves, and women, with the aim of coercing their obedience. Although imprisonment of citizens as punishment was officially ruled out in the imperial period, Tiberius and others continued to employ this method of coercing their opponents or law-breakers. Away from the large cities, smaller prisons served as places for light punishment or for confinement of those in transit to provincial headquarters or to Rome. Those accused of military violations were kept in custody for trial, and possible sentencing and execution. The prisoner was chained by the right wrist to the soldier's left in order to assure retention and to avoid escape, for both of which the soldier was held responsible. In nonmilitary cases, the accused could be entrusted to a surety for house arrest, either with an official or in the home of the accused, but "security and safety were paramount." Those accused who were released on their own recognizance were forbidden public appearance or travel outside the city. The magistrate was influenced in making custody decisions by the wealth and social status of both the accused and the accuser. Prisonable charges included propagation of war or rebellion or civil disturbance, as well as theft, murder, piracy, or sacrilege. But those publicly promulgating scorn of the rulers or dabbling in public prophecy and magic were also subject to official punishment. Citizens were protected in principle against torture or being condemned to death, and had the right of appeal to the emperor, although lack of funds for travel or basic needs for food and residence in Rome could preclude fulfilling that option. Thus the dignity and economic status of the appellant was an important factor, with the result that unimportant individuals were excluded from protection by appeal.[44]

25:1–12: Paul Appeals to the Emperor

Three days after Festus had set foot in his province, he went up to Jerusalem from Caesarea. The chief priests and the foremost of the Jews informed him about Paul, and appealed to him as a favor to transfer him to Jerusalem, arranging an ambush to murder him on the way. Festus replied that Paul would be kept in Caesarea, and that he himself was about to go there soon. "So then the men of power among you can go down with me," he said, "and if there is anything improper about this man, let them accuse him."

After he had stayed among them not more than eight or ten days, he went down to Caesarea, and on the next day, after taking his seat at the tribunal, he gave the order for Paul to be brought. When he had arrived, the Jews who had come down from Jerusalem stood around him, bringing weighty charges

which they could not document. Paul offered in defense, "Neither against the law of the Jews, nor against the temple, nor
against Caesar have I committed any violation." Festus, wishing to establish favor with the Jews, answered Paul and said,
"Do you wish to go up to Jerusalem to be judged by me there
concerning these matters?" But Paul said, "I am standing before the tribunal of Caesar, where it is obligatory for me to be
tried. I have in no way wronged the Jews, as you well know. If I
have done wrong and have done something worthy of death, I
am not trying to escape from dying. But since there is nothing
in what these people are accusing me of, I appeal to Caesar."
Then Festus, after having consulted with the council, replied,
"You appealed to Caesar: to Caesar you shall go!"

"Festus," the successor to Felix as governor of Judea from 59 to
62 C.E., is reported by Josephus to have confronted a surge in actions by radical Jewish activists, described as "bandits" (*sicarii*)
but more accurately identified as nationalists eager to liberate
their land from Roman domination.[45] Festus was appointed by
Nero (54–68 C.E.) to replace Felix, who was saved from severe
penalties for his greed and barbarities as procurator by the intervention of his brother Pallas, who is reported by Tacitus
(*Annals* 12.53, 13.14) as possessing enormous wealth and serving as the central financial officer during the reign of Claudius
(41–54 C.E.). Pallas was dismissed from this post by the angry
Nero in 55 (13.14), but his wealth and influence seem to have
continued, enabling him to gain support for his brother. Meanwhile, Festus's mediating role is demonstrated when he arranges
for a delegation to go to Nero to settle the dispute between the
Jews and Agrippa over a wall which the former built on the west
side of the temple to prevent Agrippa from surveying the temple
complex from his lofty palace on the western hill of Jerusalem.
Nero agrees to allow the wall to stand (*Ant.* 20.193–96), encouraged to do so by his wife, Poppea, who is a worshiper of God
(*theosebes*).[46] The charges brought by the Jewish leaders against
Paul are offered with no substantiation, and are countered by
Paul's denial of any violation of Jewish or Roman law. Festus's
proposal to transfer the hearing back to Jerusalem is an effort
to ingratiate himself with the leaders, but is thwarted by Paul's
insistence that the proper place for the hearing is in "the tribunal of Caesar." He is confident of his innocence of violation

of Roman law, and counters the false charges leveled against him by exercising his right as a Roman citizen to appeal his case to "Caesar." To this Festus simply acquiesces.

Excursus on the Right of Roman Citizens to Appeal to Caesar

Individuals who were wealthy or enterprising from among the ranks of provincial aristocrats had the possibility to bypass the governor or the local legal system and to undertake a prosecution or to defend a charge before the emperor, or someone designated by him. Cases from the provinces that reached the senate or the emperor more frequently involved administration of punishment rather than a retrial. The lower the status of the accused, the more severe the penalty. There was no binding obligation of the governor to grant the requests for transfer of venue of a case to Rome, but Roman aristocracy living abroad or with interests away from their places of residence were more likely to get a positive response to such a petition.[47] The account in Acts implies that Festus agreed to send Paul's case to Caesar because of his inability to assess the charges and the evidence, not because Paul was of demonstrably lofty social status.

25:13–27: Preparation for Paul's Hearing before Agrippa and Bernice

After some days had passed, Agrippa the king and Bernice arrived in Caesarea to welcome Festus. As they remained for many days, Festus laid before the king the things concerning Paul, saying, "A certain man is left behind as a prisoner by Felix, concerning whom the chief priests and the elders of the Jews gave me a report when I was in Jerusalem, requesting a sentence of condemnation for him. To them I replied that it is not the Roman custom to dispose of anyone before the accused has opportunity to meet his accusers face to face and to offer a defense concerning the charge. When they came together here, I did not in the least hinder the matter, but on the next day sat at the tribunal and ordered the man to be brought. When the accusers stood, they offered no ground for complaint regarding evil deeds such as I had supposed. But they had some disputes with him concerning their own religion and concerning a certain Jesus, who died, but whom Paul claimed to be alive. Since I was uncertain how to investigate these matters, I asked if he wanted to go to Jerusalem and be judged there concerning these matters. But when Paul appealed to be kept in custody for the decision of the emperor, I ordered that he be detained until I could send him to Caesar." Agrippa said to Festus, "I would like also to hear this man." "Tomorrow," he said, "you shall hear him."

So then on the next day Agrippa and Bernice came with full pageantry, and entered the hearing hall, with the tribunes and the men of prominence of the city, and Festus ordered that Paul be brought. And Festus said, "King Agrippa and all you men who are present with us, you see this man concerning whom an entire multitude of Jews appealed to me in Jerusalem and also here, shouting that he must no longer live. But I discerned that he had done nothing deserving death, but since he had appealed to the August One, I decided to send him. I have nothing specific to write to my lord concerning him, and so I have brought him before [both of] you, and especially before you, King Agrippa, so that I may have something to write about after the preliminary hearing has taken place. For it seems to me absurd, when sending a prisoner, not to designate the charges against him."

Excursus on Agrippa II and Bernice

Herod Agrippa II, son of Agrippa I and great-grandson of Herod, was being brought up in Rome at the court of the emperor Claudius (41–54 C.E.) at the time of his father's death in 44. His father had been designated by Gaius Caligula (37–41) as king of territories north and east of the Sea of Galilee (Josephus, *Ant.* 18.237), and then by Claudius in 41 as king over the larger area, including Judea and Samaria, which had been ruled by his grandfather, Herod (19.274). Agrippa II was only 17 and in Rome when his father died in 44. Because of his youth, Claudius was reluctant to name him as king, but in about the year 50 designated him as king of the tiny region of Chalcis, northeast of Damascus, and appointed a Roman procurator to govern Judea and the rest of the kingdom of Herod the Great (19.360–63). Agrippa scandalized the Jews by living with his sister, Bernice, as his wife after the death of Herod of Chalcis. In 53 Claudius assigned to him parts of Galilee and the districts to the north and east, to which Nero (54–68 C.E.) added Tiberias and adjacent regions.[48] Although Agrippa frequently intervened with the Roman authorities on behalf of the Jews, his ultimate loyalty was to Rome, the base of his power and wealth. Accordingly, when his attempts to halt the Jewish revolt that began in 66 C.E. failed, he worked with the Romans to defeat the revolutionaries and welcomed the leaders of the Roman armies who came to repress the revolt — especially Titus.[49] Agrippa is reported by Josephus to have delivered a speech to the Jews informing them that their motivation for revolution was misguided, that all the great nations of the Mediterranean and European regions had already come under Roman power, that the inevitable outcome of this foolish effort would be the destruction of the city and the temple, and that they should pay their tribute to Rome. The revolutionaries, however, drove him out of the city (*Wars* 2.344–407). The date and circumstances of his death are not known, but it was probably during the reign of Domitian (81–96).

●

Agrippa and Bernice journeyed from their residence, presumably in Tiberias, to "Caesarea" to greet the newly appointed Roman procurator, "Festus." This matches the earlier successful efforts of Agrippa to ingratiate himself with the Romans and thereby to confirm his own favored status. During their extended stay Festus is reported as recounting to them the plot of the Jewish leaders — "priests and elders" — to achieve the condemnation and execution of Paul. Festus has observed due process in accord with Roman law by hearing their charges, but refuses to accede to their demands to sentence Paul until he has an opportunity to hear and to weigh the accusations responsibly. Further, Festus has found nothing warranting Paul's condemnation, but instead hears only intra-Jewish religious disputes, including one about a Jew named Jesus, who had been put to death, but whom Paul claims is still alive. Festus does not raise any question about the occasion for the death of Jesus, nor about Paul's claim that Jesus has been raised from the dead. Both these aspects of the debate are on issues within Judaism, and they represent no trace of violation of Roman law. If Paul were demonstrably a violator of Jewish law, his case could in principle have been referred appropriately to the Jewish council in Jerusalem, but Paul insisted as a Roman citizen that it be transferred to Rome and heard by Caesar. To this demand, Festus has acceded, and was keeping Paul in protective custody until he could be sent off to Rome. But now he has agreed to arrange for Paul to present his case to Agrippa.

The hearing is depicted as taking place in a formal setting: located in the official hall for hearing cases, even though this was not a formal trial; attended by three kinds of distinguished individuals: (1) the Roman governor and the military tribunes, (2) the royalty from an adjacent region, and (3) "men of prominence" from the capital city of Caesarea. Once more, the author of Acts is making the point that what is happening in this new movement is taking place in public view, not secretly in a corner, as Agrippa is soon to be told by Paul (26:26). The dual purpose of the hearing is to enable Agrippa to be informed directly about the charges made against Paul and possibly to provide Festus with grounds for action on this case, so that he can avoid the awkward situation of sending off an accused person concerning whom no substantive accusations have been articulated. Clearly the author of Acts wants once more to make the point indirectly, but vividly, that Paul is indeed innocent of violation of Roman law.

26:1–32: Paul's Defense before Agrippa and Bernice

Agrippa said to Paul, "It is permitted for you to speak in your own behalf." Then Paul extended his hand and offered his defense: "I consider myself to be divinely privileged that I am about to make my defense today before you in response to all the accusations by Jews, King Agrippa, since you are the most knowledgeable about all the Jewish customs and disputes. So I plead that you hear me with forbearance.

"That from my youth my manner of life took place from the beginning among my own people and in Jerusalem, all the Jews have known. From the outset they have known, if they are willing to bear witness, that according to the strictest segment of our religion I have lived: as a Pharisee. And now I stand on trial for the hope in the promise which was made to our fathers by God, in which our twelve tribes hope to participate, as they worship night and day. I am being accused by Jews concerning this hope! Why is it considered incredible by any of you that God raises the dead?

"I convinced myself that I had to do many things against the name of Jesus of Nazareth, and I did so in Jerusalem. I not only locked up in prison many of the saints by the authority of the high priests, but when they were seized for execution, I cast my vote against them. And in all the meetings, seeking repeatedly to have them punished, I was forcing them to blaspheme. Filled with overwhelming rage, I pursued them to cities both within and beyond [our land]. To these ends I traveled to Damascus with authorization and full power from the high priests. At midday as I was on the way, O king, I saw a light brighter than the radiance of the sun shining on me from heaven and on those who traveled with me. When we had all fallen to the ground, I heard a voice saying to me in the Hebrew language, 'Saul! Saul! Why are you persecuting me? It is difficult for you to kick against the goads!' And I said, 'Who are you, sir?' And the Lord said, 'I am Jesus, whom you are persecuting. But get up and stand on your feet, for I have appeared to you for this purpose: I have handpicked you to be an agent and a witness of the things which you saw and which I shall disclose to you. I will rescue you from the [Jewish] people and from [gentile] nations to which I am sending you, in order to open their eyes and to turn them from darkness to light, and from the power of Satan to God, so that they might receive forgiveness of sins and a share with those who are consecrated through faith in me.'

"For this reason, King Agrippa, I was not disobedient to the heavenly vision, but first in Damascus and then in Jerusalem and in every section of Judea and even to the Gentiles, I proclaimed that they should repent and turn back to God, doing deeds that are fitting for repentance. On account of these things Jews seized me while I was in the temple, and tried to lay violent hands on me. Since I have had help from God to this day, I stand testifying to small and great, saying nothing but what the prophets and Moses said was going to take place: that the Messiah should suffer; that he would be the first [to experience] the resurrection of the dead; that the light was going to be proclaimed both to the [Jewish] people and to the nations."

As he was offering these things in his defense, Festus said in a great voice, "Paul, your massive learning is leading you into madness!" But Paul said, "I am not going mad, most excellent Festus, but I am uttering words of truth and rationality. For the king has understanding about these things, and to him I am speaking freely, for I am persuaded that none of these things has escaped his notice. For this was not accomplished in a corner! Do you believe the prophets, King Agrippa? I know that you do believe." But Agrippa said to Paul, "Are you convinced that you can make me a Christian in such a brief time?" And Paul said, "Whether in a brief or a long time, I wish to God that not only you but also all who hear me this day might become such as I am — with the exception of these fetters."

The king arose, as well as the governor and Bernice and those who were sitting with them. And after they had withdrawn, they were talking to one another, saying, "There is nothing deserving death or fetters that this man has done." Agrippa said to Festus, "This man could have been released if he had not appealed to Caesar."

Agrippa observes the Roman policy of a citizen's right to present his or her case when involved in defense against legal charges. Paul's gesture when he "extended his hand" as he prepares to deliver his apology is the stylized action of an orator in the Roman period,[50] and is matched by the flattering remarks he makes concerning Agrippa. Paul declares himself to be *makarios*, which means "granted special privilege by divine favor." This opportunity to present his case before the civil and religious authorities is portrayed in Acts as further attestation that it is God who is working out his purpose through Paul, which is the antithesis of the claim of his opponents that he is subverting the covenant tradition of God with his people Israel. The omission of the definite article before *Ioudaion* twice in 26:3 indicates that the charges against Paul are from certain Jews — the official leadership — but not from Jews as a whole. Agrippa's well-known dual role of supporting Jewish rights before the Roman authorities and backing the Romans when they oppose what he regards as unwise and unwarranted schemes — especially the Jewish nationalist revolutionary efforts — makes him a uniquely appropriate instrument for hearing Paul, for understanding him, and for interpreting his ideas and actions to the Roman authorities.

Paul then proceeds to make a case for his claim that his present convictions and activities are in the distinctive Jewish tradition, and are not subversive. The locus and the focus of his training have been in a Jewish setting, with regard to both his family upbringing and his subsequent training in Jerusalem. Indeed, his commitment has been shaped, not by a peripheral movement, but by the mainstream: in the "strictest" Jewish "segment," the Pharisees. It is the "hope" of the "twelve tribes" of Israel, the promise of deliverance and renewal made by God to his people, which ironically has become the basis of the current leadership's violent hostility toward Paul. The most controversial feature of this hope, which Paul's assembled critics[51] "consider incredible," is the one which he here highlights: "that God raises the dead." He asserts that the hope of cosmic renewal and sharing in the future fulfillment of God's purpose are formal and constantly repeated features of individual and corporate Jewish "worship," in keeping with the prophetic tradition. The chief cause of the violent hostility that Paul is experiencing from the Jewish leadership is his conviction that the prime agent through whom the hope of God's people is being accomplished is "Jesus of Nazareth." It is this name that Paul had so vehemently opposed, and he had done so by "authority" granted to him through the chief "priests."

The initial setting for his ferocious hostility toward those whom he now styles as "saints" was Jerusalem. This was the primary locus of authority of members of the Jewish council, whose sphere of decision and action was granted by the Romans, as noted above.[52] There Paul had been engaged in imprisoning and even executing members of this new movement, and when they sought to escape, he had pursued them to other "cities" both in Palestine and in regions "beyond." The implication is clear that the council in Jerusalem was granted authority by the Romans to maintain control of the Jewish community and to enforce conformity to its traditional laws far beyond the vicinity of Jerusalem, including the wider region of Syria-Palestine, which earlier had constituted the Seleucid realm. It was to the major city of Syria — Damascus — that Paul went with the necessary "authorization" to try to destroy the Jesus movement that had taken root there. As in the initial report of Paul's conversion in Damascus (9:1–19), there is no indication as to how the new community began there. Luke does not include Mark's mention

of Jesus' circuit through the cities of the Decapolis after his journey to Tyre and Sidon (Mark 7:31), which might have included a
visit to the best known of the cities of the Decapolis: Damascus.
There is no indication as to the identity of those who launched
"the Way" in that city (9:1–2), but it was to Jerusalem that they
were to be taken and called to account by the Jewish leadership.
Details of this report of Paul's confrontation by the risen "Lord"
differ from those earlier in Acts (9:1–18, 22:3–16). In 9:1–2, Paul
seeks and gains authorization from the "high priest" to bind and
bring to Jerusalem those who belong to "the Way"; in 26:12 the
commissioning is said to be by "the high priests." In 9:4 and
22:7, the light shines on Paul, who hears the voice and falls "to
the ground." In 26:14 all fall to the ground, but only he hears
the voice, while in 9:8 the men hear the voice but see no one.
Only here is the risen Jesus quoted as noting the difficulty Paul
is having in "kicking against the goads" (26:14). Ironically, the
voice that Paul is reported as hearing is said to address him in
"Hebrew" (which would more likely have been Aramaic), repeating his name twice, as in other apocalypses of the late first or
early second centuries C.E.[53] The image of kicking against the
goad — which means resisting moral reproof or guidance — has
its best known occurrence in Greek in Euripides (*Bacchus* 795).
Philo also uses the goad image in depicting how human emotions are stirred up, such as pleasure or sorrow.[54] Ps. Sol. 16:4
refers to God as prodding Solomon like a horse to keep him
awake, and hence as his savior and protector at all times.[55] The
proverbial saying in 26:14, said to be in Hebrew but in fact re-
calling the imagery of Euripides, reinforces the impression that
the author of Acts is deeply influenced by hellenistic culture and
traditions. In the earliest account of Paul's conversion he is told
that he is to bear witness to what he has already seen concerning
Jesus, as well as to other visions of Christ that he is yet to experience (26:16). Further, he is promised deliverance from the hands
of those who will oppose him, both leaders of the Jewish people
and of the Gentiles (26:17). It is clear that the mission of Paul is
here pictured as the outworking of a divine plan through which
Jews and Gentiles alike will be called to turn to God (26:18).

Not mentioned in the account in Acts 26 are such features of
earlier accounts of Paul's conversion as Ananias's laying hands
on Paul, and his instructions concerning Paul's mission (Acts
9:10–19). On the other hand, only in 26:16–18 are to be found

other details of Paul's commissioning for that mission, the warning about opposition from his own people and from the Gentiles, and the four themes of his message: (1) opening the eyes of his hearers, (2) turning them from the powers of darkness, (3) receiving forgiveness of sins, and (4) sharing in the life of the consecrated people of God (26:18). Sketched here is also a summary of the several locations in which Paul's mission was carried out. The list includes not only Damascus and Jerusalem, but "every section of Judea" (mission activity that is not recounted in Acts), as well as his reaching out "also to the Gentiles," which constitutes a major part of Acts. The epitome of the response that Paul seeks from all these hearers is here said to be twofold: (1) repent and turn to God; (2) perform deeds "fitting for repentance" (26:20). A final resume of his message is uttered in more explicitly christological terms than in Paul's other addresses in Acts and with the emphatic claim that all these events are in accord with the words of Moses and the prophets: the suffering of the Messiah; his resurrection as a prototype of the hope of his people; and the outreach of this message to both Jews and Gentiles (26:23). Except for the brief mention in 28:23 of Paul's effort in Rome to persuade the Jewish community there concerning Jesus, the rest of the discourse material in Acts focuses on Paul's journey to Rome and the impending trial there.

The responses of the Roman governor and of the puppet king of the Jews to Paul's message serve the author of Acts as models of the range of ways in which the Christian claims about Jesus will be received. Festus, while complimenting Paul for his "massive learning," dismisses the substance of his message as "madness." To this Paul responds with the claim that his message — which is neither subversive of Jewish tradition nor "madness" from the Roman perspective — is expressed in "words of truth and rationality," as the king who is informed about the Jewish biblical tradition should recognize. He goes on to imply that Agrippa not only knows the "prophets," but even believes their message. The king refuses to indicate that he is being speedily persuaded by Paul's message, but Paul invites all who hear to believe it and to become members of the new people of God. Although Agrippa and Bernice offer no public reaction to Paul and his invitation to share in his faith, they agree with the governor in private conversation that there is no evidence that Paul has committed a capital crime or even that he deserves imprisonment — by either Jewish or Roman standards. Nevertheless, his "appeal to Caesar" must be respected, although their own judicial decision would have been to "release" him. Clearly, the author of Acts is adding facets to his picture of Paul as one who is by no means an ignoramus but is knowledgeable in both Jewish and wider Greco-Roman learning, and who is wholly innocent of legal violations. He also portrays the Roman authorities as models of fairness and legal responsibility. Clear is the apologetic utility of this account of the hearing for Christians in the later first century who were increasingly being charged with violations of Jewish and Roman law.

27:1–6: The First Stage of the Journey to Rome

When it was decided that we should sail to Italy, they handed over Paul and certain other prisoners to a centurion of the imperial cohort by the name of Julius. Boarding a ship from Adramyttium, which was about to sail to places in Asia, we put to sea. With us was Aristarchus, a Macedonian of Thessalonica. The next day we called at Sidon, and Julius, acting benevolently toward Paul, gave him permission to go to his friends and be cared for. After putting to sea from there, we sailed under the lee of Cyprus, because the winds were contrary. When we had sailed across the sea which is off Cilicia and Pamphylia, we arrived at Myra in Lycia. When the centurion found there a ship of Alexandria on the way to Italy, he put us on board it.

In order to effect the transfer of Paul's case to Rome, he was turned over to a "centurion" by Festus, along with an undesignated number of other "prisoners," the charges against whom are not indicated in Acts. The name of the centurion, "Julius," and his membership in the Augustan cohort[56] confirm the official Roman framework in which are depicted the legal factors in this case: Paul's appeal to the emperor, the nature of the accusations against him, and the procedure by which he was held and brought to trial. Due process in the imperial mode is being observed fully.

Although the narrative at this point resumes the "we" mode, there is only one person identified as being permitted to travel with Paul: "Aristarchus." No information is given here about him, other than his place of origin: "Thessalonica" in "Macedonia."

Excursus on Aristarchus

The term used with reference to Aristarchus as Paul's traveling companion, *sunekdemos*, occurs with similar connotations in Josephus (*Life* 14) and Plutarch (*Cato Minor* 5). But he is most likely the same Aristarchus as the one who reportedly sailed with Paul from Philippi to Troas, Miletus (20:13–16), and on to Tyre and Caesarea (21:5–8). He is also most probably to be perceived as identical with the man of that name mentioned in Philemon 24 as Paul's co-worker and in Col. 4:10 as his fellow-prisoner. As noted above,[57] it is in these passages that Luke is also depicted as an associate of Paul's, which indicates why Acts was very early linked with Luke, and why it has been attributed from early on as the product of this reported companion of Paul.

•

The ship that Paul was placed on, its calling at several ports along the Syrian and Asia Minor coasts, his transfer to another ship, and the changing routes that it followed, as well as the evidence of divine protection and provision in the course of the journey, are all familiar features of sea travel in the Mediterranean as reported in popular literature of the Greco-Roman period.[58] The home port of the first ship, "Adramyttium," was well up on the western side of Asia Minor, north of Pergamum and east of Troas. After a brief journey and a call at "Sidon," where Paul was permitted to visit with a presumably Christian community not previously mentioned in Acts,[59] the journey was to the west, along the north side of the island of Cyprus in order to avoid the onset of winter winds. On the mainland of Asia Minor to the north were Cilicia (where the chief city was Tarsus, Paul's home) and Pamphylia (where the splendid chief city, Perga, had been visited by Paul; Acts 13:13, 14:24–25). Then this stage of the journey ended at "Myra," which was at that time the most important port "city in Lycia," the province located at the southwestern corner of Asia Minor. A ship there from Alexandria, which is due south of Myra across the Mediterranean on the African shore, was presumably loaded with grain produced in

Egypt and destined for the market in Rome. This vessel provided the centurion with an ideal means of transporting the prisoner and his associate(s) to the imperial hearing in the capital of the empire.

27:7–44: The Journey Halted by a Shipwreck

For some days we sailed slowly, and with difficulty we came off Cnidus. Since the wind did not permit us to go farther, we sailed under the lee of Crete opposite Salmone. Sailing past it with difficulty, we came to a place called Fair Havens, which was near the city of Lasea. Since much time had gone by and the voyage was dangerous because the Fast had already passed, Paul made a recommendation, saying to them, "Men, I perceive that this voyage is going to take place with much disaster and heavy loss, not only of the cargo and the ship, but also of our lives." But the centurion was persuaded more by the captain and the ship-owner than by the things Paul said. And since the harbor was not suitable for wintering, the majority reached the decision to depart from there, so that they might be able to reach and spend the winter at Phoenix, a harbor on Crete which faced the northwest and southwest. When the south wind blew gently, they assumed that their plan had worked, and departed and sailed along close to Crete. But before long a typhoon called the northeaster struck from there. Since the ship was tossed about and was unable to face the wind, we gave up and were driven [by the wind]. Having sailed under the lee of a small island named Cauda, we barely managed to keep control of the little boat. After hoisting it up, they tried to provide supports as braces for the ship, and fearing that we might run aground on the Syrtis, they put the sails in position, and so were driven along. Since we were extremely tossed about in the storm, on the next day they began jettisoning [the cargo], and on the third day with their own hands they threw out the ship's gear. Because the sun and stars were not visible for many days, and since it was no small storm that beset us, all hope for us to be saved was finally abandoned.

Since they had been without food for a long time, Paul then stood in their midst and said, "You should have followed my advice not to depart from Crete and would have escaped injury and loss. Now I urge you to cheer up: not a single soul among you shall be lost, but only the ship. For this night there came to me from God — whose I am and whom I serve — an angel, who said, 'Have no fear, Paul! It is necessary for you to stand before Caesar, and see, God has granted to you all those who are traveling with you.' So cheer up, men! For I trust God that everything will be just as was told to me. But we must run aground on a certain island."

When the fourteenth night came, as we were drifting in the Adriatic Sea, about midnight the sailors assumed that we were approaching land. And when they took a sounding, they found [they were] at twenty fathoms. Fearing lest we drift onto rough places, they lowered our anchors from the stern and prayed for day to come. When the sailors were seeking to escape from the ship and let down the boat into the sea, under pretext of preparing to put out anchors from the bow, Paul said to the centurion and the soldiers, "If these people do not remain in the ship, you are not able to be saved." Then the soldiers cut away the ropes of the boat and allowed it to drift.

When day was about to come, Paul was urging everyone to take some food, saying, "This is the fourteenth day that you have continued in expectancy and without food, and have taken nothing. So now I plead with you to take some food, for this will be your deliverance: not a hair of your head will be lost." When he had said these things, he took bread and gave thanks to God in front of them all, and breaking [the bread], he began to eat. Then they all became encouraged and they too took food. We were a total of two hundred and seventy-six in the ship. When they had had enough to eat, they lightened the ship by throwing the wheat out into the sea.

When day came, they did not recognize the land, but they perceived a bay which had a beach, to which they wanted — if possible — to bring the ship safely. So they cast off the anchors into the sea, at the same time loosening the ropes of the rudders and letting them go into the sea. Then hoisting the foresail into the wind, they headed for the beach. But striking a reef, they ran the vessel aground: the prow of the ship stuck fast and remained immobile, and the stern was smashed by the violence of the surf. There was a plan among the soldiers that they would kill the prisoners so that none of them could escape by swimming away. But since the centurion wanted to keep Paul safe, he prevented them from [carrying out] what they planned. He gave orders that they should head for the shore: those who were able to swim should first throw themselves overboard, and the rest [should float] on planks or on pieces remaining from the ship. And so it happened that all did escape to the shore.

The next stage of the voyage was slow and frustrating because of the hostile winds. After passing the small islands off the coast of Asia Minor, including Cnidus, the route taken was past Salmone at the northeast corner of Crete and along the southern coast of the island to Fair Havens (or Harbor), about five miles west of the city of Lasea, which may be the city of Lasos mentioned by Pliny (*Natural History* 4.12.5). The area has never been excavated adequately. Since sea travel was dangerous in the winter, there was anxiety about proceeding farther. The "Fast" that had already passed was presumably the Day of Atonement, which by the lunar calendar took place on the tenth day of the seventh month (Tishri), but by the solar calendar would fall during the months of September or October. From classical writers it can be inferred that travel after mid-September was dubious and should be halted by early November.[60] Paul is reported as giving an explicit warning that to resume the voyage will result in "much disaster and heavy loss," including the cargo, the ship, and the lives of those aboard. The immediate goal was to reach the much safer harbor at the western end of Crete: Phoenix.[61] But the centurion was persuaded by the "captain and ship-owner," and with the coming of a gentle wind from the south, which could have served to send them toward Italy, they left the harbor. A fierce northeastern storm drove them past "Cauda" (probably Gaudos), a small island located some twenty miles south of Crete. Fearful that further travel in a southerly direction would bring them disaster on the North African coast at Syrtis, they raised the sails and were driven in a northwesterly direction. Efforts to control the direction of the boat by throwing overboard their cargo were futile, and the heavy clouds prevented them even from seeing sun or stars to perceive what their course ought to be. In despair and lacking food for some days, Paul reminded them of his earlier advice not to depart from Crete, but sought to reassure them that they all would survive. The message from God conveyed to Paul by an angel assured him that there was a divine necessity that he make his case before Caesar, and hence all his fellow-travelers would be spared, and the ship would "run aground on a certain island." The point is made that even in seeming disaster and in the fiercest trials, God's hand and purpose are at work, and are certain of fulfillment.

As the sailors sensed the ship's approach to land, the anchors lowered from the stern were intended to slow its movement, but they also planned to guarantee their own escape in a small boat from the rightly anticipated wreck. Aware of their scheme, Paul warned them that to do so would result in their death, and so the little boat was let loose. He also urged them to eat food after two week's abstention, so that they would have strength to meet the challenge of landing and the experience of divine deliverance of the entire crew and passengers, who are said to have numbered 276. Paul's taking bread and "giving thanks" were not only a practical necessity but a form of Christian testimony to the pagan crew and officers. Further lightening of the ship took place when the grain was thrown into the sea. Releasing the anchors and the rudders, as well as hoisting the foresail of the ship, placed those aboard at the mercy of what they saw as the forces of nature, but what the author of Acts wants to show is the hand of God. After running aground on a reef, the ship broke apart. Aware of his responsibility to escort Paul to the hearing before the emperor, the centurion thwarted the plan of the sailors to kill Paul and the other prisoners, with the result that all escaped by swimming ashore or by clinging to pieces of the shattered ship and thus being washed safely ashore. The promise of safety conveyed by God to Paul (27:22) had found its fulfillment. Every detail in this travel account is depicted as the carrying forward of the divine plan and purpose.

28:1–10: Paul on the Island of Malta

After we had escaped, we learned that the name of the island was Malta. The natives granted us human kindness beyond the usual sort, kindling a fire to welcome all of us, because of the rain that had started and because of the cold. When Paul had collected a bundle of brush and thrown it on the fire, a viper came out because of the heat and fastened on his hand. When the natives saw the beast hanging from his hand, they said to one another, "By all means, this man is a murderer! Even though he has been rescued from the sea, justice has not permitted him to live." But then he shook off the beast into the fire and suffered no harm. They were expecting him to swell up suddenly or fall down dead. When they had waited for a long time and saw that nothing unusual happened to him, they changed their minds and were saying that he was a god. In that vicinity were lands which belongs to the chief man of the island by the name of Publius, who welcomed us and treated us hospitably as guests for three days. It happened that the father of Publius lay sick, stricken with fever and dysentery. Paul went in to him, prayed, laid his hands on him, and healed him. After this had taken place, the rest of those on the island who had ailments also came and were cured. They showered us with many honors, and as we were departing, they provided us with the things we needed.

Only after being washed ashore do Paul and the other travelers find that they have reached the island of Malta. It had been occupied for nearly four thousand years by the time of Paul, and was for a long time a trading center for the Phoenicians, whose culture continued to dominate the island. This is reflected in the term *barbaroi* — meaning nonspeakers of Greek or Latin — applied to the natives, whose language was presumably semitic. The humane cordiality (*philanthropia*) of the Maltese people was evident in their building a fire to offset the combined difficulties of the arrivals' escape from the shipwreck and the onset of cold, wet winter conditions.

Both the compassion of Paul toward those in need and the divine power at work through him are dramatically attested in details of the account at this point. The reptile[62] that fastened on Paul as he sought to build up the bonfire was initially interpreted by the local onlookers as a sign of divine punishment for one they suppose to be a "murderer," and they expected some fatal consequence. But the divine vindication was perceived by them as coming when he was not struck dead, and their estimate of him was reversed: he must be a "god" in human guise. The kindness and generosity of the inhabitants of Malta were further evident in the generosity and hospitality of "Publius," who is identified as "chief man [*protos*] of the island," which is a term found in inscriptions there with reference to the resident imperial authority, in one of which he is depicted as benefactor, magistrate, and chief priest of the imperial cult (CIG 14.60). Paul is enabled to respond to the ruler's kindness and to demonstrate the divine power and purpose at work through him in healing the official's father of "fever and dysentery" by "prayer" and the imposition of his hands. The whole segment of the island population that was ailing is pictured as being brought to Paul for healing, to which the beneficiaries respond by "showering with honors" (or an abundance of gifts) Paul and his companions as they prepared to sail forth on their continuing journey to Rome. The one who had been first thought to be the target of divine judgment had turned out to be the instrument of health and renewal, and these people who had no background in Jewish tradition responded to the divine healing with appropriate acts of gratitude.

28:11–16: Paul Reaches Rome

After three months we sailed off in a ship which had spent the winter at the island; it was Alexandrian and bore the insignia of the Dioscuri. After having landed at Syracuse, we remained there for three days. Casting off from there, we reached Rhegium. After one day, a south wind came up, and on the second day we came to Puteoli, where we found brethren and were invited to remain with them for seven days. And thus we came to Rome. The brethren from there, when they heard the things concerning us, came as far as the Forum of Appius and the Three Taverns to meet us. When Paul saw them, he gave thanks to God and took courage. When we entered Rome, it was permitted to Paul to remain by himself, with the soldier assigned to guard him.

The stay on Malta continued for three months, until the threat of winter storms had passed. The fact that this abstention from sea travel was the norm is evident in the added detail that another Alexandrian ship had spent the winter in the harbor there and was now ready to resume its journey to Italy. The ship's insignia was the "Dioscuri": Castor and Pollux, the twin sons of Zeus who by the first century C.E. were called "the savior gods" and were believed to help those at sea endangered by storms, as attested by the Stoic philosopher Epictetus (2.18.29). The voyage took the ship first to Syracuse, a prosperous and beautiful port city on the east coast of Sicily, located in part on a small island as well as on the Sicilian mainland, on each of which there were harbors. Ruins of temples there show that they were built to honor Apollo and Athena. The three-day stay may have been the result of waiting for improvement in the weather, or perhaps part of the (probably grain) cargo was un-loaded there. The next stop was at Rhegium, located at the tip of the boot of Italy on the narrow isthmus that separates Sicily from the mainland.[63] Near the city are the two famous whirlpools, Scylla and Charybdis, which may account for the importance there of the worship of the Dioscuri, as evident on local coins. These twin divinities were believed to come to the aid of sailors in response to petitions for favorable winds. Such subtle references show how well the author of Acts knows the Roman world and its traditions, and how skilled he is in making implicit contrasts with the widespread popular claims made for these divinities and the demonstrable power of God at work in behalf of Paul in connection with the coming of the gospel to the capital of the Roman world. With the cooperative emergence of a south wind, the voyage was readily completed to Puteoli, the port city just west of Neapolis (Naples), from which the most famous of Roman roads, the Appian Way, led to the capital city itself.

In Puteoli there was already a Christian community ("breth-ren"), with whom Paul and the others were permitted to visit for a week before journeying north toward Rome. The report of the coming of Paul and his associates reached the new commu-nity in the capital before Paul did, and a delegation came south from Rome along the Appian Way to meet and welcome Paul and the others. The places where they met are of symbolic sig-nificance for the arrival of this apostolic agent in Rome. Both are on the Appian Way, the most famous and most heavily trav-eled access route to Rome, which was constructed in the fourth century B.C.E. The Forum of Appius was a town located about forty miles below the capital, at the convergence of this main highway and an important canal that led south from Rome to Puteoli, the major port through which grain was imported from Egypt, and Roman products (glass, oil, fine wine, pottery) were exported. The Three Taverns, about thirty miles south of Rome near the famous Pontine Marshes, served as an important stopping point for travelers to and from the capital. These details of Paul's itinerary serve to highlight the cultural and economic importance of Rome, and thus the dramatic climax that his arrival in Rome represented. Yet the message about Jesus had already been received there, and the nucleus of the new people of God was already operative in this center of world culture. Paul was understandably grateful and encouraged to meet these representatives of the new community, and hence offered thanks to God.

28:17–22: Paul's Invitation to the Local Jewish Leaders in Rome

It happened that after three days he convened those who were the top people among the Jews. When they had come together, he said to them, "Men and brothers, although I had done nothing contrary to the law or our paternal customs, in Jerusalem I was turned over as prisoner into the hands of the Romans. After they had interrogated me, they wanted to release me, since there was no charge against me requiring capital punishment. But when the Jews spoke in opposition, I was obligated to appeal to Caesar, even though I had no accusation to bring against my nation. It is for this reason, therefore, that I requested to see you and speak with you, since it is on account of the hope of Israel that I am bearing this chain." They said to him, "We have not received any letters from Judea concerning you, nor have any of the brethren who have arrived here reported or said anything evil concerning you. We think it is fitting to hear from you the views which you hold. For concerning this sect, it is known to us that everywhere it is opposed."

One can infer multiple motivations in Paul's convening the Jewish leaders so soon after his arrival in Rome. There is the obvious objective of hoping that all or at least some of them would believe his message concerning Jesus as God's agent for renewal of his people. Even if they rejected the good news, it would be evident to them and to the Roman authorities that what was being debated was a cluster of issues within the Jewish tradition, and that this new movement should be granted a sanction and tolerance similar to that enjoyed by Judaism. Paul is also explicit that he does not want to bring any general accusation against his own people, the Jews as a whole. The combination of these features is evident from his initial denial that he has in any way violated the Law of Moses or the subsequent development of "paternal customs." The Roman authorities in Palestine clearly agree with his conviction concerning the close connection between his message and the Jewish traditions, in that they exonerated him from any capital charge. The opposition of the Jewish leaders there, however, has clouded the issue, with the result that he has to take advantage of his status as a Roman citizen and appeal his case to the emperor. The central issue between him and his opponents is therefore evidently intra-Jewish, springing from the incompatibility of his understanding of God's purpose at work through Jesus and the antagonism to this claim on the part of the Jewish officials. The controversy epitomized by Paul here as a debate over "the hope of Israel" serves as the basis for his continuing custody by the Romans after his having been transported by them to Rome.

There was no initial hostility toward Paul or his message from the side of the Jewish leaders who accepted Paul's invitation to come to his lodgings. They had received no negative reports from Judea concerning Paul, either by letter or by direct statements made by Jews who had come to Rome from that land. Yet the incipient Jesus movement, which they labeled as a "sect" or "dissenting faction" (*hairesis*), was being denounced and controverted (*antilegetai*) not only in Rome but "everywhere." They seem to have had no detailed knowledge as to what it was about the movement that was so controversial and divisive, and so they invited Paul to express his own "views" on the subject. The Jewish leaders in Rome wanted to provide Paul with as large a group as possible to hear his public presentation on this issue, rather than to have him speak to them informally and spontaneously. Since his mobility was so strictly limited as a result of his being in Roman custody, they designated a day on which they would come to him to hear his case as he presented it before the resident Jewish community in Rome.

28:23–31: Paul's Case as Presented to the Jewish Community in Rome

When they had designated a day for him, large numbers came to him at his lodging, to whom — from morning to evening — he made a presentation, bearing witness concerning the kingdom of God, seeking to persuade them from the law and the prophets concerning Jesus. There were those who were persuaded by the things he said, and there were those who disbelieved. Being at variance with each other, they departed, after Paul had made one statement:

"The Holy Spirit spoke well through Isaiah the prophet when he said to your fathers, 'Go to this people and say,

" 'You shall surely hear and not understand, and you shall surely see, but not at all perceive. For the heart of this people has become dull, and they are hard of hearing, and have closed their eyes, so that they should not perceive with their eyes and hear with their ears and understand with the heart, and turn to me so that I might heal them.' [Isa. 6:9–10]

"Let it be known to you, therefore, that to the Gentiles this salvation of God has been sent: they will give heed."

He remained there two whole years in his own rented lodging, and welcomed all those who came to him, proclaiming the kingdom of God and teaching the things concerning the Lord Jesus Christ, with full confidence and without hindrance.

When the day chosen for the interchange with the leaders of the Jewish community arrived, large numbers of them came to his rented residential space.

Excursus on Paul's Lodging in Rome

The term for Paul's living accommodations in Rome, *xenia*, often is in Greek literature an abstract term, meaning "hospitality," but here and in its only other occurrence in the New Testament — at Philemon 22 — it is most plausibly understood to be space where visitors could gather. Since we read in 28:20 that he was living "in his own rented lodgings," one can assume that he chose the kind of space that he wanted. The space seemingly preferred by the apostles as Acts depicts them was a *hyperoon*, traditionally translated as "upper room," but which means "upper story." This term does not appear here, but the fact that "large numbers came to him" and remained throughout the day to hear his message indicates that his rented accommodations were spacious, and hence comparable to those depicted in Acts 1:12–14 as housing the entire core of the new community in Jerusalem.

•

Paul's extended message consisted of his personal testimony concerning "the kingdom of God," which is a major theme in the Gospel of Luke[64] and which serves as an epitome of the post-resurrection message of Jesus in Acts 1:3. It is a major emphasis in the preaching of the good news among the Samaritans, where Philip associates it with the power of "the name of Jesus" (8:12).

On Paul's return to Syrian Antioch, his effort to strengthen the members of the new community so that they may "continue in the faith" includes a warning that it is through "many painful experiences" that one must "enter the kingdom of God" (14:22). Paul's debate with the Jews in Ephesus had as a central theme "the kingdom of God" (19:8). Here in Rome, his extended presentation to the Jews concentrates on his personal witness of the meaning and power of "the kingdom of God." Its primary strategy is to seek to persuade his Jewish hearers concerning Jesus and his role in the establishment of God's rule in the world by appeal to "the law and the prophets." Once more, the author of Acts is making the central point that Jesus and the movement he launched are not to be regarded as subversive of the Jewish tradition or of the history of the disclosure of God's purpose to Israel, but its culmination.

Both the defining of God's people in the Law of Moses and the hopes of renewal of his people articulated by the prophets find their fulfillment in Jesus, he claims. The response from his Jewish hearers is mixed: some are "persuaded" by Paul's arguments, while others refuse to believe his message. Since there is a serious division among them, they decide to leave — some from hostility to Paul and his claims about Jesus, and some who now feel alienated from their own traditional community. But prior to their departure Paul issues a solemn message of warning, couched in the language of the prophet Isaiah (28:26–27 = Isa. 6:9–10), which describes the actions of the unbelieving hearers of the claims concerning the kingdom of God and Jesus. Addressed to the people themselves, it is the prophet's warning that the inability of many who hear the message to accept its claim is the consequence of their own refusal to see and hear and understand it. They will not turn to God in faith, and so they will not experience the healing that God is offering to them. Since many of the traditional people of God have refused to receive this message, it is God's purpose to offer now to the Gentiles both the good news and the transforming renewal ("salvation") which it bestows on those who receive it.

The Acts narrative ends with the report that Paul and his associates remained for two years in these rented quarters, although there is no hint of why it apparently ceased after that period of time. The positive aspect of this period of activity is threefold: (1) the twin message concerning the kingdom of God and the "Lord Jesus Christ" continued to be proclaimed in Rome; (2) the results seem to have given Paul and his associates continuing "confidence" of the truth and the dynamic potential of this message; and (3) the author of Acts continues his subtle apologetic for the message of Paul concerning Jesus and its transforming efficacy, and does so without either religious or political interference, and with no evidence of overt opposition. The clear implication is that this witness and the community that it is creating are manifestations of the purpose and power of God, and that they are certain to continue until the divinely intended consummation of the ages. In preparation for that, the newly defined covenant community is reaching out across ethnic, ritual, and cultural boundaries — "to the end of the earth" (Acts 1:8).

Abbreviations

AB	Anchor Bible (Commentary Series)
ABD	*Anchor Bible Dictionary*, ed. D. N. Freedman
ANRW	*Aufstieg und Niedergang der römischen Welt,* ed. W. Haase
CIG	Corpus inscriptionum graecarum
CIL	Corpus inscriptionum latinarum
EThL	*Ephemerides Theologicae Lovanienses*
HDB	*Hastings' Dictionary of the Bible*, 4 vols., ed. by J. Hastings et al. Edinburgh and New York, 1899–1904.
IGRR	Inscriptiones Graecae ad Res Romanas pertinentes
JSNT	*Journal for the Study of the New Testament*
LCL	Loeb Classical Library
NovT	*Novum Testamentum*
NTS	*New Testament Studies*
SBL	Society of Biblical Literature
SJLA	Studies in Judaism in Late Antiquity
SNTSMS	Society for New Testament Studies Monograph Series
TDNT	*Theological Dictionary of the New Testament*
WUNT	Wissenschaftliche Untersuchungen zum Neuen Testament

Notes

Introduction

1. The text of the Muratorian Canon was reconstructed by H. J. Cadbury in *The Beginnings of Christianity,* Part 1: *The Acts of the Apostles,* ed. F. J. Foakes-Jackson and K. Lake, vol. 2, *Prolegomena II: Criticism* (London: Macmillan, 1922), 210.

2. The we-sections are 16:10–17, 20:4–16, 21:1–18, and 27:1–28:16.

3. According to Eusebius, *Ecclesiastical History* 6.25.6, 12.

4. Ibid., 3.4.6–7.

5. Jerome, *Commentary on Isaiah* (in Migne, *Patrologia Latina* 24.98); *De viris illustribus* 14.1.11–12.

6. A useful, comprehensive survey of the history of the interpretation of Acts has been prepared by W. Ward Gasque, *A History of the Interpretation of the Acts of the Apostles,* republished with an addendum (Peabody, Mass.: Hendrickson, 1989). Extended excerpts and critical analyses of earlier New Testament critical scholarship concerning Acts are offered in W. G. Kümmel, *The New Testament: A History of the Investigation of Its Problems,* trans. H. C. Kee (Nashville: Abingdon, 1972). Other important surveys of critical studies of Acts are mentioned below in analyses of various themes.

7. Johann Salomo Semler, *Abhandlung von freier Untersuchung des Canons [Treatise on Free Research in the Canon],* 4 vols. (Halle, 1771–75), preface.

8. Quoted from Kümmel, *New Testament,* 133.

9. Bruno Bauer, *Die Apostelgeschichte. Eine Ausgleichung des Paulinismus und des Judentums innerhalb der christlichen Kirche* (Berlin, 1850).

10. W. M. L. de Wette, *Kurze Erklärung der Apostelgeschichte,* 4th ed., ed. [and largely rewritten by] Franz Overbeck (Leipzig, 1870).

11. James Smith, *The Voyage and Shipwreck of St. Paul* (London, 1848; 4th ed., 1880).

12. Luke is mentioned in Philemon 24, and as "the beloved physician" in Col. 4:14, as well as in the Deutero-Pauline 2 Tim. 4:11.

13. W. J. Conybeare and J. S. Howson, *The Life and Epistles of Paul* (London, 1852; New York: Scribner's, 1855).

14. In an appendix to Lightfoot's critical *Essays on Supernatural Religion,* published in 1878; and in an article contributed by him to Smith's *Dictionary of the Bible* (London, 1893), 1:25–43.

15. A. C. Headlam, *HDB* 1:35.

16. W. M. Ramsay, *The Bearing of Recent Discovery on the Trustworthiness of the New Testament* (London, 1915), 89.

17. Adolf von Harnack, *Die Apostelgeschichte,* in *Beiträge zur Einleitung in das Neue Testament* (Leipzig, 1908), 222.

18. F. J. Foakes-Jackson and Kirsopp Lake, eds., *The Beginnings of Christianity, Part 1: The Acts of the Apostles,* 5 vols. (London: Macmillan, 1920–35). Vols. 4 (commentary on Acts) and 5 (notes on the commentary by Lake and Cadbury) have been reprinted (Grand Rapids, Mich.: Eerdmans, 1966).

19. Cadbury's *The Making of Luke-Acts* was published in New York in 1928, and twice reprinted (1958, 1961); *The Book of Acts in History* was published in London and New York in 1955.

20. An important group of these was collected and translated into English: *Studies in the Acts of the Apostles* (London, 1956).

21. Jacques Dupont, *The Sources of Acts: The Present Position* (London, 1964), 167.

22. Philipp Vielhauer, "Zum 'Paulinismus' der Apostelgeschichte," in *Evangelische Theologie* (1950–51), 10:1–15; translated by V. P. Furnish and W. C. Robinson Jr., in *Studies in Luke-Acts,* ed. L. E. Keck and J. L. Martyn (1966; repr. Philadelphia: Fortress Press, 1980), 33–50.

23. Vielhauer, "Zum 'Paulinismus,'" 44.

24. Hans Conzelmann, *Die Mitte der Zeit,* 5th ed. (Tübingen, 1964); Conzelmann, *The Theology of St. Luke* (New York: Harper and Row, 1961).

25. For example, Matt. 24:34; Mark 9:1; 1 Cor. 15:51.

26. Ernst Haenchen, *The Acts of the Apostles: A Commentary,* trans. R. McL. Wilson (Philadelphia: Westminster, 1971); original version: *Kritische-exegetischer Kommentar über das Neue Testament. 3. Die Apostelgeschichte,* 10th ed. (Göttingen: Vandenhoeck and Ruprecht, 1956; 15th ed., 1968).

27. Haenchen, *Acts of the Apostles,* 49.

28. This third section Haenchen considers to be written in the style of the hellenistic romance.

29. *Studies in Luke-Acts,* ed. Keck and Martyn.

30. W. L. Knox, *St. Paul and the Church of Jerusalem* (Cambridge, 1925); Knox, *The Acts of the Apostles* (Cambridge: Cambridge University Press, 1948); F. F. Bruce, *The Acts of the Apostles* (Grand Rapids, Mich.: Eerdmans, 1952; 3rd rev. ed., 1990).

31. Charles Talbert, *Literary Patterns, Theological Themes, and the Genre of Luke-Acts,* SBL Monograph Series 20 (Missoula, Mont.: Scholars Press, 1974), 134.

32. Mikeal C. Parsons and J. B. Tyson, eds., *Cadbury, Knox, and Talbert: American Contributions to the Study of Acts* (Atlanta: Scholars Press, 1992).

33. David Aune, *The New Testament in Its Environment,* Library of Early Christianity (Philadelphia: Westminster Press, 1987).

34. Gerd Lüdemann, *Early Christianity according to the Traditions in Acts,* trans. John Bowden (Minneapolis: Fortress Press, 1989), 5–18.

35. David Magie, *Roman Rule in Asia Minor to the End of the Third Century after Christ,* 2 vols. (Princeton, N.J.: Princeton University Press, 1950; repr., New York: Arno, 1975); Peter Garnsey and Richard Saller, *The Roman Empire: Economy, Society, and Culture* (Berkeley: University of California Press, 1987); Geza Alföldy, *The Social History of Rome* (Baltimore: Johns Hopkins University Press, 1988).

36. A. N. Sherwin-White, *Roman Society and Roman Law in the New Testament* (Oxford, 1963; repr., Grand Rapids, Mich.: Eerdmans, 1978). A recent example of a classical historian's drawing on Acts as a basic source of information appears in the recent study of Caesarea, *Caesarea Maritima: Retrospective after Two Millennia,* ed. Avner Raban and Kenneth G. Holum (Leiden: Brill, 1977). A summary of the volume is offered below in the excursus on Caesarea in chapter 3.

37. Stephen Mitchell, *Anatolia: Land, Men, and Gods in Asia Minor* (Oxford: Clarendon Press, 1993), 2:3.

38. Jacob Jervell, *Luke and the People of God* (Minneapolis: Augsburg Press, 1972). Dubious, however, is Jervell's thesis set out in his essay "The Church of Jews and God-fearers" (in *Luke-Acts and the Jewish People,* ed. J. Tyson [Minneapolis: Augsburg Press, 1988]), that the only Gentiles Luke wants to "find in the church" are those who have already made a prior commitment to Judaism as God-fearers. This ignores, however, the evidence from Acts for participation in the new community by those who have given no indication of taking on ritual or dietary obligations like the proselytes: the Philippian jailer (16:31–34), Dionysius the Areopagite in Athens (17:34), or the "Greeks" mentioned in 19:10. Rather, the open invitation proclaimed by Paul is extended not only to Jews and proselytes, but also to those wholly outside the boundaries of Jewish piety.

39. Halvor Moxnes, *The Economy of the Kingdom: Social Conflict and Economic Relations in Luke's Gospel* (Philadelphia: Fortress Press, 1988).

40. Examples of these tendencies are to be found in Bruce Malina, *The New Testament World: Insights from Cultural Anthropology* (Atlanta: John Knox Press, 1981); and Jerome Neyrey, *The Social World of Luke-Acts: Models of Interpretation* (Peabody, Mass.: Hendrickson, 1991).

41. Philip Esler, *Community and Gospel in Luke-Acts: The Social and Political Motivations of Lucan Theology,* SNTSMS 57 (Cambridge: Cambridge University Press, 1987). Esler's more recent study of Acts, *The First Christians in Their Social Worlds* (London and New York: Rout-

ledge, 1994), regrettably employs the categorizing methods of Neyrey and Malina.

42. H. C. Kee, *Who Are the People of God? Early Christian Models of Community* (New Haven: Yale University Press, 1993), 179-207.

43. R. J. Cassidy, *Society and Politics in the Acts of the Apostles* (Maryknoll, N.Y.: Orbis, 1987).

44. David L. Tiede, *Prophecy and History in Luke-Acts* (Philadelphia: Fortress Press, 1980); Marion L. Soards, *The Speeches in Acts: Their Content, Context, and Concerns* (Louisville, Ky.: Westminster Press, 1994).

45. Craig Evans and James A. Sanders, *Luke and Scripture: The Function of Sacred Tradition in Luke-Acts* (Minneapolis: Fortress Press, 1993). Gert J. Steyn, *Septuagint Quotations in the Context of the Petrine and Pauline Speeches in Acta Apostolorum* (Kampen: Kok Pharos, 1995); this study has great importance for the analysis of the evolution of the text of the Septuagint as well as for the use of scripture in Acts.

46. Steyn, *Septuagint Quotations*, 248, 23-24.

47. In *Luke's Literary Achievement*, ed. C. M. Tuckett, *JSNT* Suppl. 16 (Sheffield: Sheffield Academic Press, 1995), 180-81.

48. Colin J. Hemer, *The Book of Acts in the Setting of Hellenistic History*, ed. C. H. Gempf, WUNT 49 (Tübingen: J. C. B. Mohr [Paul Siebeck], 1989); Gregory E. Sterling, *Historiography and Self-Definition: Josephos, Luke-Acts, and Apologetic Historiography*, Suppl. to *NovT* 64 (Leiden and New York: E. J. Brill, 1992).

49. Earl Richard, *New Views on Luke and Acts* (Collegeville, Minn.: Liturgical Press, 1990); C. H. Talbert, ed., *Luke-Acts: New Perspectives* (New York: Crossroad, 1984); Aune, *New Testament in Its Environment*, 77-115, 116-57.

50. Bruce W. Winter, ed., *The Book of Acts in Its First-Century Setting* (Grand Rapids, Mich.: Eerdmans, 1993-): vol. 1, *Ancient Literary Setting*, ed. Bruce W. Winter and Andrew D. Clarke (1993); vol. 2, *Graeco-Roman Setting*, ed. David W. J. Gill and Conrad Gempf (1994); and vol. 3, *Paul in Roman Custody*, ed. Brian Rapske (1994).

51. Sterling, *Historiography and Self-Definition*, 53-54. Two of the major producers of this Greek historical type are Hekataios of Abdera (fl. 320-290 B.C.E.) and Megasthenes (351-281 B.C.E.).

52. Ibid., 223, 308-10.

53. Lucian, *How to Write History*, LCL 6, sec. 7-54 (Cambridge, Mass., 1968).

54. The insights into sociology of knowledge have been provided by T. S. Kuhn, in his *Structures of Scientific Revolution*, 2nd ed. (Chicago: University of Chicago Press, 1970); by Peter Berger and Thomas Luckmann, in *The Social Construction of Reality* (Garden City, N.Y.: Doubleday, 1967); and by Peter Berger, in *The Sacred Canopy: Elements of a Sociological Theory of Religion* (Garden City, N.Y.: Doubleday, 1969).

The implications of this understanding of knowledge for New Testament interpretation I have sketched in *Knowing the Truth: A Sociological Approach to New Testament Interpretation* (Minneapolis: Fortress Press, 1989), and in *Who Are the People of God?* 1–16.

55. For an analysis of the Pharisaic background for the rise of rabbinic Judaism, see excursus on Pharisees, p. 83.

56. For a sketch of the evolution of the *synedrion* see the excursus on the *Synedrion* in chapter 1, p. 68.

57. Aune, *New Testament in Its Environment,* 124. He refers to this feature in Polybius 36.11-12. The we-passages in Acts include 16:10-17, 20:5-15, 21:1-18, and 27:1-28:16.

58. Ibid., 125.

59. Statistics from G. H. R. Horsley, in "Speeches and Dialogue in Acts," *NTS* 32 (1986): 609-14.

60. Soards, *Speeches in Acts,* 160-61.

61. (1) Charles Talbert, "Biographies of Philosophers and Rulers as Instruments of Religious Propaganda in Mediterranean Antiquity," *ANRW* II.16.2, Religion, ed. H. Temporini and W. Haase (New York, 1978), 1619-51. The first type is exemplified by Lucian, in the *Life of Demonax.* (2) As in Xenophon, *Memorabilia,* to correct the common image of Socrates. (3) Lucian, *Alexander the False Prophet.* (4) Talbert's sole example of this model is the writings of Diogenes Laertius, but Aune has correctly noted that this material is much later than Luke-Acts (ca. 250 C.E.), and that not all the lives include the features noted by Talbert (*The New Testament in Its Literary Environment,* 78). (5) Porphyry, *Life of Plotinus;* also in Philo, *Life of Moses.*

62. Embodying the feature of divinization of the central figure is Philo's *Life of Moses,* which depicts Moses as ascending to heaven.

63. Moses Hadas, *Three Greek Romances* (Indianapolis: Bobbs-Merrill, 1964); Reinhold Merkelbach, *Roman und Mysterium in der Antike* (Munich and Berlin: Beck, 1962); Pierre Grimal, *Romans Grecs et Latins* (Paris: Gallimard, 1958); Albert Henrichs, *Die Phoinikika des Lollians. Fragments eines neuen griechischen Romans* (Bonn: Habelt, 1972). A volume including useful accessible English translation of nine of these romances, as well as summaries and fragments of others, has been edited by B. P. Reardon, *Collected Ancient Greek Novels* (Berkeley: University of California Press, 1989).

64. Thomas Hagg, *The Novel in Antiquity* (Oxford: Blackwell, 1983), 103. Merkelbach finds a similar intent in the romance *Chariton,* and in Apuleius's *Metamorphoses,* where the Isis cult is fostered by the tale.

65. Richard I. Pervo, *Profit with Delight: The Literary Genre of the Acts of the Apostles* (Philadelphia: Fortress Press, 1987), 96.

66. Douglas Edwards, in *Religion and Power: Pagans, Jews, and Christians in the Greek East* (New York: Oxford University Press, 1996), offers perceptive comparative analyses of Josephus, Chariton's *Chaereas and*

Callirhoe, and Luke-Acts. In all three of these documents he notes the importance of geographical location as the setting for the manifestation of the divine purpose in human history (81), which manifests itself in the realm of politics (97). The political importance of the cities of Jerusalem, Caesarea, and Rome is central for the intention of Acts. The agents through whom this purpose is carried out are chiefly the elites of the eastern Roman Empire (100). But specific agents of divine power are evident in the history of the Jews (Moses, David, the prophets) as well as in contemporary individuals and officials such as the high priest, and even Josephus, who portrays himself as an intermediary between his people and the Roman authorities. In Luke-Acts, Jesus is the agent of divine power, which is transmitted by the Holy Spirit to the apostles (111). The confirmation of the divine message and purpose is given through signs and miracles (104, 112). An important theme in the romance of Chariton is the manifestation of divine power (Aphrodite), including speeches in the presence of pagan rulers (112). The course of human history, including the triumphs of earthly rulers, are manifestations of Aphrodite's sovereign power (115). One can see from this perceptive comparative analysis how effectively Acts was aimed at the educated readership of the Roman world and employed the strategies of popular literature.

67. My analysis of the phenomena of superhuman action in the Greco-Roman world, especially healing, is offered in my *Medicine, Miracle, and Magic in New Testament Times,* SNTSMS 55 (Cambridge: Cambridge University Press, 1986; rev. ed., 1988).

68. Aune, *New Testament in Its Literary Environment,* 133–36.

69. Enjoined are abstinence from "polluted things offered to idols, from what is strangled and from blood" (15:29).

70. Steyn, *Septuagint Quotations,* 22–23. Speeches in Acts are discussed above in the introduction, p. 15.

71. The phrase also appears in 14:22 and 19:8, where Paul's message is being epitomized.

72. *Pais* is the term used in the Suffering Servant passage in Isa. 52:13ff., rather than *doulos,* but the atonement implications are not developed in Acts as they are by Paul in Philippians 2.

73. By Vielhauer, in "Zum 'Paulinismus'"; and by Haenchen, in *Acts of the Apostles,* based on his commentary begun in 1946.

74. In addition to the conservative scholars who want to achieve a complete reconciliation of the evidence about Paul from his letters and that offered in Acts, critical scholarship has become more inclined to identify historical material preserved in Paul which significantly supplements what can be inferred from his letter. A prime example of the latter type approach to the issue is that of Martin Hengel, in *Acts and the History of Earliest Christianity,* trans. John Bowden (Philadelphia: Fortress Press, 1980).

75. R. L. Brawley, "Paul in Acts: Lucan Apology and Conciliation," in *Perspectives on Luke-Acts*, ed. C. H. Talbert (Danville, Va.: Association of Baptist Professors of Religion, 1978), 129–47.

76. John Clayton Lentz Jr., *Luke's Portrait of Paul*, SNTSMS 77 (Cambridge: Cambridge University Press, 1993).

77. Ibid., 4, 19–20, 62–63, 170–72.

78. J. H. Ropes, *The Beginnings of Christianity*, ed. Foakes-Jackson and Lake, vol. 3, *Text of Acts* (London: Macmillan, 1922).

79. A notable instance of a variant in the Western text is its omission of "and from what is strangled" in 15:29, which has led many interpreters to claim that the minimal legal requirements mentioned here did not include ritual matters, and the "blood" is to be understood as "shedding blood," and hence, as murder.

80. This and other adaptations of the Greek to the Latin text are noted by Haenchen, in *Acts of the Apostles*, 52–58.

81. W. A. Strange, *The Problem of the Text of Acts*, SNTSMS 71 (Cambridge: Cambridge University Press, 1992).

82. Two important contributions to this study are those of E. J. Epp, *The Theological Tendency of Codex Bezae Cantabrigiensis in Acts*, SNTSMS 3 (Cambridge: Cambridge University Press, 1966), and E. Haenchen and P. Weigandt, "The Original Text of Acts?" *NTS* 14 (1968): 469–81.

83. Thus Barbara Aland, in "Entstehung, Charakter und Herkunft des sog. westlichen Textes untersucht in der Apostelgeschichte," *EThL* 62 (1986): 5–65.

84. Entrances: 5:21–22, 11:28, 21:16; exits: 5:18, 12:23, 14:18, 28:29; motives for action: 8:1, 14:7, 15:34, 18:2, 20:14; edificatory notes: 2:41, 14:7, 15:34, 18:2, 20:15.

85. Summarized from Strange, *Problem of the Text of Acts*, 171–73, 189.

86. *Novum Testamentum Graece* (Stuttgart: Deutsche Bibelgesellschaft, 1993).

Prelude

1. Or, "eating with them."

2. This perception of Matthew's distinctive aim in his gospel is set forth in my *Jesus in History*, 5th ed. (Fort Worth, Tex.: Harcourt Brace Jovanovich, 1996), 168–71.

3. For details on the apostleship of Paul, see the discussion in my *Understanding the New Testament*, 3rd ed. (Englewood Cliffs, N.J.: Prentice-Hall, 1993), 258–63.

4. A classic study of these two locations for the post-resurrection appearances of Jesus is that of R. H. Lightfoot, *Locality and Doctrine in the Gospels* (New York: Harper and Row, 1938).

5. Cloud. The divine radiance that embodies the presence of God with his people in the wilderness appears to them "in a cloud" (Exod. 16:10), and a "thick cloud" signifies that presence on Mount Sinai (Exod. 19:9, 16; 20:21; 24:15-16; 33:9; Deut. 5:22) and as the journey continued toward the Promised Land (40:34-38; Num. 10:12; 14:14; Neh. 9:12; Ps. 99:7). This is recalled by Paul in 1 Cor. 10:1-2. The cloud of divine glory also filled the temple (2 Chron. 5:13-14), but departed when disobedient Israel was sent by God into exile (Ezek. 10:4-5). At the transfiguration of Jesus (Mark 9:5-7; Matt. 17:5; Luke 9:34-35), the presence of God with Jesus is represented visually by the cloud that overshadowed him, and is articulated by the voice from the cloud acclaiming Jesus as God's son. The faithful are to meet Jesus in the clouds when he returns in triumph (1 Thess. 4:17), an image found in Revelation as well (Rev. 1:10, 14:14-16).

6. This list of disciples, like the one in Luke 6:13-16, varies at two points from the list in Mark 3:16-19 and Matt. 10:2-4: Simon is called "the Zealot" rather than "the Cananaean," and instead of Thaddaeus we find "Judas the son of James." The Aramaic term from which "Cananaean" derives means "zealous" or "wholly devoted." Only in the later first century was the term used for the Jewish nationalists who wanted to free the land from Roman control (see Richard A. Horsley, *Sociology and the Jesus Movement* [New York: Crossroad, 1989], 139). It is unwarranted to assume that Jesus was a political revolutionary, or that he attracted as followers those of that persuasion.

7. Martin Hengel, *The Synagogue: Studies in Origins, Archaeology, and Architecture,* ed. Joseph Gutman (New York: Ktav, 1975), 27-54.

8. So Rachel Hachlili, "Diaspora Synagogues," in *ABD* 6, ed. D. N. Freedman (New York: Doubleday, 1992), 260-63.

9. The dating of only three Palestinian synagogues to the Second Temple period is affirmed by Eric Meyers, in his article on "Synagogue" in *ABD* 6, ed. Freedman, 255. Joseph Gutman remarked that at Masada and Herodium the rooms are merely meeting halls, and that "there is no proof of piety or of a definite place of worship other than the wishful thinking [of the excavators]" (in *The Synagogue,* ed. Gutman, xi).

10. See the more complete analysis of this term in my essay, "Defining the First-Century C.E. Synagogue: Problems and Progress," *NTS* 41 (1995): 481-500.

11. Not "having a synagogue," as in the LCL translation of this text.

12. Women. Luke gives special attention to the role of women in the new community, both in his gospel and in Acts. There are unique stories in Luke about the role of women in the coming of John the Baptist and Jesus to fulfill their roles in the purpose of God (Luke 1-20), and especially in the report of the women of means who contribute support to Jesus and his disciples (Luke 8:1-3), and the story of Mary

and Martha (10:38–42). Special note is taken in Luke 23:55–56 of the role of the women followers from Galilee who prepare his body for burial, and of their names as witnesses of the empty tomb (24:10–11). Only Acts within the New Testament uses the female equivalent term for disciple, *mathetria*: Tabitha (Acts 9:36). Paul's first convert in Europe is a wealthy businesswoman, Lydia (Acts 16:13–14). In Thessalonica (17:4), in Beroea (17:12), and in Athens (17:34) the new community soon includes "not a few of the leading women."

13. *Omothumadon* is an adverb that indicates that unity of purpose is the major factor in a gathering of people. In Acts it is used with three different connotations. (1) The emphasis is on the assembling of a group, as when the crowds gather in Samaria to listen to the preaching of Philip (8:6) and when the people of Tyre and Sidon convene before Herod Antipas, seeking peace (12:20). (2) A second group of texts employs the term in connection with hostile gatherings intent on wreaking vengeance on their opponents, as when the crowd in Jerusalem rush together to seize and execute Stephen (7:57), when Jews in Achaia convene to discredit Paul before the proconsul, Gallio (18:12), and when the hostile crowd assembles in the theater of Ephesus to attack Paul and his associates for discrediting Artemis (19:29). (3) But the primary function of this term in Acts is to indicate the unity of the new community, as they are united in prayer after witnessing the ascension of Jesus (1:14), when they unite in temple worship and breaking of bread (2:46), when they join to praise God following Peter's defense before the council (4:24), when they are gathered in the Portico of Solomon (5:12), and when they unite in support of James's pronouncement of the apostolic policy on the legal obligation of Gentiles who join the new community (15:25).

14. The theme of the *plan* of God for the formation of his new people that was worked out through the death and resurrection of Jesus runs throughout Acts: 2:23, 4:28, 5:38, 13:36, 20:27.

15. Not only does Judas die differently in Matthew's account (27:3–9), but a different scripture is appealed to as justification for using the bribe he had received to purchase the place for his burial (Zech. 11:13, although it is attributed to Jeremiah).

16. The Hebrew word for "office" in Ps. 109:8 is translated in the LXX text quoted in Acts as *episkope,* which makes it especially appropriate for the role for which an early Christian reader is to be chosen.

Chapter 1. The Launching of the Inclusive Community

1. Crete was known as Caphtor in the days of ancient Israel, and was the home of the Philistines (Gen. 10:14; Deut. 2:23; Amos 9:7). Titus 1:5 implies that Paul went to Crete and then left Titus behind to

set things in order with the church leadership there. There is a quotation from the Cretan poet Epimenides, which is severely critical of the Cretans. The ship transporting Paul to Rome is reported in Acts 27:8 to have called at Fair Havens on the southern coast of Crete.

2. Paul's eagerness to come to Rome is articulated in his Letter to the Romans: 1:13–15; 15:22, 30–32.

3. Over the past twenty years, a series of studies has been published which seek to define the relationship between the people of God in Acts and in the Jewish tradition. An important contribution to this discussion is Jervell's *Luke and the People of God.* Debatable is his proposal that Paul's activity among Gentiles was limited to "Gentile-Christian proselytes" (172), a thesis that he has repeated in his more recent essay, "The Church of Jews and God-fearers," 11–20. An unwarranted representation of Acts as simply anti-Jewish has been offered by Jack T. Sanders in *The Jews in Luke-Acts* (Philadelphia: Fortress, 1987). A most perceptive study of the central importance of Luke-Acts' portrayal of the founding of the new community by Jesus in terms of the fulfillment prophecy in the sphere of history is that of David Tiede, *Prophecy and History in Luke-Acts.*

4. In the Hebrew text the numbering is 2:28–32a, but in the LXX it is 3:1–5a.

5. Soards, in *Speeches in Acts,* has noted this feature.

6. Soards, in ibid., has noted that although "wonders" (*terata*) are mentioned in Joel's prophecy, "signs" (*semeia*) are not, but the dual reference appears often in Acts: 2:43, 5:12, 6:89, 14:3, and 15:12.

7. Hades derives from the name of the Greek god, "The Unseen," who was thought to reside in the depths of the earth. In the LXX, the Greek term *hades* translates a number of terms related to death, including "pit," "darkness," and often *sheol.* The latter term is used for the waters of chaos that lie beneath the surface of the earth (Job 26:5; 1 Sam. 22:5), but it also refers to death as a creature that devours everything it can grasp (Prov. 30:16; Isa. 5:14). Another term for it is Abaddon, which is a place of gloom and forgetfulness (Ps. 88:10–12). In Isa. 14:9–11 the king of Babylon is warned of his destruction and banishment there and his consequent impotence. Another term for the abode of the dead, *gehenna,* is where the wicked are punished (Luke 16:23). In Matt. 16:18 Jesus is reported as telling Peter that the "gates of Hades" — that is, the powers of death — will not prevail against the "church," which is the community that is being called together. In Rev. 1:18 Jesus is said to have "the keys of death and Hades," which means that he has gained control of death through his resurrection.

8. David's tomb is mentioned by Josephus (*Ant.* 7.392–94, 13.249; *Wars* 1.61). Rabbinic tradition reports that his tomb was in Jerusalem, and a much later structure on Mount Zion came to be identified in modern times as David's Tomb.

9. In 1 Cor. 15:26 Paul describes death as "the last enemy to be destroyed."

10. The *gift* of the Spirit as experienced by Gentiles (10:45, 11:17) is confirmation that the inclusiveness of the new community is the result of God's action.

11. Detailed analysis of the miracles in the New Testament against the background of the phenomenon in the wider Greco-Roman world is offered in my *Miracle in the Early Christian World* (New Haven: Yale University Press, 1983) and in *Medicine, Miracle, and Magic.*

12. Salvation as process, rather than as a completed action, is implicit in the present participle, *sodzomenos,* which describes an ongoing action.

13. There are three proposals for the location of the Beautiful Gate. One is a gate that gave access to the temple on the east side from the Kidron Valley. This would have been convenient for the apostles if they were staying in Bethany, as Jesus did in the Markan tradition (Mark 14:3). But in the gospel tradition, the Passover is celebrated by Jesus and the disciples in a guestroom in Jerusalem ("go into the city," Mark 14:14), and Luke indicates that the disciples were based in Jerusalem (Luke 24:13, 18, 33). If this was in the older, southern section of the city, then entrance from there to the temple would be by the Portico of Solomon. Some scholars think that the Beautiful Gate was not through the external wall of the larger temple area, but from the Court of the Gentiles into the temple proper, or from the Women's Court into the Court of Israel. The greatest supply of potential donors to the lame man would have been at the Portico of Solomon, whether that was the actual location of the Beautiful Gate or not.

14. See the excursus on "the Name" in Acts, p. 63.

15. Quoted is Isa. 53:7–8. Isa. 53:9, concerning his burial, is quoted in Matt. 27:57.

16. The anointing of David as king: In the historical and prophetic writings, there is a repeated theme that God's ultimate renewal of his people and of the world will be achieved through a descendant of David, the one initially anointed by Samuel to be king of Israel (1 Samuel 16). This was followed by his anointing as king of Judah (2 Sam. 2:1–7) and then of all Israel (2 Sam. 5:1–5). That kingdom is to endure forever over the people of God (2 Sam. 7:12–13). This theme is repeated throughout the historical books (2 Kings 21:7, 22:2; 2 Chron. 21:7, 23:3) and the psalms (Ps. 89:3–4, 132:10–17). It is also an important motif throughout the oracles of the prophets of Israel. In Isaiah the emphasis is on the justice and peace that will characterize his rule (Isa. 9:7, 11:1, 16:5). Similarly, in Jeremiah the establishment of the throne of David (17:25) will bring in an era of peace (22:4) and justice (23:5), and central for Jeremiah is the renewal of the covenant with David (33:17, 26). Similar themes appear in Amos 9:11 and

Zech. 12:7–12, but the cosmic dimensions of the future reign of God's anointed one are set forth in Ezekiel 37, which culminates in the establishment of the Davidic kingship. It is not surprising, therefore, that Paul identifies Jesus as "descended from David according to the flesh" (Rom. 1:4).

17. See the excursus on "the Name" in Acts, p. 63.

18. The title *strategos* is used in this period as the equivalent for several types of Roman officials or for local officials collaborating with the Romans: *praetor,* consul, proconsul, military and civilian governors, and chief magistrates. The variety of modes of civil and judicial offices are described by Peter Garnsey in *Social Status and Legal Privilege in the Roman Empire* (Oxford: Oxford University Press, 1970). Further analysis of *strategos* is offered below in the notes concerning 16:22.

19. Transliterated into Greek as *Saddoukaioi,* and into English as "Sadducees."

20. Josephus, *Wars* 2.162; *Ant.* 13.293, 18.16–17, 20.199. Since the Sadducees were a significant element in the priestly group, which operated the temple and did so in collaboration with the Roman imperial authorities, it is not appropriate to refer to them as a "sect." A full and perceptive analysis of the Sadducees, as well as the Pharisees, is offered by Anthony J. Saldarini in *Pharisees, Scribes, and Sadducees in Palestinian Society: A Sociological Approach* (Wilmington, Del.: Michael Glazier, 1988).

21. Cf. Mark 8:31; Matt. 16:21; Luke 9:22 and Mark 11:27; Matt. 21:23; Luke 20:1.

22. The high priests and the years of their function in that capacity are: Eleazar, 16–17 C.E.; Jonathan, 36–37 C.E.; Theophilus, 37–41 C.E.; Matthias, 43 C.E.; Ananus II, 62 C.E.

23. Elders appear throughout the Old Testament tradition. Moses reports to "elders" his encounter with God and the disclosure of the divine name, Yahweh (Exod. 3:16). Their place of assembling is at the city gate (Deut. 25:7; Ruth 4:2), and their roles included the examination of the accused and the punishment of culprits (Deut. 19:12). They are listed with other officials when Israel has begun to settle in the land (Deut. 29:10; Joshua 23–24). It is the elders who demand in the name of the people that God give Israel a king (1 Sam. 8:4), and who enter into a covenant with David after he has become king (2 Sam. 5:3). They participate in the dedication of the temple in the time of Solomon (1 Kings 8:1) and support Josiah's effort at the reform of his people (2 Kings 23:1). Ezekiel reports the elders as fostering idolatrous practices (Ezek. 8:12). Their designation as "elders" is the counterpart of the Roman body of leaders known as the "senate," but in both cases it is social standing and not merely age that sets them apart for their role in community decisions. The formalization of this institution of the elders probably took place during the exile, as Israel looked back

on its earlier history, and is reflected in the specifying of the number of the elders as "seventy" (Exod. 24:1; Num. 11:16–21). See also n. 49, on *synedrion,* below.

24. The term used here, *euergesia,* is found elsewhere in the New Testament only in 1 Tim. 6:2, but is fairly common in inscriptions, papyri, and hellenistic literature, including Josephus and the LXX.

25. The quotation is from Ps. 118:22, but is not based on the LXX version of this text, as are the quotations of this passage in Mark 12:10, Matt. 21:42, and Luke 20:17. The similar prophecy from Isa. 28:16 about the "cornerstone" of the new community appears not only in the gospels (Matt. 21:42; Luke 20:17), but also in the letters of the New Testament: Rom. 9:33, 10:11; Eph. 2:20; 2 Tim. 2:19; 1 Pet. 4:6.

26. Hugo Mantel, *Studies in the History of the Sanhedrin* (Cambridge: Harvard University Press, 1965), 2, 52, 92.

27. As in S. Zeitlin, "Synedrion and Sanhedrin," *Jewish Quarterly Review* 36 (1945–46): 109–40.

28. *Theological Dictionary of the New Testament,* vol. 7, ed. G. Friedrich, trans. G. W. Bromiley (Grand Rapids, Mich.: Eerdmans, 1988), 860–71.

29. Anthony J. Saldarini, "Sanhedrin," *ABD* 5, ed. D. N. Freedman (New York: Doubleday, 1992), 975–79.

30. Zeitlin, "Synedrion," 109–20.

31. J. A. O. Larsen, "Consilium in Livy xlv. 18.6–7," in *Classical Philology* 94 (1948): 73–90.

32. Ps. 26:4; Prov. 11:13, 15:22, 22:10, 24:8, 26:26, 27:22, 31:23 (where the reference is to a conclave of older inhabitants of the land); Jer. 15:17 (where there is a gathering of merrymakers).

33. *Ant.* 14.82. In *Wars* 1.170, these bodies are referred to as *synodous.*

34. *Ant.* 14.91, 167–69, 170–74.

35. This transformation of Jewish leadership has been traced by Jacob Neusner in his seminal work, *From Politics to Piety: The Emergence of Rabbinic Judaism* (Englewood Cliffs, N.J.: Prentice-Hall, 1973).

36. The Greek term found here, *homothumadon,* which indicates a common gathering place or a solidly shared common point of view, is found throughout Acts. The gathering may be the assembling of a group, as when the apostles are joined in prayer (1:14), or the opponents converge on Stephen (7:57), or the Tyrians and Sidonians gather before Herod (12:20), or the Jewish opposition makes a concerted attack on Paul (18:12), or the crowds assemble in the theater in Ephesus (19:29). But in 1:14, 4:24, and most clearly in 15:25, this term for commonality is used in Acts to highlight the common identity and unity of purpose that draws and holds together the diverse individuals who have chosen to become part of the new community of God's people. This is the point of view implicit in Paul's prayer (Rom. 15:6)

that the members of the church in Rome may join with one voice in glorifying God.

37. This use of *idios* to refer to shared identity of the distinctive new community is in contrast with Acts 2:7-8, where the enormously diverse identity of the individuals gathered in Jerusalem on the Day of Pentecost is grounded on the native language of each of them as a member of one of the various ethnic groups assembled there. The miraculous translations by the Spirit enable all to hear the message "in our own language."

38. 1 Tim. 6:1; 2 Tim. 2:21; Titus 2:9; 1 Peter 2:18.

39. Celebration of God's creation is a recurrent theme in all types of Old Testament literature: pentateuchal (Exod. 20:11), historical (2 Kings 19:15; Neh. 9:6); prophetic (Isa. 37:16), and liturgical (Ps. 146:5-6), for example.

40. Not Herod the Great, but Herod Antipas, whom Luke alone in the gospel tradition reports as participating in the trial of Jesus (Luke 23:6-16).

41. A few manuscripts of Acts read here *laos Israel,* "people Israel," but the better-attested plural "peoples of Israel" indicates that the hostility of Jews toward Jesus is to be seen as widespread but by no means total.

42. The link between the death of Jesus and the Suffering Servant motif in Isaiah 53 is made explicit in Acts 8:32-33, but the designation of Jesus as servant (*pais*) is not found there.

43. The Levites were one of the twelve tribes of Israel, and were given responsibility to offer sacrifices and to administer the Law of Moses (Deut. 17:18, 33:10). For a time their role was limited to that of helpers and servants in the temple (Num. 18:2-6), but in the priestly historical accounts, 1 and 2 Chronicles, they had many functions in the temple, including caring for the ark of the covenant, leading the music in the temple services, and offering sermons.

44. The unity of the community is discussed in the discussion of Acts 4:24, pp. 73-74.

45. M. Ben Dov, *In the Shadow of the Temple,* trans. I. Friedman (Jerusalem, 1982), 77.

46. See my discussion of the characteristics of various types of wonders in *Miracle in the Early Christian World* and in *Medicine, Miracle, and Magic.* In both these studies I have noted that in contrast to the intentional and voluntary acts of healing or exorcisms attributed to Jesus and the apostles which may be more appropriately designated as miracles, there are a few passages in the gospels and Acts which describe the automatic or coercive features typical of magic. Other stories of such automatic manifestations of extraordinary healing powers are to be found in Luke 8:43-48, where a woman is cured of a bloody flow by merely touching the hem of Jesus' garment as he passes, and in

the curative and exorcistic effects of handkerchiefs or aprons that had touched Paul's body (Acts 19:11). Since the author of Acts has been influenced by the literary genre, the romance, in which magic and other manifestations of superhuman powers are featured, it is not surprising to find such narratives in this document which he produced.

47. So in NRSV version of Acts 26:5.

48. In Acts 24:5 the specific epithet attached to the Christians is "sect of the Nazarenes."

49. *Gerousia* is used for the Roman senate by Philo (*In Flaccum* 76 and 80, where the senate's name is said to imply "age [*geron*] and honor"). But in the same work (*In Flaccum* 229) the group of older members of the huge delegation that came to the Syrian governor, Petronius, to protest the plan of the emperor Gaius Caligula (reigned 37–41 C.E.), who had ordered Petronius to commission and erect in the Jerusalem temple a statue of himself (Gaius), is designated a *gerousia*. The Latin term, *senatus,* likewise derives from a term for "older": *senex*. In the Roman Republic, the senate was the major organ of government in shaping and effecting public policy. After Augustus became emperor (27 B.C.E.) he made prior governmental service (such as a higher military officer) a requirement for becoming a senator. One had to be elected to a lower public office in police, mint or other civil duties, or as a circuit judge, and to have demonstrated loyalty to the emperor, as well as having resources of at least 1,000,000 sesterces. Candidates were advanced by various tribes or regions, but all were subject to approval by the emperor. The juridical function of the senate is discussed below, under Acts 25:11, which recounts Paul's appeal to Caesar. The Jewish council convened by the high priest is the local example of the administrative system for governing provinces developed by the hellenistic rulers and then adapted by the Romans. The governors of these provinces were mostly from the senatorial ranks, but those from the next lower rank of people (the equestrians) were appointed by the emperors for a fixed term, usually about three years. Both Josephus (*Ant.* 18.55) and the gospels (Matt. 10:18; Mark 13:9; Luke 21:12) refer to the Roman governors by the general term *hegemon,* which is also used for Pilate (Matt. 27:2, 11–15, 21, 27; 28:14; Luke 20:20) and for Felix (Acts 23:24, 26, 33; 24:10) and for Festus (Acts 26:30). As Graham Burton has noted, "Cooperation of the local ruling class . . . was crucial to the administrative stability of the Empire." Therefore the essential intermediary mechanism for authority over the provincial population was the council that was formed in a city and its adjacent territory and was composed of local civic leaders, including local magistrates. These local authorities could pass laws and make judicial decisions, including regulation of local religious affairs. It was the policy of the Roman governors to reinforce the social and political hierarchy of the provinces, thereby serving to integrate the local elites into the im-

perial system (*The Roman World*, ed. John Wacher, 2 vols. [London: Routledge, 1987], 423–38). Other terms used in the New Testament, Josephus, and the LXX for a consultative council or its meeting include *symboulion* (Acts 26:4; Josephus, *Ant.* 14.192), *boule* (Ps. 1:5; Josephus, *Wars* 2.641), which is akin to the designation of a member of the council as *bouleutes* (Mark 15:43; Luke 23:50). Clearly, in the first century C.E. *synedrion* was not the technical term for a Jewish supreme religious council, as it came to be in its transliterated form, *Sanhedrin*, in later centuries. Instead, it was the designation of the local power group that collaborated with the Romans in exchange for a degree of local control.

50. Attempts to put others to death by this method are reported in Acts 14:19 (Paul) and John 8:2–11 (the woman caught in adultery). This mode of capital punishment was carried out by the community, which joined in hurling large stones to crush and bury the body of the culprit. Offenses to be dealt with by stoning included blasphemy, murder (Lev. 24:14–17), worship of other gods (Lev. 20:2–5; Deut. 13:6–10), prostitution (Deut. 22:20–21), violation of the sabbath (Num. 15:32–36), and insubordination on the part of a son (Deut. 21:18–21).

51. The syntax here, *parangelia parengeilamen,* is thoroughly semitic, thereby reinforcing the Jewish context in which this incident is described as taking place.

52. See excursus on "the Name," p. 63.

53. Exod. 6:14; Num. 10:4, 13:4; Judg. 5:15; 1 Chron. 8:28; Neh. 7:70–71. In Isa. 3:6–7 it is used for the "leader of our tribe." Only in 1 Macc. 10:47 does it appear with the connotations of prototype, where Alexander is the first of those who work for peace.

54. Plato, *Cratylus* 401.D; *Sophist* 243.D.

55. See n. 50.

56. A group of manuscripts identifies Gamaliel here as "a certain Pharisee from the council [*ek tou synedriou*]," but the best and oldest texts simply report that he made his statement "in the council." There is no indication that he was a member of the council.

57. See discussion of Gamaliel in connection with Paul's autobiographical sketch in Acts 22:3.

58. Englewood Cliffs, N.J.: Prentice-Hall, 1973.

59. Jacob Neusner, *Judaism in the Matrix of Christianity,* South Florida Studies in the History of Judaism 8 (Atlanta: Scholars Press, 1991).

60. Excellent analyses of the Pharisees in relation to other groups within Second Temple Judaism are those of Anthony J. Saldarini in *Pharisees, Scribes and Sadducees in Palestinian Society* and his article on Pharisees in the *ABD* 5, D. N. Freedman (New York: Doubleday, 1992), 289–303.

61. Jacob Neusner, *The Pharisees: Rabbinic Perspectives* (Hoboken, N.J.: Ktav, 1985), 23–58. He notes the absence from the Gamaliel rab-

binic material of the issues of table fellowship and purity rules which seem to have been paramount for the Pharisees, and the attention rather to such legal issues as property, inheritance, marriage and divorce, and rules of evidence. Accordingly, Neusner depicts Gamaliel as a public official rather than a sectarian leader (58).

62. Judas is said by Josephus in *Ant.* 18.3 to be from east of the Jordan, but in *Wars* 2.118 he is called a Galilean.

63. An older but still useful summary of these attempts to show the historical accuracy of the Acts account here is offered by H. J. Cadbury in *The Beginnings of Christianity,* ed. Foakes-Jackson and Lake, vol. 4, *The Acts of the Apostles: Translation and Commentary* (repr., Grand Rapids, Mich.: Baker Book House, 1966), 60–62.

64. See the discussion of the meeting places of Jews and Christians in Corinth on p. 221.

Chapter 2. The Initial Shaping of the New Community

1. Martin Goodman, in his essay on "Jewish Proselytizing in the First Century" (in *The Jews among Pagans and Christians,* ed. J. Lieu, J. North, and T. Rajak [London: Routledge, 1992], 53–78), concludes that there is no evidence for an active proselytizing mission by Jews in the first century. Because Judaism was a way of life, which contrasted with living like a Greek, "conversion to such a new way of life and to the new social group which went with it was a major undertaking" (70). But there was not a negative attitude among Jews toward proselytes: "The role of the Jews was simply passively to bear witness through their existence and piety; how the Gentiles reacted to such a witness was up to them" (72). Only in the second and third centuries did some Jews begin looking for converts (74). In the same volume, Tessa Rajak ("The Jewish Community and Its Boundaries," 9–28) notes that inscriptions found at Aphrodisias in Asia Minor document the association with the Jewish community on the part of "God-fearers," whom she characterizes as part-way toward becoming proselytes (20). See the excursus on Proselytes and God-fearers in chapter 3, p. 133.

2. See discussion of "the faith" on p. 162.

3. The Greek text has *synagoge,* but clearly the reference is not to either a building or a local organization; rather, what is in view is a group movement that brought together people from as far away as Africa and Asia Minor.

4. For additional details, see my essay, "The Son of Man: A Glutton and a Drunkard. Analysis of Q 7:18–35," *NTS* 42 (1996): 374–93.

5. Gen. 15:13; in 12:40 the period is given as 430 years.

6. Gen. 15:14; Exod. 2:22, 3:12.

7. Gen. 29:31–30:24, 35:16–26.

8. In the biblical accounts there is no indication of Moses having been engaged in such learning or of being unusually skilled verbally. Instead, his inability to articulate is recounted in Exod. 4:10–16.

9. Exod. 2:11 dates this event simply as "after Moses had grown up," with no indication of his specific age. The figure of 120 years given for the length of Moses' life in Deut. 34:7 seems to have served as the basis for the theory that his life was divided into three segments of 40 years each.

10. Gershom in Exod. 2:15–22, and Eliezer in Exod. 18:1–4.

11. In Exodus 7–10 and 11:29–32 are described the ten plagues that forced the Egyptians to agree to free the Israelites. Cf. Ps. 105:26–45.

12. Josh. 18:1, 19:51; 1 Sam. 2:22. The term for "tabernacle" or "dwelling place" (of God) occurs frequently in Exodus 26, and in Leviticus and Numbers, where it is seen as the embodiment of God's presence among his people. Also in Josh, 22:19, 29, and at the time of David in 2 Sam. 7:6, "dwelling place" represents God's mobile presence.

13. Literally, "stiff-necked": Exod. 32:9, 33:3–5; Deut. 9:6, 13.

14. Lev. 26:41; Ezek. 44:7, 9; Jer. 6:10.

15. 1 Kings 19:10, 14; Neh. 9:26; 2 Chron. 36:15–16; Matt. 5:12.

16. M. L. Soards, *The Speeches in Acts* (60 n. 139), has assembled a list of the passages in Acts where quotations from scripture are explicit:

1:20	Ps. 68:26, 109:8
2:17–20	Joel 3:1–5
2:25–28	Ps. 15:8–11
2:30 (?)	Ps. 131:11
2:31 (?)	Ps. 15:10
2:34–35	Ps. 109:1
3:22–23	Deut. 18:15–20; Lev. 23:29
3:25	Gen. 22:18; 26:4
4:25–26	Ps. 2:1–2
7:3	Gen. 12:1
7:6–7	Gen. 15:13–14; Exod. 3:12
7:27–28	Exod. 2:14
7:32	Exod. 3:6
7:33–34	Exod. 3:5, 7–8, 10
7:35	Exod. 2:14
7:37	Deut. 18:15
7:40	Exod. 32:1, 23
7:42–43	Amos 5:25–27
7:49–50	Isa. 66:1–2
13:22	Ps. 88:21; Isa. 44:28; 1 Sam. 13:14
13:33	Ps. 2:7
13:34	Isa. 55:3
13:35	Ps. 15:10
13:41	Hab. 1:5

13:47   Isa. 49:6
15:16a   Jer. 12:15

17. *Patriarches* translates the Hebrew words for father (*ab*; 1 Chron. 24:31), head (*rosh*; 2 Chron. 19:8, 26:12), and prince (*sar*; 1 Chron. 27:22; 2 Chron. 23:20). The only other occurrences of the term in the New Testament are in Acts 2:29, with reference to David, and in the thoroughly hellenized Letter to the Hebrews, at 7:4, referring to Abraham.

18. The rape of Dinah, daughter of Leah and Jacob, by Hamor is described in Genesis 34.

19. To translate *asteios* as "beautiful" seems inadequate, since Moses' "beauty" resides in his openness and obedience toward God.

20. For example, Exod. 39:32, 40; 40:2, 6, 7, 22, 24, 26, 29, 30, 32, 34, 35.

21. Exod. 16:34; 25:16, 21, 22; 28:31; Num. 1:50, 53; 4:5; 9:15; 10:11; Josh. 4:16.

22. Josh. 18:1; 19:51; 22:19, 29.

23. Patristic tradition concerning the persecution of the prophets is summarized in the note on Acts 7:52 in the commentary of K. Lake and H. J. Cadbury in *The Beginnings of Christianity,* ed. Foakes-Jackson and Lake, 4:82–83.

24. Judg. 2:1–23, 19:1–20:48.

25. A more individual mode of illegal action that justified stoning was for a woman to have had sex with someone before she was married (Deut. 22:20–24).

26. 8:1, 3; 9:1, 8, 11, 22, 24; 11:25, 30; 12:25; 13:1, 2, 7.

27. Although *eulabeis* is usually translated "devout," its basic meaning is "hold fast," here used in apparent contrast to those who fled from fear.

28. Ironically, some of the details of Stephen's speech match the Samaritan version of the Pentateuch rather than the Hebrew text. For example, the details about the relative ages of Abraham and his father, Terah (7:4–8; cf. Gen. 11:26–32); the quotation in 7:32 from Exod. 3:6; and the interpolation of Deut. 18:15.

29. Irenaeus, *Against Heresies* 1.23.

30. The passage from Isa. 40:3 is quoted by all three of the synoptic gospels, but in its most extensive form by Luke (3:4–6).

31. Esth. 2:3. According to Diodorus Siculus (11.69.1, 17.5.3) they functioned as chamberlains or other high officials in the Persian courts.

Chapter 3. The World Mission of the New Community

1. For example, *synedrion* in Matt. 26:59; Mark 14:55, 15:1; Luke 22:66; Acts 22:30; *boule* in Luke 23:51.

2. Although both Josephus and the New Testament refer to these provincial and subprovincial governors by the same term, *hegemon,* Roman terminology designated the governor of the whole province (e.g., Syria) as legate, or proconsul, while the governor of a section of a province (e.g., Judea) was called procurator (Josephus, *Ant.* 18.55, 19.340; Matt. 27:2; Acts 23:26).

3. Josephus, *Wars* 6.124-26.

4. Mary E. Smallwood, *The Jews under Roman Rule: From Pompey to Diocletian,* ed. J. Neusner, SJLA 20 (Leiden: Brill, 1976), 145-48.

5. Josephus, *Ant.* 18.4.84-85.

6. Josephus, *Life* 24-27. He notes that when the Jewish revolt broke out in 66 C.E., the nonrevolutionists were forced to kill those Jews who joined the revolt in Scythopolis and Damascus. Pliny (*Natural History* 5.18.74) reports the complaints to Vespasian from the "ten cities" pillaged by the Jewish revolutionaries, including Damascus.

7. So Robert Jewett, in *A Chronology of Paul's Life* (Philadelphia: Fortress Press, 1979). A summary of the evidence and a probable chronology of the life of Paul is offered in my *Understanding the New Testament,* 224-25.

8. This refers to the Nabatean kingdom of Arabia, which reached from east of Damascus through the districts east of the Jordan and southwest of the Dead Sea, ruled by Aretas IV from 9 B.C.E. to 40 C.E. Earlier (85 B.C.E.), Petra was the capital of the Nabatean kingdom, which was treated by the Romans as a client state, and it may have been restored to Nabatean control during the brief term of Gaius Caligula as emperor from 37-41 C.E. Cf. G. Bowersock, *Roman Arabia* (Cambridge: Harvard University Press, 1983), 68.

9. The scholarly debate concerning the possible architectural relationship of a window to the city wall in Damascus is surveyed by Victor P. Furnish in his commentary *II Corinthians: A New Translation with Introduction and Commentary,* AB (Garden City, N.Y.: Doubleday, 1984), 521-22, 540-42.

10. Josh. 2:15-21; Josephus, *Ant.* 5.5-15.

11. The Greek phrase *en emoi* could mean "to me," but the force of the statement is that it is Paul's personal experience of encounter with the risen Christ — "in me" — which is the ground of his apostolic call. He also refers to this experience as having "seen Jesus our Lord" (1 Cor. 9:1).

12. *Hagios* = "saints" appears twenty-six times in the authentic Pauline letters, and fifteen times in the Deutero-Pauline writings.

13. For example, in 5:30; 6:17; 8:9; 9:16, 18, 40, 43; 12:1; 18:15; 19:29; 22:11, 45.

14. For example, to Markan material: 8:9, 22; 9:14, 43; 17:1; 20:45; to the Q source: 10:23; 11:1; 12:22; 14:26; 17:22.

15. The reference here to *high priests* does not mesh with the fact that there was a single occupant of that preeminent post at any given time, but probably refers to the high priest and his immediate coterie.

16. A full and insightful discussion of the relation between Paul's account of the escape over the wall in 2 Corinthians 11 and the report here in Acts 9 is offered by Furnish in *II Corinthians*, 521–23, 540–42.

17. The most useful analysis of the term is still that of H. J. Cadbury, in *The Beginnings of Christianity*, ed. Foakes-Jackson and Lake, vol. 5, *Additional Notes to the Commentary*, ed. K. Lake and H. J. Cadbury, 59–74, who concludes that the term means those of gentile origin who became members of the Jewish community, rather than merely "Greek-speaking Jews."

18. These factors are especially evident in Paul's speech at the Areopagus in Athens (Acts 17). The kinship between Paul's apocalyptic viewpoint and that of such leading Roman Stoicists as Cicero and Seneca I have sketched under the heading "Roman Stoic Speculation about the Future," in my *Who Are the People of God?* 43–44, and in greater detail in my essay in the Festschrift for W. G. Kümmel, "Pauline Eschatology: Relationships with Apocalyptic and Stoic Thought," in *Glaube und Eschatologie*, ed. E. Graesser and Otto Merk (Tübingen: J. C. B. Mohr [Siebeck], 1985), 135–58.

19. See the excursus on Caesarea, p. 130.

20. On "saints" as a term for the community, see p. 118.

21. This is the single occurrence of the term *mathetria*, the feminine counterpart of *mathetes*. See the excursus on the Disciples in Acts, p. 118.

22. In the LXX, the term is used only three times in the Pentateuch, and relatively few times in the prophets, but is abundant in the wisdom tradition and especially in Sirach and Tobit.

23. See discussion of "upper space" on p. 37. The use of the definite article with this term in 9:39 confirms that this is the formal gathering space for the new community in Joppa.

24. See the discussion on widows on p. 89.

25. This summons to the widow to arise recalls Jesus' instruction to Jairus's dead daughter, reported in Mark 5:41: *"Talitha cumi,"* which is, of course, not a name but an address to a "little girl."

26. The inscription is found in *Inscriptiones Latinae selectae*, 3/2: 9168, ed. H. Dessau (Berlin, 1892–1916), and cited by T. R. S. Broughton in *The Beginnings of Christianity*, ed. Foakes-Jackson and Lake, 5:441–42.

27. Josephus, *Ant.* 15.331–41; *Wars* 1.408–15.

28. Lee J. Levine and E. Netzer, *Excavations at Caesarea Maritima: 1975, 1976, 1979* (Jerusalem: Qedem, 1986); R. L. Hohlfelder, "Caesarea," *ABD*, D. N. Freedman 1 (New York: Doubleday, 1992), 798–803.

The articles included in Raban and Holum, eds., *Caesarea Maritima,* are papers read at an international symposium at Caesarea, Israel, January 3–11, 1995.

29. Cf. Josephus, *Ant.* 18.84, where the difficulty of obedience to the Law of Moses while in military service is noted.

30. A full analysis of the text of the Aphrodisias inscription is offered by Joyce Reynolds and Robert Tannenbaum in *Jews and God-Fearers at Aphrodisias* (Cambridge: Cambridge Philological Society, 1987). The evidence concerning the date is discussed on p. 20.

31. Ibid., 56.

32. For analysis and lists of requirements see ibid., 58–59.

33. Ibid., 126.

34. 1 QS 8.16–17, 22. Quoted from *The Dead Sea Scrolls: Hebrew, Aramaic, and Greek Texts with English Translations,* vol. 1: *Rule of the Community and Related Documents,* ed. James H. Charlesworth (Louisville, Ky.: Westminster/John Knox, 1994).

35. Since the text of this document now exists only in Latin, one cannot ascertain the precise wording of the Greek original, but the phrase and its intent clearly match the use of *panton kurios* in Acts 10:36.

36. Only in Luke are reported the divine promise of the birth of John (1:5–25), the visit of Mary to Elizabeth, the mother of John, and the consequent assurance of fulfillment of God's promise of covenant renewal (1:39–56), the account of John's birth and the attendant promises for the new people of God (1:57–80), and the details of John's preaching of repentance, including his message to covenantal outsiders such as tax collectors, and of the coming Messiah (3:7–18).

37. Wholly missing is anything resembling the abstract terminology of the later christological confessions by which Jesus' relationship to God is described.

38. The quote is a synthesis of Deut. 27:26 and 21:22–23.

39. This motif of Jesus as the divinely appointed ultimate judge of humanity appears again in Paul's address on the Areopagus (17:31).

40. See my studies of this theme in "Roman Stoic Speculation about the Future," 43–44, and "Jews and the New People of God according to Paul," 78–82, in *Who Are the People of God?;* fuller treatment in "Facing the Future: Common Themes in Jewish Apocalyptic and Stoic Philosophy," in *Biblical and Humane,* Festschrift for John Priest (Atlanta: Scholars Press, 1997).

41. 1 Cor. 12:10, 29; 14:1, 9, 18.

42. Discussed on p. 111 in connection with the baptism of the Ethiopian eunuch (8:37).

43. Mark 10:14; Matt. 19:14; Luke 18:16.

44. *Hellenas* is a well-supported reading from papyri and early codices, as well as from patristic sources, while *hellenistas* is found

in some majuscules and many miniscules (manuscripts written respectively in large, capital letters and a mixture of large and small letters). The force of the passage would not be altered basically by selecting the latter reading, since the point remains that the message is now being carried to those under Greek linguistic and cultural influence.

45. Josephus, *Wars* 1.425; *Ant.* 16.148.

46. Josephus, *Wars* 7.9–11.

47. For example, *chrestotes* (gentleness) and *egkrateia* (self-control) occur in the Aristotelian and Platonic traditions and especially in the later adaptations of them in the first and second centuries C.E. (such as Dio Chrysostom, Lucian, and in Philo of Alexandria).

48. Tacitus, *Annals* 18.63–64. In reporting how Nero placed on the Christians the blame for the burning of Rome, he notes that the name of the movement derived from "Christos, the founder of the sect," and characterizes its members as "loathed for their vices" and for their "hatred of the human race." It was the mocking crowd that styled them as "Christians."

49. Pliny, *Letter to Trajan* 96.

50. This interpretation is compatible with the conclusion offered by Haenchen in *Acts of the Apostles,* 368 n.

51. Although the famine is said here to have affected the "whole inhabited world," the only external evidence for this event is from Josephus (*Ant.* 20.17–53), where the conversions to Judaism of Helena of Adiabene (in northern Mesopotamia) and her son, Izates, are recounted. An important event in which they participate is a famine in Jerusalem during the reign of Claudius, of which Helena learned when she visited Jerusalem to worship in the temple there and found that many were dying of starvation. She paid to have food brought from Alexandria and Cyprus, and later her son gave a generous gift to supply additional food to ease the crisis. The chronological sequence of the events reported by Josephus is confusing, but this event in Jerusalem and vicinity must have occurred in 45 or 46 C.E.

52. References to the biblical prophets include 2:16; 2:30 (David); all the prophets (3:18–15, 50); Isaiah (7:48; 8:28, 34; 28:25); Samuel (13:20); Habakkuk (13:40); 13:27; Jeremiah (15:15); 24:16; 26:22, 27; 28:23.

53. Mark 1:19, 3:17; Matt. 4:21, 10:2.

54. Mark 3:17, 5:37; Matt. 17:1; Acts 12:2.

55. Mark 1:19–20; Matt. 4:21–22; this incident is part of a much more elaborate narrative in Luke 5:10–11.

56. In Jerusalem: 5:11; 8:1, 3; 11:22; 12:1, 5; 15:4, 22; 18:22; in Antioch: 11:26; 13:1; 14:27; 15:3; in Ephesus: 19:17, 28.

57. Judea, Galilee, and Samaria: 9:31; Syria and Cilicia: 14:23; 15:41; 16:5.

58. Eph. 1:22–23, 5:24–27; 1 Tim. 3:15.

59. Exod. 23:14–17, 34:23; Deut. 16:16–17. The Passover is detailed in Exod. 12:1–49; Lev. 23:4–8; Num. 9:1–14; Deut. 16:1–8.

60. See the excursus on Caesarea, p. 130.

61. See the excursus on Caesarea, p. 130.

62. Details in Josephus, *Ant.* 19.286–91.

63. Ibid., 18.195–200, 19.343–52, 354–58.

64. In spite of the considerable textual support for *eis hierosalem* here, the logic of the document as a whole calls for choosing as the original preposition either *ex* or *apo* (from). Later minuscules and versions resolve the problem by supplying the reading *eis Antiocheian.*

65. The most frequent use of *nesteuo* in the New Testament is in Matthew, where there is a debate between modes of fasting and the self-discipline that it involves among the members of the Matthean community and those of the emergent rabbinic movement.

66. I have traced the basic differences between magic and miracle (as divine action in the world) in *Medicine, Miracle, and Magic.* The older, learned study of the evolution of magic in the Persian and Greco-Roman periods by A. D. Nock in *The Beginnings of Christianity,* ed. Foakes-Jackson and Lake, 5:151–88, is informative, but fails to take into account two basic factors: (1) the difference between the fundamental worldview embodied in magic and a theistic perspective such as that of Jewish-Christian apocalyptic, and (2) the degree to which magical features have penetrated the Christian tradition in the later New Testament writings, including Acts.

67. Convenient summary of the inscriptional evidence is provided by Alanna Nobbs in *The Book of Acts in Its Graeco-Roman Setting,* ed. D. W. J. Gill and C. Gempf, vol. 2 of *The Book of Acts in Its First-Century Setting* (Grand Rapids, Mich.: Eerdmans, 1994), 282–87. One inscription (IGRR III.930) has been shown to be too late epigraphically; on IGRR III.935 the name is not Sergius Paulus but Sergius Gaius; CIL VI.31545 mentions one Lucius Sergius Paulus, who appears as a commissioner of the Tiber in Rome during the imperial reign of Claudius (41–54). Paul's visit would have been about 50, so the chronology is possible, but the link of this Sergius Paullus (*sic*) with Cyprus is by no means implied in the inscription, and the name seems to have been common in that period.

68. Acts 3:16, 6:7, 14:22, 16:5.

69. Acts 6:5; 11:24; 14:9, 27; 15:9; 17:31.

70. Elymas could be a transliteration of a semitic word, *halima,* which means "powerful." Some manuscripts and ancient versions read Etoimas, which could be a variant spelling of the Cypriot magician mentioned by Josephus (*Ant.* 20.7.2) who negotiated between Felix the procurator and Drusilla, the daughter of Agrippa I (10 B.C.E.–44 C.E.).

71. Cf. Exod. 6:1; 32:11; Deut. 3:4; 4:34; 5:15; 6:21; 7:8, 19; 11:2; 26:8; 29:3; 2 Kings 9:24; 17:36; 2 Chron. 6:32; Ps. 136:12; Ezek. 20:33–34; Dan. 9:25.

72. This quotation adds to 1 Sam. 13:14 features from Ps. 89:20–21.

73. 1 Macc. 15:23; Philo, *Ad Gaium* 281–82.

74. A forthcoming publication, *Pisidian Antioch: The Site and Its Monuments* by Stephen Mitchell and M. Waelkens, will detail the archaeological evidence from this site.

75. Detailed analysis of this passage is offered by Steyn in *Septuagint Quotations,* 163–66.

76. Also in 1 Peter 2:24.

77. See the excursus on Proselytes and God-Fearers, p. 133.

78. Exod. 40:34–38; Num. 9:15–22, 11:25; Deut. 31:15; 1 Kings 8:10; 2 Chron. 5:13–14. This divine presence in the future is likewise depicted as a cloud in Isa. 4:2–6.

79. The routes of Paul's journeys in Asia Minor — including Acts 14, 18:22-23, and 19:1 — seem to presuppose his journeying through the southern part of the province, even when Galatia is mentioned. This region was included in the province of Galatia, although the southern districts were also known as Lycaonia and Phrygia. Iconium and these cities to the south lay on the most direct route between Syria and the western Asia Minor cities visited by Paul, such as Ephesus and Troas. The more distinctly Celtic region of the province was well to the north, and it included the districts mentioned in connection with Peter: Pontus, Galatia, Cappadocia, Bithynia, and Asia (1 Peter 1:1). Paul's principle of preaching the gospel only in areas where "Christ has not already been named" (Rom. 15:20) can explain why he did not venture into the northern regions of Galatia and Asia Minor.

80. A Jewish mode of punishment, as noted above.

81. Lycaonia was named for an indigenous people whose district became subject successively to the Persians, Alexander the Great, and the Seleucids who succeeded him, and the Romans, who in 188 annexed Lycaonia to the kingdom of Pergamum, then in 129 to the Cappadocians, in 39 to Laodicea, and in 36 to the kingdom of Galatia. In 20 B.C.E. the district was split by Augustus, with the eastern part going back again to the Cappadocians, and the western part under Roman control, colonized by Roman soldiers, and effectively linked with Galatia. Under Vespasian (reigned 69–79) the district was joined with Cappadocia and Galatia in a single province, but the east and west sections were divided again by Trajan (98–117).

82. Robin Lane Fox, in his discussion of "Pagan Cults," in *Pagans and Christians* (New York: Knopf, 1987), 100.

83. Discussed by Fox in ibid., 102–67, esp. 140.

84. For example, Gen. 37:29, 34; 44:13; Lev. 10:6; 21:10; Num. 14:6; Josh. 7:6; Judg. 11:35; 2 Sam. 1:11; 3:31; 13:19, 31.

85. *Paraleipomena of Jeremiah* 2:1, 2, 8, 10; 9:9.

86. M. L. Soards has noted that the subject of all the verbs in the declarative section of Peter's address (15:7–9) is God (*Speeches in Acts,* 90–92).

87. See the excursus on the Pharisees in chapter 1, p. 83.

88. Amos 9:11–12; Jer. 12:15; Isa. 45:21.

89. The *poor* who were to be *remembered* were not only the economically deprived, but also those who by reason of ethnic origin or social status were marginalized or oppressed. It was these kinds of people whose plight was to be remedied by the ideal king in the Israelite tradition (Ps. 72:1–4).

90. The so-called Western text of the Greek New Testament was posited by B. F. Westcott and F. J. A. Hort in their edition of *The New Testament in the Original Greek* (Cambridge and London, 1881), based on Codex D, and the Old Latin and Old Syriac versions. A feature that they noted was that in contrast to the additions that characterize these texts, at certain points they offer a shorter text, which Westcott and Hort dubbed "non-interpolations," and which they assumed to represent the original text. Both the antiquity of this text group and its existence as a definable, specific text type have been challenged in recent years, especially by Kurt Aland in *The Text of the New Testament,* trans. E. F. Rhodes (Grand Rapids, Mich.: Eerdmans, 1987). See my essay on the text of Acts in the introduction.

91. Some of the texts that omit the reference to "things strangled" include a negative version of the Golden Rule, "Whatever you do not wish to be done to yourselves, do not do to others." This confirms the nonritual, moral flavor of the passage.

92. 1 Thess. 1:1; 2 Thess. 1:1; 2 Cor. 1:19.

Chapter 4. The Outreach to the Greek World

1. Also in a letter attributed to Paul, but possibly of later date: Col. 1:1.

2. As H. J. Cadbury noted, the so-called Western text as represented by Codex D expands 11:28 to read, "And there was much rejoicing. When we were assembled, one of them by the name of Agabus ... " Not only does this variant not have credible support in the ancient manuscript tradition, but it fails to fit the pattern of locale and identified individuals associated with all the other we-sections in the Acts account. See the discussion of the text of Acts in the introduction.

3. Hengel, *Acts and the History of Earliest Christianity,* 66.

4. Stanley E. Porter, " 'We' and 'I' Passages in Luke-Acts," in *The Book of Acts in Its Graeco-Roman Setting,* ed. Gill and Gempf, 545–74.

5. Susan M. Praeder, "The Problem of First-Person Narration in Acts," *NovT* 29 (1987): 193–218.

6. According to Diodorus Siculus, 16.3.7, 16.8.6–7.

7. The issue is whether "the prime city of the Macedonian region" means that Philippi was the capital of the province, since later evidence designates Thessalonica as the capital. On this question see the still useful discussion of the textual issue in 16:13 by Kirsopp Lake and H. J. Cadbury in *The Beginnings of Christianity*, ed. Foakes-Jackson and Lake, 4:187–89.

8. See the excursus on Proselytes and God-Fearers in chapter 3, p. 133.

9. In *Embassy to Gaius* 20.132, 152. For further analysis of *proseuche* and the distinction between it and *synagoge*, see my article, "Defining the First-Century Synagogue," 481–500.

10. Analogous is Cornelius's invitation to Peter to come to his house, where he has gathered his kinsmen and close friends to hear the message about Jesus (Acts 10:22–24). These gatherings of seekers in private homes seem to reflect the phenomenon of house churches that are referred to in the Pauline letters: Rom. 16:3; 1 Cor. 16:19; Philemon 2; Col. 4:15.

11. A still notable effort to interpret this passage along these lines is that of Lake (*The Beginnings of Christianity*, ed. Foakes-Jackson and Lake, 4:192–93), where the speech of the diviner is compared with that of a ventriloquist, but not identified with it as a deceptive human accomplishment by which speech *seems* to come from a certain source.

12. Garnsey, *Social Status and Legal Privilege in the Roman Empire*, 140–41, 197, 221.

13. Some scholars have proposed that the magistrates showed their horror at the accusations by tearing off their own clothing. Although the reference of *auton* in v. 22 is not specific, it is far more plausible to see it as referring to the clothing of the apostles, who are thereby visibly and physically prepared for the beating that the magistrate ordered and which follows.

14. A *lictor*, the Latin term for law-enforcement agents, was identifiable by *fasces*, a bundle of sticks from which an axe projected, which was carried as a symbol of their authority to put into effect judicial decisions reached by the magistrates. The Greek term here, *hrabdouchos*, means "rod" or "staff," and serves as the equivalent for lictor.

15. A compact but comprehensive analysis of Roman citizenship is that of Mark Hassall, "Romans and Non-Romans," in *Roman World*, ed. Wacher, 2:685–700.

16. See analysis at 15:40, and the excursus on Silas/Silvanus in chapter 3, p. 185.

17. *Politarches* is the designation of these officials. G. H. R. Horsley (in "The Politarchs," in *The Book of Acts in Its Graeco-Roman Setting*, ed. Gill and Gempf, 419–31) has analyzed the inscriptional evidence from Macedonia in which this term appears, and presents a convinc-

ing case that "the politarchate was a senior, annual magistracy, attested predominantly in the cites of Macedonia after Roman intervention in the second century B.C." The term is found elsewhere but the majority of the evidence is from Macedonia, and more than 40 percent of it is from Thessalonica. Judging by the lists on the inscriptions, there seem to have been five politarchs in office most frequently, although one inscription indicates that there was in one year a single eponymous holder of the office of politarch. Their assignments included convening and presiding over the civic council (*boule*) as well as the citizen assembly (*ekklesia*), and one of their specific roles was the dedication of public temples and shrines to various gods and goddesses. Their function was seen by the Romans as essential to the maintenance of law and order, especially in a province that bordered on Greece to the south and on a people to the north who were not under Roman dominance.

18. Details concerning Thessalonica, including surveys of the history of the city in the earlier and later (Roman and early Christian) periods are provided by Holland Hendrix, with bibliography, in his article on "Thessalonica," in *ABD* 6, ed. D. N. Freedman (New York: Doubleday, 1992), 523–27, which has been drawn upon for this sketch of the city.

19. An outline of the debate and a bibliography are offered by Edgar M. Krentz in his study of 1 Thessalonians, in *ABD* 5, 515–16.

20. See the excursus on Proselytes and God-Fearers in chapter 3, p. 133.

21. An insightful analysis of urban elites, including women, is offered by David W. J. Gill in an essay, "Acts and the Urban Elites," in *The Book of Acts in Its Graeco-Roman Setting*, ed. Gill and Gempf, 105–18. The section concerning women is on pp. 114–17. The theory that the incipient movement first caught on among those who today would be termed "middle class" is challenged by Gill, who cites W. A. Meeks as assuming this to be the case in his *The First Urban Christians* (New Haven: Yale University Press, 1983). Meeks asserts that there are none from the top levels of Roman society (senators and *equites*) and none from the bottom ("the poorest of the poor") who are identified as members of the new community, but he does take into account the relatively wealthy, who had slaves, traveled extensively, and provided accommodations for itinerant apostles and for meeting places (72–73).

22. See n. 17 above.

23. The Romans permitted Jews to be exempt from the empire-wide requirement that all subjects participate in the imperial cult. This policy, which was inaugurated by Julius Caesar and Augustus, was revoked by Caligula, and later by Nero. The sanctity of the Jerusalem temple was guaranteed by the Romans, as Josephus attests (*Wars* 6.124–26). Although ultimate power and decisions rested with the Syrian governor, the Jerusalem council (*synedrion*), like others throughout the

empire, operated on the basis of Jewish law, and had the power to enforce it. "The constitution was an aristocracy and the high priests were entrusted with the leadership of the nation...under the aegis of the Roman governor" (Smallwood, *The Jews under Roman Rule*, 148–49).

24. L. Michael White, *Building God's House in the Roman World: Architectural Adaptation among Jews, Pagans, and Christians* (Baltimore: Johns Hopkins University Press, 1990); Bradley Blue in *The Book of Acts in Its Graeco-Roman Setting*, ed. Gill and Gempf, 119–222.

25. For a challenge to such an assumption, see my essay, "Defining the First-Century C.E. Synagogue," 481–500.

26. *Kataluma* is used in the LXX for both lodging and dining facilities (1 Sam. Kings 1:18, 9:22; Sir. 14:25).

27. J. E. Packer, in "Housing and Population in Imperial Ostia and Rome," *Journal of Roman Studies* 57 (1967): 87. From this analysis Blue concludes that "the average domicile served only as a place to sleep and store possessions," and that most of the populace spent their time in public facilities such as streets, shops, arenas and baths ("Acts and the House Church," in *The Book of Acts in Its Graeco-Roman Setting*, ed. Gill and Gempf, n. 138).

28. *Hyperoon* is used in the Acts account of the initial gathering of the followers of Jesus in Jerusalem (1:12–26). See the discussion of the significance of this term above in my analysis of this text. The term for corresponding space for Jesus' final meal with his disciples in Mark 16:15 and Luke 22:12 is "a large upper room" (*anagaion mega*).

29. This offer of hospitality by a member of the community is consonant with the fact that a majority of the New Testament occurrences of *xenizo* (where it depicts furnishing housing for itinerants) are in Acts: 10:6, 13, 23, 32; 21:16; 28:7.

30. Cf. 4:31; 6:2, 7; 8:14; 13:5, 7, 46; 16:32; 18:11.

31. See the excursus on Proselytes and God-Fearers in chapter 3, p. 133.

32. Seneca, *On Providence* 1.5.

33. Sketched by David E. Hahm, in *The Origins of Stoic Cosmology* (Columbus: Ohio State University Press, 1977).

34. The classic historical analysis of the Areopagus as it appears in Acts is that of H. J. Cadbury, in *The Beginnings of Christianity*, ed. Foakes-Jackson and Lake, 5:212–14. A recent brief but useful survey of the evidence is offered by David W. G. Gill, in his essay on Achaia in *The Book of Acts in Its Graeco-Roman Setting*, 447–48.

35. *On the Cherubim* 42. Other translations of this text in Philo paraphrase the term *deisidaimones* "corrupt religion into superstition," thereby forcing a negative connotation on the word.

36. For example, the universality of God's creation: Gen. 1:31; Exod. 20:11; Wisd. 9:1; God's creation of the archetypal human: Gen. 1:26; Wisd. 2:23; Sir. 17:1–16; the divine ordering of time and

space: Deut. 32:8; Ps. 74:12–17; Wisd. 7:17–19; humans seeking God: Deut. 4:27–31; Ps. 145:18–20; Isa. 55:6; Wisd. 13:5–9.

37. The attempt to trace the phrase to the sixth-century B.C.E. Cretan poet and philosopher Epimenides is not persuasive.

38. In spite of the absence of the phrase *en andri* from many of the ancient versions and patristic sources, the strong attestation in the oldest and best Greek sources heighten the probability of its authenticity. The fact that the noun is *aner* (male) rather than *anthropos* (human) makes more emphatic that Jesus is a complete human being, as evidenced by his sexual identity, and not merely an ideal or timeless model of humanity.

39. Greco-Roman religions often had a dualistic view of human existence—matter and spirit—and offered hope of the immortality of the human soul, liberated from the limitations it experienced in the mortal human body. This was sometimes understood as sharing in the life of a deity. Others denied the existence of humans beyond the temporal limits of earthly life. For those convinced of such religious views, resurrection of the body would be utter nonsense.

40. *Anthypatos* = head of government in a Roman senatorial province.

41. This is true whether or not one accepts the theory that in 2 Corinthians are preserved fragments of other Pauline letters to that community, as discussed by Hans-Dieter Betz in "Second Corinthians," *ABD* 1 (New York: Doubleday, 1992), 1148–54.

42. J. Murphy-O'Connor, "Corinth," *ABD* 1 (New York: Doubleday, 1992), 1134–39; Furnish, *II Corinthians*, 4–22.

43. H. J. Cadbury long ago made the point that, although "tentmaker" is the obvious literal meaning of *skenopoios*, it was used in ancient Greek and by the church fathers with reference to leatherworkers (*Beginnings of Christianity*, 4:223). An effort has been made by R. F. Hock to interpret this reference to the term literally (*The Social Context of Paul's Ministry: Tent-Making and Apostleship* [Philadelphia: Fortress Press, 1980], 41). But B. M. Rapske has pointed out that such an occupation required carrying extensive and weighty equipment, which is most unlikely for such a highly mobile individual as Paul. He also notes that the tools for a leather-worker were far simpler and easier to transport ("Acts, Travel and Shipwreck," in *The Book of Acts in Its Graeco-Roman Setting*, ed. Gill and Gempf, 6–7).

44. In four of the six references to this couple in the New Testament (Acts 18:2, 18, 26; Rom. 16:3; 1 Cor. 16:19; 2 Tim. 4:19), Priscilla (or Prisca) is mentioned first, which may imply that hers was the more significant role of this pair in the fostering and support of the new community.

45. Josh. 2:19; Judg. 9:24; 1 Kings 2:9, 32; Jonah 1:14. The precedent for putting the blame for judgment on those guilty of executing the

agent of God matches David's pronouncement on the Amalekite who killed Saul (2 Sam. 1:1–16).

46. From this point on in Acts, Paul's relationship with Jews is depicted as increasingly confrontational: in Ephesus (18:28, 19:9, 20:3) and climactically in the Jerusalem temple (21:28). Yet his vigorous efforts to persuade Jews concerning "the kingdom of God" continue according to 19:8.

47. The legal processes operative in the Roman Empire are discussed in detail by A. N. Sherwin-White in *Roman Society and Roman Law,* 99–100.

48. The excavation was reported by F. J. de Waele in *Corinthe de Saint Paul,* Les Antiquités de Grèce (Paris, 1961), and its judicial function was confirmed by an inscription described by J. H. Kent, in *The Inscriptions, 1926–1950: Results of Excavations Conducted by the American School of Classical Studies at Athens VIII.3* (Princeton, N.J.: Princeton University Press, 1966).

49. Some scholars have raised the question whether the haircutting was done by Paul, or Aquila or Priscilla, but the participle (*keiramenos*) is masculine and the most plausible interpretation is to attribute the vow and the consequent haircutting to Paul.

50. Another feature of the Nazirite vow of separation was abstinence from wine and strong drink, as is said to be the case with John the Baptist—only in Luke 1:15.

51. A perceptive survey of the impact of Hellenism on the wider Greco-Roman world, but especially on the culture of Alexandria and specifically on Judaism there, is provided by M. Hengel, in *Judaism and Hellenism,* vol. 1, English trans. John Bowden (London: SCM Press, 1974), 65–70.

52. In the other two gospel accounts of Jesus' baptism (Mark 1:10; Matt. 3:16), the term *"Holy* Spirit" is not used.

53. Philostratus (170–245 C.E.), *Life of Apollonius* 8.7.

54. See L. Michael White, "Urban Development and Social Change in Imperial Ephesos," in *Ephesos: Metropolis of Asia,* ed. Helmut Koester, Harvard Theological Studies (Valley Forge, Pa.: Trinity Press International, 1995), 27–79.

55. For example, Dieter Knibbe (in "Via Sacra Ephesiaca: New Aspects of the Cult of Artemis Ephesia," in *Ephesos,* ed. Koester, 141–55) credits Croesus (560–540 B.C.E.) with having given Artemis authority in place of Cybele, thereby becoming the Asian equivalent of the Great Mother of the gods in Rome.

56. The temple measured 360 by 200 feet, with 127 marble pillars 60 feet high, of which many were capped with sculpture and gold. Details are reproduced on Roman coins from the reign of Claudius to that of Valerian. See further Magie, *Roman Rule in Asia Minor,* 1:75, 2:75–76 n. 88.

57. Described by the first/second-century C.E. writer, Dio Chrysostom (31.54).

58. So Steven Friesen, "The Cult of the Roman Emperors in Ephesos," in *Ephesos,* ed. Koester, 228–50.

59. White, "Urban Development and Social Change," 57–59.

60. The gift of tongues as a confirmation of membership in God's new people of those who have believed in Jesus and been baptized is also promised in the longer ending of Mark (16:16–17).

61. This understanding of magic as primarily technique, as distinct from miracle, which involves trust in the deity to act in response to need or petition, is set forth in my study *Medicine, Miracle, and Magic,* esp. 95–125.

62. This is the sole occurrence of *exorkistes* in the New Testament, although the phenomenon of exorcisms is common in the gospels especially. An indication of the references to Jewish names and cultural features in the Magical Papyri of this period is offered by Hemer in *Book of Acts in the Setting of Hellenistic History,* 121 n. 54.

63. Also mentioned in 2 Tim. 4:20.

64. Difficulties with the identification of this Erastus with the one mentioned by Paul in Romans 16, or with the *aedile* (the title of a Roman public officer in charge of streets, traffic, markets, and public games) named in an inscription found at Corinth have long been noted, as by Cadbury in *Beginnings of Christianity,* 4:244–45.

65. See analysis of this term for the Jesus movement in my discussion in chapter 3, p. 113.

66. Noted by Hemer in *Book of Acts in the Setting of Hellenistic History,* 121, based on IGRR 1.467. Codex Vaticanus does not include the detail that the shrines were silver.

67. The nomenclature for these provincial governors varies, as did the fact that some were subject to the senate and others to the emperor: proconsuls in the larger provinces, with procurators as assistants or as responsible for part of a province. Also there were puppet rulers, such as Herod Agrippa.

68. See n. 17 above, for description of *politarchs.*

69. The Feast of Unleavened Bread (which originated in an agricultural setting) is already combined in the Pentateuch with the Feast of Passover (which presupposes a nomadic, herding culture). The divergences of these traditions and their historic merging in Jewish tradition are well documented by Baruch M. Bokser in his article, "Unleavened Bread and Passover, Feasts of," in *ABD* 6, ed. D. N. Freedman (New York: Doubleday, 1992), 755–65.

70. Reported, but wrongly interpreted by Adolf Deissmann as referring simply to pious Jews, in *Light from the Ancient Past* (1922; repr., Grand Rapids, Mich.: Baker Book House, 1965), 451. A useful survey of the archaeological evidence concerning Miletus is offered by Edwin Ya-

mauchi in *The Archaeology of New Testament Cities in Western Asia Minor* (Grand Rapids, Mich.: Baker Book House, 1980), 114–27.

71. The image of God purchasing or redeeming his people is familiar in both the prophetic and the wisdom tradition of Israel (Isa. 41:14; Ps. 74:4).

72. Quoted by Plutarch, *Moralia* 778C.

73. Ibid., 173D.

74. Quoted by Claudius Aelian, *Varia Historia* 13.13.

Chapter 5. The Arrest of Paul and the Outreach to the Center of the Roman World

1. An excellent survey of the history of Tyre is offered in the article on this city in the *ABD* 6, 286–92. Especially useful is Douglas R. Edwards's study of Tyre in the Greco-Roman period, 690–91.

2. Fierce hostility toward the Jews on the part of hellenistic-oriented residents in Acco is reported in the Maccabean period (1 Macc. 5:14–23).

3. See the excursus on Caesarea in chapter 3, p. 130.

4. Matt. 10:3; Mark 3:18; Luke 6:14; John 1:43–51, 14:8–11; and Acts 1:13.

5. For a broad discussion, see the excursus on "the Name" in Acts in chapter 1, p. 63.

6. This suggestion was offered by Johannes Munck in his Anchor Bible commentary: *Acts* (Garden City, N.Y.: Doubleday, 1967), 209.

7. The inscription, discovered in the last century, is in the museum in Istanbul, and published by A. Deissmann, in *Light from the Ancient East*, rev. ed., trans. L. R. M. Strachan (New York: Harper, n.d.). Josephus reports these warnings, although his wording is slightly different (*Wars* 5.193; *Ant.* 15.417).

8. See the excursus on Caesarea in chapter 3, p. 130.

9. A detailed analysis of the ancient sources and of scholarly discussion of the subject of modes of custody in the Roman world is offered by Brian Rapske in chapter 2 of his study, *The Book of Acts and Paul in Roman Custody*, vol. 3 of *The Book of Acts in Its First-Century Setting*, ed. Bruce Winter (Grand Rapids, Mich.: Eerdmans, 1994). A summary of this analysis by Rapske is offered below in the excursus on Roman modes of legal custody.

10. These Assassins were militant nationalists, seeking liberation of their land from the Romans.

11. Most of the Greek manuscripts here convey the meaning, "I looked up," but the thread of the narrative implies that Paul saw Ananias, and some manuscripts add that phrase.

12. See the excursus on Tarsus in chapter 3, p. 148.

13. See the excursus on Roman Citizenship in chapter 4, p. 200.

14. This would be Gamaliel I, as identified in the later rabbinic tradition, who appears to have been a significant interpreter of the Torah in the middle of the first century C.E. Gamaliel II in the later first and early second century was a major figure in the adaptation of Jewish tradition following the destruction of the temple and the disappearance of the priesthood.

15. See the excursus on Pharisees in chapter 1, p. 83.

16. This historical understanding has been abundantly documented by Jacob Neusner in his many studies of the Pharisees, beginning with *The Rabbinic Traditions about the Pharisees* (Leiden: Brill, 1971). An important study building on Neusner's insights, but specifying the import for New Testament interpretation, is that of Anthony J. Saldarini in *Pharisees, Scribes, and Sadducees.*

17. The term used here, *presbyterion,* is apparently a synonym for *synedrion,* and both refer to the district councils established by the Romans to gave a degree of local autonomy through locals with power or prestige. See the excursus on the *Synedrion* in chapter 1, p. 68.

18. The customary translation of *anthropous* as "men" ignores the fact that this term means humans, as opposed to other forms of life, while maleness is implicit only in the term *aner.*

19. Garnsey, *Social Status and Legal Privilege,* 268.

20. In *Wars* 5.194 Josephus confirms the existence and the intent of the tablets in the temple warning intruders that violation of the precincts was a capital crime, and he also quotes Titus reminding the Jewish revolutionaries occupying the Tower of Antonia during the Jewish revolt of 66–70 C.E. that the Romans had given Jews the right to execute intruders.

21. The decrees are reported in Josephus, *Ant.* 14, including Jews in Delos (231), Ephesus (238), Sardis (235), and Laodicea (241).

22. Garnsey, *Social Status and Legal Privilege,* 266. The emperor Caracalla (211–17 C.E.) decreed that all council members everywhere were citizens. Garnsey observes that it is possible that Roman citizenship was more highly regarded in mid-first-century Judea than in such regions as Bithynia in the early second century.

23. Sherwin-White, *Roman Society and Roman Law,* 154–55.

24. Garnsey, *Social Status and Legal Privilege,* 268.

25. See the excursus on the *Synedrion* in chapter 1, p. 68.

26. Josephus, *Wars* 2.243, 245, 441; also *Ant.* 20.131–32, 134–37. Agrippa II is mentioned in Acts 25:13.

27. The term *syneidesis* appears in the Septuagint only in the later wisdom tradition (Eccl. 10:20; Wisd. 17:11; Sir. 42:18). See the discussion of conscience in the excursus on Epicurean and Stoic Philosophy, p. 212.

28. 2:4, 17–18; 8:29; 10:19; 11:12; 16:7; 19:21; 20:22; and 21:4.

29. 5:19; 7:30–38; 8:26; 10:3, 7, 22; 11:13; 12:7–11; 27:23; in 12:23 an angel is the instrument of divine punishment.

30. 1 Sam. 8:17, 15:24; 1 Kings 1:34.

31. See the excursus on Caesarea in chapter 3, p. 130.

32. The meaning of *dexiolaboi* is uncertain.

33. Tacitus, *Annals* 12.54; *History* 5.9.

34. Josephus, *Ant.* 2.147; *Wars* 247–52.

35. Josephus, *Ant.* 160–61, 168.173–77; *Wars* 259–60, 266–67.

36. Antipatris, which was named by Herod the Great for his father, Antipater, was known as Aphek in the earlier history of Israel, reaching back to the early Bronze period (3200 B.C.E.). As noted by Martin Hengel, at this time Antipatris was an important military post, located as it was in a district that bordered on Joppa and Apollonia to the west, Lydda to the south in the toparchy of Judea, Samaria to the east, and Caesarea to the north (*Between Jesus and Paul* [Philadelphia: Fortress Press, 1983], 119).

37. For a description of the city, see the excursus on Caesarea in chapter 3, p. 130.

38. The praetorium is not one of the buildings described by Josephus in his extended accounts of Caesarea, but it has now been located by archaeologists. The excavations at Caesarea in the past two decades concentrated primarily on the harbor and on such external features as the city water supply. Recently, however, excavation of the Herodian palace on the promontory overlooking the harbor has been carried out, and the elaborate structure has been found which was Herod's palace, and was then adapted as the seat of the Roman governor. See the excursus on Caesarea in chapter 3, p. 130.

39. "Nazarene" may be derived simply from Nazareth, the town where Jesus was in residence with his family (Luke 2:39, 4:16). Or it may come from one of two Hebrew roots, *netzer* or *nazar.* The former means "shoot," and is usually linked with Isa. 11:1, identifying Jesus with the promised messianic "shoot from Jesse," which is the likely import of Matt. 2:23, where scriptural support is claimed for the term. *Nazar* means "dedicate," and is the basis for the term "Nazirite," which is used for a special mode of consecration, such as that of Samson (Judges 13). It is the latter significance that was attached to the term later by a group of Christians who insisted that all should obey fully the Law of Moses, and were denounced by Epiphanius (ca. 375 C.E.) and Jerome as wanting to be both Jews and Christians.

40. See the excursus on Epicurean and Stoic Philosophy in chapter 4, p. 212.

41. Details of these features of Stoic influence on the ethics of Paul are offered in my essay "Facing the Future: Common Themes in Jewish Apocalyptic and Stoic Philosophy," in *Biblical and Humane,* Festschrift for John Priest (Atlanta: Scholars Press, 1997).

42. See the excursus on Belief in the Resurrection, p. 263.

43. There are differences in detail between Tacitus (*Annals* 12.54) and Josephus (*Ant.* 20) as to the scope of Felix's jurisdiction, especially as to when he ruled Galilee.

44. Rapske, *Paul in Roman Custody,* 9, 15–19, 25, 31, 34, 39, 41–43, 51–55.

45. An extensive description of Felix and his action in the office of procurator is offered by Josephus in *Ant.* 20.182–96. Only a minor note appears in *Wars* 2.271–72.

46. Josephus's designation for describing her, *theosebes,* is the equivalent of the term the author of Acts uses for Gentiles who have united with Jews in the understanding and worship of God (2:5, 8:2, 22:12).

47. Illuminating discussion of this process is offered by Garnsey in *Social Status and Legal Privilege,* 75–76, 97, 263–68.

48. Josephus, *Life* 32–38; *Ant.* 20.158–59.

49. Tacitus, *History* 2.1–2, 81; 5.1.

50. In *Metamorphoses* 2.21 Apuleius describes a guest at dinner who, when invited to recount his life story, sat on the couch and "held out his right hand in the manner of an orator, shutting down the two smaller fingers and stretching out the other three, and pointing up with his thumb a little."

51. The pronoun "you" is here plural, *humin,* which indicates that he is addressing all his auditors, not merely Agrippa.

52. See the excursus on the *Synedrion* in chapter 1, p. 68.

53. E.g., 4 Ezra 14:1; 2 Bar. 22:2.

54. Philo, *The Worse Attacks the Better* 46.

55. The term for goad, *kentron,* is used in canonical and deuterocanonical texts with reference to the actions of God or of others in stimulating, chastising, or rebuking his people (Prov. 26:3; Sir. 38:25; Hosea 5:12, 13:14; 4 Macc. 14:19).

56. The text of Acts identifies the centurion's military group as *speireis Sebastes.* There are frequent references in Josephus to cohorts *Sebastenon,* where the troops were recruited from Sebaste, the chief city of the Samaritans (e.g., *Ant.* 19.365, 20.122; *Wars* 2.52). The reference here might be to such troops of local origin, but inscriptional evidence from Syria designating Roman troops serving in the region as the Augustan cohort (*speira sebaste*) has long been known, as T. R. S. Broughton has shown (*Beginnings of Christianity,* 5:443–44).

57. See the excursus on the We-Passages in Acts in chapter 4, p. 189.

58. These features are familiar in the hellenistic romances, such as *Chariton* and *Ephesiaca* (translations in *Collected Greek Novels,* ed. B. P. Reardon [Berkeley: University of California Press, 1989], 17–169).

59. In the synoptic tradition, hearers of Jesus are said to have come in large numbers from such places as Sidon (Mark 3:8), and his preaching tour as sketched in Mark 7:31 (Matt. 15:29) included visiting the

region of Tyre and Sidon. In the Q tradition (Luke 10:13–14) Tyre and Sidon are cited as being more open to repentance when confronted by the works of Jesus than were the cities of Bethsaida and Chorazin. The existence of a Christian community in this city very early, therefore, is by no means historically implausible.

60. The peril of sea travel in winter is a feature of the narrative in the romance of Chariton, *Chaereas and Callirhoe* 3.5.1., and is specified by the fourth-century C.E. Latin writer Vegetius in *Concerning Military Matters* 4.39 as being perilous after mid-September and impossible after early November.

61. The location of the harbor was probably not the one east of Cape Mouros, which faces east, but one which is now shallow (perhaps from seismic shifts) and faces southwest and northwest, as specified in 27:12.

62. *Echidna* is the term for the reptile that clung to Paul. Though often translated "viper," it is used in classical Greek for a variety of snakes and small reptiles, so the fact that vipers are not found on Malta does not demonstrate the historical unreliability of Acts.

63. The name of the city may derive from the Greek word *rhegnymi,* meaning "split," and was given to it in the belief that Sicily had been split off from the main part of Italy by an earthquake.

64. Eighteen occurrences of the phrase, including the central claim in Luke 11:20 that Jesus' exorcisms are a manifestation of the presence and power of the kingdom of God.

Bibliography

History of New Testament Interpretation (especially Acts)

Bauer, Bruno. *Die Apostelgeschichte. Eine Ausgleichung des Paulinismus und des Judentums innerhalb der christlichen Kirche.* Berlin, 1850.

Gasque, W. Ward. *A History of the Interpretation of the Acts of the Apostles.* Republished with an addendum. Peabody, Mass.: Hendrickson, 1989.

Kümmel, W. G. *The New Testament: A History of the Investigation of Its Problems.* Trans. H. C. Kee. Nashville: Abingdon, 1972.

Powell, Mark Allan. *What Are They Saying about Acts?* Mahwah, N.J.: Paulist Press, 1991.

Richard, Earl. *New Views on Luke and Acts.* Collegeville, Minn.: Liturgical Press, 1990.

Semler, Johann Salomo. *Abhandlung von freier Untersuchung des Canons* [*Treatise on Free Research in the Canon*]. 4 vols. Halle, 1771–75.

Commentaries on Acts

Bruce, F. F. *The Acts of the Apostles.* Grand Rapids, Mich.: Eerdmans, 1952; 3d rev. ed., 1990.

Cadbury, H. J. *The Acts of the Apostles: Translation and Commentary.* Vol. 4 of *The Beginnings of Christianity,* ed. F. J. Foakes-Jackson and Kirsopp Lake. 1932; repr., Grand Rapids, Mich.: Baker Book House, 1966.

de Wette, W. M. L. *Kurze Erklärung der Apostelgeschichte.* 4th ed., Leipzig, 1838. Edited and largely rewritten by Franz Overbeck, 1870.

Dunn, James D. G. *The Acts of the Apostles.* Narrative Commentaries. Valley Forge, Pa.: Trinity Press International, 1996.

Haenchen, Ernst. *The Acts of the Apostles: A Commentary.* Trans. R. McL. Wilson. Philadelphia: Westminster Press, 1971. Original version: *Kritische-exegetischer Kommentar über das Neue Testament. 3. Die Apostelgeschichte.* 10th ed. Göttingen: Vandenhoeck and Ruprecht, 1956; 15th ed., 1968.

Johnson, Luke Timothy. *The Acts of the Apostles.* Sacra Pagina 5. Collegeville, Minn.: Liturgical Press, 1992.

Knox, W. L. *The Acts of the Apostles.* Cambridge: Cambridge University Press, 1948.

Historical Analyses and Reconstructions of Acts

Cadbury, H. J. *The Book of Acts in History.* London: A. & C. Black; New York: Harper, 1955.
————. *The Making of Luke-Acts.* New York: Macmillan, 1928; repr., 1958, 1961.
Conybeare, W. J., and J. S. Howson. *The Life and Epistles of Paul.* London, 1852; New York: Scribner's, 1855.
Dupont, Jacques. *The Sources of Acts: The Present Position.* London, 1964. English translation of *Les Sources du Livre des Actes.* Bruges, 1960.
Foakes-Jackson, F. J., and Kirsopp Lake, eds. *The Beginnings of Christianity,* Part 1: *The Acts of the Apostles.* London: Macmillan, 1920–35.
    Vol. 1: F. J. Foakes-Jackson and K. Lake. *Prolegomena I: The Jewish, Gentile, and Christian Backgrounds.*
    Vol. 2: H. J. Cadbury. *Prolegomena II: Criticism.* 1922.
    Vol. 3: J. H. Ropes. *The Text of Acts.* 1922.
    Vol. 4: K. Lake and H. J. Cadbury. *Translation and Commentary.* 1932; repr., Grand Rapids, Mich.: Baker Book House, 1966.
    Vol. 5: *Additional Notes to the Commentary,* ed. K. Lake and H. J. Cadbury. 1933; repr., Grand Rapids, Mich.: Baker Book House, 1966.
Headlam, A. C. "Acts of the Apostles." *HDB* 1:35.
Keck, L. E., and J. L. Martyn, eds. *Studies in Luke-Acts.* 1966; repr., Philadelphia: Fortress Press, 1980.
Knox, W. L. *St. Paul and the Church of Jerusalem.* Cambridge, 1925.
Lüdemann, Gerd. *Early Christianity according to the Traditions in Acts.* Trans. John Bowden. Minneapolis: Fortress Press, 1989.
Ramsay, W. M. *The Bearing of Recent Discovery on the Trustworthiness of the New Testament.* London, 1915.
Smith, James. *The Voyage and Shipwreck of St. Paul.* London, 1848; 4th ed., 1880.

Historical and Social Setting of Acts

Cassidy, R. J. *Society and Politics in the Acts of the Apostles.* Maryknoll, N.Y.: Orbis, 1987.
Esler, Philip. *Community and Gospel in Luke-Acts: The Social and Political Motivations of Lucan Theology.* SNTSMS 57. Cambridge: Cambridge University Press, 1987.
Fox, Robin Lane. *Pagans and Christians.* New York: Knopf, 1987.
Friesen, Steven. "The Cult of the Roman Emperors in Ephesus." In *Ephesos,* ed. Koester.
Hendrix, Holland. "Thessalonica." In *ABD* 6, ed. D. N. Freedman, 523–27. New York: Doubleday, 1992.

Hengel, Martin. *Judaism and Hellenism.* 2 vols. Trans. John Bowden. London: SCM Press, 1974.

Kee, H. C. *Who Are the People of God? Early Christian Models of Community.* New Haven: Yale University Press, 1993.

Knibbe, Dieter. "Via Sacra Ephesiaca: New Aspects of the Cult of Artemis Ephesia." In *Ephesos,* ed. Koester.

Koester, Helmut, ed. *Ephesos: Metropolis of Asia.* Harvard Theological Studies. Valley Forge, Pa.: Trinity Press International, 1995.

Meeks, Wayne A. *The First Urban Christians.* New Haven: Yale University Press, 1983.

Mitchell, Stephen. *Anatolia: Land, Men, and Gods in Asia Minor.* 2 vols. Oxford: Clarendon Press, 1993.

Moxnes, Halvor. *The Economy of the Kingdom: Social Conflict and Economic Relations in Luke's Gospel.* Philadelphia: Fortress Press, 1988.

Murphy-O'Connor, J. "Corinth." In *ABD* 1, ed. D. N. Freedman, 1134–39. New York: Doubleday, 1992.

Raban, Avner, and Kenneth G. Holum, eds. *Caesarea Maritima: Retrospective after Two Millennia.* Leiden: Brill, 1977.

White, L. Michael. "Urban Development and Social Change in Imperial Ephesos." In *Ephesos,* ed. Koester.

Winter, Bruce W., ed. *The Book of Acts in Its First-Century Setting.* 6 vols. Grand Rapids, Mich.: Eerdmans, 1993– (vols. 4–6 forthcoming).
Vol. 1: *Ancient Literary Setting,* ed. B. W. Winter and Andrew D. Clarke. 1993.
Vol. 2: *The Book of Acts in Its Graeco-Roman Setting,* ed. David W. J. Gill and Conrad Gempf. 1994.
Vol. 3: *Paul in Roman Custody,* ed. Brian Rapske. 1994.

Yamauchi, Edwin. *The Archaeology of New Testament Cities in Western Asia Minor.* Grand Rapids, Mich.: Baker Book House, 1980.

Historical and Sociological Method

Berger, Peter. *The Sacred Canopy: Elements of a Sociological Theory of Religion* (Garden City, N.Y.: Doubleday, 1969).

Berger, Peter, and Thomas Luckmann. *The Social Construction of Reality.* Garden City, N.Y.: Doubleday, 1967.

Hemer, Colin J. *The Book of Acts in the Setting of Hellenistic History.* Ed. C. H. Gempf. WUNT 49. Tübingen: J. C. B. Mohr [Paul Siebeck], 1989.

Horsley, Richard A. *Sociology and the Jesus Movement.* New York: Crossroad, 1989.

Kee, H. C. *Knowing the Truth: A Sociological Approach to New Testament Interpretation.* Minneapolis: Fortress Press, 1989.

———. *Who Are the People of God? Early Christian Models of Community* New Haven: Yale University Press, 1993.

Kuhn, T. S. *The Structures of Scientific Revolutions*. 2nd ed. Chicago: University of Chicago Press, 1970.

Sterling, Gregory E. *Historiography and Self-Definition: Josephos, Luke-Acts, and Apologetic Historiography*. Suppl. to *NovT* 64. Leiden and New York: E. J. Brill, 1992.

Acts in the Context of Judaism in the Greco-Roman Period

Bokser, Baruch M. "Unleavened Bread and Passover, Feasts of." In *ABD* 6, ed. D. N. Freedman, 755–65. New York: Doubleday, 1992.

Collins, John J. *The Apocalyptic Imagination: An Introduction to the Jewish Matrix of Christianity*. New York: Crossroad, 1987.

Evans, Craig, and James A. Sanders. *Luke and Scripture: The Function of Sacred Tradition in Luke-Acts*. Minneapolis: Fortress Press, 1993.

Gutman, Joseph, ed. *The Synagogue: Studies in Origins, Archaeology, and Architecture*. New York: Ktav, 1975.

Hachlili, Rachel. "Diaspora Synagogues." In *ABD* 6, ed. D. N. Freedman, 260–63. New York: Doubleday, 1992.

Horsley, Richard A. *Archaeology, History, and Society in Galilee*. Valley Forge, Pa.: Trinity Press International, 1996.

Kee, H. C. "Defining the First-Century C.E. Synagogue: Problems and Progress," *NTS* 41 (1995): 481–500.

———. "Facing the Future: Common Themes in Jewish Apocalyptic and Stoic Philosophy." In *Biblical and Humane*, Festschrift for John Priest. Atlanta: Scholars Press, 1997.

Lieu, J., J. North, and T. Rajak, eds. *The Jews among Pagans and Christians*. London: Routledge, 1992.

Mantel, Hugo. *Studies in the History of the Sanhedrin*. Cambridge: Harvard University Press, 1965.

Meyers, Eric. "Synagogue." In *ABD* 6, ed. D. N. Freedman, 251–60. New York: Doubleday, 1992.

Neusner, Jacob. *The Pharisees: Rabbinic Perspectives*. Hoboken, N.J.: Ktav, 1985.

———. *From Politics to Piety: The Emergence of Rabbinic Judaism*. Englewood Cliffs, N.J.: Prentice-Hall, 1973.

Reynolds, Joyce, and Robert Tannenbaum. *Jews and God-Fearers at Aphrodisias*. Cambridge: Cambridge Philological Society, 1987.

Saldarini, Anthony J. *Pharisees, Scribes, and Sadducees in Palestinian Society: A Sociological Approach*. Wilmington, Del.: Michael Glazier, 1988.

———. "Sanhedrin." In *ABD* 5, ed. D. N. Freedman, 975–79. New York: Doubleday, 1992.

Smallwood, Mary E. *The Jews under Roman Rule: From Pompey to Diocletian*. Ed. J. Neusner. SJLA 20. Leiden: E. J. Brill, 1976.

Steyn, Gert J. *Septuagint Quotations in the Context of the Petrine and Pauline Speeches in Acta Apostolorum*. Kampen: Kok Pharos, 1995.

Tyson, J., ed. *Luke-Acts and the Jewish People*. Minneapolis: Augsburg Press, 1988.

The Roman World: Structure, Administration, and Culture

Alföldy, Geza. *The Social History of Rome*. Baltimore: Johns Hopkins University Press, 1988.

Bowersock, G. W. *Hellenism in Late Antiquity*. Ann Arbor: University of Michigan Press, 1990.

———. *Roman Arabia*. Cambridge: Harvard University Press, 1983.

Edwards, Douglas. *Religion and Power: Pagans, Jews, and Christians in the Greek East*. New York: Oxford University Press, 1996.

Garnsey, Peter. *Social Status and Legal Privilege in the Roman Empire*. Oxford: Oxford University Press, 1970.

Garnsey, Peter, and Richard Saller. *The Roman Empire: Economy, Society, and Culture*. Berkeley: University of California Press, 1987.

Magie, David. *Roman Rule in Asia Minor to the End of the Third Century after Christ*. 2 vols. Princeton, N.J.: Princeton University Press, 1950; repr., New York: Arno, 1975.

Millar, F. *The Roman Near East: 31 B.C.–A.D. 337*. Cambridge: Harvard University Press, 1993.

Sherwin-White, A. N. *Roman Society and Roman Law in the New Testament*. Oxford: Oxford University Press, 1963; repr., Grand Rapids, Mich.: Eerdmans, 1978.

Wacher, John, ed. *The Roman World*. 2 vols. London and New York: Routledge, 1987.

Literary Models in the Greco-Roman World

Aune, David. *The New Testament in Its Literary Environment*. Library of Early Christianity. Philadelphia: Westminster Press, 1987.

Grimal, Pierre. *Romans Grec et Latins*. Paris: Gallimard, 1958.

Hagg, Thomas. *The Novel in Antiquity*. Oxford: Blackwell, 1983.

Horsley, G. H. R. "Speeches and Dialogue in Acts." *NTS* 32 (1986): 609–14.

Merkelbach, Reinhold. *Roman und Mysterium in der Antike*. Berlin and Munich: Beck, 1962.

Parsons, Mikeal C., and J. B. Tyson, eds. *Cadbury, Knox, and Talbert: American Contributions to the Study of Acts*. Atlanta: Scholars Press, 1992.

Pervo, Richard I. *Profit with Delight: The Literary Genre of the Acts of the Apostles*. Philadelphia: Fortress Press, 1987.

Soards, Marion L. *The Speeches in Acts: Their Content, Context, and Concerns*. Louisville, Ky.: Westminster Press, 1994.

Talbert, Charles. "Biographies of Philosophers and Rulers as Instruments of Religious Propaganda in Mediterranean Antiquity." Re-

ligion, ed. H. Temporini and W. Haase. *ANRW* II.16.2 (1978):
1619–51.

————. *Literary Patterns, Theological Themes, and the Genre of Luke-Acts.*
SBL Monograph Series 20. Missoula, Mont.: Scholars Press, 1974.

Paul in Acts

Brawley, R. L. "Paul in Acts: Lucan Apology and Conciliation." In *Perspectives on Luke-Acts*, ed. C. H. Talbert, 129–47. Danville, Va.:
Association of Baptist Professors of Religion, 1978.

Furnish, Victor. *II Corinthians: A New Translation with Introduction and Commentary.* Anchor Bible. Garden City, N.Y.: Doubleday, 1984.

Hengel, Martin. *Acts and the History of Earliest Christianity.* Trans. John
Bowden. Philadelphia: Fortress Press, 1980.

————. *Between Jesus and Paul.* Trans. John Bowden. Philadelphia:
Fortress Press, 1983.

————. *The Pre-Christian Paul.* Trans. John Bowden. Minneapolis: Fortress Press, 1991.

Jewett, Robert. *A Chronology of Paul's Life.* Philadelphia: Fortress Press,
1979.

Kee, H. C. *Understanding the New Testament.* 5th ed. Englewood Cliffs,
N.J.: Prentice-Hall, 1993.

Lentz, John Clayton, Jr. *Luke's Portrait of Paul.* SNTSMS 77. Cambridge:
Cambridge University Press, 1993.

Theological Themes in Acts

Conzelmann, Hans. *The Theology of St. Luke.* New York: Harper and
Row, 1961.

Jervell, Jacob. *Luke and the People of God.* Minneapolis: Augsburg Press,
1972.

Kee, H. C. *Medicine, Miracle, and Magic in New Testament Times.* SNTSMS
55. Cambridge: Cambridge University Press, 1986; rev. ed., 1988.

————. *Miracle in the Early Christian World.* New Haven: Yale University
Press, 1983.

Tiede, David L. *Prophecy and History in Luke-Acts.* Philadelphia: Fortress
Press, 1980.

On the Son of Man

Borsch, Frederick H. *The Son of Man in Myth and History.* Philadelphia:
Westminster Press, 1967.

Kee, H. C. "The Son of Man: A Glutton and a Drunkard. Analysis of Q
7:18–35." *NTS* 42 (1996): 374–93.

Moule, C. F. D. "The Son of Man: Some of the Facts." *NTS* 41 (1995):
277–79.

Ancient Sources

Apuleius. *Metamorphoses* (LCL).

Charlesworth, J. H., ed. *The Dead Sea Scrolls: Hebrew, Aramaic, and Greek Texts with English Translations.* Vol. 1: *The Rule of the Community and Related Documents.* Louisville, Ky.: Westminster/John Knox, 1994.

Collected Ancient Greek Novels, ed. B. P. Reardon. Berkeley: University of California Press, 1989.

Dio Cassius. *Roman History.*

Eusebius. *Ecclesiastical History* (LCL).

Hadas, Moses. *Three Greek Romances.* Indianapolis: Bobbs-Merrill, 1964.

Henrichs, Albert. *Die Phoinikika des Lollians. Fragments eines neuen griechischen Romans.* Bonn: Habelt, 1972.

Irenaeus. *Against All Heresies.*

Jerome. *Commentary on Isaiah* (in Migne, *Patrologia Latina*).

Josephus. *Antiquities of the Jews* (LCL).

———. *Wars of the Jews* (LCL).

Kee, H. C. *Cambridge Annotated Study Apocrypha.* Cambridge: Cambridge University Press, 1994.

Lucian. *Alexander the False Prophet* (LCL).

———. *How to Write History* (LCL 6).

Philo. *Embassy to Gaius* (LCL).

———. *Life of Moses* (LCL).

Plato. *Cratylus* (LCL).

———. *Sophist* (LCL).

Pliny. *Letter to Trajan* (LCL).

Plutarch. *Moralia* (LCL).

———. "On the 'E' at Delphi" (LCL).

Porphyry. *Life of Plotinus.*

Tacitus. *Annals* (LCL).

The Text of Acts

Aland, Barbara. "Entstehung, Charakter und Herkunft des sog. westlichen Textes untersucht in der Apostelgeschichte." *EThL* 62 (1986): 5–65.

Aland, Kurt. *The Text of the New Testament.* Trans. E. F. Rhodes. Grand Rapids, Mich.: Eerdmans, 1987.

Epp, Eldon J. *The Theological Tendency of Codex Bezae Cantabrigiensis in Acts.* SNTSMS 3. Cambridge: Cambridge University Press, 1966.

Haenchen, E., and P. Weigandt. "The Original Text of Acts?" *NTS* 14 (1968): 469–81.

Ropes, J. H. *The Text of Acts.* Vol. 3 of *The Beginnings of Christianity*, ed. F. J. Foakes-Jackson and Kirsopp Lake. London: Macmillan, 1922.

Strange, W. A. *The Problem of the Text of Acts.* SNTSMS 71. Cambridge: Cambridge University Press, 1992.

Index of Scriptural Texts

Index of Ancient and Modern Authors

Index of Subjects

Antioch: description of, 147–48, 166
"apostle": use of the term in the NT, 32–33
Aristarchus: excursus on, 287
Athens: description of, 209–10, 211–12
attribution of Acts, 1–2

baptism: centrality of the theme in Acts, 25, 53; as a link to the new community, 229, 257; as a symbol of the community's shared life, 39; term used for, 111
biography, 7–8, 16–17
blood of Jesus: excursus on, 241–42
breaking of the bread: implications of, 54; Paul's participation in, 237; summary of the theme in Acts, 25; as symbol of community's shared life, 39
"brethren": discussion of the term, 123–24

Caesarea: description of, 130–32, 335n.38
Christos: discussion of the term, 73, 140, 150
circumcision: accusations against Paul regarding, 249; controversy in new community regarding, 145, 148, 178–79, 180, 181–82, 183, 186; as sign of covenantal relation, 97
citizenship, Roman, 200–201
Corinth: description of, 218–19
Cos: description of, 245
council in Jerusalem (Jewish political institution): blamed for Jesus' death, 81; composition of, 69, 261–62; examination of apostles by, 80–86; functions of, 79–80, 114–15, 315–16n.49; Stephen before, 90–102
crucifixion, 52, 81–82, 141–42

Damascus: description of, 120; likelihood of Christian community at, 115–16; Paul's preaching in, 121
date of composition of Acts, 13–14
Derbe: description of, 175
"disciples": discussion of the term, 32–33, 119–20, 149
divination, 195–97
dramatic narrative, as a model for Acts, 17–18

ekklesia: discussion of the term, 152
Ephesus: description of, 226–28
Epicureanism, 211–14
eucharist, the: 25, 55. *See also* breaking of the bread '
exorcism, 231, 314–15n.46

fasting, 159, 175
form criticism, 5–6

Gamaliel I, 14, 83, 84–85, 316n.56, 317n.61, 334n.14
Gamaliel II, 84–85, 334n.14
Gentiles: the opening to the, 166, 168–69; relation to Jewish community, 134–36; requirements for their entering the Christian community, 176–84, 248–49; response to the good news, 127–43
God-fearers, 25, 133–36, 238, 303n.38, 317n.1

healing: inclusiveness of, in Acts, 77–78; magic and, 314–15n.46; the name of Jesus and, 57–58, 64, 71; Paul's methods of, 230–31; Peter and, 59, 124–27
hellenism/hellenists, 88–89, 122–23, 146, 322–23n.44
Herod Agrippa I, 155–57
Herod Agrippa II, 278–86
Herod Antipas, 151–53

359